Chögyam Trungpa

*His Life
and Vision*

Chögyam

HIS

LIFE

Trungpa

AND
VISION

FABRICE MIDAL

Translated by Ian Monk

Foreword by Diana J. Mukpo

SHAMBHALA

BOSTON & LONDON 2004

Shambhala Publications, Inc.
Horticultural Hall
300 Massachusetts Avenue
Boston, Massachusetts 02115
www.shambhala.com

9 8 7 6 5 4 3 2 1

First Edition
Printed in the United States of America

♾ This edition is printed on acid-free paper that meets the
American National Standards Institute z39.48 Standard.
Distributed in the United States by Random House, Inc.,
and in Canada by Random House of Canada Ltd

Library of Congress Cataloging-in-Publication Data
Midal, Fabrice, 1967–
[Trungpa. English]
Chögyam Trungpa: his life and vision / Fabrice Midal; translated
from the French by Ian Monk.—1st ed.
p. cm.
Translation of: Trungpa: biographie. Paris: Seuil, 2002.
Includes bibliographical references and index.
ISBN 1-59030-098-x (hardcover: alk. paper)
1. Trungpa, Chögyam, 1939– 2. Lamas—China—Tibet—Biography.
I. Title.
BQ990.R867M5313 2004
294.3'923'092—dc22
2003027653

CONTENTS

Chapter Three
MEDITATION AND THE IMPORTANCE OF SITTING 61

Chapter Four
EXPERIENCE, MODERNITY, AND TRADITION 81

Ceremonies
Midsummer's Day
Shambhala Day
Chögyam Trungpa's birthday
Marriages

FOREWORD

I AM DELIGHTED TO BE ABLE to say a few words about the wonderful book that Fabrice Midal has written about my husband, Chögyam Trungpa, and his life's work. It is quite extraordinary that such a clear, accurate, and heartfelt portrait of Trungpa Rinpoche's life and his achievements has been created by someone who never knew him. To the best of my knowledge, everything that Fabrice has written here is completely accurate.

This is precisely the book about Trungpa Rinpoche that has been needed for a long time. I feel that it is absolutely what Rinpoche would have wanted written about his major accomplishments and teachings. My husband was so brilliant in being able to use many different media to express his teachings. Rinpoche demonstrated that the awakened mind can be expressed in many ways, through various art forms, as well as in all the forms and details of everyday life. His approach made the buddhadharma available to all kinds of people who have different interests in their lives. As well, it is a hallmark of the vajrayana teachings that you fully engage everything in your world. My husband was a master of this, and Fabrice Midal has beautifully captured this quality in his book.

On behalf of my family and myself, I would like to commend Fabrice Midal and to thank him for having written this book. I am quite amazed by the amount and the quality of the research that he did. He has really looked into every corner of Rinpoche's life. It is clear that Fabrice has put tremendous effort into this project, and the results speak for themselves.

It is interesting that the first book about my husband's life has been written in French, a language that he did not speak. This shows how far his teachings and influence have spread. I hope that *Chögyam Trungpa: Sa vie et son oeuvre* will be translated and published in many other languages, as I think it will be of interest to many people—those who knew my husband and studied with him, as well as many who never met him. I think that readers will find it to be helpful, enjoyable, and illuminating, as I did myself.

With the blessings of the Mukpos, I remain,

Diana Judith Mukpo
PROVIDENCE, RHODE ISLAND
27 DECEMBER 2001

PREFACE

I WROTE THIS BOOK IN THE HOPE that, at a time when people are so disoriented that they are open to all sorts of charlatans, the depth and the brilliance of Chögyam Trungpa's vision may help them to rediscover their true path.

Beyond the Buddhism that he inherited, beyond any religion, Chögyam Trungpa shows us how we can transform our own existence within our own culture, to discover a sacred world and establish an enlightened society.

My understanding of Chögyam Trungpa's work and teachings is so limited that all the reader will find here is an overview. By reading, by gathering testimonials and encounters, I have simply tried to gather together what was disparate in order to help the reader understand the life and work of one of the greatest spiritual masters of our time.

My "encounter" with Chögyam Trungpa goes back to 1989, when I attended a center in Paris set up by a couple of his American students.

During the subsequent years of practice, numerous meetings with his close disciples, and visits to various centers and meditation and study programs whose content and form he had devised, I was constantly exposed to the extraordinary brilliance of his teaching and its manifestation.

When I started practicing, I found the concrete nature of meditation reassuring—there were no theories or new systems of thought to absorb; instead we were asked to examine ourselves with ever greater curiosity and gentleness. This encouragement to refuse all dogmas delighted the rather short-sighted atheist that I was at the time, devoted to freedom of thought and refusing any kind of manipulation as practiced by the various churches. But as the years went by, thanks to Chögyam Trungpa my preconceptions were obliterated. He opened my eyes. He opened my heart. The existence of a variety of paths allowing human beings to reach attainment appeared to me in places and contexts that I would never have been able to appreciate before. Chögyam Trungpa showed me the true meaning of Tradition.

Without him, I would never have become a Buddhist, because still today I find I have more in common with paths that have nothing to do with that tradition than with various Buddhist groups whose religious, even dogmatic, character is totally alien to me.

When I go to certain Buddhist centers, I may appreciate what goes on there, but I often feel lost and homesick—for the Kingdom of Shambhala that Chögyam Trungpa founded. I miss its freedom, which is like the garuda, a mythical bird that never needs to land on earth.

If I am referring to my personal experience, despite the ignorance I realize it reveals, it is because it proves that it is possible to enter into contact with the teaching of Chögyam Trungpa even though he is no longer physically among us. Chögyam Trungpa continues to open the eyes, hearts, and minds of numerous people, and his presence often overwhelms me.

INTRODUCTION

Chögyam Trungpa was a Buddhist teacher who was born in Tibet in 1940 and died in Nova Scotia, Canada, in 1987. He was one of the first to teach Westerners, even living with them and sharing their lives.

There are numerous gurus who are known to be true heirs of the Tibetan Buddhist tradition. But there is something unique about Chögyam Trungpa. It is difficult to define what is so singular about him, but this book offers an approach.

It is important to note that no other Tibetan guru has so distanced himself from his original culture. A commonly held belief is that spiritual practice is inseparable from its cultural context.

For many years, Zen masters considered that it was impossible to teach Buddhism to Westerners. So their first European disciples took up a Japanese lifestyle.

Chögyam Trungpa never wanted his students to become Tibetan. He believed that when Buddhism is transmitted to the West, it should give rise to a Western Buddhism, and this could only occur after profound reflection about the language and the culture in which the dharma could be established. Such was the huge task that Chögyam Trungpa undertook by immersing himself in the Western world. As he himself explained, becoming a Buddhist is not a matter of trying to live up to what you would like to be, but an attempt to be what you are: "This possibility is connected with seeing our confusion, or misery and pain, but not making these discoveries into an answer. Instead we explore further and further and further without looking for an answer. It is a process of working with ourselves, with our lives, with our psychology, without looking for an answer but seeing things as they are—seeing what goes on in our heads directly and simply, absolutely literally. If we can undertake a process like that, then there is a tremendous possibility that our confusion—the chaos and neurosis that goes on in our minds—might become a further basis for investigation."[1]

With this in mind, Chögyam Trungpa paid constant attention to education. He set up several schools and a university; he organized interreligious meetings at a time when they were scarce (while showing a profound interest in Christianity and Judaism, as well as other schools of Buddhism that were little known in Tibet); he was extremely sensitive to the role played by artists, poets, painters, and musicians with whom he regularly worked. He met numerous members of the avant-garde of the time; he analyzed the West's economic situation and how he could make a significant contribution to it; he gave thought to medicine and how to assuage the ills of the body as well as the mind; he became passionate about politics as a means of living in community and thought deeply about ecology and our relationship with our environment.

In many ways, Chögyam Trungpa is reminiscent of those stained-glass windows, made of a large number of facets, that decorate Gothic cathedrals. Like them, he dazzles you. The only inappropriate aspect of this analogy is that while such prolific richness can seem dazzling, such brilliance can also provoke the greatest terror when it exposes the depth of our own imbecility.

The word *imbecile* comes from the Latin *imbecillus*, which means "not having a stick." An imbecile is someone with no leaning post. Caught in the web of thought's changing fashions and habits, he has been lost in obscurity. This is just what Buddhism means by *samsara*, an endless circle spun by our beliefs and opinions, without the slightest attention to what really is.

The basis of Buddhism, like all authentic practices, is the affirmation

---

1. *Crazy Wisdom*, pp. 9–10.

that it is possible to find a genuine stick to lean on, that a real world does exist beyond the one we build for ourselves and try to adhere to, come what may.

In a period marked by cynicism, there is a good deal of provocation in the idea that there is a path that can reveal the possibility of living otherwise—in other words, that the aim of life is not to become a good consumer or producer.

In reality, such an idea is often downplayed. Most of the press, books, and seminars devoted to spirituality set about doing so, for various reasons. Buddhism is often presented as being an atheistic—or at best agnostic—teaching, which is scientific and rational, which can be diluted into the "values" of modern society. It is also presented as a form of psychological therapy leading to a better existence, or else as a bulwark providing cheap and easy protection against the stress of modern life.

When Buddhism is mingled with the West in such a way, not much of it is left.

But if more attention is paid to how Buddhism can be introduced into the West without being watered down by the media machine and the world of show business, then the work of Chögyam Trungpa becomes vital, because he was the first to warn us with prophetic clarity against the swamp we are sinking into ever deeper.

Chögyam Trungpa presented Buddhism in such a way that it can take root anywhere. He wanted its teachings to become part of everybody's daily life and meaningful in our society.

Buddhism is not a religion, as he frequently explained; it is a way of life.[2] Spirituality must not be a specific field, excluded from the social and ooºular world.

A presentation of Chögyam Trungpa cannot be limited to the work of the man, no matter how exceptional he was. It also entails examining a truly historic event: a completely novel meeting between the East and the

---

2. See, for example, "Buddhism is not a national religious approach," *Crazy Wisdom*, p. 55, and "I don't think Buddhism should be regarded as a religion, but as a social realization," in *Annual Report to the Sangha*, 1985–1986, Vajradhatu Publications.

West. Beyond Buddhism, Chögyam Trungpa decided to become an intrinsic part of our destiny so as to transform it—in other words, to liberate its dignity and greatness.

In writing this book, I considered several possible ways of presenting Chögyam Trungpa. I immediately excluded the idea of writing a biography, because such a psychological approach seemed both reductive and inappropriate to the very notion of egolessness as explained in Buddhist teaching.

Furthermore, who can pretend to know what Chögyam Trungpa thought?

Walter Fordham lived with him for a long time and organized his domestic life. When I interviewed him, he told me that every time Chögyam Trungpa came back from a trip, Walter felt as though he didn't know him anymore. He had changed so much that he seemed like a stranger. When you thought you knew who Chögyam Trungpa was, when you believed you had grasped your relationship with him, he broke down all your convictions. He never stayed still. As Walter told me: "I never knew who he was; he'll always be a mystery for me. The trap some of his students fell into was to believe they had a personal relationship with him. No one was ever at ease with him. His relationship with us was more intimate than that. He completely saw through all of us, but at the same time the whole situation was so light. He was so passionate about who you were, while at the same time it didn't matter." This is why it seemed to me that describing Chögyam Trungpa's personal experience would be impossible. No book could ever pretend to "grasp" such a man.

There was another possible approach: to produce a namthar, a traditional tale describing the life and teachings of a guru, written by his disciples. Such a project would imply a realization of his teachings, which is beyond my powers. Furthermore, it could not become truly meaningful in our modern world without being adapted and transformed, and thus disfigured.

Instead, I decided to sketch a series of portraits that would serve as a series of entrances into the world of Chögyam Trungpa.

Chögyam Trungpa is not a historical figure belonging to the past. He remains present in his works and continually offers us new ways to touch our hearts here and now.

Each chapter has been conceived as a facet of this work, capable of revealing a sacred vision—the capacity to see the beauty and space of all experience. The entirety of Chögyam Trungpa's life and work was devoted to transmitting the spirit of enlightenment, and no encounter with him is ever superficial. This is why, wherever he went, people were waiting for him, lining up to greet him. This should not be seen as the expression of fanaticism or mere protocol, but instead as the burning desire to enter into contact with that space.

The life of Chögyam Trungpa surpasses all comparison. As we shall see, it shocked many people and continues to disturb others.

Great spiritual masters abandon all conventions and require no recognition. They are ready to take any number of risks in order to communicate enlightenment to their disciples: The master "constantly challenges his students to step beyond themselves, to step out into the vast and brilliant world of reality in which he abides. The challenge that he provides is not so much that he is always setting hurdles or egging them on. Rather, his authentic presence is a constant challenge to be genuine and true."[3]

But such excess cannot become meaningful only in the context that produced it. Certain surprising things he did can seem shocking today, and may also have seemed brutal or crazy at the time, but thanks to them the persons they were aimed at were able to open fully. It is thus difficult to judge them now. But any attempt to conceal his more disconcerting side would also water down the character of Chögyam Trungpa. I have tried to find a happy medium between this and the essential message of his work, while constantly examining the question of how Chögyam Trungpa had the power, and still has the power today, to enlighten us.

---

3. *Shambhala: The Sacred Path of the Warrior* (Shambhala Library, 2003), p. 210.

Chapter One

PORTRAIT OF
CHÖGYAM TRUNGPA
IN 1970

This person called Mr. Mukpo here is a very ordinary person. He has simply escaped out of Tibet because of the Chinese communist suppression. He is looking for possible ways to relate with the world outside of that Tibetan world and trying to share with people how he feels about his own practice, and his own feelings about what he has studied, what he has learned. That's simply what we're doing right here.[1]

—CHÖGYAM TRUNGPA

1. Encounter with Hippie America

Chögyam Trungpa meets the hippie generation

In March 1970, Chögyam Trungpa Rinpoche moved to the United States after seven years' residence in England.[2] The hippie movement was in full swing. An entire generation had made its mark with its distinctive lifestyle, spirit of spontaneity, and rejection of the Establishment. Young

---

1. Chögyam Trungpa, "Speaking to the Sangha on His Birthday," February 1979, unpublished.

2. Chögyam Trungpa arrived with his wife, Diana Pybus Mukpo, in Toronto, Canada, in January. They then had to wait a few months in Canada until they obtained visas. Chögyam Trungpa taught in Montreal before going to Barnet, Vermont, where his students had bought the property that was to become the first Kagyü Buddhist meditation center in the United States.

people were questioning and protesting their elders' way of life. The result was a unique moment in Western culture. Inspired by writers of the Beat Generation, such as Jack Kerouac, Allen Ginsberg, and William Burroughs, the hippies ridiculed narrow-minded middle-class conformity and advocated the use of "mind-expanding" drugs such as marijuana and LSD as keys to freedom. The hippie lifestyle varied from "back to the land" communes or communal city "pads" to nomadic wanderings across the United States. Many were "flower children" who engaged in antiwar demonstrations under the sign of peace and love. Hippies were involved in a variety of experimental practices ranging from psychedelics and free love to art and mysticism, all in a spirit of highly undisciplined curiosity. Among the spiritually inclined, Hindu chanting, yoga, and Zen became popular as counterculture alternatives to conventional religious teachings and practices.

No matter how naive these young people were in their desire for a world of "peace and love," their open-mindedness—and even their confusion—created a fertile ground for the arrival of Buddhism. It was in just this context that Rinpoche (Chögyam Trungpa's honorific title, meaning "precious jewel" in Tibetan) succeeded in setting up one of the first-ever communities of practitioners of Tibetan Buddhism in the West, which is still among the most important ones today. His achievements were prodigious: he introduced the Buddhist tradition in all its depth and trained one of his Western followers to become his successor and regent; founded a university (Naropa Institute, now called Naropa University), schools for children, and a program of secular education (Shambhala Training); started a new tradition of contemplative psychology (Maitri Space Awareness) and a theater school (Mudra Space Awareness); and published many books and collections of poetry as well as creating artworks as a calligrapher and photographer.

But all of this is not purely the work of one isolated individual; it is rather the result of a meeting between a man and a generation, whose deepest aspirations he was able to embody. In entering into direct contact with the hippie movement, Chögyam Trungpa responded to the quest for authenticity and freedom that the hippies had expressed in such a confused way.

As early as 1970, Chögyam Trungpa was speaking the same language as the young; he dressed in the same casual attire as they, and partook of the alcohol and drugs they favored. He ate the same food and slept in houses with them, sometimes on a bare floor. Chögyam Trungpa did not want to be seen as a distant master to be placed on a pedestal, but rather as someone with whom it was possible to have a frank, direct relationship. Moreover, at the time, Tibetan Buddhism was practically unknown in the West, and so it made sense to abandon the exotic trappings of a lama and meet people on their own ground.

True communication beyond hypocrisy

Diana Pybus Mukpo, whom Chögyam Trungpa had just married in Scotland,[3] recalls an encounter that illustrates her husband's manner at the time. They had not been in the States for very long when, one day, a young American hippie dressed as an East Indian came to their house. He went upstairs, saw Chögyam Trungpa, and asked, "I've come a long way to see the guru. Where is he? I need to see him!" Chögyam Trungpa replied that he didn't know and that the young man must have been given the wrong address. The American went back downstairs, disappointed. Diana advised him to go back up and take a second look.

To be sure, it was hard to imagine that this man, then aged thirty-one, wearing jeans and sometimes a rather loud cowboy shirt left unbuttoned at the top, was a guru. He even smoked and drank whiskey. His very appearance upset conventional ideas of what constituted a spiritual master.

In his early years in the United States, Chögyam Trungpa thus presented himself very simply. He met people in the most direct manner possible. Being an honest person, he did not hide the fact that he was not bound by ordinary conventions, whether they were what Westerners typically expected of him or the conventions acquired during his upbringing. As a young tülku (incarnate lama) in Tibet, he had been waited

---

3. They were married on January 3, 1970. Diana Pybus was then only sixteen years old. A recent law had authorized marriage at that age in Scotland, without parental consent.

on by servants and had learned to sit still on an elevated throne while his visitors treated him with the respect due to his rank. Westerners had a very narrow vision of how the wisdom of Oriental sages was supposed to present itself. The commonly held opinion was, and still is, that wisdom manifests itself as disembodied calm in every circumstance.

But nothing could be farther from the true wisdom that Chögyam Trungpa taught and displayed. According to him, wisdom derives from a "complete experience"[4]—no matter what that experience may be.[5] The purpose of the spiritual path is not, as young people then imagined, to attain to some ethereal existence in which the passions of life are replaced with a superior detachment, but is instead a way of being fully human: "Spirituality, from a superficial point of view, is based on the idea of making things harmonious. But somehow . . . that approach does not apply. The idea is not so much to make things harmonious and less active, but to relate with what is happening, with whatever struggles and upheavals are going on—trying to survive, to earn more dollars, get more food, more room, a roof over our heads, and so on."[6]

Before moving to the United States, Chögyam Trungpa had been teaching in England, but without attracting more than a few serious students; few, it seems, were able to appreciate what he had to offer. People expected him to behave like the stereotypical "Oriental sage," and he found this horribly hypocritical. Their desire for him to play a role implied their avoidance of any real contact with what he was saying. He described the period in England as "the first time I had been the object of that fascination which is noncommunicative and nonrelating, being seen

---

4. *Transcending Madness*, p. 294. Wisdom, *jnana* in Sanskrit and *yeshe* in Tibetan, is not at all a matter of no longer being troubled but is instead a relationship with "pure emotion, which is the original flash of instantaneous experience." *Journey without Goal*, p. 122.

5. Chögyam Trungpa gave this description of the fundamental idea we generally have of enlightenment: "An enlightened person is supposed to be more or less an old-wise-man type: not quite like an old professor, but perhaps an old father who can supply sound advice on how to handle all of life's problems. . . . That seems to be the current fantasy that exists in our culture concerning enlightened beings. They are old and wise, grown-up and solid." *Crazy Wisdom*, p. 25.

6. *Orderly Chaos*, p. 16.

as an example of a species rather than as an individual: 'Let's go see the lamas at Oxford.'"[7] Throughout his life, Chögyam Trungpa refused to conform to common social clichés.

In India and Tibet, generations of practitioners had dedicated their lives to perpetuating what the Buddha taught. In the West, should such efforts result in their spiritual heir becoming an exotic figure invited to perform for a few exclusive circles of "right-thinking" people? Was it for this that the Buddha taught? In Chögyam Trungpa's mind, the answer was clearly no.

Chögyam Trungpa could have had many disciples in England, been greatly respected, and led a comfortable life, as some of his fellow exiles did. But that was not what he wanted. His aspiration was to introduce the Buddha's teachings in all their authenticity, holding back nothing of what he himself had learned. For this, he was ready to give up everything. He was incapable of deception. He thus decided to play down his religious status so as to be able to communicate directly with the people he met. He thus entered the everyday lives of his students. As one early student, Chuck Lief, recalls, when Chögyam Trungpa stayed at his home in Boston, he washed the dishes and helped with the household chores.

For anyone who knows the formality and ceremony that surround many Tibetan masters, this is rather surprising. Chögyam Trungpa had sacrificed his thrones, servants, and all the ceremony that traditionally surrounds a master. When he realized that these aspects of his culture were meaningless in his new American context, he dropped them.

Buddhist teachings insist on the importance of total renunciation. Such abandonment is a precondition of freedom. Chögyam Trungpa did not simply teach this basic precept; he was one of its most striking exemplars. He cast off his culture, his Tibetan background and habits, in order to touch people's hearts more easily.

In his early years in the United States, one major activity in addition to his teaching of seminars consisted in entering into direct contact with all those who wanted to see him. It was an intense round of interviews,

---

7. "Epilogue to the 1971 Edition" of *Born in Tibet*, in *The Collected Works of Chögyam Trungpa*, vol. 1 (Boston: Shambhala Publications, 2003), p. 280.

dinners, parties, and encounters. At the time, Chögyam Trungpa used to stop people in the street and ask them if they had heard of meditation or Buddhism. If they asked him questions, he would answer at once, offer them meditation instruction, and give them a copy of his book *Meditation in Action*, which he often carried with him.

He kept abreast of the country's political and social life and questioned all sorts of people with great curiosity. He paid close attention to everyone's life and asked his students to correct his English. He became their friend.

A challenge to inauthenticity

During that period, while Chögyam Trungpa displayed an extraordinary openness to those who wanted to meet him and study with him, he was implacable when confronted with arrogance and hypocrisy. One day, he was invited to a gala reception with several VIPs in attendance.[8] There, he met an art collector who owned a large body of Tibetan work, from which Trungpa wanted to borrow for an exhibition he was planning. The collector came over to Chögyam Trungpa and said in an offhand way: "So, how is life treating you?" Chögyam Trungpa ignored him and went rapidly around the room before returning to where he had been standing. He looked the collector straight in the eye and said, "Life doesn't treat me, I treat her, and I'd say that I treat her quite well." And he left the room. Chögyam Trungpa refused to corrupt his vision, even if this meant alienating certain intellectuals and wealthy people who might have helped him.

On another occasion, in late 1970, he was invited to give a lecture on Tibetan art and iconography at the prestigious Asia Society in New York. Some of his students told him that this was a good opportunity for him to get to know some wealthy people who were at least interested in the culture of Tibet, even if they were not drawn to its religion. Many invitations were sent out. At the appointed time, the hall filled with smart, well-off, middle-aged New Yorkers, all apparently curious to find out what this brilliant young Buddhist master, who spoke such excellent English, would

---

8. At the Dharma Art Festival in 1974.

have to say about this exotic art form. The time for the lecture arrived, but Rinpoche was not there. Time passed. The audience grew restless, and people began to walk out.

Downstairs, Chögyam Trungpa, who had arrived on time, was seated in his car. He asked the student who had come with him to drive around the block. The exodus upstairs continued until Rinpoche finally made his appearance, all smiles, over an hour late. He sat down and started to talk about the practice of meditation, without mentioning the announced topic. An irritated member of the audience in the front row loudly opened his program to demonstrate his annoyance. People continued to leave. Finally, when there was just a smattering of people left in the hall (most of whom were his students), Rinpoche smiled and said, "Well, yes, some of you here may well be interested in Tibetan art and iconography, and in what the images mean. But I can assure you that this is pointless without practicing meditation. If your aim is just to collect antiques, then you will probably become one yourself."

Whatever the circumstances, Chögyam Trungpa was unyielding. He refused to flatter people. He never set out to deceive, and he promised nothing. True dharma cannot be presented by wrapping it up in cultural exoticism.

He never hesitated to tell the truth, even if this meant provoking the audience. At a talk in San Francisco in the fall of 1970, he began by saying: "It's a pity you came here. You're so aggressive."

According to Jerry Granelli, who was in charge of organizing many of Chögyam Trungpa's early visits to the West Coast, as soon as the audience for a lecture had taken their seats, Jerry would go and hide the box office takings in his car. He knew that some of the audience would be furious and demand a refund. Chögyam Trungpa would often arrive very late or speak only for a few minutes, as at the Dharma Art Festival lecture he gave in 1974, for which the audience of over fifteen hundred had paid five dollars each. People wanted answers, but Chögyam Trungpa refused to cater to their expectations. His purpose was to unravel the tangle of beliefs in which they had ensnared themselves. He thus exposed as purely artificial the hidden foundation on which most people's experience is based.

When teaching, instead of reassuring those present, he often warned them: "Be careful; if you start practicing, there's no going back." He presented the spiritual journey as no pleasant stroll, but rather a painful process of exposure: "The Buddhist path is ruthless, absolutely ruthless, almost to the point of being uncompassionate. What we could say is that we are not looking for pleasure. The journey is not geared for finding pleasure; it's not a pleasure trip."[9]

His desire to communicate freely and intensely and his efforts to break through hypocrisy are two sides of the same coin, because hypocrisy makes any real heart-to-heart relationship impossible. During the seventeen years he taught in the United States, and regardless of the changing forms his teachings took, Chögyam Trungpa never hesitated to take risks or overturn convention if this could help people to understand themselves. He thus allowed them to experience his world directly and completely. He did not present himself in a polished way; he was willing to be shocking, incredible, strange, unexpected, or disturbing—for such was the nature of the teachings with which he was entrusted.

But though some people were put off, many were attracted to him, and the more Chögyam Trungpa came across as irascible, the more they were won over by the open, direct contact they had with him and the more eager they were to study with him and learn to develop the dignity he had unveiled within them.

2. His Following Increases

Chögyam Trungpa's *Meditation in Action*, first published in London in 1969, was at the time one of the few books about the practice of Buddhist meditation available in the West. It had rapidly become a work of reference for anyone wanting to study Buddhism. In it, Chögyam Trungpa presents a surprising approach to "spirituality." The way of the Buddha is described with disarming simplicity. As he explains: "As far as the teaching is concerned, it is always open; so open in fact, so ordinary and so simple, that it is contained within the character of that particular person

---

9. *The Lion's Roar*, p. 6.

[who seeks to awaken]. He may be habitually drunk, or habitually violent, but that character is his potentiality."[10] Chögyam Trungpa does not present the spiritual path in terms of the acquisition of some precise, external wisdom, but as the capacity to face our true selves as directly as possible, leaving aside social or moral conventions.

Tail of the Tiger

The first place where Chögyam Trungpa lived in the United States was a 400-acre farm in Vermont, found by four of his students who had met him at Samye Ling, the center he had set up in Scotland. They moved to the farm in March 1970 to prepare for his coming. With Chögyam Trungpa's blessing they named the place Tail of the Tiger, after an oracle drawn from the *I Ching: The Book of Changes*. Chögyam Trungpa himself arrived in May of 1970.

Tania Leontov, who had studied with him in Britain and taken the Buddhist name Kesang Tönma, was then his secretary. She was an American and knew lots of people in New York, whom she invited to Tail of the Tiger. In July, Chögyam Trungpa gave his first seminar at Tail. His manner was extremely mild and humble. Chuck Lief first met him at this time and remembers how gracious he was. He was even rather shy, surprised and pleased to see so many unfamiliar faces that had come to meet him.

After a few months, about twenty permanent residents were living at Tail of the Tiger. Almost a thousand visitors had been there, attended seminars, received instruction in meditation, gone into retreat, or shared the community life there. The atmosphere that prevailed at Tail of the Tiger was a cross between a hippie community and a Buddhist monastery and practice center, even if, at the time, the first element was still dominant.

Colorado and the lack of a private life

After his stay in Vermont, a tour in California, and visits to several American cities, Chögyam Trungpa went to Colorado in the early fall of 1970.

---

10. *Meditation in Action*, p. 18.

He was delighted by the little house his students had chosen for him in the mountains. In December, he moved to another house, in Four Mile Canyon near Boulder.

He had been invited to Boulder by several people at the University of Colorado, including Karl Usow, who had written to him in England about it. There were other offers, but Diana Mukpo remembers that her husband accepted this invitation because he liked the mountains pictured on the postcard. They reminded him of Tibet.

In Rinpoche's house, people came and went and sometimes even moved in. One day, he and Diana quarreled over whether people should be required to knock on their bedroom door before entering. Visitors who had nowhere else to go would stay in the house and sleep wherever they could, sometimes just outside the room where Chögyam Trungpa and his wife slept. Chögyam Trungpa had no private life. At Tail of the Tiger, things went so far that occasionally someone would even follow him into the bathroom and sit down on the floor beside him to carry on asking him questions.

In December 1970, some of his students decided to settle together in Boulder in a house that Chögyam Trungpa called Anitya Bhavan, "House of Impermanence." His first seminar in Colorado was held there, but neighbors complained so much about the noise that they had to finish the program in Rinpoche's house. (A series of talks beginning at this time and concluding in the spring of 1971 was to become the basis for the book *Cutting Through Spiritual Materialism*, published in 1973.) In September 1971, Karma Dzong—a center for meditation and Buddhist studies—was founded at 1111 Pearl Street.

Rocky Mountain Dharma Center

In 1971, a decision was made to buy a large piece of land in order to found a rural residential center. After an initial search, the site the students showed to Chögyam Trungpa greatly appealed to him. The contract was signed on September 16, and the site was named Rocky Mountain Dharma Center (RMDC).

A group of hippies living in a community in Boulder, known as the Pygmies, became Rinpoche's disciples very soon after meeting him. They adopted the motto "We're bodhisattvas and we live on East Arapahoe." (*Bodhisattva* is a Sanskrit term for an enlightened being whose life is dedicated to the benefit of others.) Despite an early heavy snow, at Chögyam Trungpa's invitation the Pygmies moved to RMDC on September 20, to live on the land. Many of them built their own houses there. The meditation room was the sitting room of one of the houses. When it was time to meditate, they simply covered the television with a piece of cloth. To earn a living, the Pygmies made buttons from deer antlers that they found on the land. They also made looms to spin cloth. In 1971, at least a dozen people were living at RMDC.

A rapid expansion

Just after the purchase of Rocky Mountain Dharma Center, the Buddhist community was given another property. A couple, Roger and Louise Randolph, presented Chögyam Trungpa with some land in the mountains of southern Colorado. They wanted this site to be preserved and not disfigured with buildings. It was called Dorje Kyung Dzong (Vajra Garuda Fortress). Small huts were constructed there for individual retreats.

At Jackson Hole in Wyoming, another group of followers took over a hotel, the Snow Lion Inn.[11] From 1972 to 1974, when the hotel was closed during the off season, Chögyam Trungpa taught there. In 1972 he taught a seminar on Crazy Wisdom and in 1973, the first Vajradhatu Seminary was held there.

The activities of the community were thus taking various directions. Chögyam Trungpa taught constantly, conducting endless discussion

---

11. The Snow Lion was named after the animal that is the emblem of Tibet. It was here that in 1972 the "Crazy Wisdom" seminar was held (later published as a book with the same title), then the first Seminary presenting the three yanas in 1973, which brought together sixty people for three months.

groups and seminars,[12] without the slightest attention to his own health or well-being. He took so little time off that he seemed to defy common sense. He appeared to be beyond the measure of a normal human being.

Study and meditation centers were set up in major cities of the United States and Canada where Chögyam Trungpa had taught: New York, Boston, and San Francisco, then shortly afterward Chicago, Berkeley, Los Angeles, Denver, Montreal, and Toronto.

People practiced little in 1970 and did more or less what they felt like.

---

12. To give an idea of his activities, here is an approximate list of what he taught in 1971. At Boulder he gave the talk "Dealing with Emotions," and at Tail of the Tiger several talks were given to the community: "Community Energies," "Crazy Wisdom," "Negativity," and a seminar titled "Practice of Meditation."

At the University of Colorado in Boulder he taught a series of six courses. In Boulder, he also gave several talks: "Battle of Ego," "Surrendering: Taking Refuge," "The Guru Scene," "Initiation," "The Hard Way," "Self-Deception," "The Open Way," "Sense of Humor," "The Marriage of Wisdom and Compassion," and "Mandala."

In New York he taught "Awareness," then in Boston in February, "The Six Chakras" and "The Four Karmas," now published as *Secret Beyond Thought* (Halifax: Vajradhatu Publications, 1991.)

Back in Boulder, he gave a seminar "Milarepa Film Workshop," devoted to what was to be his unfinished film about Milarepa.

In April he went into retreat with two of his older students in Wisconsin. From May 9 to 29, he toured California, where he taught in San Francisco, Berkeley, Davis, and Los Angeles as well as giving a seminar on the houseboat of the Zen popularizer Alan Watts. During this time he presented "The Nature of Mind," "Sense of Humor," and a longer seminar, "Meditation," "Ambition to Learn," "Battle of Ego," "Meditation and Shunyata," and "The Open Way."

In Allenspark, Colorado, he gave a seminar "The Six Bardos." It was the first time a residence was rented where several people could stay for the seminar.

In August and September he gave seminars at Tail of the Tiger, including: "How to Tell a Charlatan," "Explanation of *Om Ah Hum Vajra Guru* Mantra," and "Dialogue with Ego," as well as a detailed presentation of the abhidharma and the *Tibetan Book of the Dead*.

Between October and November he toured North America: in New York he presented "Approach to the Spiritual Path: Examining What's Here First"; in Boston, "The Mandala of the Five Buddha Families," "The Theory and Practice of Tibetan Buddhism," and "The Growth of Spiritual Energy in the U.S."; in Montreal, "Passion and Aggression"; in Toronto, "Searching for Spirituality" and "Meditation in Action"; in Washington, "The Three Marks of Existence"; and finally he went to Chicago.

Between mid-November and mid-December he gave another seminar of nine talks, entitled "Tibetan Buddhism and American Karma," at Karma Dzong, Boulder, before leaving for Estes Park, Colorado, and then San Francisco, where he presented "The Eightfold Path."

There was no format or procedure for receiving and guiding new arrivals. Chögyam Trungpa received each student individually.[13] When he invited a group of Zen practitioners from the San Francisco Zen Center to organize a nyinthün (an entire day of meditation) at Tail of the Tiger, everyone was amazed by the realization that it was possible to stay sitting during an entire weekend.

In 1971, Trungpa asked that each student meditate for at least an hour a day, and that those present at Rocky Mountain Dharma Center not kill animals such as the deer they found there. Slowly, without even realizing it, his students were becoming Buddhists. By the end of 1972, the discipline was becoming more precise. As with other aspects of his work, the process was gradual. He worked with the situation and took his time. For example, one day, during a community meeting at Tail of the Tiger, someone suggested that it might be good idea to set a time limit on the evening discussions, which sometimes lasted through to the next morning. Chögyam Trungpa agreed. He did likewise when it was proposed that alcohol should be drunk only at the end of the day. On another occasion, someone suggested that the group draw up a daily schedule and allot a specific time for practice. Chögyam Trungpa always encouraged these efforts to build a genuine Buddhist community, while leaving the initiative to his students. But sometimes he went further and surprised everyone. One day, someone asked if they should limit the amount of time they could listen to music. Chögyam Trungpa replied: "Just one evening a week!"

Finally he returned to Tail of the Tiger, where he gave three talks on the Maitri Project before giving a seminar of seven talks titled "The Six Realms of Existence."

The diversity of the subject matter is impressive. It must be stressed that when he presented the same theme several times, each talk was totally different. For example, he gave three seminars called "The Six Realms of Existence," one in Colorado and two in Vermont. Two have been published in *Transcending Madness*. The first, given at Allenspark, associates each realm with a specific bardo. In this case, the worlds are described as islands, while the bardos are culminating points that reveal each island. However, the seminar given at Tail of the Tiger emphasizes the process through which we continue to pass. In this perspective, each world contains the full cycle of bardos, which helps it reinforce and maintain its power.

13. In 1971, at Tail of the Tiger, there were just five instructors capable of presenting the practice of meditation when Rinpoche was not there, and none at all at Boulder.

3. Teaching Buddhism: From a Seminar on The Jewel Ornament of Liberation to "Work, Sex, and Money"

The first seminar Chögyam Trungpa gave after arriving in the United States lasted one week. It was a commentary on a text by Gampopa, one of the great masters of the past, entitled *The Jewel Ornament of Liberation*—one of the classic texts used by masters to guide beginners on the Buddhist path. Such texts are known as lamrim, the Tibetan term for a group of texts that offer a full presentation of the different steps on the spiritual path.

Chögyam Trungpa gave twice-daily talks that sometimes lasted as long as three hours. Teachings flowed from him like water from a fountain. What is striking is how different the teaching style was from the one he would adopt a few weeks later. During this brief period, Trungpa adhered closely to the Tibetan practice of offering many teachings but few instructions for concrete practice. In the Tibetan tradition, teaching usually consists of presenting a text, then explaining it line by line. In general, a basic work is used, such as *The Jewel Ornament of Liberation* by Gampopa, or *The Great Perfection* by Paltrül Rinpoche, or one of the lamrim gathered by Tsongkhapa. Such teaching, which dwells principally on the existence of suffering (the Buddha's "first noble truth") and the need to develop compassion, is addressed to all levels of understanding. It is thus assured that the teaching is appropriate to the situation.

But soon Chögyam Trungpa began to teach far more freely. A few months later, in Boston, he presented a program entitled "Work, Sex, and Money," which marked a profound change in approach compared with the earlier seminar on Gampopa. Now he no longer made explicit references to Buddhist doctrine[14] but instead tried to deal directly with the most burning issues of the day. His concern was to show that the Buddha's teachings were not aimed at a particular sort of person at a particular time, but at all of us, here and now. He had discovered his voice,

---

14. Even if we can now recognize in it a classic Buddhist presentation of the three poisons: aggression, passion, and ignorance.

characterized by a relaxed, free tone, plenty of humor, and a deep desire to share his own experiences. Instead of simply repeating acquired knowledge, he directly communicated his own state of being. He had an extraordinary capacity to address an audience and answer people's questions directly, in such a way that a genuine encounter took place. His teaching was an extremely powerful evocation of everybody's experiences. Chögyam Trungpa was so clear and accurate that he was like a hook that caught his students' hearts.

Several influences explain the revolution he was to bring about, which would leave an indelible mark on the way Buddhism is taught in the West, even while his own style remained inimitable. First, one of his masters, Khenpo Gangshar, taught him to compose poems and speeches spontaneously. This apprenticeship offset the more scholarly nature of the education he had received. Chögyam Trungpa was also profoundly interested in the seminars given in the Theravada school, the Buddhism of Southeast Asia. There, monks give teachings on various subjects in return for the food they receive. Chögyam Trungpa was struck by the way his spiritual friend the Zen meditation master Shunryu Suzuki gave seminars in a free, spontaneous way. Finally, his education in Oxford from 1963 to 1966 provided him with an example of teaching methods that are extremely different from those used in Tibet.

It is difficult to determine which of these various influences was most important in the development of the distinctly personal style that Chögyam Trungpa now adopted. His simplicity and closeness to his students were striking for the period, even more so than the content of the teachings themselves. People felt the warmth he had for them all and were deeply affected. For the first time in their lives, they discovered what being loved really meant. Chögyam Trungpa manifested a love that, without asking anything in return, recognizes and welcomes the person we are deep down. It was the force of this love that allowed him to break through everything that makes genuine encounters impossible. He identified these obstacles as "spiritual materialism." This notion has become so closely bound with his teaching that the two are often identified as one. We must now try to set it in its context.

4. Cutting Through Spiritual Materialism

The retreat in Bhutan and the realization of the universality of spiritual materialism

A retreat that Chögyam Trungpa took in Bhutan in 1968 was a decisive moment in his life. For years, in Tibet, India, and then Britain, he had experienced intense frustration at the widespread corruption of true spirituality and at his own inability to reveal Buddhism in all its authenticity.

This is the darkest hour of the dark ages. Disease, famine, and warfare are raging like the fierce north wind. The Buddha's teaching has waned in strength. The various schools of the sangha are fighting amongst themselves with sectarian bitterness;[15] and although the Buddha's teaching was perfectly expounded and there have been many reliable teachings since then from other great gurus, yet they pursue intellectual speculations. The sacred mantra has strayed into Pön [Bön], and the yogis of tantra are losing the insight of meditation. They spend their whole time going through villages and performing little ceremonies for material gain. On the whole, no one acts according to the highest code of discipline, meditation, and wisdom. The jewel-like teaching of insight is fading day by day. The Buddha's teaching is used merely for political purposes and to draw people together socially. As a result, the blessings of spiritual energy are being lost. Even those with great devotion are beginning to lose heart. If the buddhas of the three times and the great teachers were to comment, they would surely express their disappointment.[16]

---

15. In reply to a student's question, Chögyam Trungpa specified that he was not just talking about conflicts between Tibetan schools of Buddhism but among all schools: "The Theravadins were at odds with the Sarvastivadins; the Burmese were quarreling with the Sinhalese."

16. Chögyam Trungpa, *The Sadhana of Mahamudra Which Quells the Mighty Warring of the Three Lords of Materialism and Brings Realization of the Ocean of Siddhas of the Practice Lineage*, trans. Nālandā Translation Committee (Halifax, 1990), p. 5. Those familiar with Tibetan Buddhism will be interested to know that this text was received by Chögyam Trungpa as a

Chögyam Trungpa's attempts to confront this distressing situation can be seen throughout his work. At the beginning of his retreat, everything seemed ordinary. But Chögyam Trungpa felt increasingly frustrated because he was searching for spiritual inspiration, and nothing seemed to be happening. He had no idea what to do to arouse energy. Then suddenly, one night, he experienced a profound spiritual inspiration and started writing *The Sadhana of Mahamudra Which Quells the Mighty Warring of the Three Lords of Materialism,* whose introduction has just been quoted. This retreat altered him profoundly. He could now face up to the distressing trend of our times, which he had seen at work in both the East and the West without being able to name it or deal with it. The obstacle that had constantly stopped him from being able to present Buddhism correctly was *spiritual materialism.*

Many observers have, with good reason, denounced the materialism of our times. For example, the French metaphysician René Guénon, in *The Crisis of the Modern World* (1927), stated that in our day everyone's preoccupation has turned toward the material.[17] In his definition, to be materialistic was to be consciously centered on the material world and related preoccupations: "Modern civilization is truly what might be termed a quantitative civilization, which is another way of saying that it is a material civilization," Guénon wrote. "If one wants to be further convinced of this truth, then it is sufficient to examine the immense importance the world of economics has in the existence of both peoples and individuals: industry, commerce, finances; it would seem that they alone matter, which confirms my earlier point that the sole social distinction that remains is based on material wealth."[18]

Chögyam Trungpa knew that it was necessary to root out materialism in its more subtle and dangerous forms than those based purely on material comfort.

---

terma ("treasure"), a teaching that is concealed by a great teacher of the past for the benefit of a future generation, to be discovered by a qualified person when the time is right.

17. René Guénon, *La crise du monde moderne* (The Crisis of the Modern World) (Paris: Gallimard, 1973), p. 146.

18. Ibid., p. 153.

The Three Lords of Materialism

In his book *Cutting Through Spiritual Materialism*, published in 1973, Chögyam Trungpa distinguishes three aspects of materialism, called the Three Lords of Materialism. We are constantly being deceived by the Lord of Form, the Lord of Speech, and the Lord of Mind. These three figures are metaphors for our relationship with the world.

The Lord of Form corresponds to all our efforts to gain comfort and security. It involves "manipulating physical surroundings so as to shield ourselves from the irritations of the raw, rugged, unpredictable aspects of life. Push-button elevators, prepackaged meat, air conditioning, flush toilets, private funerals, retirement programs, mass production, weather satellites, bulldozers, fluorescent lighting, nine-to-five jobs, television—all are attempts to create a manageable, safe, predictable, pleasurable world."[19] Such efforts are expressed in the constant pursuit of wealth. But extreme asceticism is also a manifestation of this aspect of materialism: you can deprive yourself of many things and impose an extremely harsh lifestyle on yourself without necessarily renouncing egocentrism, and with the sole aim of acquiring greater comfort. Such materialism is based on the desire to control the world and to avoid all possible sources of irritation in our physical environment.

The Lord of Speech is the use of intellect to control our universe better. We adopt concepts as if they were levers we could use to control phenomena. We see the world only through them. They become filters that block any direct perception of reality. In order to maintain a world in which we feel secure, we seek to understand everything. With this intention, any ideology or doctrinal system can become materialistic: nationalism, communism, existentialism, Catholicism, Buddhism. All these "isms," when seen as panaceas for our ills, become the instruments of this Lord.

But the most sophisticated Lord, the Lord of Mind, does not restrict himself to the rather flagrant maneuvers of the previous two. He perverts the spiritual desire to become more conscious and aware. Many forms of meditation and spiritual practices in general are used with the sole aim of

---

19. *Cutting Through Spiritual Materialism* (1973), p. 6.

reaching a state of pleasure or happiness, in the attempt to "live up to what we would *like* to be."[20] On the contrary, genuine spirituality is based on a realistic approach to oneself and to the world.

Analysis of these three Lords shows that everything can be used in the service of materialism, and that it is not so simple as "the reign of quantity," to use Guénon's term characterizing our degenerate age. The desire for a certain material comfort, the intellectual effort to understand the world or a spiritual experience, are not intrinsic problems. They only become problematic if what motivates us is the desire to make ourselves invulnerable and to avoid fear or insecurity. Materialism consists in thinking that our existence should be improved. We ask ourselves how we can let go of ego and open up, but "the first obstacle is the question itself: 'How?' If you don't question yourself, don't watch yourself, then you just do it."[21]

The three forms of materialism derive from the effort the ego makes to reassure itself of its own existence. In Buddhism, the word *ego* does not have the same meaning as it does in Western psychology. It is an illusion that sets out to prove the solidity of its existence. In this sense, the ego is not a true entity, but instead an accumulation of habits and confusions, a set of hopes, fears, and dreams. Our entire relationship with the world thus passes through this filter, which checks out whether what is going on is advantageous to us or not. In such a perspective, undertaking a spiritual quest is merely the personal desire to gratify our ego, whereas it should, on the contrary, open us ever more deeply to what truly exists and provide "a way of subjugating or shedding our ego."[22]

One of Buddhism's most basic teachings shows the pointlessness of all the efforts we make to satisfy the Three Lords. As Pema Chödrön, one of

---

20. *Crazy Wisdom*, p. 6. The first chapter of this book is devoted to spiritual materialism. The author explains how the ego, in its spiritual quest, leads to "the transcendental unknown," a marvelous expression used to describe a pole where we project all our desires, a "something about the world or the cosmos that corresponds to this 'something' that we are" but which we have never made the effort to confront honestly.

21. *Cutting Through Spiritual Materialism* (1973), p. 49.

22. *Training the Mind and Cultivating Loving-Kindness* (1993), p. 148.

Chögyam Trungpa's students, put it: "There's a common misunderstanding among all the human beings who have ever been born on the earth that the best way to live is to try to avoid pain and just try to get comfortable."[23] Being honest and recognizing the reality of our suffering is the only way to break with the process. The spiritual way can then turn into personal experience.

The catastrophe of our time is that it has become difficult to distinguish between authentic spirituality and materialism. The confusion between them is a sign of the times.

The persistence of spiritual materialism

Spiritual materialism is an obstacle to any authentic spiritual path: "There are numerous sidetracks which lead to a distorted, ego-centered version of spirituality; we can deceive ourselves into thinking we are developing spiritually when instead we are strengthening our egocentricity through spiritual techniques."[24]

Such criticism is not aimed uniquely at the West. Many Tibetans and Westerners have presented an idyllic image of Tibet, where so many people were supposed to be following the path of enlightenment. But Chögyam Trungpa, while remaining profoundly attached to his native land, often spoke of the corruption that was rife there. In 1975, in a seminar devoted to *The Sadhana of Mahamudra* entitled "The Embodiment of All the Siddhas,"[25] he explained: "We definitely had a lot of spiritual problems in my country. People just conducted their little spiritual business affairs: they conducted marriage ceremonies; they conducted funeral ceremonies; they conducted ceremonies for the sick; they conducted ceremonies for the unfortunate. But there was no real practice going on; it

---

23. Pema Chödrön, *The Wisdom of No Escape and the Path of Loving-Kindness* (Boston: Shambhala Publications, 1991), p. 3.

24. *Cutting Through Spiritual Materialism* (1973), p. 3.

25. Chögyam Trungpa, "The Embodiment of All the Siddhas," Karmê Chöling, September 1975, unpublished.

was a big racket."[26] Materialism, especially in its spiritual form, is just as present in the East as in the West.

In the United States, the situation in the 1970s was like a huge supermarket where you could go in and pick whatever captured your fancy: watered-down versions of authentic traditions, drugs, fake gurus and other assorted charlatans, a taste of Zen or Hinduism, even Tibetan Buddhism, freshly delivered. Many masters of the time, particularly those from India, followed this trend. They thus established their own territory and confirmed that of their disciples. To their followers, they promised ultimate well-being. They thus formed a mutual conspiracy that was denounced by Chögyam Trungpa. As he put it on arriving in the United States: "Spiritual interest is coming out more strongly in people now because of the character of this century; the river of materialism has overrun its banks. Not only are there endless gadgets and machines, but there is pervasive spiritual materialism under which the great traditions have become just so much milk in the marketplace. The twentieth century is the age of ego."[27]

Chögyam Trungpa felt that many of the spiritual masters who had come to the United States did not offer a true discipline that would allow us to rid ourselves of our constant egocentricity. Their approach was incomplete. He even denounced those who claimed to exemplify a discipline by, for example, wearing white robes, being vegetarian, or speaking softly. All of these approaches could easily be just a means to conceal spiritual arrogance.

Chögyam Trungpa thus undertook a campaign that deeply marked the first years of his teaching. As early as the first issue of his magazine *Garuda*,[28] which came out in 1971, he devoted an important arti-

---

26. Chögyam Trungpa, *Sadhana of Mahamudra Sourcebook* (Boulder: Vajradhatu Publications, 1979), p. 7.

27. Chögyam Trungpa, "The Common Heart," Centre Monchanin, Montreal, December 4, 1970, unpublished.

28. Garuda is the name of a mythical animal, a sort of heavenly eagle. It symbolizes enlightenment because it hatches fully developed from its egg.

cle to this subject, entitled "Transcending Materialism." Whatever the circumstances, he never hesitated to attack materialism. When answering a questionnaire sent to him through the mail about what he thought of the "Age of Aquarius," he said, "I have heard this expression, but I don't think that it has any particular significance. It would be presumptuous to predict the future, but it seems that what is happening is that this New Age will develop a height of supermaterialism and that during this time, man's search will continue beyond that state."[29]

Everywhere, he cut through the mystification he witnessed. Once, over dinner, an extremely elegant lady was foolhardy enough to ask him: "Rinpoche, my guru has taught me the practice of White Tara, but he hasn't explained what it is. What is White Tara?" Chögyam Trungpa replied: "It's cottage cheese." Then, after a few moments of silence, he pointed at another dish in front of him and added: "And Green Tara is spinach."

5. From Cynicism to Gentleness

No more "trips"

With ruthless accuracy, Chögyam Trungpa cut through everyone's "trip." This expression is typical of the hippie culture of the time. It suggests that we leave on a trip each time we depart from reality with a sensation of "spacing out." The aim of his teaching, Chögyam Trungpa explained, was to shatter these trips and bring the student back face to face with reality—which can be a painful process, especially for those who mistake their trips for reality. Without any hesitation, but not without humor, Chögyam Trungpa destroyed people's illusions. During a visit from a student who had already met several Tibetan gurus and who, following Tibetan custom, bowed down before him, Trungpa looked at the floor and asked, "Have you lost something?" On another occasion, during a lecture in New York, a student who seemed to be on drugs stood up and started asking

---

29. Chögyam Trungpa, answer to a questionnaire on *The Voice of Aquarius*, a television show, September 7, 1970, unpublished.

an extremely long, intellectually convoluted, and clearly meaningless question. While the student was still speaking, Trungpa bent toward the microphone and blew a long *ffff* into it. Rather surprised, the student stopped. Then he took a breath and started up again. So Chögyam Trungpa interrupted him again with another even longer *fffff*, which, this time, finally brought the student to silence.

Chögyam Trungpa opened people's minds. He made fun of anything that was too serious, pinpointing the precise spot where it most hurt.

In his teachings, he explained that those who think they have found a spiritual path and are on the side of truth have simply fallen into the huge trap of looking for a savior and thus fleeing their own experience: "It's not so much that the doctrine has converted you, but that you have converted the doctrine into your own ego."[30] The aim of the teachings is for us not to learn to be "right," but instead to be ever more open to what is.

Meditation

Confronted as we are with the rampant spiritual materialism all around us, the practice of meditation is the only weapon we possess. This practice consists in looking at who we really are, thus providing us with a naked experience of our state of mind, but without trying to reach any particular goal. Meditation is not a religious practice: "The practice of meditation is based not on how we would like things to be, but on what is."[31] Given that the characteristic of the ego is to view everything in a competitive, aggressive manner, it is starved to death by meditation, which aims at nothing.

In other words, the sole alternative to the confusion created by spiritual materialism is to face up to our own experience in the present, in what Chögyam Trungpa termed "nowness." To achieve this, the only advice he gave was to practice regularly. He often repeated: "Everybody who is

---

30. Chögyam Trungpa, *Selected Community Talks* (Boulder: Vajradhatu Publications, 1978), p. 37.

31. Chögyam Trungpa, "An Approach to Meditation," unpublished lecture, Association for Humanistic Psychology, Washington, D.C., September 1971.

interested in any kind of pursuit of spiritual discipline should sit and meditate first."[32]

Embacing the situation that he found on arriving in the United States, Chögyam Trungpa did not ask anyone to become vegetarian, take monastic vows, or adopt any particular beliefs. It was simply necessary to meditate and learn to be here, just as we are.

The second phase: open your heart

Within two years, Chögyam Trungpa had created a genuine community of practicing Buddhists, both at Tail of the Tiger and in Boulder. He had also established a close relationship with each of his students. He had learned to appreciate them. The complete trust that he had in them is one of the most striking aspects of his approach. He adapted himself to their energies, their difficulties, and their personalities. He did not set out to transform them; instead he encouraged them to develop themselves and become what they really were. During one of the seminars he regularly held in the community, he told the participants: "I am sorry to be so crude, so emotional, but I feel I would like to make love to everybody in the community, and I feel that you can understand what I'm trying to say. . . . I am putting my trust in you."[33]

On June 16, 1972, Chögyam Trungpa gave a seminar entitled "Phase Two." He remarked that the initial step of his teaching had been marked by a growing cynicism, based on the refusal to accept anything without close scrutiny. Cynicism, he explained, is a way to unmask everything that is preordained or doctrinal, everything that is imposed from the outside, such as the set of habitual mental reflexes we have developed ourselves, our own "school of thought" in which we are locked. His students were indeed ready to question everything that was explained to them and believe nothing. Together, they had put together a series of critiques on the

---

32. Chögyam Trungpa, "Buddhism and the Spiritual Energy of America," Boston, April 6, 1976, unpublished. These were the closing words of the seminar, after the replies to questions.

33. Chögyam Trungpa, "Trust Run Wild," July 10, 1972, in *Selected Community Talks*, p. 28.

various spiritual approaches then present in the United States so as to expose their materialism and hypocrisy.

However, too much cynicism means we turn self-destructive. So it was now time to start the second stage of implanting Buddhism in the West and thus create the possibility of establishing honest relationships among people. Mutual help was required: "we have to develop a kind of romanticism. This is equally important as the cynical approach we have been taking up till now."[34]

This was hard to swallow for the hard-boiled cynics that many of Chögyam Trungpa's students had become, and there was much debate. But he pressed his point on numerous occasions: the students had to develop more compassion. While cynicism is the means to destroy the beliefs of the ego, Chögyam Trungpa showed how compassion could also destroy ego by cutting through our arrogance. In a seminar entitled "Cynicism and Devotion," he explained the importance of discovering the fresh continent of mystic experience, which had hitherto been a taboo subject: "Mystical experience in this case has nothing to do with astral traveling or conjuring up ritual objects in your hand or turning the ceiling into the floor. Mystical experience in this case is discovering a hidden warmth—the larger version of home."[35]

Chögyam Trungpa brought about the destruction of spiritual materialism and cut through to the heart of the sardonic game that ego plays with itself in order to create "a sense of beauty, and even of love and light."[36] This deepening of his teaching inaugurated a new phase, the first in a long series of changes. Year after year, Chögyam Trungpa cast doubt on what had previously seemed to be the core of the teaching, while always finding new ways to enter the heart of the truth.

---

34. "Crazy Wisdom" seminar, Jackson Hole, Wyoming, December 1972. See *Crazy Wisdom*, p. 64.

35. Chögyam Trungpa, *Selected Community Talks*, p. 39.

36. *Crazy Wisdom*, p. 65.

Chapter Two
CHILDHOOD
AND EDUCATION

My teachers, namely two persons in my life, Jamgön Kongtrül and Khenpo Gangshar, were always able to catch me. Whenever I came up with little spikes or sparks of every possible way of making myself well known and maintaining my ego, they would constantly throw a web or net of some kind over me.

At the time it was miserable and painful. I felt that instead of such torture, why didn't they just kill me on the spot, execute me on the spot? I requested them to do so many times, but they said, "You'll be more useful later on if we don't kill you." [1]

—CHÖGYAM TRUNGPA

THE SIMPLE PRESENCE of this man who spoke so directly seemed to place a magnifying glass over all the little games and tricks we use in order to feel good and avoid facing the truth. Yet he came from a very different world, faraway Tibet, and was raised in the tradition of Buddhism as it is practiced in that region.

---

1. Chögyam Trungpa, *1976 Seminary Transcripts: Vajrayana* (Boulder: Vajradhatu Publications), p. 27.

1. Finding the Eleventh Trungpa and the Notion of Tülku

Chögyam Trungpa was born in February 1940,[2] in a small village on the high plateau of northeastern Tibet. Above it, the famous Mount Pagö Pünsum, often called "the pillar of the sky," rises abruptly at a height of over eighteen thousand feet. It looks like a large arrow, and the eternal snow on its peak glitters in the sun. This is the region of Kham, Eastern Tibet, which, while belonging to the Land of Snow (as Tibetans call their country), enjoyed a certain independence from the central power in Lhasa.

Like all the inhabitants of their village, Chögyam Trungpa's parents were nomads. Together, the nomads made up a large family who lived in tents, moving from place to place with their yaks and sheep. Many Tibetans traveled around like this, on horseback or else on foot if they were poor.

"I was born in a cowshed in Eastern Tibet," Chögyam Trungpa recalled, "where people have never seen a tree. The people of that particular region live on pastureland without any trees or even bushes or greenery. They live on meat and milk products throughout the whole year. I was a son of the genuine earth, the son of a peasant."[3]

In this country known for the severity of its climate, there is a profound bonding between people and nature. Because they believe that human beings are intimately linked with the environment, Tibetans generally do not try to alter or interfere with the world around them. Their relationship to the sacred and to one another takes a completely different form than ours does in the West.

---

2. "There has been some confusion about Chögyam Trungpa's precise date of birth. *Born in Tibet* gives it as the full-moon day of the first month of the Earth Hare year, 1939. Other autobiographical sources, including an important doha (song) that he wrote in Tibet, suggest that he was born in the year of the Iron Dragon, 1940. Later in his life, he himself considered this to be his birth year." *The Collected Works of Chögyam Trungpa*, vol. 2 (Boston: Shambhala Publications, 2003), introduction by Carolyn Rose Gimian.

3. Chögyam Trungpa, *1979 Kalapa Assembly Transcripts* (Boulder: Vajradhatu Publications), p. 15.

When Chögyam Trungpa was thirteen months old, he was recognized as a tülku, the incarnation of a Buddhist master of great importance. In order to explain this rather mysterious notion, it will first be necessary to explain a few fundamental Buddhist ideas. Although unique to Tibet,[4] the institution of tülku derives from the traditional Buddhist doctrine of karma[5] and rebirth. While these terms are often used in the West, they are generally misunderstood. They need elucidation.

In Buddhism, each being has countless existences. However, these lives possess no intrinsic reality, in contrast to the way reincarnation is sometimes viewed in the West. While there is a continuum of consciousness, this does not constitute a "soul" or an autonomous entity. Thus the doctrine of karma does not provide us with an eternity during which we can eventually perfect ourselves. On the contrary, the doctrine of karma is the understanding that birth and death are continual.

It is thus rather inaccurate to talk about reincarnation in Buddhism: a better term would be *rebirth*.[6] Buddha understood that suffering was the lot of humankind, as well as of all other sentient beings. The desire to propagate one's own individuality is one of the main forces that keeps us

---

4. The tradition of tülkus was inaugurated by the Karmapas, the spiritual leaders of one of the main lineages of the Kagyü school, known as Karma Kagyü, to which Chögyam Trungpa belonged.

5. *Karma* literally means "action." According to this universal law of cause and effect, our experience now is the result of our actions in the past. Our karma is also the potential that guides our behavior and influences our present and future actions and thoughts. All karma is the seed of other karmas to come. We reap the results of our actions in terms of joy or suffering, according to the nature of our thoughts and deeds. In this way, our future condition depends on the way we live now. At each moment, we create our future karma.

6. Chögyam Trungpa explained this misunderstanding as follows: "Oriental wisdom has made an enormous impact and given tremendous promise to the Western philosophers and the Western mind in general. This began when Theosophy was first introduced in the West. Since that time, a lot of Westerners have thought, 'We don't have to be highly accomplished as such, because we have constant hope of becoming a better person all the time.' They think that Oriental wisdom and meditation involve just being open and doing nothing. 'Just sit and meditate. You're going to be okay as long as you sit and relax.' So the idea of reincarnation has been a problem, as well as a promise, in Western thinking—particularly in the case of Westerners who think in terms of Oriental traditions." Chögyam Trungpa, *Karma Seminar* (Boulder: Vajradhatu Publications, 1973), p. 50.

chained to this suffering. Renouncing the "I" and recognizing the illusory nature of our rebirths allow us to gain freedom.

In the case of tülkus, the forces that shape their existence are rather different and are not solely conditioned by karma. Such beings are basically free because they are enlightened. Their rebirth is a direct expression of their bodhisattva vow, their wish to return to earth to benefit others. Whereas for certain Buddhist schools the end of the path is freedom from confusion and suffering (leaving behind samsara), in Tibetan Buddhism it is necessary to go beyond your own liberation and to devote yourself to the freedom of all beings. In this way, the institution of tülkus is the perfect accomplishment of the aspirations of all practitioners, which are often expressed in the form of four great vows:

> However innumerable beings are, I vow to save them;
> However inexhaustible the passions are, I vow to
> transform them;
> However limitless the dharma is, I vow to understand
> it completely;
> However infinite the Buddha's truth is, I vow to attain it.

Inspired by such a perspective, the ambition of practitioners is not to reach enlightenment for themselves. Their primary preoccupation is to devote themselves to all living beings and to help free themselves from their fundamental ignorance, which is the cause of their suffering.

When an important master dies, the head of the lineage is often charged with finding his new rebirth. He will then receive in dreams or visions precise indications as to where to find the child. For example, in the case of Chögyam Trungpa, the sixteenth Karmapa[7] indicated that the tülku of the tenth Trungpa had been born in a village five days' walk from Surmang, the house had a south-facing door, the family had a large red dog, and the father's name was Yeshe Dargye and the mother's Chung Tso. Because the mother had remarried, there was some confusion when iden-

---

7. The sixteenth Karmapa was Chögyam Trungpa's hierarchical superior, just as previous Karmapas had been for prior Trungpas.

tifying the child—the name of the man she was living with was not the same as that of Chögyam Trungpa's father as revealed in the prediction.

When Chögyam Trungpa was finally identified, he was tested, as is customary. He was presented with several objects of the same type, only one of which had belonged to his predecessor. Without any hesitation the child identified the correct one. The indications given by the Karmapa were right. Chögyam Trungpa said that he could clearly remember events in the life of his predecessor, the tenth Trungpa, until the age of thirteen.

However, even if young children recognized as tülkus have great potential, they have not fully realized this potential. They must be educated in a very strict and rigorous fashion, far more so than ordinary monks. When he was eighteen months old, Chögyam Trungpa had to leave his village to live in a monastery. At the age of five, he began his formal education.

2. The Tradition of Surmang and the History of the Lineage

The union of the Nyingma and Kagyü lineages

Tibetan Buddhism is divided into several schools. The oldest, the Nyingma, goes back to the eighth century. Because its practitioners (known as Nyingmapas) lived in isolated hermitages, it survived the waves of persecution that led to the destruction of many monasteries in the ninth century. The eleventh century saw the development of the Kadam and Sakya schools, which originated in conventional Indian monasticism. The Kagyü school also emerged around then as a more purely tantric movement, passed on from master to student, so that initially it was less institutionalized than the other schools. In the fourteenth century, the great scholar Tsongkhapa founded the Geluk school as a reform version of the Kadam movement. The Gelukpas emphasize study, exercises in logic, scholarship, and monasticism; their best-known representative is the Dalai Lama. So the four main Tibetan schools of Buddhism are the Nyingma, Sakya, Kagyü, and Geluk.

As the inheritor of the Trungpa lineage, Chögyam Trungpa was recognized as a holder of the Kagyü tradition. However, his root guru, or main teacher (Sechen Kongtrül), belonged to the Nyingma school. Trungpa thus was a primary inheritor of two traditions. This dual allegiance is not unusual, as the Kagyü and Nyingma traditions have always been very close. Both emphasize the practice of meditation, which they consider to be the sole way to gain an unobstructed, direct experience of truths that the texts can only suggest.

The Kagyü school is particularly associated with the teaching known as mahamudra, whereas the older Nyingma tradition is linked to the teachings of ati, or dzogchen. As Chögyam Trungpa contrasted them, mahamudra entails "working on your own basic ground as you are," whereas with ati you "approach your work with the inspirations of your fruition, your enlightenment experience."[8] Such a perspective implies that "the ati vision generally looks to a much greater level of various situations, fully and thoroughly; while the mahamudra vision always looks for the colorful aspect of the phenomena of your journey."[9]

Chögyam Trungpa explained: "My presentation of Buddhism in America has been an expression of bringing together the two schools. The teachings are capable of reaching people's minds properly, without any cultural sophistries, because of the saving grace of both those wisdoms. Those teachings transcend the conceptual level: they are able to communicate with us as human beings."[10]

The union of politics and spirituality

As the eleventh Trungpa, the young child had to become the secular leader of the Surmang monasteries and the spiritual holder of the teachings practiced there.

---

8. Chögyam Trungpa, *1973 Seminary Transcripts: Vajrayana* (Boulder: Vajradhatu Publications), p. 130.

9. Chögyam Trungpa, *Collected Vajra Assemblies*, vol. 1 (Halifax: Vajradhatu Publications, 1990), p. 14.

10. Chögyam Trungpa, *Sadhana of Mahamudra Sourcebook* (Halifax: Vajradhatu Publications, 1979), p. 37.

Surmang is the name given to a group of monasteries founded by the great master Trung Ma-se Lodrö Rinchen. Born in the far east of Tibet, he was the son of the king of Minyak[11] but renounced his kingdom in the hope of finding a guru. He traveled to different monasteries, finally arriving at Tsurphu in Central Tibet, where he met the fifth Karmapa, Teshin Shekpa (1384–1415). He studied under his direction and remained in a retreat for ten years in conditions of great austerity.

The fifth Karmapa was a truly great guru. He was invited to China by the Ming emperor, Yung-lo, who became his disciple. Because of the great respect he felt for him, the emperor gave him the title of Imperial Teacher and presented him with the famous "black hat," or vajra crown, which was to become the symbol of the Karmapas. This vajra crown represents his spiritual attainment. Even today, during a very special ceremony, the Karmapa places this crown on his head while meditating for a period of time. He is then Avalokiteshvara personified, the embodiment of compassion. Teshin Shekpa had a great influence on Chinese spiritual and cultural thought.

After several years in his company, the Karmapa[12] asked Trung Ma-se to set up a new center of practice and study. Trung Ma-se then traveled around before returning to his birthplace in East Tibet. When he arrived in the Yöshung Valley, he had the feeling that this was the place. He stayed there in solitary retreat for six years before starting to teach a few

---

11. The term *king* here does not imply a political role as in the West. A Tibetan king was above all a landowner. His mission was not to rule over his subjects, but rather to act as property administrator. Thus his relationship with his people was more like that of a landlord with his tenants.

12. Teshin Shekpa gave Trung Ma-se the teachings of the Kagyü and Nyingma. From the Kagyü school, he introduced him to the mahamudra and in particular the practice of Chakrasamvara and Vajrayogini. This had been transmitted from a guru to a single disciple for thirteen generations, according to the instructions of Naropa, the Indian master. This sort of transmission is called *chig gyü*, which means transmission by a single lineage holder. Trung Ma-se was the thirteenth generation, and he became the first to transmit the tradition to more than one student.

He also received the Nyingma teachings of the *Khandro Nyingthik*, "the quintessence of the dakinis," which Guru Padmasambhava conferred to his consort and closest disciple, Yeshe Tsogyal.

students. They lived and practiced together in an extremely primitive reed hut.

Because of his attainments, more and more disciples gathered around him. A monastery was created.

Künga Gyaltsen, the first Trungpa

The first Trungpa was born into a prominent family but left it to study with Trung Ma-se. He stayed by his teacher's side for twenty years, serving him and studying under his direction. Then the time came for him to leave his guru, who advised him to find his own place and teach others. He was offered a castle belonging to Adro Shelubum, a rich landowner and one of his disciples. But, at the same time, the first Trungpa always desired to maintain a nomadic existence.

Meanwhile, Trung Ma-se had gathered an even larger number of students around him. His hut-monastery was now overcrowded and so was transferred to a fort called Namgyal Tse, much larger than Dütsi Tel and also a gift from Adro Shelubum. A large amount of land was included with the donation, as well as some rocky mountains containing several caves suitable for secluded meditation. Trung Ma-se, who was proud of his irregularly shaped hut, adopted the name Surmang ("many-cornered") for the entire region where these activities were taking place.

Before dying, Trung Ma-se said that he would not be reincarnated, because "his teaching was both his incarnation and his portrait."[13] At the time of his death, Surmang included Namgyal Tse, Dütsi Tel, and several smaller monasteries, each with its own spiritual head.

From the second to the ninth Trungpa

When the second Trungpa was recognized by His Holiness Karmapa, a new lineage of incarnations began.

The third Trungpa, Künga Öser, focused on structuring the monastic life of Surmang, which was still mainly conducted nomadic style, using

---

13. *Born in Tibet*, 4th ed. (2000), p. 33.

tents and caravans, which allowed practitioners to travel according to climatic conditions. The library was transported by mules, and the assembly hall was a large tent. Over a hundred monks traveled together. This conception of monastic life was very common in Tibet at the time; Tsurphu, the Karmapa's home monastery, was also formed in this way.

Chögyam Trungpa drew on this tradition when teaching in the United States. During many important programs conducted at Rocky Mountain Dharma Center in the mountains of Colorado, he lived in a tent or a simple trailer, because he loved "tent culture" and its insecure simplicity, expressing the principles of a simple life and a direct relationship with nature.

The fourth Trungpa, Künga Namgyal, is of considerable importance for the entire Kagyü school because of the depth of his understanding and attainment. He wrote three large volumes on mahamudra meditation, unlike anything previously composed, and also a number of other treatises. He was a musician, famed for the chants he composed. Thanks to his reputation, the monastery of Dütsi Tel became extremely prestigious, even though it was smaller than Namgyal Tse. However, Künga Namgyal decided to hand over direction of his monastery to his brother, and went to live as a hermit in a cave for six years before setting out on long pilgrimages. The contemporary guru Tenga Rinpoche has described him as follows: "Trungpa Kunga Namgyal, after attaining complete mastery and realization, was in the habit of putting his mala [prayer beads] and his books and so forth simply in the air in front of him, where they would remain. When he was in retreat in a cave he didn't have to rely on the door; he had attained transparency or unimpededness, so he could simply go right through the wall to where he wished to be."[14]

Thanks to their considerable spiritual influence, the succeeding Trungpas were to play an important political role. They became supreme abbots of all the monasteries in Surmang. The spiritual and cultural situation developed to such an extent that the government in Central Tibet, controlled by the Gelukpas, was very uncomfortable with power being assumed by

---

14. Tenga Rinpoche, address to the Karma Dzong community, Halifax, in *Vajradhatu Sun*, December 1985, p. 28.

monasteries or groups anywhere else in Tibet. In league with the extrem-
ist Mongol leader Gusri Khan, they decided to put a stop to the influence
these masters had in the region. In league with the fanatical followers of
Gusri Khan, they ravaged the province of Surmang and imprisoned the
seventh Trungpa for many years.[15]

But, thanks to their spiritual realization, the Trungpas survived.

The tenth Trungpa

The tenth Trungpa, Chögyam Trungpa's direct predecessor, led a life of
great austerity. After being brought up in a prosperous and influential
family, he became a monk and refused all honors. His humility was legendary. For example, he never mounted a horse, because he found such
an attitude haughty and proud. While still young, he rebelled against his
instructors, who wanted him to become a fundraiser for the monastery.
For a monastery to thrive, custom demanded that its spiritual leader
travel to gather offerings to enrich the community. The tenth Trungpa refused this role. He thought it more important to devote himself to the
practice of meditation and to deepen his understanding of the teachings.
Because of the pressure he was under, one night he decided to run away
alone, on foot, and join Jamgön Kongtrül the Great, one of the most em-
inent gurus of the time. He stayed with him and studied for many years.
Once his training was over, he remained in retreat, under Kongtrül's direction, for six more years, before returning to Surmang. He was now a
famous teacher, and many disciples came to study under him, including
Dilgo Khyentse and Jamgön Kongtrül of Sechen. They in turn were to become the gurus of Chögyam Trungpa. The continuation of the lineage
was thus preserved.

The history of the tradition of Surmang allows us to understand the
specific nature of the training Chögyam Trungpa received. Because of the
particular way in which tantric Buddhism is transmitted orally from
teacher to disciple, each monastery develops its own tradition to some ex-

---

15. See *Born in Tibet*, 4th ed. (2000), p. 35, and "Line of Trungpa," Karmê Chöling, January
26, 1975, sixth talk.

tent, even if the ultimate approach is the same. The teachings that Chö-gyam Trungpa presented in the West were not invented by one man. They came from the unbroken lineage to which he was heir. Here we cannot provide an exhaustive list of the teachings that were specific to Sur-mang;[16] Chögyam Trungpa did not aim to transmit them all. He was far more than the spiritual head of Surmang. Once he had moved to the United States, he surpassed the specific nature of the functions associated with his title. He presented the very heart of Buddhism, without neces-sarily explaining all of the rituals and practices he had learned. Numer-ous teachers, on coming to the West, present the characteristic teachings that they hold and in which they are in some ways the experts. Custom-arily, an abbot in Tibet would focus mainly on transmitting the special-ties of his monastery. Instead, Chögyam Trungpa resolved to teach shamatha-vipashyana meditation, which he saw as the necessary founda-tion for presenting dharma in the West.

3. Recognition of the Eleventh Trungpa and His Training

Chögyam Trungpa was enthroned as the eleventh Trungpa by the six-teenth Karmapa. Over twelve thousand monks and laypeople from all over East Tibet came to attend the ceremony, during which the child took refuge in the Buddha (an example of an enlightened being), in the dharma (the Buddha's teachings, which lay out the path), and in the sangha (the community of practitioners). This ceremony is a key moment in the life of all Buddhists, but this occasion was a particularly solemn event given the importance of the eleventh Trungpa.

At the moment when the Karmapa approached with his scissors to cut a lock of the child's hair, thus symbolizing his commitment, a blast of

---

16. The Kagyü tradition of Surmang in particular includes the commentary of the fourth Trungpa on mahamudra, the practice of chö, and the practice of Chakrasamvara transmit-ted by the fifth Karmapa along with an extensive cycle of dances specific to this tradition and linked to this yidam. This practice was transmitted as a visionary revelation to one of the first Trungpas.

thunder was heard, it began raining, and a rainbow appeared. These were seen as good omens.

The Karmapa gave him his new name: Karma Tendzin Trinle Künkhyap Pal Sangpo. All those who take refuge in the Karma Kagyü lineage receive the first name Karma as a sign of belonging to this tradition. *Tendzin Trinle Künkhyap Pal Sangpo* means "the universal action of the holder of the Doctrine, the gloriously good."

After this ceremony, Chögyam Trungpa remained living with his mother, surrounded by servants who looked after him. Then, when he turned five, it was decided that the time had come to begin his instruction. A tutor named Asang Lama was chosen for him, a very kind and gentle man whom Chögyam Trungpa loved deeply. He taught the boy to read and write, introduced him to the arts, and told him stories about the main teachers of the lineage, which greatly inspired the young Trungpa tülku.

It was then decided that life at Dütsi Tel was too full of distractions, and he was sent to Dorje Khyung Dzong, a retreat center.

When he was seven, Chögyam Trungpa was taken back to Dütsi Tel so that he could receive the ritual authorization to study all of the Kangyur, the texts containing the teachings of the Buddha.[17] The regent abbots of the two monasteries, dissatisfied with the tutor Asang Lama because they considered him a little too indulgent, appointed a replacement, Apho Karma. This new tutor put a stop to painting lessons, reduced the time devoted to writing, and asked Chögyam Trungpa to work harder at his memorization. The separation from the man who had become like a father to him was extremely painful, and Chögyam Trungpa was delighted when he was finally free from the control of Apho Karma. Later on, it was always with much emotion that Chögyam Trungpa spoke of his education: "I had been brought up strictly from infancy, from the age of eighteen months, so that I had no other refer-

---

17. The canonic texts of Buddhism are divided into two large groups: the Kangyur, which contains the sutras, abhidharma, vinaya, and tantras of the Buddha in 103 volumes, and the Tengyur, which contains commentaries by various Indian masters, consisting of over 230 volumes, translated into Tibetan mainly from Sanskrit.

ence point such as the idea of freedom or being loose. I had no idea what it was like to be an ordinary child playing in the dirt or playing with toys or chewing on rusted metal or whatever. Since I did not have any other reference point, I thought that was just the way the world was. I felt somewhat at home, but at the same time extraordinarily hassled and claustrophobic."[18]

The regent abbot monk of Dütsi Tel, Rölpa Dorje, also played an important part in the instruction that Chögyam Trungpa received at Surmang. In particular, he transmitted to him the practice of Vajrayogini, a basic practice of the Kagyü school that Chögyam Trungpa would subsequently present in depth in the West.

4. Jamgön Kongtrül of Sechen and the Student-Teacher Relationship

The importance of the teacher

Chögyam Trungpa's initial training remained basically theoretical. Given that the heart of the Buddhist teachings lies in the relationship between teacher and disciple, the essential part was still to come.

It may be hard for Westerners to understand what a spiritual teacher stands for. It is necessary first to realize that the guru lies at the crux of tantric Buddhism and that there is no real equivalent to this role in Western religion: "Without such a teacher," Chögyam Trungpa explained, "we cannot experience the world properly and thoroughly."[19] There is no better statement of what a teacher is. The ego is so blind that, without a guide, it is impossible to be free and recognize the nature of reality.

However, a teacher is not a static entity carved in stone. He (or she) assumes different roles as the disciple progresses.

---

18. *Journey without Goal,* pp. 97–98.

19. Ibid., p. 61.

First, the teacher is an instructor, or tutor. The dharma cannot be understood without a direct, personal relationship with a teacher. This is often misunderstood, and yet at a basic level we can accept it. Consider the experience of seeing a play performed brilliantly at the theater. It is absolutely unlike reading the script at home. The written word takes on a completely different dimension. So, to an even greater degree in the spiritual world, if teaching is to be genuine and alive, then personal contact with a teacher is vital.

At the next stage, the teacher enters into a closer relationship with our fundamental nature, and our state of mind, and assumes the appearance of kalyanamitra, or "spiritual friend." A loving relationship begins between him and his disciple.

Finally, the teacher may become the student's "vajra master," or guru.[20] The Sanskrit word *guru* means "heavy," referring to being heavily laden with good qualities. The Tibetans use the word *lama,* which means "one who is above," because it describes someone who has a panoramic vision of his students' situation and who can thus guide them correctly.[21] A guru is not just worthy of respect; he embodies the spirit of enlightenment that can be experienced directly. He is the spokesman for the world of phenomena: "The master makes your perceptions, your thoughts, your confusion so vivid. . . . You see red is so red and gold is so gold and yellow is so yellow and blue is so blue. You begin to have this perception of pain as extremely painful maybe, and pleasure as extremely pleasurable. There is an experience of real reality taking place."[22]

Without a teacher, enlightenment could turn out to be an object *we* want to attain, rather than an experience beyond any limit.

In Tibetan Buddhism, enlightenment is manifested in a human being

---

20. The symbolic emblem of indestructible reality is also called vajra. It is a sort of scepter depicting the skillful ways of tantra.

21. The term *lama* has become an honorary title given to a rather wide variety of teachers. Incarnate masters, or tülkus, are called Rinpoche, "precious one."

22. Chögyam Trungpa, "Sacred World," Boulder, May 1980, in *Collected Vajra Assemblies,* vol. 2 (Halifax: Vajradhatu Publications, 1991), p. 7.

who serves as an example for others. The fundamental point about a teacher is not the fact that he has knowledge but that he enters into the deepest possible relationship with his disciples. For this reason, he must be of flesh and blood, and thus capable of personally experiencing our suffering and our joy.

And yet, at the same time, the guru is merely a manifestation of the inner guru. The true teacher is none other than our own basic intelligence. The external teacher's task is to allow the disciple to enter into contact with the teacher who exists within: the universal primordial wisdom in each human being.

Devotion as the heart of an authentic spiritual attitude

Because the teacher is the living example of complete openness, the relationship with him becomes the path of the disciple.

Devotion is the way to connect with the guru and to open oneself to reality as it truly is. But the word *devotion* is a poor translation of the Tibetan *mögü*. In English it means "the fact of being devoted to religious practices,"[23] while the Tibetan term means "opening." A traditional image likens this to a flower allowing itself to be soaked by the rain so that it can blossom fully later on.

Mö means to desire, to want; it is the thirst to receive what the teacher can give. *Gü* means humility, absence of arrogance, and implies a notion of respect. So *mögü* describes the union of burning desire and humility, a combination of respect, longing, allegiance, and commitment.

Devotion to a teacher does not, as is often thought in the West, mean blind submission. On the contrary, an authentic relationship is possible only if we are willing to be our true selves when we are in his presence.

The guru is no "savior"; he can only point to all the work we still have to accomplish.

---

23. *Oxford English Dictionary*. Nor does the meaning "unreserved attachment" that the word has in vulgar Latin give an idea of the Tibetan word.

Jamgön Kongtrül the Great, the Ri-me movement, and the denunciation of corruption

Chögyam Trungpa's teacher was Jamgön Kongtrül of Sechen, the incarnation of the famous Jamgön Kongtrül the Great (1813–1899), also known as Lodrö Thaye, a major figure in the history of Tibetan Buddhism.

Because of his decisive influence on Buddhism, it is necessary to say a few words about Jamgön Kongtrül the Great. Chögyam Trungpa always referred to him with the greatest reverence and often relied on his works as references when teaching. It would be impossible to comprehend Chögyam Trungpa's work without understanding its sources.

Jamgön Kongtrül the Great was born in Derge province, a region that lies at the heart of the intellectual and artistic life of Kham. After studying the Bön tradition, the indigenous religion of Tibet, with his nominal father, and then traditional medicine, he went to the Nyingma monastery of Sechen, where he was ordained a monk in 1829.

In 1833 he was sent to the Kagyü monastery in Palpung,[24] where he met his root guru.[25] He was then asked to take his vows as a monk once again, which he did reluctantly, as he states in his memoirs.[26] Why take the same vows again? He could not understand the lack of unity that reigned between the various schools, which seemed to him to run against the very nature of Buddhism. What was the reason for the conflicts that then existed between schools that were in fact working toward the same goal? Jamgön Kongtrül the Great decided to transcend such partisan points of view and restore a more open form of Buddhism, which would be truer to its mission.

In nineteenth-century Tibet, Buddhist teachings had often become

---

24. This monastery of the Kagyü school was the seat of Situ Pema Nyingje (1774–1853), a great teacher who became his root guru.

25. Each practitioner may have several teachers, each of whom transmits an aspect of the teachings. But among these teachers, the disciple has a stronger connection with one, who is called his or her root guru.

26. See *Jamgon Kongtrul's Retreat Manual,* translated and introduced by Ngawang Zangpo (Ithaca, NY: Snow Lion Publications, 1994).

doctrinaire and were the source of numerous disputes. It was the sign of profound corruption. As Chögyam Trungpa often explained, at this time Tibet had broken off all foreign relations and did not invite any great teachers from abroad. It had closed in on itself: "In that atmosphere spiritual materialism began to develop. Abbots and great teachers were more concerned with building solid gold roofs on their temples, constructing giant Buddha images, and making their temples beautiful and impressive than with the actual practice of their lineage. They sat less and did more business. . . . Jamgön Kongtrül the Great was like a jewel in a pile of manure."[27]

Jamgön Kongtrül studied with 135 different teachers, representing all the various schools. Like Jamyang Khyentse Wangpo (1820–1892), another master who shared the ideal of nonsectarianism, he traveled throughout Tibet for many years in order to gather together the numerous practices, teachings, and initiations of the varied Buddhist traditions and lineages, many of which had almost disappeared. Jamgön Kongtrül and Khyentse Wangpo organized these teachings carefully in over 150 volumes that form five collections. For the sake of future generations, they undertook to guarantee their continuing transmission. By saving such a large number of teachings from oblivion, they encouraged a genuine renaissance of Buddhism in all of Tibet.

They initiated an important spiritual movement called the Ri-me ("nonsectarian") perspective. The idea was not to bring every faction into a single unity but to promote all the genuine contemplative traditions, in order to preserve and propagate the particular richness of each lineage. The decisive contribution of the Ri-me movement was to restore emphasis on meditation, retreat practice, and realization instead of the simple collection of initiations. Jamgön Kongtrül the Great was the teacher of the tenth Trungpa Tülku, and when this instruction was complete, the tenth Trungpa in turn became the guru of two incarnations of Jamgön Kongtrül the Great: Jamgön Kongtrül of Palpung and Jamgön Kongtrül of Sechen.

Jamgön Kongtrül of Palpung was the son of the fifteenth Karmapa,

---

27. *Journey without Goal*, pp. 90–91.

who was, to everyone's surprise, the first Karmapa to marry and have children.

As for Jamgön Kongtrül of Sechen, Chögyam Trungpa described his situation in this way: "Jamgön Kongtrül of Sechen had gone through enormous hardship. He was said to be the incarnation of the Great Jamgön Kongtrül, but at the same time nobody would make any physical commitment to provide hospitality to him. He ended up living day to day, camping around the homes of the monks of Sechen monastery. Certain householders or monks there formed a kind of committee, the Kongtrül Helpers, who worked together to decide which night he would stay with which particular monk and who was going to feed him. When they needed to buy him a horse to ride, or clothes to wear, the Kongtrül Helpers would get together and collect money. So, within Sechen monastery, a little scene developed to help Jamgön Kongtrül, who otherwise might have been turned out into the street. . . . Finally, when Gyaltsap Rinpoche became the abbot of Sechen monastery, he took control of the situation and created a proper headquarters for Jamgön Kongtrül of Sechen."[28]

After devoting himself to the austere practice of meditation of the Kagyü and Nyingma schools until the age of twenty-five, Jamgön Kongtrül of Sechen took over the spiritual direction of the monastery.

While it was Jamgön Kongtrül of Palpung who ordained Chögyam Trungpa and gave him his first teaching, it was Jamgön Kongtrül of Sechen who became his main teacher. Thus it was that an authentic spiritual tradition was kept alive. A teaching cannot be transmitted in writing; the transmission must occur between two human beings who come together physically, emotionally, and spiritually. It is precisely this full encounter that allows teachings to be truly embodied. The point is to be one with the teaching, to be the dharma itself. It was through this sort of relationship with his teacher that Chögyam Trungpa was able to become an accomplished practitioner who could in turn guide disciples along the difficult path to enlightenment.

---

28. Chögyam Trungpa, "Jamgön Kongtrül," unpublished talks, Boulder, December 1974, fourth talk.

The role of the teacher is not necessarily to innovate but to transmit as precisely as possible what he himself has received. However, the teacher cannot simply hide behind a tradition. His task is to see how deeply he has integrated the heritage he has been given and if he has understood it well enough so that, when he explains it, it communicates his own experience well. This experience then becomes inseparable from that of the teachers who preceded him. The teacher *is* the teachings, and this is what makes him precious.

With Jamgön Kongtrül of Sechen

Chögyam Trungpa devoted several seminars to explaining his relationship with his teacher. They provide a precious opportunity to understand the path he followed. As was his custom, Chögyam Trungpa dropped the usual clichés and presented his education in an extremely lively way.

Chögyam Trungpa was nine when he first met Jamgön Kongtrül of Sechen, who was visiting Dütsi Tel. As soon as he saw him, the young Trungpa felt moved. "He was a big, jolly man, friendly to all without distinction of rank, very generous and with a great sense of humor combined with deep understanding."[29] Spiritual attainment had so often been presented to Chögyam Trungpa as something serious and rigid that he was surprised and relieved to find that such an accomplished man was also spontaneous and humorous. Jamgön Kongtrül was "outrageously spontaneous, and he embarrassed people somewhat."[30] Holiness is not a matter of becoming divine or superhuman, but rather of being purely and simply human. Chögyam Trungpa would never forget this first lesson.

During his visit, Jamgön Kongtrül instructed him in the ultimate simplicity of meditation practice. When Chögyam Trungpa asked him what

---

29. *Born in Tibet*, 4th ed. (2000), p. 51.

30. Chögyam Trungpa, "Jamgön Kongtrül," unpublished talks, Boulder, December 1974, fifth talk. Chögyam Trungpa taught two seminars on his own guru that are among the most moving documents on his education.

enlightenment meant, Jamgön Kongtrül answered: "Well, there is no such thing as enlightenment, and this is it."[31]

A few years after this initial meeting, Chögyam Trungpa decided to go and study with him in Sechen, ten days' journey from his own monastery. He arrived there on the day of his thirteenth birthday.

After such a strict education, he could respond to any logical argument on any subject. He was brilliant. But instead of praising him for his accomplishments, Jamgön Kongtrül appeared highly displeased. Chögyam Trungpa did not understand what was wrong until Jamgön Kongtrül finally told him: "You should watch your step. You might become a brilliant logician, but we don't have warfare happening in this country at this time, and there is no such job for anybody. Think about it."[32] Chögyam Trungpa said that after this incident, he began to gain a more experiential understanding of the teachings, instead of purely appreciating their logic.

In his teaching, Jamgön Kongtrül emphasized the importance of understanding the meaning of what we do, and of not studying or practicing in a mechanical way. He criticized the attitude of those who study it as if they were milkmen. For, as he put it, they sell bottles of milk in the market without ever having tasted it, and without having had the slightest contact with a cow.[33] The teachings are not just an intellectual apprenticeship in which you can simply repeat your lessons until you get the point.

At one point, Jamgön Kongtrül told his student: "There is something wrong here. You use very polite language, of course, but fundamentally you aren't understanding what the teachings are all about. You seem too naive. You still want to practice something higher, more profound, but there is no such thing." Chögyam Trungpa was shocked. He wasn't sure whether the teacher was trying to confuse him because he didn't want to give him the higher teachings, or whether he was really trying to tell him that he was doing something wrong. In fact, the problem was that

---

31. Ibid.

32. Ibid.

33. Chögyam Trungpa, "Jamgön Kongtrül," Karmê Chöling, April 1975, third talk.

Chögyam Trungpa was unable to cut through his anxiety and ego orientation in order to receive the teachings. He asked Jamgön Kongtrül if perhaps he should practice for longer periods or try ascetic practices such as fasting. Jamgön Kongtrül replied, "No, there's something more than that." So then Chögyam Trungpa suggested that he could study Madhyamaka, profound Buddhist philosophy, so that he would understand what his teacher wanted. Jamgön Kongtrül was completely disappointed by that suggestion. He said to his student, "You are much too eager to get something out of this. That is not the way of the contemplative tradition." Finally, it dawned on Chögyam Trungpa that he was missing the point. There was no problem with his sense of devotion, but he was being too faithful. His hard-core, solemn approach was getting in the way of genuine experience. At that point, he discovered the true meaning of freedom. It was a profound relief.[34]

One day, the tutor Apho Karma, who had accompanied Chögyam Trungpa to Sechen, told him that he should ask for his final teachings from Jamgön Kongtrül of Sechen; in that way they could then go back to Surmang and not have to stay too long in this strange monastery. Apho Karma gave Chögyam Trungpa the traditional white scarf, some gold coins, and everything that is required when making such a request.

Chögyam Trungpa reluctantly did as his tutor requested. But Jamgön Kongtrül was no fool, and with his legendary humor he looked at him and broke into boisterous laughter. After a moment, he asked: "You've just repeated what your tutor told you to say, haven't you?" Chögyam Trungpa agreed: "Yes, my tutor wanted me to make this request. He thinks we don't have much time left if we want to go home. Our reserves are running low, and the season is going to change and make travel impossible. He doesn't want to stay here another year." Jamgön Kongtrül became angry. He summoned the tutor, who thought that he too was going to be invited to receive the final teachings. He was delighted.

He came back furious and asked Chögyam Trungpa: "You told him everything? About our lack of supplies and everything? Don't you understand anything about diplomacy? You should have told him you were

---

34. Chögyam Trungpa, "Jamgön Kongtrül," Boulder, December 1974, sixth talk.

dying to receive his teachings." Right from childhood, Chögyam Trungpa was incapable of playing the hypocrite.

After he had studied with Jamgön Kongtrül intermittently over many years, the time to return to Surmang for an extended period approached. Chögyam Trungpa showed his teacher some commentaries on sacred texts that he had written, feeling proud at having found his own style. Jamgön Kongtrül encouraged him and said, "From this time onward, you don't have to ask anybody's approval. You are the holder of the lineage already."[35]

Chögyam Trungpa suddenly panicked: "Does that mean that I'm not going to meet you again in this life? Are you going to abandon us?"

"No, no," Jamgön Kongtrül reassured him; "we're going to meet again. Come and visit me in Central Tibet [where he was going in the attempt to escape the Chinese]. We're going to take a journey to India. When the situation gets worse, I'll go ahead and you just follow me." Those were his last words.[36] Some time later, Jamgön Kongtrül was captured by the Chinese, thrown into prison, and never seen again.

But Chögyam Trungpa always kept his memory alive. At a seminar he explained, "He's my rider. He trained me since the age of nine, when I was not even a teenage horse but a little colt. I feel that he's still riding me. I not only *feel* that, but he *is* riding me constantly, all the time."

In 1967, in Scotland, Chögyam Trungpa composed a contemplative invocation to his guru, "The Sadhana of the Sun of Wisdom," which says:

> Lord, your actions are like a child's—
> That is a sign of being without inward inhibitions.
> Your mind possesses the superknowledge which is free
>   from lust and hesitation;
> You are the yogi who sees all of whatever appears as pure
>   and equal—
> Quickly bring down the continual rain of your blessings.

---

35. Ibid.

36. Ibid.

. . . .

You are the lord especially loving to the lowly—
That is the sign of freedom from arrogance and pride.
Yours is the compassion which holds others dearer than
    oneself.
Lord, like the full moon among a myriad of stars,
You are most beautiful among the many.
You are like the lotus which is free from the slime—
That is a sign of having gone completely beyond samsara
    and nirvana.

. . . .

Lord, you are gone into taintless space.
Your children, myself and the rest, are foundering in the
    mire of the dark age,
Thought ridden in grief.
In the real space of genuine devotion
Ours is the song of an only child who cries out to its
    mother.
With this song of sorrowful yearning, with steadfast faith,
I call to you the authentic guru—
Bring down the great radiance of your luminous wisdom
    body,
Grant the great abhisheka of your self-existing mind![37]

5. Leaving Tibet

The extension of the seminary and Khenpo Gangshar

Once he was back in Surmang, Chögyam Trungpa took his responsibilities as a spiritual master to heart. Despite the worrisome situation in Tibet, he decided to build a new seminary at Dütsi Tel and to open it to monks from other monasteries. In *Born in Tibet*, he explained, "Even if

---

37. Chögyam Trungpa, *Sun of Wisdom* (Boulder: Nālandā Translation Committee, 1967). In tantric Buddhism, a sadhana is a text that serves as a support for meditation practice. Abhisheka is a ceremony of transmission from teacher to student.

the Communists destroy the whole place, the seeds of knowledge in our hearts cannot be destroyed. Even if we build today and our building is torn down tomorrow, I will not regret the spending."

To carry out his project, he had to contradict the elders who questioned its relevance. Throughout his life, Chögyam Trungpa was confronted with "common sense" whose aim was to oppose the vast vision he was attempting to put into practice. This never discouraged him.

Chögyam Trungpa presented his plans to the head of the lineage, Gyalwang Karmapa, when they met in Palpung in 1955, during a meeting devoted to the situation in Tibet.[38] The Karmapa encouraged him in his mission. With gentle conviction, Chögyam Trungpa brought the administration of Surmang around, and the building was completed in 1958. For him, carrying out this project was also a way of fulfilling the wish of the tenth Trungpa, who had initiated the idea.

It is revealing that one of the first important decisions he made was to go against the inertia of the times and to try to renew the way the teachings were presented. To help him in his task, Chögyam Trungpa invited Khenpo Gangshar, who became his private tutor as well as the director of the seminary.

From his early childhood, Khenpo Gangshar had been raised by Jamgön Kongtrül of Sechen, who regarded him as his spiritual son. Reginald A. Ray, the author of *Buddhist Saints in India*, described him as follows:

> As a young monk, the Khenpo was renowned for his scholarly training and rigorous, indeed faultless, observance of the vinaya [monastic rules]. At one point, however, he became extremely sick, was given up for dead, and finally passed away. His corpse was laid out in a small room. Some time later, he suddenly and most dramatically revived, leaping up and throwing open the shutters of the tiny cell where he had been put.
>
> From that moment on, he seemed to have become an entirely different person. He took a female consort, renounced his vows,

---

38. *Born in Tibet*, 4th ed. (2000), pp. 100ff.

and behaved in a bizarre fashion. He was said to be able to tell people's inner thoughts immediately by just looking at them. Many who met him found his attainment self-evident and became disciples and devotees. Others were troubled and embarrassed at this strange behavior, were uncomfortable in his presence, and criticized and avoided him.[39]

Khenpo Gangshar defied and overturned the reassuringly secure vision of themselves and the world that people construct. After becoming enlightened, he had an aura that terrified everyone—disciples and detractors alike—and he had done things that seemed immoral according to conventional norms.[40]

Confronted by the increasing Chinese oppression, Khenpo Gangshar stopped limiting access to instruction to the monks in the seminary. He decided that all the region's inhabitants, both monks and laypeople, should receive the dharma. It would soon be impossible to teach publicly: it was thus necessary to present the heart of the Buddhist teachings in an extremely direct way, outside the usual forms and specific rites.

He emphasized the importance of altruism and compassion. In a situation where the dharma was under threat, dogma was useless and all that mattered was experience. As he explained: "Quotation is no use in itself; we can all repeat scripture by heart. You must demonstrate loving-kindness by your actions."[41]

However, what was most surprising was his ability to present the heart of the teachings directly, before large crowds of followers. Such transmission is the ultimate basis for the establishment of stable, pro-

---

39. Reginald A. Ray, quoted in Jeremy Hayward, *Sacred World: A Guide to Shambhala Warriorship in Daily Life* (New York: Bantam New Age, 1995), p. 208.

40. See Reginald A. Ray, "Gone beyond Lhasa," review of the book *Civilized Shamans: Buddhism in Tibetan Societies* by Geoffrey Samuel, *Shambhala Sun*, September 1994. In this article, Ray underlines the continuity between the teachings of Chögyam Trungpa and those of Khenpo Gangshar, both of which lie outside the monastic way with their vision of "crazy wisdom," which has always been considered one of the fundamental elements of the Tibetan tradition.

41. *Born in Tibet*, 4th ed. (2000), p. 124.

found practice. It is usually presented only to the fortunate few. Khenpo Gangshar decided to transmit it to as many people as possible.

He visited hermits who had taken vows to live the rest of their lives in solitude. He advised them to return to the world and learn to remain in retreat within themselves.

Khenpo Gangshar ignored cultural conventions in order to go straight to the core of Buddhism. Chögyam Trungpa was extremely impressed by such an approach and began working in a similar way during the two years they taught together at Surmang.

The Chinese invasion

The Chinese threat grew increasingly alarming. The Communists had taken over China in 1949. Soon afterward, they declared their intention to annex Tibet, which they considered to be a Chinese province given over to a barbarian religion, and convert it to Marxism.

On January 1, 1950, the Chinese announced their determination to "liberate Tibet from foreign imperialists and reunite it with the mother country." An immense army invaded the Land of Snow.

At the beginning, the Chinese thought they would be welcomed as liberators from imperialism and feudalism. But, on the contrary, the Tibetans reacted with great hostility. China concluded that the only way to "liberate" Tibet was to destroy it.

In 1955, a system of land collectivization was introduced. Chinese troops confiscated weapons and property and eliminated all forms of possession. They publicly tortured and killed monks and nuns. These measures led to a rebellion, especially in the regions of Kham and Amdo, where units of guerrillas had formed. It was put down violently, because the Chinese were both more numerous and better armed. The days of a free Tibet were numbered.

In 1959, the situation worsened. Tensions rose when it was announced that the Dalai Lama, the spiritual leader of all Tibet, might be kidnapped. On March 28, Zhou Enlai announced on the radio that the Tibetan government had been dissolved and that China had taken over. The Dalai Lama fled to India, disguised as a soldier.

To return to Surmang or leave for India?

Chögyam Trungpa was then just nineteen years old. He had to face up to events that were not then so clear to him as they now seem to us, with the benefit of hindsight. He was isolated and ill-informed as to the intentions of the Chinese. At a very young age, he had to make decisions with far-reaching consequences. In particular, should he stay or should he leave his country?

The leaders of Surmang were pressuring him to stay with them. His bursar, Tsethar, refused to admit the gravity of the situation and blindly hoped and believed that everything would return to normal.

Chögyam Trungpa traveled to the province of Chamdo, where he met with Khamtrül Rinpoche, the head of the Khampa Gar monastery near Lhathok, which oversees two hundred monasteries of eastern Tibet. Chögyam Trungpa felt close to him at once. When Khamtrül Rinpoche asked him to join in his undercover escape to India, Chögyam Trungpa hesitated: "Any decision I might make would affect not only myself, but all the monasteries in the district, particularly those connected with Surmang, as well as the lay population. Everyone looked to me as their authority and were prepared to follow my lead."[42] He declined the invitation and instead followed the suggestions of his bursar, who had a great influence over him. In *Born in Tibet*, Chögyam Trungpa described how he was caught between the need to leave Tibet, in order to save the precious teachings he had received, and the advice of his bursar, whom he found it difficult to oppose and who refused to recognize the catastrophe befalling the country.

The situation worsened daily and Chögyam Trungpa soon realized that the bursar's arguments were mere expressions of fear. He learned that the Chinese had invaded Surmang, Namgyal Tse had been destroyed, and a large number of monks had been murdered.

Chögyam Trungpa had already gone into hiding before this. He was giving an empowerment at a neighboring monastery, some days away from Surmang, when he received news of fighting around Surmang. Eventually it became clear that he could not return to Surmang, so he

---

42. Ibid., p. 145.

withdrew and practiced in a remote valley awaiting further news. He sent his bursar back to Surmang, where he discovered that the Chinese had desecrated the tomb of the tenth Trungpa.

Before long, Dütsi Tel also came under attack; Chinese troops entered the library and threw all its precious books onto the floor. The treasures on the altars, such as statues and lamps, were smashed and their metal sent to China. The tomb of the tenth Trungpa Tülku was defiled and his embalmed body left in the open air. Surmang became part of the Chinese province of Qinghai.

Chögyam Trungpa was being hunted by the Chinese as a political enemy. In such conditions it was impossible to return to Surmang; if he did so, he would expose himself and his community to even greater persecution.

It was necessary to flee. Despite everything that was happening, the bursar still held on to the belief that the tragedy engulfing Surmang did not affect the entire country.

Escape to India

At first, Chögyam Trungpa left for Lhasa. But when he learned that the Dalai Lama had gone into exile, he decided also to leave for India at the head of a group of refugees. Starting out with nine companions, he soon had three hundred people in his group. To guide them, he often used divination.[43]

The journey was long and dangerous. It lasted almost ten months in extremely difficult conditions. While trying to avoid the Chinese, who were tracking them, the refugees often had to walk all day, from dawn to dusk, and sometimes even at night. Chögyam Trungpa thought of this journey as a kind of pilgrimage, a return to the Buddha's homeland, and he devoted a certain amount of time to religious practice, despite the dif-

---

43. Chögyam Trungpa was considered to have considerable powers of divination. For example, he carried out prasena, a form of divination practiced by only a few initiates. Like many other masters, the Dalai Lama frequently consulted him on important questions.

ficulties. He explained to his companions: "It is fortunate for us that our way is hard and that we are struggling against greater difficulties than the pilgrims of the past, for by this means we shall learn and profit the more from our journey."[44] Chögyam Trungpa sought to transform the chaos he encountered into a spiritual experience. When they reached the Indian border with Assam, only nineteen members of the group remained. During the long journey from Tibet, several had taken ill, others were too old for such an arduous walk and had died of exhaustion, and many had been taken prisoner.

At last they left the mountains and reached the tropical zone. As they had nothing to eat, they were reduced to boiling their leather bags. They didn't dare touch the bananas they saw growing, because they had never seen such fruit and were not sure if it was edible.

Now that he had successfully escaped from Tibet, Chögyam Trungpa had also been separated from its many traditions and way of life. He had now left his home behind for good, aware of the fact that he would never return.

The young man who arrived in India in 1960 was an exceptional person, but not only because of his status as a tülku or his unusual upbringing; it was more because of the decisions he had already made. He was willing to make any sacrifice that would allow him to fly the victorious flag of the teachings he had received, which had transformed his life. Buddhism was not external to him; he and the teachings were one.

---

44. *Born in Tibet*, 4th ed. (2000), p. 208.

Chapter Three

MEDITATION
AND THE IMPORTANCE
OF SITTING

The main purpose of our being together here is purely the practice of meditation. And also the main purpose of my personal existence on this planet, so to speak, is the practice of meditation. That without that we have no working basis at all. And such a working basis is very delightful.[1]

—CHÖGYAM TRUNGPA

CHÖGYAM TRUNGPA CONSTANTLY repeated: "If you don't sit, there is no point in my teaching you. It is simple as that."[2] In order to study how he presented Buddhism in the West, it is thus necessary to start by examining how he presented the practice of meditation.

1. The Need to Return to Simple Practice

As early as 1970, during his first months in the United States, Chögyam Trungpa emphasized this point. It is a very basic experience: to sit down and be with yourself, to look at *who* you are beyond all dogma and belief. As we have already said, such an experience tends to reduce the tempta-

---

1. Chögyam Trungpa, "Community Talk," Karmê Chöling, February 28, 1977, unpublished.

2. Chögyam Trungpa, "View, Meditation and Action," *Vajradhatu Sun*, December 1979, p. 8.

tion to use spirituality to attain some particular goal, and it thus breaks through spiritual materialism.

Every time students asked Chögyam Trungpa for some esoteric teachings, he reminded them of the necessity to start out by quite simply sitting down. In a lecture in which she mentions a few personal memories, Diana Mukpo told what happened during the first days after she and Chögyam Trungpa arrived in North America. Because they had no money, they had to move into a tiny apartment renting at twenty-four dollars a week. A few people who had studied under the direction of Chögyam Trungpa at Samye Ling had discovered land for a meditation center near Barnet, Vermont. They were already living there, waiting for Chögyam Trungpa and Diana Mukpo to arrive.[3] They phoned Chögyam Trungpa in Montreal to say they wanted to come and visit.

In Diana Mukpo's words: "So they drove up to Montreal, because we didn't have the immigration visa to come into the United States. We also met Cyrus Crane in Montreal. He was about seventy at the time, one of Rinpoche's oldest students, chronologically speaking. He was wonderful. He had his first meditation interview with Rinpoche in Montreal. He said, 'Rinpoche, I need some advice. First I did the mahamudra and then I did the maha ati [very advanced practices that take years to accomplish]. Now that I've done both of those, what should I do next?' Rinpoche told him, 'I'm going to teach you to meditate.'"[4]

This anecdote not only reflects the style and content of Chögyam Trungpa's early teachings, it also shows the direction he constantly followed. In his vivid way, he always explained: "By meditation here we mean something very basic and simple that is not tied to any one culture. We are talking about a very basic act: sitting on the ground, assuming a good posture, and developing a sense of our spot, our place on this earth."[5]

---

3. This was the center called Tail of the Tiger, now known as Karmê Chöling.

4. Diana J. Mukpo, unpublished interview, 2003.

5. *Shambhala: The Sacred Path of the Warrior* (Shambhala Library, 2003), p. 20.

2. The Basis of the Path

In Tibet, the path was generally monastic: one began by taking monastic vows and becoming involved in regular ritual practices and liturgies. Chögyam Trungpa realized that it would be meaningless to import such practices into the West, so he decided to return to the very source of the path: the practice of meditation as it was taught by Buddha himself. The Buddha experienced enlightenment while meditating beneath a tree. The simplicity of such an approach, devoid of any desire to achieve a result, allows us to contact the fundamental nature of ourselves and who we are. The idea of Buddhism is that, in such an experience where we connect completely with what is, a gap can appear in the defenses of the ego, thus allowing naked, compassionate consciousness to break through in all its brilliance. The ego is the constant effort we all make to "maintain the basic myth of solidity."[6] It is a habitual and doomed mechanism that locks us ever more tightly into a struggle to establish a situation of comfort that can never be maintained. When meditation dissolves this struggle, it allows us to discover the primordial wisdom present within us, as in all human beings. It is not intrinsically linked to a particular culture or even to a spiritual tradition. It is a way for all people to communicate with their true being. As Chögyam Trungpa put it: "Ego is that which thrives on the security of your existence. Beyond that there is intelligence that sees the foolishness in trying to thrive on your security."[7]

The true spiritual path is not a matter of reaching some particular state of consciousness; it is a gradual process of letting go: "We discover the nonexistence of self through the practice of meditation."[8] Because of its simplicity, such a discipline is the only solid "ground" it is possible to rely on, because it is a constant insult to the ego.

---

6. *Cutting Through Spiritual Materialism*, p. 9.

7. *The Lion's Roar*, p. 101.

8. *Journey without Goal*, p. 4.

While most teachers present different practices depending on the occasion and the students, giving numerous initiations, Chögyam Trungpa decided that all his students should return to this ground, the fundamental basis of understanding.

We must always "go back to square one," as he often said.[9] From the time he arrived in America, the sitting practice of meditation was the first practice he introduced to any student who wanted to study under his direction. Studying with him meant first of all practicing meditation.

This insistence on basic meditation for beginners had no equivalent in Tibet, nor in any of the other centers of the Tibetan tradition in the West. As Chögyam Trungpa explained frequently: "We should be quite clear that ordinary Tibetans don't sit very much, which is a degeneration of the teaching in the country. . . . Even in the monasteries it sometimes is very hard to make people sit, and the actual serious sitters are people in various retreat centers. . . . Intense sitting practice was done in the early times a great deal. That's what we're doing, what we've been doing."[10]

Today, when people first arrive in one of the centers set up by Chögyam Trungpa, they are often surprised to discover that the main activity is meditation practice. Even before understanding how the center is organized or what Buddhism is, they are asked to sit down on a cushion and meditate. During teaching programs, and even during the visits of great masters, most of the time is devoted to meditation.[11]

---

9. Chögyam Trungpa's decision to emphasize the shamatha-vipashyana practice of sitting meditation was in part inspired by his deep knowledge of different forms of Buddhist meditation. He greatly appreciated Zen and the satipatthana (foundations of mindfulness) of the tradition of Burmese vipassana (the Pali word for vipashyana), both of which utilize the simple practice of sitting meditation—which is not generally the case in the Tibetan tradition. He recommended to his students the books *Zen Mind, Beginner's Mind* by Shunryu Suzuki and *Heart of Buddhist Meditation* by Nyanaponika Thera. Chögyam Trungpa had an excellent knowledge of other Buddhist schools, and he never hesitated to mention them in his own teachings and to invite their representatives to meet his students.

10. Chögyam Trungpa, *Manual for Shamatha Instructors*.

11. This is one of the main differences with the way most other Tibetan centers are run. When there is a visiting teacher, the students make the most of listening to him teach, and the time for meditation, if any, is reduced to a minimum.

3. Description of the Practice

To practice, you need to drop your activities for a time and take a break from your daily routine. This does not imply trying to escape from your problems, leave yourself and the world behind, or attain a new state of mind; on the contrary, you try to contact as directly as possible your true self and the world as it really is.

The posture

The starting point of meditation is making a relationship with your body.[12] You sit on a cushion, keeping your spine as straight as possible, with your head in line with your spine. A straight back represents the courage we need to confront our own existence, while an open, vulnerable chest or front expresses the gentleness we need to be able to reach it. The posture is a proclamation: it is possible to rid ourselves of our defenses and the protection mechanisms that stifle us, in order to be touched by everything that happens.

Your eyes are open, directed slightly downward, without staring at anything in particular. Numerous other meditation techniques insist on closing the eyes in order to enter more easily into oneself, but in this case the emphasis is on cultivating an increasingly direct relationship with the world.

In this form of practice, posture is a vital point. As Chögyam Trungpa put it, when we're in a theater and the movie is interesting, we naturally sit up. The meditation posture should reflect the same attitude of openness and attention to each moment. Chögyam Trungpa wanted his students to be intently aware of their bodies and posture, but without being rigid or unnatural.

---

12. It is extremely important to understand that this description is not an instruction on how to meditate. Anyone who wishes to practice meditation must receive personal instruction from a qualified teacher. The magic of the lineage cannot be transmitted in any other way. For this reason, I do not attempt to be exhaustive here but instead pay close attention to certain aspects that were particularly emphasized by Chögyam Trungpa.

Breathing

Your posture having been established, you begin to attend to your breathing. Like our changeable minds, which are always seeking out new possibilities, respiration is not stable but constantly comes and goes. When we are tired, it becomes more difficult, but if we are relaxed, we breathe more easily. The breath is a simple, intimate, and changing point of reference that we can rely on.

Chögyam Trungpa placed a great deal of importance on attending to the out-breath in meditation. There is a moment when, by following the exhalation, we dissolve into space. It slowly draws our attention further and further away from ourselves. But the in-breath does not require our attention; it can take care of itself. As he explained: "There is a constant going out with the out-breath. As you breathe out, you dissolve, you diffuse. Then your in-breath occurs naturally; you don't have to follow it in."[13]

The more you give yourself over to this discipline, the more the moment of dissolving becomes essential relaxation. This practice is not a matter of concentrating but instead "of trying to become one with the feeling of breath."[14]

In this process, there is a gap, a moment when you stop, when your attention dissolves, when there's no one at home: "So it's out, dissolve, gap; out, dissolve, gap; out, dissolve, gap. You are constantly opening, abandoning, boycotting something in you that wants to hold on or follow through. So *boycotting* in this case is a very significant word. If you hold on to your breath, you are constantly holding on to yourself. Once you begin to boycott the end of the out-breath, then there's no world left—except that the out-breath reminds you to tune in with it. So you tune in, dissolve; tune in, dissolve; tune in, dissolve; tune in, dissolve."[15]

---

13. *Shambhala: The Sacred Path of the Warrior* (Shambhala Library, 2003), p. 24.

14. *Meditation in Action*, p. 77.

15. Chögyam Trungpa, *1974 Seminary Transcripts: Hinayana-Mahayana* (Boulder: Vajradhatu Publications), p. 5.

The mind

When following this discipline, you pay more attention to the way your mind works. You sit down, and nothing is happening, but all sorts of things occur in the mind: memories, expectations, hopes, fears, various ideas. One thought arises, then a second, then another, sometimes in floods. You then realize, sometimes for the first time, that you never stop talking to yourself and that you are caught up in an internal commentary on everything you do. Then, along with thoughts, feelings arrive—of irritation, boredom, or jealousy. Such emotions are also thoughts, only more energetic and colorful than the others.

You then realize that it is difficult to remain mindful, to avoid being swept away by the waves of chatter. The technique consists first in understanding this fact and examining it. You notice how, when silence falls, you feel awkward and immediately want to fill the gap. The realization of our possible nonexistence sets off a feeling of panic. Inner dialogue creates the impression that someone else is there and that we must sort things out with this inner companion—rather like a cat chasing its own tail.

As Chögyam Trungpa explained, the ego is a sort of central government, while "the emotions are the highlights of the ego, the generals of ego's army; subconscious thought, daydreams, and other thoughts connect one highlight to another. So thoughts form ego's army and are constantly in motion, constantly busy."[16] With such an army, we strive to remain in control.

In meditation, when "thoughts" (daydreams, reflections, emotions) appear, we are instructed to simply observe them. The idea is not to try to get rid of them, but just to recognize their transitory and "translucent nature."[17] The technique consists in realizing that you are thinking and then discreetly labeling this activity by mentally saying to yourself: "thinking." Then you return attention to the breath. Recognizing that you

---

16. *The Myth of Freedom*, pp. 22–23.

17. *Meditation in Action*, p. 77.

are thinking reminds you of what you are doing and brings you back to the breath, back to the cushion.

It is not necessary to analyze the thoughts we have. Their content has no particular importance. The sole objective is to understand their nature and to use the awareness of thinking to bring us back to the cushion instead of following thoughts, responding to them, or acting on them. Being annoyed at how uptight we are or congratulating ourselves on our calm state of mind is quite simply another type of thought, which we must label before we can return to an unmanufactured space.

Meditation is not an unbroken process of concentration: "Fixation or concentration tends to develop trance-like states. But from the Buddhist point of view, the point of meditation is . . . rather to sharpen perceptions, to see things as they are."[18] States of grace are fleeting. Meditation is a matter of dissolving fixation and not making it more solid. So it is important not to fixate on your experience, whatever it might be. The effort lies in cultivating a feeling of welcome or acceptance toward whatever occurs, in allowing your naked presence to create a breeze of delight.

4. The Practice of Shamatha and Vipashyana

When he arrived in the United States, Chögyam Trungpa presented the practice of meditation in the simplest possible way: "sit down and be aware of space." He did vary his instructions with different students, but this was the essential point. Then, during the 1973 Seminary (an advanced formal program of practice), he made a more detailed and unified presentation: "So far the practices that we have been doing, including meditation in the retreat situation, have been individualistic in style. . . . I feel we need a somewhat systematized, uniform practice."[19] He

---

18. Chögyam Trungpa, in Herbert V. Guenther and Chögyam Trungpa, *The Dawn of Tantra*, p. 22.

19. Chögyam Trungpa, *1973 Seminary Transcripts: Hinayana-Mahayana* (Boulder: Vajradhatu Publications), p. 1.

then explained meditation as the unification of shamatha and vipash-yana (*shi-ne* and *lhakthong* in Tibetan). These two elements were explained one after the other to make them easier to understand for his students, but he also pointed out that for practitioners they are inseparable: "In the Buddhist tradition, meditation practice is generally total involvement: body, speech, and mind are completely, totally involved. That is the shamatha practice. And the vipashyana practice is total involvement of body, speech, and mind, plus you are also totally involved in awareness of the environment around you. You are involved so much that there is no individual entity left to watch itself anymore."[20]

The word *shamatha* means "the development of peace," and here the word *peace* "refers to the harmony connected with accuracy rather than to peace from the point of view of pleasure rather than pain."[21] Practitioners develop a clear experience of things as they are. They have an extremely direct relationship with the *details* of their own experiences: bodily sensations, the simplicity of breathing, and the experience of various kinds of thought. As Chögyam Trungpa wrote: "The shamatha meditation, the beginning point of the practice, could be described as sharpening one's knife. It is a way of relating to bodily sensations and thought processes of all kinds; just relating with them rather than dwelling on them or fixing on them in any way."[22]

"Having established the precision of details, one begins to experience the space around them."[23] This is the experience of vipashyana. The Tibetan term is *lhakthong*, which literally means "superior vision" or "perfect vision." This word is generally translated as "insight," but Chögyam Trungpa deliberately decided to translate it as "awareness." While vipashyana is often presented as being an analytical investigation or examination of the nature of things—for example, examining the nature of self and of thought—Chögyam Trungpa explained vipashyana awareness

---

20. Ibid.

21. *The Path Is the Goal*, p. 14.

22. In Herbert V. Guenther and Chögyam Trungpa, *The Dawn of Tantra*, pp. 22–23.

23. Ibid., p. 24.

as an absence of technique that occurs naturally from the practice of shamatha: "In discussing vipashyana, we are talking about the sense of precision that could arise from the sitting practice of meditation and that could slowly infiltrate our everyday life situation. There seem to be two different schools, one which talks about the purely analytical contemplative way, and the other which talks about the nonanalytical, experiential way. The first school talks about the possibilities of becoming more aware if you ask more questions, or further examine the nature of reality and one's own state of mind. But in our tradition, in accordance with Jamgön Kongtrül, we talk purely in terms of a nonanalytical approach, just simply an experiential approach, which is the style of the practicing lineage."[24]

5. No Promises

When we start to practice in this way, we discover just how confused we are and how much our thoughts constantly swirl around inside us. Our nonstop subconscious chatter suddenly appears to us as a cloudbank of fog that we usually don't even notice. The difficulties we have in life do not derive from our mood swings, our aggression, our jealousy, our selfishness, or our pride, but from the fact that we pretend that our problems do not exist. We soon become experts in the little game of lying to ourselves.

The practice of meditation gives us, often for the first time, access to a space where we can discover who we really are. We no longer have to pretend. This is the beginning of a true feeling of making friends with ourselves. Whatever the situation, it becomes possible to see it as it is and work on it. We are not defenseless. Such a friendship is not just a pleasant acquaintance. It crosses hurdles.

It is born from the practice of meditation because it allows us to enter into a nonjudgmental relationship with whatever occurs: "Don't regard having sexual fantasies in the middle of your sitting practice or having ag-

---

24. Chögyam Trungpa, *1974 Seminary Transcripts: Hinayana-Mahayana*, p. 66.

gression fantasies—how you're going to punch your enemy in the nose—as your problems. They are regarded as a promise, in fact."[25]

Instead of living in fear of our weaknesses, failings, and confusion, we look at them as they are. It is possible to cultivate a less conflicted attitude toward ourselves. For Chögyam Trungpa, spirituality is not a question of using a stick or a carrot, but instead begins with this discovery of friendship with ourselves: to experience who we are, no matter how great our confusion.

By focusing on everything that arises during meditation, we also begin to see that mental processes are neither permanent nor solid. Chögyam Trungpa often described the ego as "building sand castles,"[26] or as "the control tower" or even "central headquarters," [27] but this centralizing desire has no real existence. Our belief in an ego is not only mistaken, it is also the origin of the pain and suffering we inflict on ourselves and on others.

In contrast to certain commonly held ideas, the purpose of meditation is not to annihilate the individual self and dissolve into some sort of vague oneness with all. This initial misunderstanding leads to a further one: the idea that practice makes people weak and indecisive, cut off from the material realities of life. But practice does not make us flee from the world. On the contrary, meditation allows us to be in closer touch with things as they really are. It frees us. As Chögyam Trungpa said, "for the first time we are able to see ourselves completely, perfectly, beautifully as what we are, absolutely as what we are."[28]

Chögyam Trungpa constantly returned to this basic point: there is no goal to be reached, and we should simply *be*—like a rock or a mountain touched by water or wind. This sort of meditation practice is no tranquilizer; in fact, it brings our emotions and fears to the surface. It leads not to mastery but to an ever more poignant revelation.

---

25. *The Path Is the Goal*, p. 12.

26. *Crazy Wisdom*, p. 77.

27. *The Myth of Freedom*, p. 21.

28. *The Path Is the Goal*, p. 15.

6. From the Simplicity of Shamatha to the Primordial Nature of Mahamudra and Maha Ati

Meditation practice is not rigid. It is a living process that evolves with the student's personal development and life context. Chögyam Trungpa presented sitting meditation not as a purely preliminary practice but as a discipline to be followed throughout the path.

He adopted two different but complementary approaches to explain this. The first, which has already been explained, is based on simultaneously developing shamatha and vipashyana, attention and awareness, in their indivisible unity.

However, in a 1972 teacher-training seminar, he explained that the practice can also be seen as being divided into different steps: shamatha, vipashyana, mahavipashyana, mahamudra, maha ati. The experience of precision that belongs to shamatha and that of totality in vipashyana join together and so give birth to mahavipashyana, the experience of emptiness. In *Cutting Through Spiritual Materialism*, he explained: "In mahavipashyana meditation there is a vast expanse of space between us and objects. We are aware of the space between the situation and ourselves, and anything can happen in that space. . . . awareness becomes very precise and all-encompassing."[29]

This understanding opens a path that leads from highly focused, precise attention toward the fullness of space, from which the spontaneous experience of enlightenment, which belongs to mahamudra, can arise.

The perspective of mahamudra

In the practice of meditation, we discover gaps[30] that interrupt the continuity of our thoughts. We can thus see beyond the workings of the mind and begin to notice the space in which appearances take form. And what

---

29. *Cutting Through Spiritual Materialism*, p. 168.

30. "Meditation practice has this particular quality of providing a pure gap and not feeding on concepts of any kind." *Illusion's Game*, p. 48.

an alive space it is: "Sitting meditation is *being*, a way of being in open space."[31]

But it is not just a matter of grasping the insubstantial nature of thoughts, which simply pass through the mind; it is also necessary to experience our thoughts as the very texture of space. In other words, Chögyam Trungpa joined the perspective of mahamudra to the practice of shamatha-vipashyana, because it allows us to have a far more direct relationship with the very qualities of our minds: "Mahamudra is very sharp, not just full alone. It's colorful. Shunyata [emptiness] fullness is rather gray and transparent and dull, like London fog."[32] The idea is not at all to be devoid of thought, but instead to see the primordial openness of the mind, both when it is calm and when it is agitated. Thus, to emphasize the point once more, stopping discursive thought is not the objective of the practice. It comes about through the liberation of thoughts at their source, through the realization that they emerge as the creative force of awakened nature and are simply its offshoots. Recognizing their absolute nature makes it possible to free thoughts as they emerge at the source, in such a way that they leave no traces.

The practice consists in allowing space to infiltrate us completely. In such an experience, "forms become solid and definite forms, colors become bright and definite colors, sounds become definite sounds. Thought processes also become, in some sense, real, because at this point there is no longer any reason to condemn thoughts or try to mold them into a different pattern. It is just a spontaneous thinking of thoughts."[33]

This way of describing meditation is typical of Chögyam Trungpa's style. He always insisted on the naked, "awake" nature of all authentic experiences. Thanks to this practice, we learn to appreciate the texture of each experience, whether pleasant or unpleasant, by always connecting ourselves to its most salient quality, like a portrait painter who does not

---

31. *Transcending Madness*, p. 15.

32. *Illusion's Game*, p. 130.

33. Chögyam Trungpa, in Herbert V. Guenther and Chögyam Trungpa, *The Dawn of Tantra*, p. 36.

choose always to paint beautiful faces but instead tries to depict his subjects as they are deep down.

The aim is not to attain enlightenment.[34] Far more radically, it is a
matter of allowing primordial space to dissolve all of our expectations. It
is not we ourselves who have the experience of this openness. Ego cannot
even imagine it. If we manufacture this experience, it will fade and we will
find ourselves embracing a corpse.

Meditation is an invitation to rest in the nature of the mind, free of all
limitations. It is a situation of welcome and openness. Goals are super-
fluous. Chögyam Trungpa always returned to this basic quality of meditation, to this utter surrender to the living present, so simple and yet so
far-reaching. One of his favorite expressions when asked a question about
how to do something was "Just do it." Anybody can utter such a phrase,
but Chögyam Trungpa's unshakable conviction transformed the person
he so addressed.

7. Nyinthün, Dathün, and Meditation Instructors

At the beginning of the 1970s, when people asked to study with him,
Chögyam Trungpa often sent them to undertake an intensive session of
sitting meditation in solitary retreat. For example, Sherab Chödzin
(Michael H. Kohn), who first met Rinpoche in the fall of 1970, was advised to undertake a three-month solitary retreat. Sherab agreed and
built the first retreat hut at Tail of the Tiger. Sarah Coleman remembers
the moment when Chögyam Trungpa asked her to go on a two-week retreat. After she tried to explain how impossible this was and how she was
not ready to embark on such an obviously unfeasible project, he told her
at once that if she wanted to study with him, then she must go on retreat
for one month.

---

34. This is seen as being too dualistic a vision. As Chögyam Trungpa put it: "The idea of the
attainment of enlightenment is based on ignorance, which is the opposite of enlightenment." "You are not going to liberate yourself in order to attain enlightenment. You have to
give up the notion of liberation at the beginning." *Glimpses of Shunyata* (seminar given at
Karmê Chöling, April 1972) (Halifax: Vajradhatu Publications, 1993), pp. 1 and 13.

The young students he met at the time tended to use Buddhism as a way of maintaining their illusions. David McCarthy was a young artist who had been practicing for a few months in Boston when he first asked to meet Chögyam Trungpa. The conversation took place in a large room with a long table in the middle surrounded by chairs. In a corner of the room, Chögyam Trungpa was sitting on a sofa. He asked David McCarthy to sit down next to him, which pleased the young man, who felt proud to be receiving so much attention. He began by telling Rinpoche about his practice and the extraordinary visions he had while meditating. After a while, Chögyam Trungpa interrupted him and asked him to move one of the chairs, which was not in line with the others. McCarthy stood up and went to dispose of this little chore as quickly as possible so that he could continue sharing his marvelous experiences with the master. But he sensed that Chögyam Trungpa was watching him, and so he tried to slow down a little. Under observation, he felt awkward.

When he came back, Chögyam Trungpa asked him to sit down on a chair in front of him. Now distanced, McCarthy felt rejected. He was crestfallen and laid bare in an extremely profound way. He could no longer carry on creating an image of the person he wanted to be. Instead of continuing what now seemed like playacting, he spoke more authentically.

At that instant, Chögyam Trungpa asked him, "Do you have time to go on a retreat?"

"Yes," McCarthy replied.

"At once?"

"Yes."

"For three weeks?"

"Yes."

Chögyam Trungpa then told him to call Tail of the Tiger immediately and go that very day.

McCarthy was worried and asked him why he had to go on a retreat at once: "Am I in danger of dying soon?" Chögyam Trungpa then explained to him that his mind was fundamentally healthy and clear, but that it was covered over with so much garbage that he should sit down and practice as soon as he could. He gave him very few instructions, apart from the fact that he should fix his gaze on the visions at the moment they arrived in order to recognize their transparent nature. David McCarthy remembers how he soon found them extremely dull and how they vanished of their own accord during the three weeks of practice.

In 1973, Chögyam Trungpa asked all of his students to undertake a dathün (a month's group meditation) at Rocky Mountain Dharma Center, in order to give them a tangible experience of practice. At the beginning, all the participants were afraid that they wouldn't be up to it. Then, once they had committed themselves to the project, they were delighted. Such an experience becomes a unique opportunity for self-discovery and for allowing the mind to mingle with the magic of the teachings. In such a context, free from all other preoccupations, everyone can savor the depth of meditation practice.

Chögyam Trungpa also introduced the practice of nyinthün, one full day of meditation per week, during which he encouraged the entire community to gather together and practice.

David Rome, Chögyam Trungpa's personal secretary, remembers how furious Rinpoche was when he, the Regent (Rinpoche's appointed successor), and other close Western disciples did not attend the nyinthüns. He insisted that everyone participate actively.

Without practice, without this direct contact with oneself, free from all concepts, the path turns into just another mental game. Without such discipline, the Buddhist teachings are merely one more novelty in an existence already cluttered with other projects.

In 1975, the first training course for meditation instructors was organized. Before that time, students became instructors by simply asking. Meditation instructors are, in the words of Chögyam Trungpa, "instructors in a very strict sense; their role is not to theorize or analyze but just to transmit what they themselves have learned and understood."[35] They are not gurus, and yet they play a decisive role, because meditation is at the heart of all the activities that take place in a center. They help the students to return to the simplicity and precision of meditation in order to explore its depths.

---

35. Epilogue to *Born in Tibet* (1977), p. 261.

Authorizing meditation instructors was an important contribution that Chögyam Trungpa made. His students thus have to share their understanding with others. This is a formidable experience that pushes them into examining ever more closely their own experiences in the light of the teachings. Each new student is given a meditation instructor, and they enter into a regular personal relationship.

To conclude this chapter, we can only make sense of Chögyam Trungpa's work in the light of meditation practice and the discovery and experience of egolessness. Without this, the rest becomes a mere set of mental constructs, which may be more or less interesting but remain divorced from the living source that alone makes authentic experience possible.

Chapter Four

EXPERIENCE,
MODERNITY,
AND TRADITION

In the twentieth century, we talk about democracy, individualism, personal heroism, and all kinds of things like that. While all of those ideals are excellent in one sense, they are the creation of a culture that does not appreciate arduous and long training in a traditional discipline. Throwing away tradition and wisdom that have been developed through many centuries is like tossing the extraordinary exertion and sacrifice that human beings have made out of the window, like dirty socks. This is certainly not the way to maintain the best human society.[1]

—CHÖGYAM TRUNGPA

1. Thinking Takes a Modern Turn

A traditional master

Chögyam Trungpa might have appeared, at first sight, to be very modern and up-to-date in his approach to the teachings. He had abandoned the external signs of the Tibetan monastic tradition. He drank whiskey, smoked cigarettes, and wore Western clothes. He had a frank, often provocative way with words and ignored the normal conventions of a guru.

But nothing could be further from the truth. For Chögyam Trungpa

---

1. Chögyam Trungpa, "Proclaiming the Living Strength of the Practice Lineage," in Ösel Tendzin, *Buddha in the Palm of Your Hand* (Boston: Shambhala Publications, 1982).

was arguably the most traditional of all Tibetan masters. The word *tradi-tion* must be understood here in the precise sense of being associated with the *source* of the teachings.[2] It thus has nothing to do with the desire to maintain the past for the past's sake. As Chögyam Trungpa explained, with a humorous touch, "Tradition does not mean dressing up in robes and playing exotic music or having dakinis dancing around us, or any-thing like that. Tradition is being faithful to what we have been taught and to our own integrity. From this point of view, tradition is being awake and open, welcoming but at the same time stubborn."[3] Thus, an authentic re-lationship with Tradition[4] is a matter of purity of heart and not of being a conservative. It is inseparable from the freedom to return, beyond all conventions, to the source.

This distinction between two meanings of the word *tradition* is of fun-damental importance; it allows us to understand the entirety of Chögyam Trungpa's work as an effort to liberate the first utterance of the teachings from the swamp of habits, customs, and commentaries and from all that is familiar. Chögyam Trungpa reinvented the dharma while remaining absolutely faithful to the Tradition.

Such a paradox is nevertheless possible because the *source* does not be-long to the past but resides in the living present. The Buddha is nowhere if not here, on this patch of earth, now, at this very moment.

Modernity

Can we characterize Chögyam Trungpa's presentation of the dharma in such a profound and unexpected way as an adaptation of Buddhism to the West?

No. Such an explanation is far too simplistic. If we really want to un-

---

2. The ultimate source of a tradition is not a human one. For the Kagyü school, it was Vajra-dhara. Vajradhara is understood not as a deity exterior to oneself, but as the ultimate ex-pression of the spirit of enlightenment.

3. *Journey without Goal* (2000), p. 50.

4. From here on, I shall spell the word *Traditional* with a capital *T* to mean the preservation of the inspiration of the lineage, in order to distinguish it from its vaguer common use.

derstand what he was trying to do and get a glimpse of the true scope of his work, it is necessary to go further. Chögyam Trungpa did not *adapt* Buddhism to the West. He did not start with an existing doctrine—Buddhist teachings—that had to be presented in a new way. Rather, he reinvented Buddhism by virtue of his capacity to go to the heart of its authentic source. He saw the *modern revolution* that was transforming our world and giving rise to a new way of being.

But how to understand the word *modern* in this context? Not in its usual sense, certainly. Chögyam Trungpa was always opposed to modernity, if it is understood as the rule of materialism and individualism, which are intrinsically opposed to any authentic tradition: "We can't convert America to Buddhism by converting Buddhism into American desires. We can't make everything modern. We have to have some old-fashioned truth. That's very important."[5]

To understand the meaning of this word, it is necessary to separate it from its temporal sense. Modernity is not a characteristic of a recent era or the present time;[6] it is a term used for artists who, like Rimbaud, Baudelaire, or Hölderlin, display a *way* of being that is closely related to the *truth* of our epoch.

Hölderlin, for example, explained that modern destiny is not as *imposing* as ancient destiny, but instead is *more abyssal*.[7] Unlike a gulf, an abyss has no bottom; it is not a place where we fall, but one where we

---

5. Chögyam Trungpa, "Ground, Path, and Fruition," April 1976, in *Collected Vajra Assemblies*, vol. 1 (Halifax: Vajradhatu Publications, 1990), p. 9.

6. Note that the word *modern* is not a philosophical term; Nietzsche, for example, was always sarcastic about anything "modern," while Heidegger carefully avoided the word and used other terms in his writings. At the same time, Nietzsche paid close attention to this phenomenon. He saw the need to overcome the decadence that was enveloping the West. For Nietzsche, a modern revolution should lead not to a renewing of morality but instead to a new way of being. Chögyam Trungpa, unlike most spiritual teachers, also did not make an appeal to morality or try to claim that Buddhist morality could fill in the gaps left after the collapse of Christian morality. Above all, he stressed the importance of practicing meditation, which allows us to *experience* our own humanity, in all its fragility and dignity, in a constantly fresh manner.

7. See François Fédier, "Hölderlin Révolution Modernité," in *Regardez Voir* (Paris: Les Belles Lettres/Archimbaud, 1995), pp. 118–139.

must learn to walk without "ground or leaning post."[8] Hölderlin showed that modernity means learning to live without a stable base.

Chögyam Trungpa understood this loss of ground that is typical of our times. In 1970 he explained the positive aspect of the situation: "The twentieth century brings all religions closer because it forces you to look deeper and then you discover the same things. Spiritual interest is coming out more strongly in people now because of the character of this century; the river of materialism has overrun its banks. . . . So now people want personal and direct spiritual experiences rather than handed-down ones. The religious instinct in all human beings is the same, but the dogma is the obstacle to that spiritual instinct, that primeval intelligence in all religions. It is the obstacle because things are worked out beforehand rather than just being experienced spontaneously."[9]

This is an important statement and indicates the tone of Chögyam Trungpa's approach: as it is no longer possible to rely on an authority, the truth of the teachings must be revealed in each person's direct experience. Such is life in an abyssal world.

In Chögyam Trungpa's work, Buddhism is no longer seen as an established truth that we are required to respect and follow. It is reinvented anew each time.

For Chögyam Trungpa, Buddhism was not starting to take root in the West in order to replace Christianity, which was now incapable of defining the limits in a world stripped of morals.

Chögyam Trungpa did not want to remove the impossibility of finding any foundation or clearly defined identity, which is so typical of our time. On the contrary, he made use of this chaos, which he saw as a way to understand the dharma.

In this point of view, Chögyam Trungpa was able to exploit two per-

---

8. Martin Heidegger, *De l'essence de la liberté humaine: introduction à la philosophie* (The Essence of Human Freedom: An Introduction to Philosophy), trans. from the German by Emmanuel Martineau (Paris: Gallimard, 1987), p. 116.

9. Chögyam Trungpa, "The Common Heart," Centre Monchanin, Montreal, December 4, 1970, unpublished.

sonal discoveries that had marked him. First, his guru Jamgön Kongtrül of Sechen had taught him that the way does not consist in trying to become a sage, but instead in trying to become what you are—the only way to transcend hypocrisy. Second, as Khenpo Gangshar showed him, in moments of distress the only resource is to rely on your own experience as the doorway that may lead to the inner guru.

Returning to experience does not mean being condemned to sentimental mysticism. On the contrary, through this involvement with the living present, the way lies in finding the heart of the true Tradition here and now.

Such is the meaning of modernity: the possibility of freely establishing a relationship with this disappearance of authority. The great modern artists are examples of warriors of modernity. Their work teaches us how to remain at the heart of the abyss, vulnerable and with no reference point.[10] They do not regret this "loss of values" or the fact that our society has "lost its sense of direction" and that there is therefore nothing we can transmit to our children. They do not try, as we spontaneously do, to find a way to avoid this abyss. Instead, like Kasimir Malevich, they say: "I have broken through the blue lampshade of the constraints of color. I have moved into the white. Sail after me, fellow aviators, into the abyss."[11]

The courage of Chögyam Trungpa in experimenting with this absence of any solid ground is disturbing and explains the depth of his work. The journal he kept in 1967 illustrates this aspect of his life:

> *I have no home,*
> *Home, I have none,*
>
> I have no home.

---

10. Such as Paul Cézanne, whose space was no longer the coherent construct of Renaissance perspective. Or the composer Edgar Varèse, who opened up a new musical space, leaving behind the well-tempered system based on fixed scales of sound. In his search for "pure sounds," it could almost be said that his music is not made of notes.

11. Kasimir Malevich, *Suprematism*, exhibition catalog (Moscow, 1919).

While growing up, since I was little up to now, I have never had a family. Having no family seems very sad, but when I think how I have no home, it is very strange. . . . Therefore, since I have no ultimate heart friend other than myself alone, I think that it is definite that no one can create an ultimate home or family for me. Still, strangely, this home of being homeless is my home wherever I go. Everything is my home, the great home of being homeless.[12]

Like no other spiritual teacher, Chögyam Trungpa insisted on the vital importance of remaining in the heart of chaos: "Practice more and experience further loss of ground, but without confusion. . . . The shaky ground is something that you should look forward to."[13]

Such is the nature of space: an unknown opening that both nourishes and panics us. When things seem uncertain, we tend to become more conceptual and discursive in an attempt to fill space. At the beginning of the path, Chögyam Trungpa led his students to make use of such gaps, which are openings through which space dissolves solidity.

As soon as he arrived in the United States, Chögyam Trungpa presented himself as simply as possible, without relying on any form of external authority. This is one reason why, when in England, he decided to abandon his monk's robes. By so doing, he threw off an important barrier that might separate him from Westerners, while also removing any fascination with the exotic. But what a strange situation to be in and what a curious period it must be, if religious dress—whether it frightens or fascinates—is more of an obstacle to understanding than a help! If wearing a monk's robes creates an unbridgeable gap, then this is a precise example of the consequence of the disappearance of any intrinsically legitimate authority.[14]

---

12. Unpublished journal (1967), quoted in Diana J. Mukpo, "Stories That Need Telling," *Shambhala News* (September 2000), p. 5. Translated by the Nālandā Translation Committee. Used by permission of Diana J. Mukpo.

13. Chögyam Trungpa, "Shambhala Day Address, 1982," *Vajradhatu Sun*, April/May 1982, p. 28.

14. The reason is that for us, religious vestments often seem to be just a mask concealing pure hypocrisy. This idea was even one of the aims of twentieth-century thought, a striking

In other words, it is because of the very nature of modernity that the profoundest way to present the truth of Buddhism is to live without recourse to any preestablished forms. As Chögyam Trungpa explained:

> I had a serious accident. I was driving a Triumph 13, a little car which had been recently purchased. It cost 1,000 pounds in England. A sudden blackout overwhelmed me, and I ran into a joke shop and went through the door. . . . That was a kind of very interesting, extraordinarily powerful message to me personally speaking, about how one could be personally involved. There was still a faint hesitation in working on oneself, still wondering whether to simply trust and take refuge in one's reputation, in one's robes, in one's monastic vows alone, relying on one's credentials. That's basically what it boiled down to. I think what was expressed there was that there was a certain fear in me, myself personally, wondering: Suppose I give up my paraphernalia, my outfit, then I'm going to be a fish without water. . . . It took some time to recover from that message, but it was an extraordinarily important message . . . : unclothe yourself, be naked.[15]

There can be no better description of the experience of a lack of solid ground, which is essential to modernity, than in this ordeal of nakedness. This experience of nakedness is not humility but a complete exposure to the world.

His car accident was not just another event in his life. It was a turning point: it transformed the way the dharma was transmitted to the West.

In the twentieth century, there were many teachers coming from different traditions who manifested qualities of presence and compassion in moving and inspiring ways, thus incarnating the ultimate truth of the teachings. But Chögyam Trungpa was the only one who deliberately took

---

example of which can be seen in the film *L'Age d'or* by Luis Buñuel and Salvador Dalí. It is then necessary to rediscover the meaning of an authentic existence outside the church or any other institution.

15. Chögyam Trungpa, "Jamgön Kongtrül," Boulder, December 1974, sixth talk, unpublished.

a long step back to provide an explicit overview of all the teachings. The teachings of Christ and the Buddha, he said, "have been handed down as authority—take it or reject it. And it has been very much based on a dictatorial one person's voice, one person's discovery."[16]

Chögyam Trungpa's teaching and manifestation were not just brilliant and extraordinary; they were also a clear response to a crisis in the West that was becoming general. It was no longer possible to effectively present a spiritual path using the established forms of the past. Chögyam Trungpa opened a new way for people to rediscover a true bond with the sacred and a possibility of freedom. His example goes far beyond Buddhism. His explanation of the dharma reveals and unfolds all of its resonances because it is related through a constant revelation of his own relationship to it. Such is the profoundly modern aspect of his work that makes his words so personal and original.[17]

Chögyam Trungpa never simply recycled what he had learned in Tibet. He reinvented the dharma, placing himself in a position where he could look critically at his heritage. As a critic, he tried to separate what is important from what is not. This distinction could only be made in the light of the unflinching gaze that Chögyam Trungpa focused on himself and on his own path.

Chögyam Trungpa the revolutionary

Because Chögyam Trungpa had access to the source of all forms of spirituality, he was a Buddhist teacher of great historical importance—in the sense that his work transformed interpretations of Buddhism. But this is not because he presented anything that was *new* to the Tradition, but

---

16. "Community Energies," Tail of the Tiger, January 6, 1971, unpublished.

17. In the same way, a truly great writer reveals his own relationship with himself so precisely that his readers have immediate access to what he says—whereas, in general, people's relationships with themselves are extremely imprecise. A good example is the work of Marcel Proust. In the unmodern world, there is always a canon with norms that all work must respect.

because his teaching had a direct relationship with the very beginning that gave birth to Buddhism.[18] The establishment of such a relationship with the very beginning required a true revolution.[19] A revolution changes, as the philosopher François Fédier wrote, "everything that seems to us to be the most solid inheritance from the past—but not to 'make it new,' but instead to remain faithful to the origins we are claiming as ours."[20] In Buddhist terms, it can be said that the origin is the root or germ of all phenomena, their most intimate core.

This statement may be surprising. It is generally thought that the opposite applies, that those who want to *conserve* Tradition preserve it, and it is by revolution that others try to destroy it. But this is a rather naive idea. As Martin Heidegger put it: "The beginning . . . is not safeguarded— it is not even reached—by conservatives. It is only from what has already occurred that such people produce what must regulated and ideal."[21] In other words, conservatives want to keep intact what was, for the simple reason that it has been, without any regard for its true worth.

By being both extremely modern, as only an artist can be, and wholly traditional, as only an authentic spiritual teacher can be, Chögyam Trungpa provided a new interpretation of Buddhism. But what exactly do we mean by *interpretation* in this context? In general, it is understood as something reductive, providing an unambiguous meaning, like the Freudian interpretation of Leonardo da Vinci's painting. Freud saw in it what he already wanted to see.

But in its broader sense, interpretation is a matter of giving full life to

---

18. It is certainly no coincidence that his first book, *Meditation in Action*, opens with a chapter titled "The Life and Example of Buddha," a text of quite breathtaking beauty, with a childlike freshness to it.

19. The word *revolution* comes from an Indo-European root *wel*, "to roll." A revolution is the "return to the starting point." Initially, it had a cosmic meaning, e.g., the revolution of heavenly bodies (Copernicus).

20. François Fédier, *Interprétation* (Paris: P.U.F., 1985), p. 41.

21. Quoted by François Fédier, "Reconstitution" in *Regarder Voir* (Paris/Archimbaud: Les Belles Lettres, 1995), p. 312.

what is under consideration. Thus does a great musician reveal the music he is playing. For example, Glenn Gould played Bach like no one before. In a sense, he did nothing original; he was simply being faithful to the score. But he allowed it to manifest itself in a new way.

Chögyam Trungpa had the talent of a artist when he made the meaning of Buddhism appear in a new light, even if, like a brilliant musician, he was playing a score he did not need to invent.

Chögyam Trungpa and Paul Cézanne

As we have pointed out, the historic movement launched by Chögyam Trungpa's work is very much like the work of an artist.

Paul Cézanne[22] was one of the most important modern painters: "From one generation to another, Cézanne has cast his shadow over nearly all modern painters' workshops. From Gauguin to Picasso, from Bonnard to Malevich, from Matisse to Klee, from Braque to Kandinsky, or from Marcel Duchamp to Jasper Johns, all of them had an intense relationship with Cézanne, and almost all of them, when they could, had a Cézanne in their collection. Cézanne was not only 'the father of us all' (Picasso), 'the master par excellence' (Klee), but also a spiritual master, 'a sort of god of painting' (Matisse), the producer of a 'mystic construction' (Franz Marc), whose use of form had 'given back a soul' to painting (Kandinsky)."[23] He changed the course of art history. With Cézanne, a new era started, to such an extent that it was no longer possible to paint the same way after him as before him. Yet Cézanne never claimed he had produced work that was new. As he put it, he was simply trying to paint like "a natural Poussin."[24]

---

22. Cézanne was born in Aix-en-Provence on January 19, 1839. He claimed that his work as a painter only really began when he had reached the age of forty. Cézanne's true point of departure happened when what was to be called Impressionism exploded onto the scene, even though he soon began to live alone in Aix and distanced himself from any artistic group so as to devote himself to his work.

23. Françoise Cachin and Joseph J. Rishel, "Il est celui qui peint," *Cézanne* (Paris: Réunion des Musées Nationaux, 1995), p. 15.

24. *Conversations avec Cézanne*, presented by P. M. Doran (Paris: Macula, 1978), p. 122.

It is important to understand that Cézanne's artistic revolution was a way for him to remain faithful to the tradition—which he felt to be incarnated by Nicolas Poussin more than anybody else. As Clement Greenberg, the renowned art historian, put it: "This is exactly the idea I have of modernity and the avant-garde. Manet, Flaubert, and Baudelaire wanted to be as good as the best of their predecessors. But they could not imitate the past. In this way, it could be stated that the avant-garde is a salvage operation on the Western tradition."[25]

Cézanne thus tried to reveal painting as it really is: "I owe you the truth in painting, and I shall tell it to you." His modernity was not a rejection of the past but was born of his passionate quest for the truth.

With this in mind, Cézanne established a relationship with his own experience. Such is the meaning of the word *natural* for Cézanne: to paint directly what he felt. And so modernity was born. No matter how much he admired his predecessors, "He might want to resemble them, but he *cannot* resemble them. In reality, he could only find his discipline within himself," as the writer C. F. Ramuz observed.[26]

Like Cézanne, Chögyam Trungpa was long condemned to isolation by the official Academy, which was frightened by the experience of freedom he offered. Both men shared a common desire to bring out the truth in an authentic way, without any regard for conformity. In the words of David Rome, the longtime secretary to Chögyam Trungpa and a connoisseur of modern art: "These two men manifested the same basic quality and the same almost brutal power. With exemplary courage, genius, and persistence, they never gave up transmuting the base earth into a new gold that no one had been capable of seeing before."

---

25. Clement Greenberg, *L'École de New-York* (catalog), *Les années 50* (Paris: Centre Georges Pompidou, 1988), p. 57.

26. See C. F. Ramuz, *Paul Cézanne* (Lausanne: Bibliothèque des Arts, 1995), p. 26.

2. Translation

Teaching in English

In the new relationship with the Tradition that Chögyam Trungpa began, the question of translation was of course paramount. By affirming the need to present the dharma in his students' native tongue, Chögyam Trungpa was working against a trendy fascination with the far-off and the exotic.

A large part of Chögyam Trungpa's work consisted in presenting the essential doctrinal teachings directly in English—his students' language—and translating a large amount of scripture. He was thus among the first to present the dharma in a Western language, without using an interpreter, and the first to ask his students to practice in their own tongue: "It would be good to have an American students' version of the whole thing, which would be much more dynamic and very personal. And that is precisely one of the reasons why we have meditation instructors from among my own students, people who have been entrusted and have actually been developing themselves somewhat. And sometimes dharma is heard in your own language, your own tongue, your own accent is very inspiring, unless you are into some kind of Orientalist trip."[27]

Buddha himself probably used a vernacular language rather than Sanskrit or Pali. Consistent with his criticism of the caste system, he insisted on the importance of teaching everyone, and not just priests, who were the only ones who understood Sanskrit. In this regard, Buddhism distinguishes itself from Judaism, in which Hebrew is the sacred language that contains the divine presence. There is no "Buddhist" language.

In order to carry out this immense task of transferring the Tradition from one language to another, Chögyam Trungpa went back to Sanskrit, because it is the lingua franca, the common tongue in all Buddhist countries, even China and Japan.

For there was nothing new about this translation of Buddhism into another language. It had already been done by the Tibetans themselves. Between the seventh and eight centuries CE, they had translated the en-

---

27. Chögyam Trungpa, "Jamgön Kongtrül, " Boulder, April 1974, second talk, unpublished.

tire Indian canon into Tibetan. Before translating it once more into English, Chögyam Trungpa thought it very important to consult the original Sanskrit.

He even decided, wherever possible, to choose Sanskrit terms over Tibetan ones (for example, for the practice of mindfulness, Chögyam Trungpa used the Sanskrit term *shamatha*, while other teachers preferred the Tibetan *shi-ne*). Furthermore, along with Greek and Latin, Sanskrit is one of the roots of all our Indo-European languages; it is thus not completely foreign to us. Some terms, such as *Buddha, bodhisattva, karma*, and *yoga*, have even become household words and entered our Western dictionaries. Chögyam Trungpa wanted the same to happen to far more words.

He also wanted his students to pronounce Sanskrit correctly, as the Brahmans do, and not like Tibetans, who do not read Sanskrit properly and pronounce it rather strangely; for example, they pronounce the term *vajra*—the indestructible quality—as if it were spelled *benza*.

By making such decisions, Chögyam Trungpa tried to create a specific Buddhist tongue based on the vernacular: "I have heard people say that English is the language of barbarians and that is why we have to learn Tibetan or Sanskrit. If both languages convey what is, I see no reason to distinguish between them. In fact, what is more inspiring is that we transcend the racial and cultural divisions: as we are, we can penetrate directly into the heart of it. This is the penetration of wisdom cutting through the fascination."[28]

What is translation?

How could a Tibetan, coming from such a different culture from ours, present to us a spiritual tradition that lies outside Western culture? If we take this question to heart and avoid facile answers, it becomes clear that it is of fundamental importance. It is not just a question of finding English words to say what the Tibetan says; more deeply, translation means

---

28. Chögyam Trungpa, "Cutting Through," *Garuda II: Working with Negativity* (Tail of the Tiger, Barnet, VT, and Karma Dzong, Boulder), Spring 1972, p. 6.

thoroughly thinking over what we mean (in another relationship with the world constructed by language itself). Thinking is always a form of translation: in other words, an explanation of what we want to say.[29]

Translating Tibetan Buddhist thought means thinking in both the source and target languages. It is not enough to have a merely functional relationship with language. Language is not just a means of transmitting a message from a sender to a receiver. It is a profound way of experiencing the world. In this sense, the work of Chögyam Trungpa should be thoroughly examined, because he paid exceptional attention to this problem.[30]

His teachings are a constant effort not to remain satisfied with what has already been said. His discourse was alive, because it had a direct relationship with what it aimed to express.

In this aspect of his work, one of the signs of Chögyam Trungpa's genius is the systematic way he avoided the vocabulary of Western metaphysics and any habitual use of language—two things that would have missed what is original about what the dharma can tell us.

Avoiding the concepts already expressed in Western philosophy and Christianity is no easy task, because there is a strong tendency to recycle concepts that have already proved to be of great worth. But the risk would then be to mix different orders of meaning and obscure both of

---

29. Friedrich Schleiermacher (1768–1834), the famous translator of Plato into German, had this to say: "When a discourse is transported from one language to another, it manifests itself to us in a variety of ways. . . . If the productions of a language that has been dead for centuries can be embraced by another language, we do not then have to go outside the domain of a single language in order to encounter such a phenomenon. For not only are the dialects of the different groups of a single nation . . . already, in a narrower sense, different languages requiring a complete oral transposition, but contemporaries who are not separated by dialect, who simply belong to different social classes and have little mutual contact, are extremely different from one another in their upbringing, and often need just such mediation if they are going to communicate. Do we not often have to translate the words of another person, who is quite like us, but whose sensibility and temperament are different? . . . Even more: we sometimes have to translate our own discourses after a certain time if we want to be able to reappropriate them easily." *Des différentes méthodes du traduire* ("On the Different Methods of Translation") (Paris: Éditions du Seuil, 1999), p. 31ff.

30. The Tibetan word for translator, *lotsawa,* literally means "eye of the world."

them. Buddhist thought is different from Western metaphysics, so to think about one via the other would be to run the risk of losing touch with both of them.[31]

As regards the massive task of translating the Tibetan texts that were required for his students' studies and practice, Chögyam Trungpa decided to assemble a group of practitioners who were not professional translators (that is, they were not Tibetologists) and have them work together. This situation was a singular one. The translation group met with Chögyam Trungpa and, line by line, discussed with him the translation they had drafted. In this way, they had long and thorough discussions of the experience behind a given term. When a text describing a spiritual experience was translated, Chögyam Trungpa manifested the very nature of the teaching. In this way, the work was no longer purely linguistic, but instead an exercise in entering into relationship with the experience itself.

What he wanted was a change in how his students experienced language—"the most intrinsic mode in which a human can exist."[32] In a context of transmitting Buddhism to the West, it was necessary to open up a space so that the word could take root within language itself—so that English could start to be spoken dharmically.

In his book *Regarder Voir* the philosopher and translator François Fédier put the meaning of the act of translation into a clear perspective. Translating, he explained, is not a matter of passing from one linguistic system into another, as is generally thought. To understand this fundamental point, which means that no computer will ever be able to really

---

31. This is what Heidegger clearly explained about Christianity: "A Christian philosophy is a square circle and a misunderstanding. There is of course elaboration, through a questioning thought concerning the world we have experienced as Christians, in other words, with faith, and this means theology. Only those eras that no longer really believe in the hugeness of theology's task conceive the ruinous idea that theology might in some way be rejuvenated with the help of philosophy." Martin Heidegger, *Introduction to Metaphysics*. The same applies to Buddhism. The notion of "Buddhist philosophy" is a contradiction in terms, which deforms both philosophy and Buddhism.

32. François Fédier, "Traduire les Beiträge . . . ," in *Regarder Voir* (Paris: Les Belles Lettres, 1995), p. 84.

translate, two levels of translation must be distinguished. The first, which he called *translatability*, is where "language reaches the limits of the word."[33] This is the sort of translation that goes on inside each language, when it speaks truly. We then have to pass from a utilitarian, habitual, and immediate use of language to a more fundamental relationship with it. The second is the level of translating from one language to another. Its source lies in the initial translation. So translating is not a matter of looking for equivalents, but instead of "rediscovering the initial situation, where we must find the way of speaking that suits what must be said."[34] In other words, it is allowing your language to say what there is to be said: "Which nevertheless presupposes the fact that the people who translate from one language to another are led, by their translation, to perceive, in one way or another, the original that lies at its source."[35] It is just this original that Chögyam Trungpa tried to bring out and use as the basis of what needed to be said.

Chögyam Trungpa returned to the direct experience of what he explained. If, for example, he spoke about compassion, he communicated the need to leave behind what we usually understand by this term, to abandon our presuppositions and go directly to the heart of the notion: "*Karuna* is usually translated as 'compassion.' However, the word *compassion* is filled with connotations in English which have nothing to do with karuna. So it is important to clarify what is meant by enlightened compassion and how it differs from our usual notion of compassion. Usually we think of a compassionate person as someone who is kind and gentle and who never loses his temper. Such a person is always willing to forgive our mistakes and to comfort us. But enlightened compassion is not quite as simple-minded as that notion of a kindly, well-meaning soul."[36] He

---

33. Ibid., p. 104.

34. Ibid., p. 98. Cf. Marcel Proust, *Le Temps retrouvé* (Time Regained): "this essential book, the sole true book, a great writer has no need to invent in the common sense of the term, because it exists inside us all; what he does is to translate it."

35. François Fédier, "Traduire les Beiträge . . . ," p. 104.

36. *The Heart of the Buddha*, p. 17.

proceeded in the same way with many other terms, as here with the word *patience*: "In the English language, patience ordinarily means 'wait and see,' to endure the wait. In the Shambhala context, patience means to be there. It is simply being there, always being there. There is no connotation of being so painfully there."[37]

When Chögyam Trungpa used Tibetan words, he nearly always defined them using their original meanings. In order to establish an intimate relationship with a word's original meaning, as well as with its use and current sense, he often used the etymology of English words and regularly consulted his beloved twelve-volume *Oxford English Dictionary*.

Chögyam Trungpa was particularly enthusiastic about this creative activity, in his attempts to find the right word, or more exactly allow language to find its own terms. He devoted much time to the project.

He had a deep knowledge of English. While his syntax could be faulty, his vocabulary was extremely good, and he was highly attentive to the subtleties of the various connotations of each word.

It is basically due to him that we now use the terms *ego* and *egolessness* to translate the notions of *atman* and *anatman*. An examination of previous translations of these terms shows that they were generally taken from the Christian tradition—which explains the choice of the word *soul*. One of the remarkable insights he had was to see that equivalences to Buddhist thought were perhaps easier to find in psychology rather than religion, which explains why he mined this area for his vocabulary. For example, he spoke of anxiety as a way of expressing the first noble truth and used the notions of sadness and depression. He did not translate the Tibetan word *dikpa* as "sin," which had excessively Christian connotations, but as "blockage."

In the same way, to translate *soldep* as "pray" seemed too heavily nuanced; he preferred the word *supplicate*. He spoke more of "sacredness" than "holiness." Even when he spoke directly of his experiences and religious customs, he was careful to select the least theistic word possible. This opened the Buddhist way to an entirely new and different audience,

---

37. *Great Eastern Sun*, p. 87.

thanks to a vocabulary that sounded right in the culture in which it was used.[38] He deliberately chose to use the language of poetry, literature, and the pop culture of his time.

This allowed him to coin evocative phrases that stayed with people, for example: "back to square one," "riding on a razor blade," "cutting through spiritual materialism," "transforming confusion into wisdom." Chögyam Trungpa used onomatopoeia extensively, in the hope of joining sound and sense. At different levels and in different ways, he showed how firmly he believed that the word is linked to the sacred.

Chögyam Trungpa thus created a new language or, to be more precise, a new relationship with our own language: the words *compassion, patience, ego, meditation, suffering,* and *hope,* as well as *fear, sadness,* and *bravery,* no longer have the same meaning as they once did in our daily lives.

In the 1980 foreword to *The Rain of Wisdom*—translations of the songs of the teachers of the Kagyü lineage, which he had worked on with his students—he noted: "I am realizing for the first time that the basically theistic English language has now been blessed by the Practice Lineages and is becoming a great medium for expressing the nontheistic, enlightened dharma."[39]

---

38. During his conduct of the Vajradhatu Seminary, Chögyam Trungpa devoted considerable time to translation. For example, in 1976, he translated the sadhana of Vajrayogini with his group; in 1978, the Chakrasamvara; in 1979, *The Rain of Wisdom*, a collection of devotional texts and songs; and in 1980, *The Life of Marpa* as well as several of the texts belonging to the cycle of Shambhala teachings.

39. Foreword to *The Rain of Wisdom*, p. xi. To conclude this chapter, it is interesting to note that Chögyam Trungpa was very keen for his teachings to be translated into other Western languages, in the same spirit he had adopted.

Chapter Five
HOW CHÖGYAM TRUNGPA TAUGHT

I have been doing as much as I can in my presentation of the teachings so far to make sure you understand that each one of the dharmas I have presented to you is your personal experience. You can actually relate the dharma to what you experience on the spot.[1]

—CHÖGYAM TRUNGPA

1. To Speak from the Heart

Chögyam Trungpa is one of the most widely read Buddhist authors among the various Western practitioners of the dharma. The quality and depth of his teachings remain as vibrant now as they were when he was physically among us. His many books form a genuine body of work, with its own unity. Rinpoche hoped eventually to see the publication of 108 volumes destined for the general public, to which would be added about 40 volumes intended for more advanced students.[2]

---

1. Chögyam Trungpa, *1980 Seminary Transcripts: Hinayana-Mahayana* (Boulder: Vajradhatu Publications), p. 143.

2. Almost as soon as he arrived in the West in 1963, Chögyam Trungpa began his work as a writer. In England at the end of the sixties, he worked with Esmé Cramer Roberts on his first

For the most part, his works are based on transcripts of oral teachings. On each occasion, Chögyam Trungpa taught in relationship to the context in which he found himself and the expectations of the people who had come to hear him. But he also had in mind to present a unified group of teachings that could be edited into works that would be of use to people in the future.[3] He explained that he was teaching not just his own students but also future generations.

What makes his books so different from those of other spiritual teachers?

One characteristic of his approach was that he did not cater to people's expectations, especially when it came to preconceptions about spirituality. Without adopting a mystical or subjective approach, Chögyam Trungpa broke with both theology and metaphysics—that is, with the theoretical approach to spirituality that has dominated the West since the days of scholasticism. He also broke with the normative, moralistic discourse in which religion often cloaks itself. He wore none of the conventional masks of the "sage." His rigor was unequaled, merciless, and yet never dogmatic.

His teaching style was very different from what he had seen at Oxford.

---

book in English, the autobiographical *Born in Tibet* (first published 1966). Two other books soon appeared: *Meditation in Action* (1969) and *Mudra* (1972), both edited with the help of Richard Arthure. Today, thirty volumes of his work are in print in English.

The project to publish 108 volumes was called the Dharma Ocean Series. Carolyn Rose Gimian writes in the introduction to volume four of *The Collected Works of Chögyam Trungpa*: "All together, eight volumes in the Dharma Ocean Series have been published, which leaves only 100 more to come! This seems like an enormous number of books, but given Chögyam Trungpa's prolific activity as a dharma teacher, it is not at all out of the question. He gave several thousand talks that were recorded and archived during his seventeen years in North America, no two of which are the same. There is more than enough material in this collection to complete the volumes in the Dharma Ocean Series."

3. Chögyam Trungpa never repeated himself. There are no two identical seminars in his entire output. To give just one example, he gave four seminars on the life of Naropa: in New York and at Tail of the Tiger in 1972, then another the next year at Tail of the Tiger, and a final one in 1976 at RMDC. On each occasion, he approached Naropa's life in a different way. The first and third have been published in the book *Illusion's Game: The Life and Teaching of Naropa*. Given the utter coherence of Chögyam Trungpa's teaching, it is a pity that the other two were not included.

Nor did he adopt the traditional Tibetan style, which generally consists of the line-by-line explanation of a classic text and commentaries by a great teacher of the past.

During the first few years, he taught in an extremely direct and free manner, aiming at the heart of everyone's experience: "We are going back to the original style of how Buddhism was practiced in the time of the Buddha, so that people live the dharma, they live impermanence on the spot. They actually live the whole thing, properly and fully. That seems to be the only way to make everything real."[4]

Despite the deep comprehension and realization of other teachers, many of them are stuck in a web of concepts embedded in their traditions. This makes them hard to understand for those who were brought up outside those traditions. This is why Chögyam Trungpa decided to speak so directly. If Buddhism is to be a description of how we can free ourselves from conceptual thought—or, more precisely, our set of beliefs concerning reality—Chögyam Trungpa showed the way. He constantly cut through abstractions in order to reveal our most concrete experiences of their ultimate depth. He invented a new language that allowed him to provide simple explanations for complicated, advanced teachings.

Apart from the brilliance of his teaching, there was another, even more touching factor: Chögyam Trungpa spoke directly about his own experience, sharing his heart with his entire audience. He thus removed the distance that Tibetan tradition maintains between teacher and disciple. In this way, as explained in the preceding chapter, Chögyam Trungpa leaped into modernity: "So I thought I shouldn't be too methodical or scholarly in expounding the vajrayana to you, and that I should speak from my heart."[5] He did not mean "from my heart" in the sentimental sense, but in a spirit of complete openness and involvement. Over and above being a guru, he was a human being entering into a relationship of friendship with another human being.

---

4. Chögyam Trungpa, "Confidence and Enlightenment," September 1978, second talk, unpublished.

5. Chögyam Trungpa, *1982 Seminary Transcripts: Hinayana-Mahayana* (Boulder: Vajradhatu Publications), p. 5.

This quality is particularly noticeable in the inimitable way he answered questions. The typical Tibetan teacher gives a scholarly, often very long, precise, and technical answer to each question, taking the opportunity to reiterate some doctrinal point.[6] Chögyam Trungpa answered the person directly. When you read these answers later, they often seem to be off the point. But if you watch the videotape of the question-and-answer session, then everything becomes clear. The visual image reveals the special atmosphere of an encounter between two people. Chögyam Trungpa replied not just to the meaning of the words in the question, but to what the person was really trying to ask and had concealed behind the words. He did not try to give the "right" answer according to Buddhist doctrine; instead, he pointed to the space out of which the question came, in order to open his student's mind further.

His teaching had nothing technical or philosophical about it. Chögyam Trungpa liked to surprise and touch his audience. When listening to him, or when reading his words today, there is always a moment when a flash of his intense brilliance suddenly hooks you. To take one example, while he was presenting a seminar on the life of Naropa, one of the greatest teachers of the Kagyü lineage, he began by explaining: "It seems that in relation to the whole thing we are talking about, Naropa's attainment of enlightenment is not that important. It is Naropa's confusion that is important for us as ordinary people."[7] Thanks to this turnabout, he cut through the usual logic in order to show what had previously been hidden but which is of vital importance: while everyone was expecting to find in Naropa a primary example of spiritual accomplishment, Chögyam Trungpa emphasized that it was the way Naropa coped with his confusion that is truly edifying. Thus we follow the path not by imitating an external model but by establishing authentic contact with

---

6. I am not criticizing this extremely authentic traditional method, which is a generous and precise manner of taking a student's question seriously. I only wish to emphasize how unusual Chögyam Trungpa's teaching style was by comparison.

7. *Illusion's Game,* p. 20.

who we really are. It is while we are listening that we are suddenly disarmed and opened out to an even vaster dimension than the one we had perceived initially—and there is nothing conceptual about such an experience.

He never appeared to teach out of a sense of duty. This was surely the secret of the freedom he manifested. He wanted to enter into a relationship with students that was as direct as possible. At the end of a talk, he often would devote some time to meeting those who had come to listen to him. A line of people formed, everyone waiting to exchange a few words with him personally. Even though it was just for a few minutes, he was so available and concerned about who you were that people were profoundly moved by just a short contact. He thus radically changed the lives of those he encountered. Susan G., one of his students, remembers the moment when she was introduced to him: "I was stunned, as if I had received an electric shock. He held out his hand to me, and when I took it I felt the most unbelievable feeling of gentleness I had ever known. In contrast, my own energy felt painfully aggressive. Then I looked into his eyes. There was a softness and kindness exuding from him which I had never experienced before and, beyond that, a depth I could not fathom. I couldn't find the person beyond those eyes. The effect on me was tremendously powerful. It was as if this man could see through to my deepest core, and yet he accepted me. I felt I had been penetrated by loving but X-ray eyes—my mask unraveled in the light of his being so real."[8]

Most university professors, many scholars, and some religious personalities adopt a particular tone of voice and look when they speak, as if they are playing a part. So nothing was more moving than to listen to someone speak without this layer of protection distorting his humanity. Chögyam Trungpa, with his high voice,[9] burning with love for all of us, was there before us, naked and cosmic.

---

8. Quoted in Jeremy Hayward, *Sacred World: A Guide to Shambhala Warriorship in Daily Life* (New York: Bantam New Age, 1995), pp. 212–213.

9. His voice became particularly high-pitched after his car accident.

An uncompromising teaching

But it would be wrong to think that his teaching was always simple and accessible. On the contrary, some seminars, such as those collected in *Transcending Madness* and *Orderly Chaos*, are extremely difficult. They are even perhaps the most challenging texts yet published in the West concerning the vajrayana tradition.

But the problem does not lie in the use of difficult concepts that only advanced students could understand. Each sentence is comprehensible, there is no obscure jargon, and we easily form the impression that we are following what is being said. But we rapidly become lost. Chögyam Trungpa's use of language is not based on familiar concepts. Because his words are unmarked by the "bureaucracy of ego"[10]—ego's constant desire for something "higher" and "more spiritual"—they take on an unexpected meaning. The logic that he follows has nothing to do with our logic. It is the pure unfolding of space.

Sometimes it is difficult for us to retain or grasp any ideas from his teaching that we can make use of. As he put it one day, "There is no hope of understanding anything at all. There is no hope of finding out who did what or what did what or how anything worked. Give up your ambition to put the jigsaw puzzle together. Give it up altogether, absolutely; throw it up in the air, put it in the fireplace. Unless we give up this hope, this precious hope, there is no way out at all."[11] We must make the leap of understanding reality in terms of openness, rather than based on our confusion. Such a prospect throws us into a panic.

Experience transmitted in this way is extremely direct, even if at first we understand nothing. The paradox is that when teachers present—at least in public—the highest teachings, such as those of dzogchen, they do so using a list of categories, based on a very strict logic. But even when Chögyam Trungpa presented basic teachings, he did not adopt this approach. He plunged his listeners and readers into the very heart of the

---

10. An extremely expressive phrase that Chögyam Trungpa often used; see, for example, *Cutting Through Spiritual Materialism*, p. 15.

11. *Crazy Wisdom*, p. 84.

experience of his teaching. The Dorje Löppon (one of Chögyam Trungpa's students)[12] remembers how, during a seminar about the six realms[13] given in December 1971, each talk created a different space, in which the listeners became absorbed: "We all felt so absorbed, as though locked into a particular experience. Chögyam Trungpa made us see how experience is born, and how it can become confused. He always taught in such a way that his entire audience could remain in a state of spiritual realization." More than just presenting the content of his teaching, Chögyam Trungpa created the space that corresponded to it, which everyone could experience.

The difficulty of his teaching lies also in its intensity, for he cut the ego to pieces in order to free our naked hearts. For Chögyam Trungpa, teaching always meant freeing his students *at once*, and he was ready to take any risk in the hope of succeeding. He often precisely described of the way the people who were listening to him were manipulating their experiences even while he spoke. As a contrast, a world appeared that was vaster, more colorful, and more lively than our everyday world. On the one hand, he held up a merciless mirror that reflected us as we are; on the other, he allowed us to see a world that is so blindingly brilliant it is almost off-putting. His students were thus torn in two, forced to let go and accept reality as it is.

2. Three Styles of Transmission

As with all truly great spiritual teachers, the essence of his teaching was not just in its content, but in its immediate and personal transmission. Let us take a very simple example in order to understand what is meant

---

12. The Dorje Loppön, Lodrö Dorje, is one of Chögyam Trungpa's students who was given the job of overseeing the Buddhist teachings and practices in all of his organizations. In a Tibetan monastery, the dorje loppön is traditionally the master of rites.

13. The six realms are a classic part of Buddhist teaching. They are the world of hell beings (naraka), hungry ghosts (preta), animals, human beings, jealous gods (asura), and gods (deva).

by this sort of transmission. We have all known someone who has told us about a book they cherish, and the love for it that they transmit to us opens a door allowing us access to their experience. For instance, I can remember a teacher to whom I explained my inability to see sculpture properly and how that art form generally left me indifferent. He advised me to go see the work of Julio González (1876–1942), one of the greatest artists of the twentieth century. "With González," he told me, "you will understand the excellence of sculpture: pay attention to the space it opens up. Sculpture should not be looked at in the same way as painting; you have to feel it with your solar plexus." Following his advice, and his way of showing me physically how to place myself before such a work of art, I was at last able to really see sculpture. For the first time, my eyes opened to a dimension that had formerly been obscure to me.

With spirituality, this approach is of vital importance, despite the fact that it is currently absent from our culture. What really matters is not the theoretical knowledge that the teacher possesses, but the way in which he or she understands not only a given text, but the world in general.

This could be described as the transmission of a spiritual influence whose primary characteristic is that it affects our entire being. Such transmission is not so much a matter of communicating a message as it is an entrée into the way the teacher experiences the world so that we can feel the same way.

In the tradition of tantric Buddhism, it is said that transmission takes place in three styles.[14] The first style of the transmission of enlightenment uses words, or more generally concepts and ideas. But just as a finger pointing at the moon is not the moon, words merely indicate an experience that we must still live out. This level of explanation is a vital yet partial contribution to teaching.

The second style of communication lies in the creation of a particular context: "All the teacher can do is to create the situation."[15] The situation in which teaching can take place is like a theater, to use a simile pre-

---

14. Chögyam Trungpa explains this point in the chapter "Dorje Trolö and the Three Styles of Transmission" in *Crazy Wisdom*, pp. 167–182.

15. *Meditation in Action*, p. 32.

sented in *Meditation in Action*. Everything is ready: the seats, the stage, the lights. When you enter the theater, you immediately sense that you are going to take part in something special. Exactly what the teacher does is of no importance; what matters is the situation he creates. As Chögyam Trungpa explained: "If you don't have the experience of winter, you have to take off your clothes and lie in the snow at night. That way you will learn a very good lesson on what winter is all about that doesn't use words. You could read a book about it, but it doesn't mean very much unless you have that very immediate and direct experience—which is frightening, very powerful."[16] Transmission at this level means allowing the student to experience the teaching directly.

Finally, at the third level of transmitting enlightenment, the teacher shares his own mind with his disciple.[17] It is an experience of space and "the most transparent energy."[18] But such space has nothing to do with a quiet, religious dimension. Instead it is provocative and full: "Transmission is merely opening up on both sides, opening the whole thing. One opens oneself completely in such a way that, although it may only be for a few seconds, it somehow means a great deal. That doesn't mean one has reached enlightenment, but one has had a glimpse of what reality is."[19] To be with Chögyam Trungpa meant experiencing reality, which is what some Buddhists call *dharmata*: "dharmaness, the isness of reality."[20] Strangely enough, reality never responds to the concepts we have of it, nor to our expectations.

Such transmission can be given formally but can also reside in the particular quality of the atmosphere that the teacher manifests. In his presence, we are exposed to the presence of enlightenment.

---

16. *Illusion's Game*, p. 123.

17. "The thought lineage is more of a presence than something happening. Also, it has an extraordinarily ordinary quality." *Crazy Wisdom*, p. 170.

18. *Crazy Wisdom*, p. 103.

19. *Meditation in Action*, p. 36.

20. *The Lion's Roar*, p. 6.

3. Commitment to a Specific School

The way Chögyam Trungpa presented Buddhism is part of a long historical tradition to which he was the heir.

We have already noted that he was very concerned about connecting the lineage of mahamudra energy, which is part of the Kagyü lineage, to the dzogchen experience of space of the Nyingma lineage.[21] Furthermore, he emphasized the mystical tradition of the siddhas, the "perfected ones," as well as the more formal lifestyle of monks.

Siddhas practice in their daily lives with little respect for social conventions. For example, Tilopa, the founder of the Kagyü school, ground sesame seeds in order to extract their oil. He didn't care that this job was normally done by the lowest castes. It became his practice and allowed him, as he expressed in verse, to extract the oil of spiritual activity from his body and fill the vase of his heart. Dombipa was another such adept. Before becoming a siddha, he worked as a laundryman, washing clothes in a river. One day a yogi passed by and asked him if he also washed his daily thoughts and kleshas (disturbing emotions). Dombipa had no answer to this and so asked how he could join his work with a practice that would allow him to reach enlightenment.

Gampopa, the fifth head of the Kagyü school, transformed this tradition of nomadic siddhas into a monastic tradition, which gave the school the monastic character it brought into modern times. He was a famous doctor, with a wife he dearly loved, whose beauty and intelligence struck everyone who met her. They had two children. Then a terrible plague carried away his wife and children, leaving him alone. Keeping a promise made to his wife, he became a monk. After years of strict practice, he heard about Milarepa,[22] one of the most famous yogis and siddhas in all of Tibet, who practiced according to the perspective of limitless tantra, and decided to study with him.

When Gampopa became Milarepa's successor, he brought together the

---

21. This does not mean that he thought them the same; on the contrary, he always emphasized their differences.

22. See Fabrice Midal, *Pratique de l'éveil* (Paris: Éditions du Seuil, 1997).

two traditions he had received: the monastic tradition based on rules and precepts, and the yogic tradition of the siddhas, which focuses on spontaneous inner realization.

Chögyam Trungpa inherited these two traditions. He was careful to build up precise structures and establish strict discipline, and to do this he created a framework allowing a large number of his students to progress along the spiritual path in gradual steps, without sacrificing the abrupt quality of the highest transmission from teacher to student.

4. Advice to Students About to Teach

Another way to understand how Chögyam Trungpa regarded teaching is to examine the advice he gave his own followers.

It has already been pointed out how important he felt was be for students to manifest their own understanding. In 1972, he invited some of them to accept this responsibility. Every Friday evening, while he was addressing the assembled community in Boulder, Colorado, he asked someone to prepare a brief presentation based on a chapter of one of his books. He wanted his students to become spokespersons for the dharma. As he wrote in *Meditation in Action*: "Putting it into words—whatever you have achieved—and giving it to someone else is the only way to develop yourself."[23] When students are placed before the assembly of practitioners, they are obliged to take things seriously and find the best way to express themselves. The slightest attempt at manipulation or hypocrisy comes across clearly to one and all.

By making his students teach, he was helping them to become one with the teachings, and to give up thinking that they are helpless and need their teacher to feed them.

The main advice he gave was to speak simply, from the heart, and not to hide behind concepts. He said that students would not necessarily remember what was said, but they would remember the teacher's presence and the environment he or she created. Although he said it was

---

23. *Meditation in Action*, p. 45.

important to know your subject well, he stressed that true prajna is the union of intuition and understanding, which comes from your connection with others rather than from transmitting information.

When David Rome had to teach in public on a number of occasions, he asked Chögyam Trungpa to critique his way of presenting the dharma. He was told that he lacked a sense of crescendo that would allow him to round off his talks. He was advised to create a space in which he could explain a particular logic. At the same time, it was necessary to abandon this logic so as to be spontaneous and passionate. The main point was to reveal the particular texture of the subject in question. In this way, David Rome learned how to maintain a state of presence when he taught. To be in space, while knowing how to modulate it, is the true way to teach, the means to reveal the dimension where it can manifest itself.

When someone presented the dharma, the students who had come to listen found themselves in a situation of great concentration. Such acute attention is fundamental to any possibility of instruction. Remaining silent can be a way of transmitting that is just as good as, if not better than, talking. The art of teaching means recognizing that what we want to teach has its own existence, independent of us.

Chögyam Trungpa often explained the importance of expressing what is true for us at the moment of speaking, and not just repeating what we already know to be true. It is not enough merely to parrot lessons.

Seminary

Chögyam Trungpa was sometimes critical of Tibetan institutions and their formal rigidity, without rejecting the basic principle of an institution. On the contrary, he set about founding new ones, to manifest the tradition to preserve his teachings, beyond his own charisma, for future generations. These institutions had to be founded on an authentic desire to spread enlightenment. One that he was most proud of was the three-month Seminary.[24]

---

24. Chögyam Trungpa conducted numerous teaching programs or seminars; the one lasting three months was called Seminary (or Vajradhatu Seminary).

Seminary was the means to institutionalize a training program that would allow students to familiarize themselves with the profundity of the teachings. It could be reconvened year after year. Even in Tibet, nothing like it had ever existed, and Chögyam Trungpa was very pleased with this innovation: "As far as I'm concerned, nobody has ever created programs like this before, so therefore it is ideal." He led the first Seminary in 1973, in Teton Village, Wyoming. After that, and until 1986—with the exception of 1977, when he was in retreat for the entire year—Chögyam Trungpa devoted three months of each year to the program. He greatly emphasized the importance of this training, saying that it was a precondition for being able to study the vajrayana in depth and begin preliminary practices (*ngöndro*).

When presenting a new teaching, Chögyam Trungpa often began by explaining the sort of experience it covered, before dealing with all the details in more intellectual terms. But at Seminary, he wanted to enter with precision into the heart of Buddhist doctrine: "As students became more completely involved with practice and study, I felt there was a need for more advanced training in the tradition of Jamgön Kongtrül the Great and of the Kagyü contemplative order. A situation was needed in which a systematic and thorough presentation of the dharma could be made."[25]

Larry Mermelstein, who often worked as a translator alongside Chögyam Trungpa, remembers this change in approach: "Chögyam Trungpa's preparation for talks varied enormously. Most seminars, especially during the first few years, never seemed to involve any preparation. Perhaps the Vajradhatu Seminary, which began in 1973, was the beginning of using notes for his more detailed presentations of the dharma, and he sometimes spent some considerable time perusing Tibetan texts and taking notes for his talks. Many of the early Seminary talks involved pages of notes."

For his students, going to Seminary was a mark of great commitment.

---

25. Chögyam Trungpa, "Epilogue: Planting the Dharma in the West," *Born in Tibet*, 4th ed. (2000), p. 260. In his Seminary teaching, Chögyam Trungpa emphasized the systematic and careful study of the three-yana journey, following the traditional lamrim (stages of the path) approach. Although he relied on many root texts, he depended most heavily on two texts as sources for Seminary talks: *The Treasury of Knowledge* by Jamgön Kongtrül the Great and a text on the nine yanas by Dudjom Rinpoche.

Attending a three-month program often put them in difficulty, because it was necessary for them not only to give up their normal lives for that period of time, but also to find enough money to live for three months, find someone to rent their apartments, leave their friends, and so on. It was impossible to attend Seminary without previous preparation, which sometimes took several years. It was also necessary to study seriously before Seminary, which started with an entrance exam.

It then became a precious experience, and as Chögyam Trungpa liked to say: "The nine-yana approach can seep through your entire system, even your bones and marrow. You can be completely and properly soaked in it, and you can actually experience the whole thing—discipline actually means discipline; learning means real learning."[26] For many students, attending Seminary was a turning point in their development and their personal involvement with Chögyam Trungpa and Buddhism.

Each month of Seminary was devoted to a yana—hinayana, mahayana, and vajrayana—and was itself divided into equal periods of intensive practice and study of the principles of buddhadharma. It was thus possible to understand and experience the continuity and coherence of the path.

In addition to Chögyam Trungpa's talks, which were the central point of the program, senior students also taught courses. Participants in Seminary generally took three courses in addition to the main course taught by Chögyam Trungpa. Usually five or six courses were offered; one or two might be required, while the third was usually an elective. The subjects varied considerably over the years and included the history of the sciences, dharma poetics, Yogachara and Madhyamaka, the *Tibetan Book of the Dead*, theism and nontheism, abhidharma, lineage and devotion, and Shambhala culture. Furthermore, when transcriptions of Chögyam Trungpa's teachings at previous Seminaries were published, it was also necessary to organize study groups in order to review what had been taught during the previous years.

Many practices were introduced at Seminary, including oryoki, a med-

---

26. Chögyam Trungpa, *1974 Seminary Transcripts: Vajrayana* (Boulder: Vajradhatu Publications), p. 2.

itative mealtime discipline borrowed from the Zen tradition; kyudo, or Japanese archery; and the service mandala of the Dorje Kasung. We shall return in detail to each of these elements that made up Chögyam Trungpa's world; what is important here is to understand that Seminary was both a general presentation of the path and the means for students to experience the world that Chögyam Trungpa had created.

John Stanley, a student of Dudjom Rinpoche and Dilgo Khyentse Rinpoche, attended the 1983 Seminary and wrote an article about his experiences there. It provides us with an interesting account by a Buddhist with a real understanding of the dharma but who was completely outside Chögyam Trungpa's community. Like its predecessors, this Seminary brought together over three hundred people and took place in a large hotel that had been reserved for the occasion. John Stanley wrote: "To anyone familiar with the presentation of Tibetan Buddhism in the West, the surprising thing about the Vajradhatu Seminary is the insistence on training. Nobody else makes this emphasis. Generally, it is left up to the individual practitioner. Here you cannot avoid the training."

John Stanley also emphasized the precision with which the various activities were conducted. Three hundred people practiced and studied with perfect discipline. While trying to understand the reason for this achievement, which he found extremely impressive because he had never seen anything like it before, he noted that it was the overall environment that transmitted the teachings: "Even if everything else is missed, the aesthetics leave an indelible impression."

He identified the two complementary approaches that Chögyam Trungpa used when teaching. On the one hand, Rinpoche presented, with rare depth, the classic perspective tinged with a "sense of transmission simultaneous with his word." "Rinpoche's other mode of teaching was an amazing display of magnetizing, enriching, and subjugating. It was dramatic, riveting and wholly unpredictable. His words, actions, expressions, gestures and presence became nakedly atmospheric and luminous. . . . One could never explain what was communicated. If the first mode was inconceivable, this one was completely inconceivable."[27]

---

27. John Stanley, "Riding the Tiger," *Vajradhatu Sun*, June/July 1983, p. 5.

Chapter Six

TEACHING THE
THREE YANAS

It seems to be very important for us to be soaked thoroughly in all three yanas and to become thoroughly Buddhist, rather than just purely becoming vajrayana practitioners alone. We are basically talking about how to become a real Buddhist: how to become a real hinayanist in the fullest sense of being tamed properly and thoroughly; and how to become a real mahayanist so that we are able to share our gratitude and devotion to other people, such as the guru and the lineage and the teachers from whom we receive our teaching.[1]

—CHÖGYAM TRUNGPA

1. The Progressive Approach of the Three Yanas

Although Chögyam Trungpa's work appeared to be unified, driven by a profound coherence, one should not assume that it followed a predetermined plan. On the contrary, Chögyam Trungpa constantly changed his approach to the teachings according to his students' reactions and their understanding. It was by remaining in constant touch with his environment that he could decide what he was going to teach and how he would present the buddhadharma.

For example, at Samye Ling in Scotland, he presented some advanced

---

1. Chögyam Trungpa, *1981 Seminary Transcripts: Vajrayana* (Boulder: Vajradhatu Publications), p. 32.

teachings that dwelled on the absolute view.[2] In North America, he soon started giving seminars on the *Tibetan Book of the Dead*, during which he described the six realms of existence.[3] His style at the time was marked by the dzogchen approach. Then, with the 1973 Seminary, he adopted a more gradual and structured approach. Using the practice of sitting meditation as the foundation, he set about presenting the path step by step, as we have seen.

With this gradual approach in mind, he adopted the classic structure of the three yanas. The term *yana*, often translated as "vehicle" in English, suggests a palanquin, "something that lifts you up and carries you." A yana is anything that takes you to a destination, such as an automobile, a train, or a plane.[4] In Buddhist terminology, a yana is the vehicle but also the road itself that allows the practitioner to follow the path to enlightenment.

Some Tibetan teachers believe that the choice of "vehicle" depends on each person's spiritual maturity. Beings of lower intelligence should use the hinayana, they say, while those with excellent potential should follow the vajrayana.

Such an approach did not suit Chögyam Trungpa; he was even opposed to it. Citing numerous traditional texts, he stressed the absolute necessity for everyone to begin the spiritual path with the hinayana, without which the rest of the path is a mere egocentric construct.[5] He never spoke of the hinayana in a derogatory way.

---

2. He taught Vajrakilaya, the bardo retreat in solitude and darkness, and dzogchen, teachings of the Nyingma lineage.

3. Such teaching is associated with the specific preliminaries of dzogchen, *khorde rushen* (roughly, "separating samsara from nirvana"), in which the practitioner experiences the six realms, or states of being. By intensifying these confused states, the practitioner perceives enlightened nature, which has become obscured by the different perceptual styles of the realms. Two of the three seminars that Chögyam Trungpa gave in 1971 are available in *Transcending Madness*.

4. The Tibetan word for *yana* is *thekpa*. *Thek* means "to lift" or "to carry," and *pa* turns it into a noun, so *thekpa* means "that which lifts you up." Chögyam Trungpa sometimes related the meaning of *yana* to the British use of the word *lift* for what in America is called an elevator.

5. Rinpoche was often extremely critical of the way the buddhadharma was frequently presented, with a dangerous naiveté and lacking the basis that would allow Western students to

Placing such an emphasis on hinayana is in fact quite unusual in Tibetan Buddhism. Tibetan teachers coming to the West, especially in these early times, often presented practices and visualizations, including recitations of mantras or ritual formulas, to anyone who requested the teachings, even very new students. For Chögyam Trungpa, such an approach was a mistake: "as I see it, Westerners are largely unprepared for the practices of the vajrayana at this point, because they have not yet assimilated the basic understanding of Buddhism. In general they do not even have the beginning notions of suffering as explained by the four noble truths. So at this point, the introduction of Buddhism into the West has to be very much on the hinayana level. People have to relate with the pain of sitting down and meditating and churning out all kinds of material from their minds."[6] He felt absolutely certain that it was necessary to begin "at square one." Without this basis, all spiritual work turns into materialism. In the Buddhist tradition, no spiritual journey is possible unless it begins with the honesty of hinayana. While Chögyam Trungpa was teaching, many Western students were becoming fascinated with dzogchen. These teachings were supposed to be more "valuable" than others. Such an attitude made him extremely angry. He found it degrading to the tradition and symptomatic of our time, which sees everything in terms of merchandise.

A complete study of the three yanas is rather like studying a map before leaving on a journey: it allows us to know where we are going and to sharpen our curiosity and intelligence once we have set off. No path has more value than any other; they all simply employ different means to the end.

---

connect with the tradition: "Some teachers from the East seem to be excited by foreignness: 'Wow! Finally we are going to teach the aliens, the overseas people.' Because of this fascination and out of naive generosity, they make unnecessary concessions. Although such teachers may be liberal enough to include Occidental students, to take them to heart and be very kind to them, their extraordinary kindness may be destructive." *Journey without Goal*, p. 50. At the same time, he made every effort to train all his students so that they could follow the path of vajrayana.

6. Chögyam Trungpa, in Herbert V. Guenther and Chögyam Trungpa, *The Dawn of Tantra*, p. 79.

To describe this path, he often used the classic image of comparing hinayana to building the foundation of a house, while mahayana is building the house itself. Tantra is then placing a golden roof on it. So it would be ridiculous to start with the roof instead of the foundation. Chögyam Trungpa set about showing how each step naturally leads to the next: each succeeding phase goes further, but retains the preceding one within it. Thus, the path does not mean advancing from one grade to another, as at school, nor is it a matter of arbitrarily deciding to follow mahayana and then vajrayana in the same way that one might decide to take a car to visit Italy, then a plane to see the jungles of Kenya. The path reveals itself according to the practitioner's experience, and the way Chögyam Trungpa demonstrated this internal logic is magnificent.

According to Rinpoche, although it is important to study one yana after another, it is not necessarily imperative to finish one yana before beginning the next one. A familiarity with the experiences of a given yana is certainly required before progressing further, but students are not expected to reach a full realization of it before going on. In the end, the three yanas exist simultaneously in everyone's practice. It is therefore not a matter of going beyond hinayana. To make this point in a striking way, Chögyam Trungpa awakened his students in the middle of the night during the last Seminary that he taught, in 1986, and when they had all gathered together, he told them: "The hinayana teaching should not be regarded as something that you can just carry out and then get rid of, or discard. The hinayana teaching is the life force that carries out our own practice and discipline, which goes on continuously. From that point of view, the hinayana should be regarded as life's strength. Okay. That's that. *Never forget hinayana.*"[7]

In this chapter, I make no claim to explain the entirety of each of the three yanas as Chögyam Trungpa presented them. I simply want to provide a few indications, while emphasizing certain crucial points; the corpus is so rich and vast that other points could easily have been chosen. In

---

7. Chögyam Trungpa, *1986 Seminary Transcripts: Hinayana-Mahayana* (Boulder: Vajradhatu Publications), p. 13.

any case, it would be absurd to limit Rinpoche's teaching of a yana to the talks he gave concerning it; whatever subject he was teaching, he always kept the profound coherence of the way in mind.

2. Hinayana: The Narrow Path

Literally, the word *hinayana* means "small or lesser vehicle," but it would be more accurate to translate it as the "narrow way": "The hinayana is small or narrow in the sense that the strict discipline of meditation narrows down, or tames, the speed and confusion of mind, allowing the mind to rest in its own place."[8] We thus reduce our existence to the essence by working in an extremely simple, solitary manner with our own minds.

The point of hinayana is to live as who we really are instead of as who we would like to be: "This possibility is connected with seeing our confusion, or misery and pain, but not making these discoveries into an answer. Instead we explore further and further and further without looking for an answer."[9] In other words, hinayana means experiencing suffering and understanding how we create it ourselves through our attachment to the physical body and our identity.

In addition to physical suffering due to birth, aging, and death, there is also psychological suffering, which derives from the unceasing cycle of joy and pain. At a more subtle level, this continuous alternation of hope and fear creates a deep layer of anxiety. We are then caught up in an endless struggle to make things turn out the way we want them to.

In this respect, hinayana can also be called the "hard way,"[10] according to another beautiful definition given by Chögyam Trungpa. Surely, through it we must face suffering, our powerlessness to escape hardship,

8. *Journey without Goal*, p. 2.

9. *Crazy Wisdom*, p. 9.

10. See *The Path Is the Goal*, p. 26: "It's very hard, very difficult. That's why we call the beginning level hinayana, the narrow path, which is very severe, extremely severe. It's not a matter of being happy and having fun, particularly. It's very difficult."

our powerlessness to find someone to save us or draw us toward enlightenment by magic. Chögyam Trungpa often stressed that the Buddhist
path is "nontheistic," and this means that no one can walk the path in our
place. It is up to us to dismantle the fundamental structure of our ego and
learn not to be trapped by our own manipulations, which pretend to help
us find comfort but in reality only create more suffering for ourselves and
others.[11]

Such a realization depends on a commitment to adhere to a discipline
(Skt. *shila*; Tib. *tsultrim*) founded by Buddha. He established the rules
that monks and nuns must follow to the letter. These rules make up the
vinaya, which literally means "taming." And indeed, "through practicing
the proper conduct of tsultrim, our body, speech, and mind are thoroughly tamed and we are able to quell, or cool off, the heat of neurosis."[12]

3. Mahayana: The Open Way

In contrast with the narrow way of the hinayana, the mahayana, or "great
vehicle," is like "a wide open highway."[13] The opening is far broader. Prac-

---

11. I have decided to bring out a few important points concerning each yana in the hope of
thus revealing their underlying logic. The hinayana corresponds to the four noble truths
(suffering, the origin of suffering, the cessation of suffering, and the path leading to cessation), as well as the three marks of existence (impermanence, suffering, and the fact that all
experience is marked by egolessness). Beyond this, the hinayana affirms the existence of nirvana, or peace. To accomplish the hinayana path, the practitioner vows to take refuge in the
three jewels, which are the Buddha (an example of someone who has taken the path), the
dharma (teaching), and the sangha (the community of practitioners). The aim is individual
liberation (*soso tharpa*). A general presentation of the hinayana also includes an explanation
of karma (to which Chögyam Trungpa devoted an entire seminar at Karmê Chöling in
1972). The doctrine of the hinayana is presented in three parts of the Buddhist canon (*tri-
pitaka*): the sutras, or word of the Buddha; the vinaya, or monastic rules; and the abhidharma, or description of the nature of reality and, more precisely, of its submergence
under the ego and its projections. (See the exceptional presentation made by Chögyam
Trungpa in *Glimpses of Abhidharma*.)

12. *Journey without Goal*, p. 2.

13. Ibid. See also chap. 7, "The Open Way," in *Cutting Through Spiritual Materialism*,
pp. 91–109; the chapter with the same title in *The Myth of Freedom*; and *Training the Mind*

titioners no longer aim to achieve enlightenment for themselves; they devote themselves to the liberation of others. In this way, mahayana goes beyond the simple hinayana ideal of personal liberation and aims at freeing everybody.

The main discipline in mahayana is to put others before ourselves, to discover that other people matter more than we do. But such an attitude "is not based on self-denial or martyrdom, but rather springs from the development of genuine warmth and compassion":[14] it is not a question of obeying moral principles.

Compassion is not a matter of feeling sorry for others, or even of sharing their suffering; it is "clarity which contains fundamental warmth."[15] It is a feeling of intelligent gentleness that radiates naturally toward all beings. Just as the sun naturally shines, without making any effort and with no favoritism, in the same way, once we have removed the veils and barriers that block its expression—which is the very path of mahayana—the compassion in our hearts flows out for the good of one and all.

To communicate this, Chögyam Trungpa borrowed the contrasting notion of "idiot compassion" from G. I. Gurdjieff,[16] which means "a slimy way of trying to fulfill your desire secretly"[17]—to make someone feel good, but in a way that adds to their illusions and weakens them.

True compassion in fact consists in seeing the situation *as it really is*, and acting accordingly.[18] It may be necessary to hurt someone in order to help them, just as you might express anger in order to stop a child

---

and Cultivating Loving-Kindness (1993), p. 4, where Chögyam Trungpa states that the mahayana is "the highway that everybody goes on, a wide way, extraordinarily wide and extraordinarily open."

14. *Journey without Goal*, p. 3.

15. *Cutting Through Spiritual Materialism*, p. 97.

16. G. I. Gurdjieff was a Greek-Armenian teacher who introduced his own spiritual path, which he taught in Europe and the United States in the first half of the twentieth century. Chögyam Trungpa admired Gurdjieff and his insights into spirituality.

17. *Illusion's Game*, p. 29.

18. He explained this as follows: "Perhaps this will put off a lot of people, but I am afraid love is not really the experience of beauty and romantic joy alone. Love is associated with ugliness and pain and aggression, as well as with the beauty of the world; it is not the re-creation

from putting its fingers in an electric socket, or administer an injection as a cure.

The power in such a vision resides in the fact that the effort to put others before ourselves is the complete opposite of our usual way of life, a radical shift from our egocentric attachment to ourselves. Developing compassion means opening our hearts by dissolving the obstacles that diminish our vision—fear, selfish preoccupations, projections, and expectations, which are simply ways of maintaining our delusions and constantly reassuring ourselves that we exist. As Chögyam Trungpa explained: "The whole point we are trying to get to is—when are we going to open, *really*? The action of our mind is so overlapping, an ingrown toenail, introverted: If I do this, then that is going to happen; if I do that, then this is going to happen."[19]

Pure compassion does not exist intrinsically in us; we have to learn to make it grow: "The obstacle to becoming a mahayanist is not having enough sympathy for others and for oneself—that is a basic point. And that problem can be dealt with by practical training, which is known as lojong practice, or 'training the mind.'"[20] One of the lojong practices that Chögyam Trungpa particularly stressed is tonglen, "sending and taking,"[21] which he introduced during the 1979 Seminary.

The practice of tonglen includes three steps. To begin, you rest your

---

of heaven. Love or compassion, the open path, is associated with 'what is.' In order to develop love—universal love, cosmic love, whatever you would like to call it—one must accept the whole situation of life as it is, both the light and the dark, the good and the bad." *Cutting Through Spiritual Materialism* (2002), p. 101.

19. Ibid., p. 93.

20. *Training the Mind and Cultivating Loving-Kindness* (1993), p. 1. While the discipline of the hinayana is basically a question of *taming* the mind, in the mahayana it is more a matter of *training* the mind.

21. This practice is based on the seventh slogan of Atisha (982–1055): "Sending and taking should be practiced alternately. These two should ride the breath." These guidelines come from Atisha's root text, *The Seven Points of Mind Training*. Atisha abandoned the palace life he had known as a youth, then studied and practiced for many years in India. He then went to Tibet, where he taught for thirteen years, until his death, presenting teachings that were to become foundation texts for various Buddhist schools.

mind briefly in a state of openness. This is like a flash of deep calm and great clarity. It corresponds to the sudden experience of emptiness and is none other than "absolute compassion."[22] This step is all the more important because true compassion can only arise from the realization that the ego is nonexistent and the recognition of emptiness, shunyata. Understanding the nature of reality leads to compassion: "When you begin realizing nonexistence, then you can afford to be more compassionate, more giving. A problem is that usually we would like to hold on to our territory and fixate on that particular ground. Once we begin to fixate on that ground, we have no way to give. Understanding shunyata means that we begin to realize that there is no ground to get, that we are ultimately free, nonaggressive, open."[23]

Second, you work on "texture." As explained by Judith L. Lief:

> You breathe in a feeling of heat, darkness, and heaviness, a sense of claustrophobia, and you breathe out a feeling of coolness, brightness, and lightness—a sense of freshness. You feel these qualities going in and out, through all your pores. Having established the general feeling or tone of tonglen, you begin to work with mental contents. Whatever arises in your experience, you simply breathe in what is not desirable and breathe out what is desirable. Starting with your immediate experience, you expand that to include people around you and other sentient beings who are suffering in the same way as you. For instance, if you are feeling inadequate, you begin by breathing that in and breathing out your personal sense of competence and adequacy. Then you extend the practice, broadening it beyond your personal concerns to connect with the poignancy of those feelings in your immediate surroundings and throughout the world. The essential quality of this practice is one of opening your heart—wholeheartedly taking in and

---

22. *Training the Mind and Cultivating Loving-Kindness* (2003), p. 13.

23. Ibid., pp. 13–14.

wholeheartedly letting go. In tonglen nothing is rejected: whatever arises is further fuel for the practice.[24]

In Tibet, practitioners are shown, by various logical arguments, the need to create more compassion within them and to stop thinking they are the center of the world. Because of the principle of karma, which states that we have all had countless lives, emphasis is placed on the fact that all beings have at some time been our own mothers, and so we should love them.[25] Such an image is an integral part of all teachings of the mahayana. Much is also made of the great teachers of the past, who went through intense suffering and were ready to cut off a slice of their thigh, or even their head, for the good of others. We must, in turn, follow their example.

Because of the particular destiny of the West, Chögyam Trungpa emphasized a different aspect of the mahayana.[26] Instead of using logical argument, he stressed compassion as an *experience* that arises when the struggle to maintain the fiction of ego ceases. It is an acceptance and a feeling of trust that spreads and radiates naturally toward others: "In the mahayana tradition we experience a sense of gentleness toward ourselves, and a sense of friendliness to others begins to arise."[27] When he taught, he made this experience felt, and it thus became more tangible and less of an intellectual ideal. There was no difference between what he said and what he was.

---

24. Judith L. Lief, Editor's Preface, in *Training the Mind and Cultivating Loving-Kindness* (2003), p. xiv. On many occasions, Judy Lief was asked by Chögyam Trungpa himself to transmit this practice.

As I have explained in connection with the practice of shamatha-vipashyana, such a description cannot be used as an introduction to real practice, which must be transmitted orally.

25. See, for example, the wonderful book by Dilgo Khyentse, *Enlightened Courage* (Ithaca, NY: Snow Lion Publications, 1993), p. 32: "It is thanks to your mother that your precious human life exists at all. If she had not been there, who knows whether you would have attained it? Therefore you should be very grateful to her. Thinking in terms not only of this but of countless lives, understand that all beings have been your mothers and have cared for you just as your present mother has done."

26. The difference, of course, lies in the approach he adopted; the teachings remained the same.

27. *Training the Mind and Cultivating Loving-Kindness* (1993), p. 1.

Such an approach, which stresses the natural character of compassion, gets around the main obstacle that seems to trouble Western students. For them, the problem is not a lack of motivation; they can easily recognize the importance of the altruistic perspective of the mahayana. But this vision seems to them to be impossible to apply. They often complain that they feel nothing, that their hearts are closed, and by trying to open up they become even more frustrated.[28]

Chögyam Trungpa insisted on students starting by connecting to their own hearts, in other words, with the situation they found themselves in, their own confusion. Having done so, from then on, they can extend that feeling of gentleness toward others. Traditionally, maitri, which he called "gentleness toward yourself" or "basic friendship," is translated as "love." With his translation of this term, Chögyam Trungpa indicated that it is impossible to develop love or compassion unless you first touch your own heart. An approach in which we help others without taking ourselves into account creates huge resentment—a far cry from genuine compassion. We can only love if we have first developed true tenderness toward ourselves.

By adopting this attitude, we cultivate what Chögyam Trungpa so profoundly called our "sore spot." Negativity, resentment, anger, and irritation are produced because we try to conceal the vulnerability of our hearts: "Whether we are crazy, dull, aggressive, ego-tripping, whatever we might be, there is still that sore spot taking place in us. An open wound, which might be a more vivid analogy, is always there. That open wound is usually very inconvenient and problematic. We don't like it. We would like to be tough. We would like to fight, to come out strong, so we do not have to defend any aspect of ourselves."[29] Chögyam Trungpa thus emphasized a positive act: if we stop protecting ourselves, it is because we are tender

---

28. Pema Chödrön, one of Chögyam Trungpa's students who teaches tonglen practice, explained this problem: "An interesting thing happens whenever I give tonglen instruction: people start going to sleep. It's hard to hear this stuff. I've never given tonglen instruction where I don't notice that at least three people are completely gone, and the others are probably all feeling extremely drowsy." *The Wisdom of No Escape and the Path of Loving-Kindness* (Boston: Shambhala Publications, 1991), p. 63.

29. *Training the Mind and Cultivating Loving-Kindness* (1993), pp. 14–15.

and deeply affected. The practice of mahayana consists of trusting that fragility, which, far from being an obstacle, is the sign of our humanity.[30]

4. Vajrayana: The Abrupt Way

While the hinayana is the way to understand your mind, and the mahayana the way to understand your emotions, the vajrayana, which means "the indestructible vehicle," allows extremely direct contact with phenomena and a recognition that the world is sacred. At this level, the practitioner connects with situations as they are, without having any other point of reference than reality itself.

While the vajrayana is distinct from the mahayana, it is necessary to understand that the underlying perspective remains the need to devote oneself to the good of all other beings. As Chögyam Trungpa said, "Trying to practice the vajrayana without compassion is like swimming in molten lead—it is deadly."[31] Understanding in vajrayana is quite simply even more direct and radical than in mahayana. The bodhisattva is motivated by a project, that of doing good and helping others. The vajrayana, however, depends on the idea that compassion should be even more immediate. Vajrayana depends on immediate, radical trust in the open, indestructible nature of our own experience. It breaks with the very idea of a path. It is thus necessary to take an apparently irrational step. You must adopt the point of view of endless space instead of the cramped position of the ego. For this reason, devotion for the teacher is fundamental. With-

---

30. In particular, the mahayana teachings contain a description of the two kinds of bodhichitta (awakened heart): relative bodhichitta and absolute bodhichitta, sometimes presented as compassion and emptiness, understanding the principle of shunyata (emptiness) and its application through the paramitas, or six transcendental activities—generosity, discipline, patience, effort, meditation, and transcendent knowledge. The ideal for the practitioner is no longer the arhat but the bodhisattva (hero for enlightenment), who is the ideal for this yana because he or she has vowed not to attain enlightenment until all beings are freed from suffering. The mahayana describes different paths the practitioner follows: the path of accumulation, the path of unification, the path of seeing, the path of meditation, and the path of nonmeditation (called "no more learning").

31. *Journey without Goal* (2000), p. 5.

out it, no one would take such a risk. Devotion teaches us to trust our burning desire for openness and to give ourselves up to it.

Even in his early days in the United States, Chögyam Trungpa presented the vajrayana. He thus showed that enlightenment and confusion are two sides of the same coin: "It is better to develop some kind of respect, realizing that your neurosis also is a message, rather than garbage that you should just throw away. That's the whole starting point—the idea of samsara and nirvana being one. Samsara is not regarded as a nuisance alone, but it has its own potent message that is worthy of respect."[32]

Even when he presented basic teachings, linked to hinayana, he did so within the nondualistic perspective of vajrayana. For example, he explained the practice of meditation as "a way of continuing one's confusion, chaos, aggression, and passion—but working with it, seeing it from the enlightened point of view."[33]

During Seminary he presented the teachings of vajrayana in an organized, precise way, but each year from a different perspective. Sharing his experience of vajrayana made him especially happy. He explained that it allowed him an even closer relationship with his students: "Without vajrayana we don't have a head. Hinayana is the feet. Mahayana is purely heart. But Buddhism without a head is dead. Therefore I feel very happy about the possibility of sharing my understanding with you. It is like discovering a new friend. It is a very moving situation for me personally."[34]

5. Restoring the Sense of Initiation

How did Chögyam Trungpa present the path of vajrayana and its associated practices?

Before we address this question, it is perhaps useful to quote one of Chögyam Trungpa's typical expressions—"Once again, I would like us to

---

32. *Crazy Wisdom*, p. 125. (This teaching was given in December 1972.)

33. *The Path Is the Goal*, p. 14.

34. *The Lion's Roar*, p. 55.

comb our hair to backtrack and take another look at what we studied earlier on"—because it is important to present the path in terms of its own evolution.

In terms of hinayana discipline, students directly encounter their suffering, frustrations, and neuroses. Thanks to mahayana, they practice putting others before themselves. A genuine encounter with the nature of reality, which is sometimes called the nature of the mind, then becomes possible. This marvelous event takes place through direct contact with the with teacher's mind. His task is to "electrify the student's vessel, so that it becomes clean and clear, free of all kinds of materialistic germs, and then to pour the essence into it,"[35] which is the very idea of transmission. Transmission is the core of the esoteric path. As René Guénon explained: "Religion views being only as an individual human state and has absolutely no aim to remove it from this situation, but instead aims to guarantee the most favorable conditions in its present state; but the main aim of initiation is to surpass the possibilities of this state and to make it actually possible to rise to superior states, and even, finally, to lead the being to a state beyond all conditioned states of being."[36]

The formal experience of transmission offers a chance for direct contact with the spiritual influence of the lineage and to encounter the spirit of enlightenment that the teacher embodies.

Chögyam Trungpa decided to present elements of vajrayana as soon as practitioners set out on the path. At the end of the three-month Seminary, which presented the three yanas, students could receive vajrayana transmission if they wished.

It is at this moment that students can start practicing the preliminaries (known as ngöndro, which must be practiced before one receives the full initiation, or abhisheka). We will not go into the details of these practices (despite the fact that the way Chögyam Trungpa presented them was

---

35. *Journey without Goal* (2000), p. 54.

36. René Guénon, *Aperçus sur l'initiation* (Perspectives on Initiation) (Paris: Éditions Traditionnelles, 1992), p. 27. This makes it clear that it is impossible to practice outside a lineage. The most basic dimension of Buddhist transmission would then be lost, no matter how great the student's motivation.

stunningly novel), as Chögyam Trungpa did not want them to be presented publicly. He thought that the esoteric path should remain sacred and reserved for those students he knew personally.[37]

In the context of this chapter, it would be interesting to quote from an unpublished letter written by Chögyam Trungpa to his tantrikas (vajrayana practitioners) on August 29, 1975, which gives an overview of the work he wanted to carry out: "I think the power of our particular approach to tantra speaks for itself. Many Tibetan teachers give American students mantras, sadhanas, seemingly tantric things. These are usually received, or presented, from a purely external viewpoint, such as one would present in Tibet to the local peasantry or the average monk. However, as for myself, I regard each of you as possible siddhas, potentially capable of identifying with the highest teachings. I am proud that in the early days we introduced only shamatha-vipashyana, emphasizing basic acquaintance with your mind. By leveling your trips and not cheating you of the raw experience of yourselves, we have prepared tremendous ground to introduce vajrayana teaching completely, undiluted."[38]

Chögyam Trungpa organized regular seminars reserved for his vajrayana students, where they were encouraged to talk about their own experiences. These early groups were popularly known as tantra groups.

Full initiation is given during an abhisheka, which is a high point in a Buddhist's life. An abhisheka is an empowerment, or ceremonial transmission of power, during which the teacher introduces the disciple to

---

37. In *The Torch of Certainty* by Jamgön Kongtrül, translated by Judith Hanson (Boston: Shambhala Publications, 1986), Chögyam Trungpa, Kalu Rinpoche, and Deshung Rinpoche answer a number of questions about the preliminaries. This allows us to appreciate the particular nature of his vision. This interview is one of the main public sources that Chögyam Trungpa provided concerning these practices. Thus, to the question "In what ways, if any, will the manner of practicing the Four Foundations here in the West differ from that followed in Tibet?" Chögyam Trungpa answered: "Because of the cultural differences, the practice of the Four Foundations will be somewhat different for Western students. Since they are not completely familiar with the cultural background of Buddhism, when they try to practice the Foundations they will encounter some cultural gaps which they will have to overcome. We must try not to impose the Tibetan tradition on them but to present them with the basic 'mind's work' of the teachings" (pp. 12–13).

38. Used by permission of Diana J. Mukpo.

the world of enlightenment in a complete way that brings together all aspects of the student's personality.

While Chögyam Trungpa was studying with Jamgön Kongtrül of Sechen, his guru transmitted to him the *Rinchen Terdzö* (Precious Treasury of Terma). The sixty-three volumes of this "treasury" include a large number of teachings and initiations that Jamgön Kongtrül the Great had gathered together.

Jamgön Kongtrül of Sechen began his preparations at four in the morning, and his students had to stay in the room from five in the morning until eight in the evening. This ceremony lasted almost six months. At the end, Jamgön Kongtrül gave Chögyam Trungpa special permission to transmit in turn the teachings he had received. He enthroned him and presented him with symbolic objects: his own robes, his ritual bell, and his dorje, the emblematic scepter of indestructible reality, as well as some of his books.

A few months later, while traveling to Drölma Lhalhang, Chögyam Trungpa was asked to give the initiation of *Rinchen Terdzö*. He accepted, after some hesitation because of his young age. The event was quite extraordinary. Even for a tülku, it was extremely unusual to give such a large number of transmissions at the age of only fourteen.

The last time he gave this teaching was in 1958, at the request of Yak Tülku. Because of the dangerous situation of the Chinese presence, the *Rinchen Terdzö* was given in just three months, before three hundred monks who had come from neighboring monasteries, and the ceremony ended very late at night.

Thus Chögyam Trungpa had the ability to give hundreds of different abhishekas—which are part of the transmission of *Rinchen Terdzö*—but he gave only two during the seventeen years he spent in the United States. Beginning in 1977, every year he gave the Vajrayogini abhisheka, and in 1986, a few months before his death, he gave the Chakrasamvara abhisheka.[39] This was clearly an important decision.

---

39. The way that sadhanas are practiced in the sangha of Chögyam Trungpa is in some ways unique. The manual for Vajrayogini practice contains several hundred pages of precise explanations, including careful documentation of all the ritual aspects, drafted by the Nālandā

In this sense, Chögyam Trungpa's attitude was revolutionary in contrast to the custom of the time. In Tibet, this consisted in giving a large number of different abhishekas. Even today, when a teacher comes to stay at a dharma center during a trip to the West, he often gives several initiations.

Chögyam Trungpa disagreed with this approach. To his mind, abhishekas were given at worst like sweets or games and at best as a way to enter into the grace of the lineage, whereas they should be the final point in a cultivation of the way of the three yanas: "Receiving hundreds and hundreds of abhishekas and constantly collecting blessing after blessing as some kind of self-confirmation has at times become a fad, a popular thing to do. This was true in Tibet in the nineteenth century as well as more recently in the West. That attitude, which reflects the recent corruption in the presentation of vajrayana, has created an enormous misunderstanding."[40] In such a situation, students can no longer experience the full disturbing force of an abhisheka, because they have not prepared themselves properly.[41] Traditionally, to receive such an initiation, the student should

---

Translation Committee after dozens of hours. As for Chakrasamvara (which is given after Vajrayogini), Chögyam Trungpa explained early on that this was the practice his students had to devote themselves to. But, in 1981, when some of them asked him to transmit it to them, he replied, as the Dorje Loppön remembers, "This business is on my desk, not yours." In October 1985, he took part in the second fire puja, of the four karmas, devoted to Vajrayogini, which is a preliminary step before receiving the abhisheka of Chakrasamvara. As he had planned for some years, he brought Tenga Rinpoche, the main expert on vajrayana ritual for the Kagyü lineage, to the West to present it in detail in 1985. The Translation Committee worked intensely to revise its translation of the sadhana and prepare the manual to explain the practice. It was only then that Chögyam Trungpa, despite his health problems, gave it to his students. Thus we find once again the same idea that we have already pinpointed: the presentation of few practices in the greatest possible detail in order to transmit the very heart of the tradition, waiting until the students are ready, a presentation of a coherent approach to the path so that students can develop a precise understanding of it, an explanation of the details of the practice, then complete trust in the intelligence of his students.

40. *Journey without Goal* (2000), p. 89.

41. He explained this point as follows: "Traditionally, in medieval India and Tibet, the date for an abhisheka was set six months in advance. In that way students would have six months to prepare. Later the tantric tradition became extremely available, and some of the teachers in Tibet dropped that six-month rule—which seems to have been a big mistake." *Journey*

have practiced for many years and carried out all the preliminaries; unlike many other teachers, Chögyam Trungpa never allowed anyone to escape from this rule and to carry out only a part.[42]

There is even a Tibetan proverb that criticizes this situation: "The practitioners of Indian vajrayana practice one yidam and realize thousands, while Tibetans practice thousands and don't even realize one." Chögyam Trungpa's idea was to reinstate the Indian idea, as he did in many other areas.

In order to create the right conditions and give his ceremonies real power, Chögyam Trungpa stirred up a situation in which no one knew what was going to happen next. This was the rationale behind the very secret of vajrayana, which he constantly stressed. The secret is what allows everyone to tread this intimate path. The less the practitioners know what they are in for, the more direct and spontaneous a relationship they will have with the practice or teaching before them, and the greater their chances will be to enter into the magic of the situation.

6. The Dzogchen Teacher: Presenting Everything from the Ultimate Point of View

Dzogchen (Tib.; Skt. *maha ati*) is the ultimate point of the path, or state of primordial perfection. Some of Chögyam Trungpa's students felt that he did not present the dzogchen teachings to them in any depth, or that he really didn't present dzogchen except perhaps during the period when he was in Great Britain before coming to America. But nothing could be more absurdly far from the truth, or more revealing of a deep misunderstanding of what real dzogchen is and the true nature of Chögyam

---

without Goal (2000), pp. 88–89. It is clear that Chögyam Trungpa, who had his students wait, reinstated the ancient approach in order to restore the transmission's basic, esoteric power, which had become obscured.

42. As René Guénon often remarked, there is a huge difference between virtual and real initiation. For initiation to be genuine, disciples must be truly ready and able to devote themselves to the work at hand.

Trungpa's work. It would be more accurate to say that he taught nothing but dzogchen, as he himself said, given that all the teachings he presented "talk of enormous space . . . not a space as opposed to a boundary, but a sense of total openness,"[43] which is appropriate to this path. This is one of the most extraordinary aspects of his teaching—though he would no doubt have preferred it be called the most genuinely ordinary, as that is the very nature of the dzogchen perspective.[44]

The maha ati, as he explained, is like standing on the top of a mountain and looking out, attracted by the panoramic view. Using this perspective, Chögyam Trungpa revealed the entirety of the path. In hinayana, he presented the practice of shamatha-vipashyana as a way of learning how to identify ourselves with space. By following our breath, after fully breathing out, we dissolve; a fleeting moment of panic follows, then we rebuild our world of beliefs. Chögyam Trungpa encouraged his students to dissolve in this tiny opening—a breach in the apparent continuity of our existence. Practitioners who thus give up their beliefs also stop doing harm to others.

In mahayana, Chögyam Trungpa taught the practice of tonglen as well as the precepts of Atisha.[45] Tonglen begins with a sudden flash of unconditional compassion, then proceeds in a continuous alternation between

---

43. *Journey without Goal* (2000), p. 134. As he says further on: "Likewise, ati is regarded as 'imperial' because, from the perspective of ati yoga, hinayana discipline is seen as spaciousness; mahayana discipline is seen as spaciousness; and the tantric yanas, as well, are seen as spaciousness. If you review what we have been discussing throughout this book, you will see that we have been taking this point of view. We have discussed everything from the perspective of ati."

44. Technically, it is said that mahamudra is an approach to the sambhogakaya path in order to realize dharmakaya as fruition. It is an upward path, leading from confusion to realization. But ati manifests the actual realization of dharmakaya, and this is how it extends through the various yanas, as that many ways of connecting with the world. Such is the approach that Chögyam Trungpa adopted in most of his teachings.

45. Atisha was born around 982 CE into a noble family in Vikramapura, eastern Bengal. He chose the religious life at a young age. After living as a yogi for twelve years, he decided to become a monk and took on important responsibilities in Nalanda, Otantapuri, and above all Vikramashila—India's three largest Buddhist monastic universities. In 1042 Atisha accepted an invitiation to go to Tibet, where he stayed until his death in 1054. It was there that

in-breaths and out-breaths that dissolve all our reference points. Atisha's precepts emerged from his mind as a fish from water and so suddenly open the heart.

Vajrayana provides us with the means to link ourselves with the magic of the unconditional opening of the limitless space of dzogchen. It is a way of experiencing the space that is present in the vividness of all experience. Peace cannot be experienced without chaos as well—such a peace would remain a dualistic construct.

Chögyam Trungpa constantly stressed the way all practices ultimately aim to dissolve every limit and so allow us to see the measureless space at the heart of all liberated experiences.

We are now stating that Chögyam Trungpa was unusual in that he taught the ultimate perspective of dzogchen, and yet we have previously dwelled on how often he stressed the importance of beginning the path with hinayana. Isn't there a contradiction here?

Not at all. Chögyam Trungpa of course made his students begin at the beginning, but the meditation practice that he presented, which corresponds to the discipline of the hard way and honesty which belong to hinayana, is thoroughly soaked in a total trust in our indestructible vajra nature.

On this subject, the Loppön remembers what happened during a trip Chögyam Trungpa made to Dao Shonu in Ireland, at the time a European retreat center. One day, twenty-five teachers of Transcendental Meditation came to see Chögyam Trungpa, who decided to give them a talk. He told them that it was necessary to start at the beginning, from square one—and so he presented them with the perspective of hinayana.

But, the Loppön recalls: "If that was the logical content of his presentation, the atmosphere he created was quite different and gave the impression of being in front of a huge cliff-face. Our minds were plunged

---

he wrote *A Lamp for the Path to Enlightenment* (*Bodhipathapradipam*). This brief work of sixty-six lines was highly influential and was studied and commented on by all the Tibetan schools. In it, Atisha glorified the ideal of the bodhisattva and the need for awareness of basic emptiness.

into an apparently limitless space. His teaching had the quality of a transmission of dzogchen, capturing your mind, giving it a point of reference before releasing it into immensity. What he said was different from what he did."

Everything he did or taught reflected what the great Saraha said: "Be unmutilated in the essential nature of immaculate Awareness!"[46]

Dzogchen is the atmosphere from which everything is unfolded: "Buddhism has a number of schools, primarily divided into the hinayana, mahayana, and vajrayana traditions, and squabbling goes on among all of them. They all speak the language of totality, and every one of them claims to have the answer. The hinayanists may say that they have the answer because they know reality. The mahayanists may say that the bodhisattva is the best person that we could ever find in the world. Tantric practitioners may say that the most fantastic person is the powerful and crazy yogi who is unconquerable and who has achieved siddhis and magical powers of all kinds. Let them believe what they want. It's okay. But what do these things mean to us personally, as students who want to experience the teachings? The maha ati practitioner sees a completely naked world, rather than skin or flesh or even bones. In the lower yanas, we develop lots of idioms and terms, and that makes us feel better because we have a lot of things to talk about, such as compassion or emptiness or wisdom. But in fact, that becomes a way of avoiding the actual naked reality of life. Of course, in maha ati there is warmth, there is openness, there is penetration—all those things are there. But if we begin to divide the dharma, cutting it into little pieces as we would cut a side of beef into sirloin steaks, hamburger, and chuck, with certain cuts of beef more expensive than others, then the dharma is being marketed. In fact, according to Vimalamitra, the reason maha ati is necessary is because throughout the eight lower yanas the dharma has been marketed as a particularly juicy morsel of food. The maha ati level is necessary in order to save the

---

46. *The Royal Song of Saraha: A Study in the History of Buddhist Thought,* translated and annotated by Herbert V. Guenther (Boulder: Shambhala Publications, 1973), p. 66, stanza 18. © 1968 University of Washington Press.

dharma from being parceled and marketed."[47] Here, cutting through spiritual materialism takes on a different appearance and becomes one of the most profound of all teachings.

Gradual way / sudden way

On the one hand, Chögyam Trungpa described the *gradual* ways of the various yanas; on the other, he presented the *sudden* way of immediacy. He showed the importance of keeping both sides together. If practitioners need to learn to identify with a path, so as to "wear out the shoe of samsara,"[48] they also need to learn to connect, on the spot, with reality as it is. The teaching of the sudden way begins with the notion of spiritual materialism, in which, as Chögyam Trungpa explained, the path is not a matter of accumulating things. Practitioners must cut through the slightest temptation to distance themselves from what is. In this way, the fruit of the teachings is total identification with the radical openness of the way. We go nowhere, but awaken to true reality.

In this chapter, we have studied the Buddhist approaches of the three yanas. However, during a Seminary Chögyam Trungpa presented the more extensive principle of *nine* yanas with great precision.[49] In 1973 in San Francisco, when he was presenting a seminar on this subject, a student asked him, "When you were a student in Tibet, were you presented with this whole road map of the nine yanas before you started studying them?"

---

47. *Journey without Goal* (2000), p. 135.

48. *The Myth of Freedom* (2002), p. 50.

49. Chögyam Trungpa often taught the nine-yanas principle, which he explained with unequaled power and clarity. But as my aim is not to present all of Chögyam Trungpa's teachings in this volume, the three-yana approach described here will suffice as a background to Buddhism. It provides an understanding of his work and his genius for presenting the tradition in a lively way. For readers interested in the nine-yanas principle, even though most of his teachings on this subject are currently reserved for close students—in particular as transcripts of the Seminaries—the best book to consult is *The Lion's Roar: An Introduction to Tantra*, which gathers together two general presentations of the nine yanas, given during seminars in San Francisco in May 1973 and in Boulder in December 1973.

Chögyam Trungpa replied, "No, I wasn't. I was highly confused. I wish they had done this. That's why I'm doing it. I wanted to look at it myself and share it with the rest of the people. The training program we had in Tibet was unorganized and chaotic."[50]

Such a choice shows how Chögyam Trungpa was attached to the tradition; he presented the heart of Buddhist teachings, without varying an inch, but without accepting the slightest compromise: "The approach presented here is a classical Buddhist one—not in a formal sense, but in the sense of presenting the heart of the Buddhist approach to spirituality."[51] Chögyam Trungpa's ambition was to restore the tradition's inherent purity, which is increasingly threatened by this age of materialism and despair.

He never concealed how hard this approach is. He never hesitated to describe the difficulties: "We have three problems . . . as far as the future student's sanity is concerned. One is that you get carried away by the culture of Tibetan-ness or the Sanskritness or the Buddhistness of India, of the East. You can get completely carried away. You would like to become Tibetifiers in the future. That's the biggest problem. The second problem is that quite possibly you will feel you have done enough tantric practice, that you don't have to work with hinayana and mahayana anymore. And the third problem is that when meditation students come to you and want to receive instruction, you give purely cryptic answers to them and don't want to work with them from the bottom up completely. Those could possibly be problems, since most of you are teachers already, or if not, you are teachers on the spot, you are would-be teachers in any case. So [avoid those] for the sake of the lineage and also for the sake of my effort I have put on you."[52]

These are three vital aspects for a full understanding of the scope of what he was trying to do. First, Buddhism is not linked to any particular culture but is a genuine path of initiation that lies beyond culture.

---

50. *The Lion's Roar*, p. 210.

51. *Cutting Through Spiritual Materialism* (2002), p. 4.

52. Chögyam Trungpa, *Collected Vajra Assemblies*, vol. 1 (Halifax: Vajradhatu Publications, 1990), pp. 83ff.

It concerns all living beings because it provides the possibility of direct contact with the nonconceptual dimension of all human experience.

Second, it is impossible to follow the path without using the three yanas and beginning with an honest examination of our own confusion. Any lack of humility at this point will distort the meaning of Buddha's teachings and could create an even subtler and more ferocious ego.

Finally, he wanted his students to transmit the dharma through honest communication and not by playing power games. The dharma could only be transmitted and take firm root in the West through genuine and simple encounters between practitioners.

These three pieces of advice remind practitioners of the need to be fully faithful to their own inner experiences and not to succumb to the temptation of conforming to external images—which is perhaps one of the greatest challenges of all for any human being.

Chapter Seven

THE TANTRIC TEACHER

Tantra introduces us to the actuality of the phenomenal world. It is one of the most advanced, sharp, and extraordinary perceptions that has ever developed. It is unusual and eccentric; it is powerful, magical, and outrageous; but it is also extremely simple.[1]

—CHÖGYAM TRUNGPA

THE WAY CHÖGYAM TRUNGPA taught, with constant attention to the three levels of transmission—the body and physical space, the symbolism of speech and the emotions, and direct transmission of the nature of the mind—made him a true tantric teacher, able to create immediate intimate contact with his students. The perspective that animated Chögyam Trungpa was always limitless tantra.

But what is tantra?

The Sanskrit word *tantra* (Tib. *gyu*) has been translated as "continuity." This notion of continuity emphasizes the fact that enlightenment is not something new to be obtained in the future, something that does not really exist yet but will only exist after an effort has been made to

---

1. *Journey without Goal* (2000), p. 19.

construct it: "This kind of continuity cannot be challenged, because this kind of continuity never depends on superficial continuity or discontinuity. It is unconditional continuity."[2] Thus the perspective of tantra does not lie in the discovery of wisdom as opposed to confusion; instead it is found in the understanding of a more primordial continuity, which runs through clarity and confusion alike.

In its fundamental nature, tantra has nothing to do with religion, no matter how you want to define the word. It provides no rules of behavior, aims at no form of transcendence, and does not bring people together. It means being in touch with reality as it is, in an exceptionally direct way.[3] When Chögyam Trungpa taught, he entered into such precise contact with the reality of what he was talking about that it immediately manifested itself through the way he behaved.

1. Tantra as Ground

During his first three years in the United States, Chögyam Trungpa presented the perspective of tantra as the basic ground for establishing and transmitting the entirety of the buddhadharma—even before he had adopted the progressive three-way approach or taught a single practice that was clearly linked to vajrayana.[4]

The basis of the spiritual journey lies beyond the distinction between samsara and nirvana, enlightenment and confusion, sacred and profane, Buddhist and non-Buddhist: "There is no middle path involved. There's a total path. This is an absolutely heavy-handed approach to things as

---

2. *Illusion's Game,* p. 64.

3. "There is a sense of personal involvement. The experience of tantra is extremely personal, rather than purely philosophical, spiritual, or religious." *The Lion's Roar,* p. 176.

4. At the beginning of his stay in the United States, he did present some tantric teachings. Successively, he directed seminars on the six realms, the experience of bardo, the *Tibetan Book of the Dead* in 1971, and then the five buddha families (at Tail of the Tiger, 1972, and Karmê Chöling, 1974).

they are."[5] Chögyam Trungpa thus indicated that our own lives, in all their fullness and confusion, are the only basis we have to rely on.[6]

Appreciating relative truth

In this respect, enlightenment has nothing to do with a special moment of calm or relaxation. On the contrary, it is necessary to have daily experiences of the most ordinary kind in order to challenge an understanding that might otherwise become contrived and lacking in spontaneity.

Tantra is linked to the ability to see poison as medicine, to find enlightened energy in confused energy. In other words, this teaching allows us to confront ourselves without *using* the teachings for any particular purpose. For this reason, Chögyam Trungpa encouraged his students to have strong personal relationships, to have children, to be active members of society, to teach others, to take responsibilities in the meditation centers he set up, to work with chaotic situations and difficult people, and so on. He insisted on the need for such commitment, because it is not possible to escape from this world. Enlightenment is possible only in this world. The strength of our neuroses (that is to say, of our minds) and that of the phenomenal world are the same. Tantra is not a precondition for following the ultimate path but a way of truly integrating it into our lives: "Experience on the tantric level corresponds to the utmost and most complete state of being that can be attained. On the other hand, tantra is not a question of attainment, but rather the actual work of relating to situations properly."[7]

It is important to manifest the teachings in daily life, whether you are a businessperson, a waiter, a professor of nuclear physics, or a computer

---

5. *Orderly Chaos*, p. 10.

6. The ground of the journey is a recognition that our lives are like a sadhana, a mandala of energy and activity, the basic mahamudra, as Chögyam Trungpa specified: "This common ground idea, or alaya, is not ground in terms of solid ground, but perpetually changing ground." *Transcending Madness*, p. 21.

7. Chögyam Trungpa, in Herbert V. Guenther and Chögyam Trungpa, *The Dawn of Tantra*, p. 6.

scientist. In terms of understanding the teachings, no career is better than any other. Such is the radical way of vajrayana, not determined or limited by moral norms and social conventions.

Intrinsically, confusion is not a problem and, in the context of practice, even becomes a potential for enlightenment. However, "the misunderstanding seems to be that tantra comes into being out of some kind of desperation; that since we cannot handle the confusion, we accept the convention of tantra as a saving grace. Then the shit of our confusion becomes pictorial—pop art. . . . If tantra merely acknowledged that samsara had to be put up with, without seeing the absolute purity and cleanness of it, tantra would be just another form of depression, and devoid of compassion."[8]

This is an essential point. Before confusion sets in, as a result of attachment to the ego, our neuroses are an (admittedly distorted) expression of enlightenment. To see the open quality of our neuroses, we must abandon all ambition, all hope. We have to surrender to reality as it is, without holding back in the slightest. Tantra imposes a perspective of total openness.

Passion, pleasure, art, and sensory perceptions

In order to see just how special Chögyam Trungpa's teaching was, let us examine the example of passion, the fact of wanting something intensely, whether it is money, sex, or chocolate cake. Most spiritual approaches stress the need to deliver ourselves from passion, as though it were salt water and the more we drank of it, the thirstier we became.[9] Whatever antidote is on offer, which varies according to the teacher or tradition, passion is something that we must free ourselves from.

In his faithfulness to the true tantric approach, Chögyam Trungpa saw

---

8. Ibid., p. 48.

9. See, for example: "Desire is like drinking salt water—the more you indulge, the more craving increases" (verse 21) from "What a Bodhisattva Does: Thirty-seven Practices," by Ngulchu Thogme Sangpo, translated from the Tibetan by Constance Wilkinson and Kiki Ekselius, © 1998, http://c-level.com/bodhi.

things differently.[10] The true nature of passion is not a matter of wanting to drag something back into your own territory: I feel gripped by passion for that chocolate cake, so I'm going to buy it, eat it, have it inside me. Chögyam Trungpa explained that there is an open and enlightened dimension to passion, which becomes confused only because we do not know how to connect with it: "That primeval background or universal unconscious— whatever you would like to call it—is not just a blank state, a vacant state of nothingness at all. That background also contains tremendously powerful energy. It is completely filled with energy. If we examine that energy, we see that it has two basic characteristics: heat and direction."[11] Thus it is not energy centered on itself, but instead a reserve of unconditional warmth. In other words, confusion—ordinary passion, for instance—is an opening being manipulated by the ego.

When seen in this way, tantra means "not running away from your pleasures, but rather identifying with them, working with them as part of the working basis. This is an outstanding part of the tantric message. Pleasure in this case includes every kind of pleasure: psychosomatic, physical, psychological, and spiritual. Here it is quite different from the way in which spiritual materialists might seek pleasure by getting into the other. In this case, it is getting into 'this.' There is a self-existing pleasurableness that is completely hollow if you look at it from the point of view of ego's pleasure orientation. Within that, you don't actually experience pleasure at all. All pleasure experiences are hollow. But if you look at it from the point of view of this nakedness, this situation of being completely exposed, any pleasure you experience is full because of its hollowness. . . . You are the embodiment of bliss, and that contains a quality of your being very powerful. You have conquered pleasure, and pleasure is yours. One doesn't have to go so far as to try to enjoy pleasure, but pleasure becomes self-existing bliss."[12]

---

10. He gave several seminars entitled "Work, Sex, and Money," including one in Boston in September 1970 and another in Burlington, Vermont, in April 1972. But he also referred to these topics in many other talks.

11. Chögyam Trungpa, "Sex," *Shambhala Sun*, January 1995, p. 43.

12. *Illusion's Game*, pp. 120–121.

Chögyam Trungpa did not just teach these principles; he embodied them. He made love to the phenomenal world, one might say, because his appreciation of it was so intense and precise. The way he held his glass during a talk was extraordinarily moving, so much so that it was often the first thing that struck those who had come to hear him. The way he lifted his glass, holding it for a moment in his hand before raising it to his lips and drinking, was paradoxically both very slow and intense. The glass came from nowhere, went nowhere—it was just a glass. The intensity in the meeting of space with space was electric.

When he smoked, there was the same quality in the way he held his cigarette. Such passion had nothing to do with grabbing things for oneself; instead it was an expression of pure warmth, true communication, a way of responding to the depth of the world with immense simplicity and astonishing intensity.

Buddhism is often characterized as a path along which we abandon all our desires and pleasures, but in fact it attempts to cut through our identification with desire, which blunts it instead of sharpening it. Buddhism, especially its tantric form, teaches us to dance passionately with the phenomenal world and so increase the brilliance of our lives.

2. Crazy Wisdom Teacher

From the tantric point of view, Buddhism can no longer be seen as a metaphysical conception or a "spiritual" path; instead it is a bold endeavor to make contact with things as they really are. A true tantric teacher like Chögyam Trungpa respects neither custom nor convention; he is willing to take any risk necessary in order to establish genuine communication with his students.

During a talk Chögyam Trungpa was giving at the Naropa Institute in 1976, before nearly nine hundred people, the Beat poet Gregory Corso started shouting insults. At first, Chögyam Trungpa tried to communicate with him by asking him what he wanted to say. But Corso, who was clearly rather drunk, just yelled louder and louder: "What you're saying is meaningless." He did not listen to Chögyam Trungpa's answer. He made no attempt to communicate with him and seemed to be there only to get himself noticed and pour out his anger.

Chögyam Trungpa stood up. Sarah Coleman remembers that he was in a state that she had never witnessed before, in him or anyone else. He pointed his vajra, a metal ritual scepter that he often held in his hand during lectures, at Corso. Then, radiating an intensely dark energy, he said in a composed voice: "Get out of here." He repeated this sentence several times, with increasing fury.

Some of Chögyam Trungpa's students went to remove Gregory, who no longer dared to utter a word. Chögyam Trungpa fell silent. The air seemed to have become solid and black. No one moved. Then, just as the door closed, Chögyam Trungpa burst out laughing. The entire atmosphere changed immediately. Nothing is solid. Chögyam Trungpa had done what needed to be done in order to make contact with Gregory Corso, by reflecting back at him the image of his pure aggression. Once Corso had gone, this aggression had no reason to go on. He picked up the thread of his talk again. At no time did he show the slightest hesitation. When the class convened again later in the week, he welcomed Corso back. Chögyam Trungpa then gave an amazing talk on the problems associated with aggression.

Instead of trying to establish a deep relationship based on a conventional approach, he adopted the perspective of great compassion and used that approach to find the best means to apply it. He had no private life. The contact he had with everyone, man or woman, was so intimate that he was always inventing new ways to allow for that contact. Any event was a pretext to radiate or share his compassion: a meeting, a one-to-one interview, a stroll on the street, going shopping, or leading a seminar. A measure of his compassion can be gleaned from the reports of a number of female students who experienced spending intimate time with him as a very precious communication. Some women reported that, even when there was no sexual intimacy involved—as was often the case in the last years of his life—they experienced spending the night with him as the greatest kind of intimacy.

Chögyam Trungpa's unbounded nature was often surprising. His mind rested in a vast space that refused to be measured. Thus, he shocked and amazed. Without the slightest hesitation or fear, with utter faithfulness to unconditional space, he constantly displayed the ground of true health, which has nothing to do with the sort of health we usually content ourselves with. He radiated a warmth that dissolved any hesitation.

Crazy wisdom

At various times throughout Tibetan history there have been crazy wisdom masters (*yeshe chölwa* in Tibetan), as illustrated by the eccentric behavior of "mad yogis." One was the famous ascetic Drukpa Künlek, "the Mad Yogi of Bhutan," who converted Bhutan to Buddhism and was particularly famous for his fondness for women and beer. In India, this tradition can be seen in the stories of the great tantric masters known as the mahasiddhas. Similar personalities can be found among the sages of China and Japan.

The classic idea of crazy wisdom refers to a form of wisdom that goes beyond all reference points, to such a degree that for ordinary people it sometimes appears insane. Such wisdom is unlimited and unconditioned, expressing itself according to the situation, without concern for conventions or politeness. It is direct and immediate, seeking to be as close to reality as possible. It is truth in action: "It cuts everything down. It does not even try to translate falseness into truthfulness, because that in itself is corruption. It is ruthless, because if you want the complete truth, if you want to be completely, wholly wholesome, then any suggestion that comes up of translating whatever arises into your terms, interpreting it in your terms, is not worth looking into."[13]

The crazy wisdom that Chögyam Trungpa manifested expressed the fullness of his compassion. To be, as he was, a buddha at any moment, is not "polite" and depends on no logic.

---

13. *Crazy Wisdom*, p. 12.

3. Inviting Chaos and Confusion

Early in 1974, to promote the Naropa Institute, which was about to open for its first program, a lecture tour around various American universities was organized for Chögyam Trungpa. As many of his students had only recently graduated from college, they still had the necessary contacts to arrange lectures at their former institutions.

For example, Larry Mermelstein recalls the visit of Chögyam Trungpa to the University of Michigan. The recent graduate was very nervous and worried about this event, which was to take place in a large lecture hall, the Rackham Auditorium, which can hold some five hundred people. All of his professors and old friends would be there. He asked Alton Becker, a professor of linguistics with a specialty in Indonesian and Burmese languages, and his wife, Judith Becker, a professor of ethnomusicology, to arrange for the lecture and host the master in their home during his stay.

On the day of the talk, the rather large entourage departed without Chögyam Trungpa for a couple of hours to visit Professor Becker's office, during which time Rinpoche met with one rather fortunate student requesting some guidance. Upon their return, the group found Rinpoche quite inebriated, having finished nearly a bottle of sake in the interim. Larry Mermelstein began to panic, as it wasn't going to be easy getting Rinpoche to the lecture hall.

As Eastern religions were quite fashionable at the time, the auditorium was packed. The lecture was very brief, so too the question-and-answer period. The talk seemed rambling and disjointed to the worried students—not at all the inspired discourse they knew was possible from their teacher. Above all, Larry was worried what his friends would think. But to his great surprise, Professor Becker told him how impressed he had been: "Chögyam Trungpa uses language to break down conceptualization. I always thought that such a thing was possible, but I'd never seen it done before." Half the audience was furious and the other half deeply moved—which was not an unusual occurrence when Chögyam Trungpa spoke.

The next day, Rinpoche left. As his talk had been the closing lecture in a series of different presentations of Buddhism, a roundtable was organized. Nobody wanted to talk about anything except Chögyam Trungpa, who had so surprised them. A specialist in Buddhism hesitated before speaking, then finally said what he thought. In his opinion, Chögyam Trungpa was not a genuine Buddhist teacher: "He drinks, he smokes, he makes things even more confusing, which is not what Buddhists do. On the contrary, their aim is to let everyone reach peace and inner calm."

But for others, including Alton Becker, Rinpoche was the only one to have spoken the truth. He was living proof that Buddhism is an affront to the conventional and confused world. Buddhism is not a comfortable religion but has a radical side to it, for it aims to tear the ego and its certitudes to shreds.

What is fascinating about this anecdote is that it shows the opposition of two approaches to the path of enlightenment. Many current psychological or spiritual teachings stress the need to avoid confusion and chaos. Thus, "for most people, who think of spirituality as based on goodness, any kind of opposition or obstacle is considered a manifestation of evil."[14] These people thus remain prisoners of a highly aggressive (though also extremely subtle) conception of spirituality.

Chögyam Trungpa shocked and provoked throughout his life, as countless stories attest. We have already emphasized the shock created by his decision to marry a young Englishwoman. It was not so much his decision to abandon his monk's vows that scandalized as it was his abandoning proper protocol in the Tibetan world. Chögyam Trungpa decided to live like a Westerner and cut across all of authority's hierarchical barriers. He would not change again. He did not want to be venerated, but wanted to touch the hearts of his students and offer them real help in mixing their daily lives with dharma. To this end, he decided to live like an ordinary person. He never stopped insisting on this point, as here in 1972: "The speaker here doesn't regard himself as a superior to the audience except that he is sitting on a platform, which does not mean anything very much."[15]

---

14. Ibid., pp. 159–160.

15. Chögyam Trungpa, "Work, Sex, and Money," Burlington, Vermont, April 1972, p. 2.

Chögyam Trungpa smoked and drank alcohol. In this, nothing about him resembles the image of a sage. His teachings can shed some light on his way of life. The danger of spirituality, he explained constantly, is to create a world apart, a holy world without ties to the solid and direct experience of each person. Such a vision of bliss can never truly help people. It is a sort of unattainable ideal that reinforces each person's feeling of psychological misery and encourages spiritual materialism. In response to a letter from someone who was surprised by such a way of life, which he found unworthy of a religious person, Chögyam Trungpa replied: "With regard to your inquiry about my lifestyle, you must understand that I regard myself as an ordinary person. I am a householder, who makes mortgage payments. I have a wife and three children whom I support. At the same time my relationship with the teachings is inseparable from my whole being. I do not try to rise above the world. My vocation is working with the world.

"You ask about the teachings. There is a fundamental idea which refuses to divide things into this or that, sacred or profane, right or wrong. That is why I write and speak of meditation in action. It is much easier to appear holy than to be sane. So the idea is to separate spirituality from spiritual materialism. This requires a practice and some courage. . . .

"By the way, what you heard is true. I do drink, smoke, and permit my students to do the same."[16] There were nonetheless an enormous number of questions about the quantity of alcohol he drank, which went beyond any ordinary measure. How could a spiritual master drink so much? Is he an alcoholic? Is this the shadow part of his personality? Shouldn't a Buddhist have morally irreproachable behavior?

There is a long tradition of teachers putting themselves at the fringes of social conventions and consuming huge amounts of alcohol—as a number of Indian mahasiddhas show us. Chögyam Trungpa is in no way an isolated case. These yogins defined the particular character of Himalayan Buddhism by transmitting their "crazy wisdom" to the Tibetans who came to study with them; they did not hesitate to work with a more relative

---

16. Unpublished letter of May 10, 1973, Shambhala Archives, copyright by Diana J. Mukpo. Reprinted by permission.

reality in order to make ultimate wisdom spring forth. They remained faithful to the bodhisattva commitment, promising to remain in the world and participate in its events through a compassion unfettered by conventions. Tilopa was known for being a procurer, living with a prostitute.

Within the countries of the Himalayas, a number of masters have manifested themselves this way as well. One thinks first of the enormously revered Drukpa Künlek, mentioned above. His taste for beer and women forms the connecting thread that runs through his adventures. R. A. Stein writes that he "gently mocks people, puts them in their place, denounces abuses wherever they proliferate, among the nobility, in the clergy, humbles pride and the complacency of imbeciles."[17] The tantric view shows us a state beyond good and bad, which alone preserves a truly vast attitude, where allegiance to the primordial space of enlightenment is unceasingly maintained and proclaimed.

Those who have the task of presenting the dharma in a new world seem more constrained to accept such an existence and abandon any private life. The life of Padmasambhava, who introduced Buddhism into Tibet and is regarded as a second Buddha, is also deeply shocking. He had sexual relations with the king's daughter while living in a monastery, and he committed a double murder.[18]

Was Chögyam Trungpa the Padmasambhava or the Drukpa Künlek of our times?

This in any case is what the highest Buddhist dignitaries maintained. They continually proclaimed him to be a perfectly enlightened master, having opened the way for them in the West. In 1976 and then in 1981, the Karmapa, head of the Karma Kagyü lineage, solemnly confirmed him as a vajra master and principal propagator of the dharma of his lineage in the West. Dilgo Khyentse Rinpoche, holder of the Nyingma lineage, wrote a supplication after his death in which he specifically named him "maha-

---

17. R. A. Stein, *Vie et chants de 'Brug-pa Kun-legs le yogin* (Paris: Éditions Maisonneuve et Larose, 1972), p. 3.

18. Padmasambhava, in the form of Pema Gyalpo, the Prince Born from the Lotus, killed the wife and son of the minister Katama. See Philippe Cornu, *Padmasambhava: La magie de l'éveil* (Paris: Éditions du Seuil, 1991), p. 71.

siddha." Tülku Urgyen, Penor Rinpoche, and a number of others have also recognized him.

The teachers all insist, nevertheless, that the path of tantra is neither easy nor open to just anybody. It encourages absolutely no egotism, but rests on an extreme ethical requirement since it is only supported by the luminous, direct character of reality. Chögyam Trungpa did not miss a chance to recall the tragic story of Rudra, who felt authorized to enjoy himself freely. His master having revealed his error, Rudra flew into a dreadful rage and killed him—thus condemning himself to "vajra hell." Crazy wisdom does not authorize an abuse of freedom but rather designates a complete renunciation, a requirement to serve all beings, without the slightest reservation. No protection or distance can be maintained anymore. The master must accept being naked before his students, sharing everything with them, in order to transmit his experience of enlightenment directly. The continuity of our open presence, of our allegiance to primordial space, is the key point in the tantric view. Alcohol can be included on this path, explains Chögyam Trungpa, who taught on a few occasions about the way to absorb it while keeping one's entire attention on one's own mind: "People who take drinking seriously relate to it as a refuge from life's hustle and bustle; they also fear they might be becoming alcoholics. In either psychological situation, there is love and hate in their style of drinking, coupled with a sense of going into the unknown. . . . There seems to be something wrong with an approach to alcohol that is based entirely on morality or social propriety. . . . The real effect of alcohol is not considered."[19]

But if a real discipline is established within a strict practice context, "The drinker experiences greater clarity because he feels more really what he is. . . . Whether alcohol is to be a poison or a medicine depends on one's awareness while drinking. Conscious drinking—remaining aware of one's state of mind—transmutes the effect of alcohol."[20]

Is this a set of indicators for understanding the way in which he

---

19. "Alcohol as Medicine or Poison," chap. 10 in *The Heart of the Buddha*, pp. 186–187.

20. Ibid., pp. 187–189.

drank? Watching him teach, for example by looking at a number of the films of him that are available, anybody can see how much alcohol he drank. Under such conditions, how could he have presented such coherent teaching, which anybody can ascertain by opening one of his books? Whereas alcoholics destroy themselves and harm those close to them, Chögyam Trungpa always sought to help people become more alive, free of any imprisonment, and to this end created a substantial organization, Vajradhatu, a new presentation of a spiritual teaching with Shambhala Training, a university, a contemplative form of psychology with Maitri, an ikebana school, and numerous publications.

What effect did alcohol have on him? Why did he drink? It seems difficult to understand this phenomenon, which remains an enigma. However, Chögyam Trungpa did not *encourage* his students to drink, and at a number of Seminaries, during the six weeks or so devoted exclusively to meditation practice, he had them apply the strict discipline of the five precepts: abstaining from destruction of life; abstaining from taking what is not given; abstaining from lying; abstaining from sexual activity (celibacy); and abstaining from alcohol or drugs. With respect to recreational drugs, Chögyam Trungpa was ruthless, firmly denouncing their use during a period when it was regarded favorably. Consuming drugs was prohibited among those who wanted to study with him. Because they make you lose contact with the earth and with reality, they are harmful and dangerous. They make you "high," which is exactly the opposite of the goal of Buddhist teaching.

Generally speaking, Chögyam Trungpa never encouraged anyone to imitate his behavior, and he was troubled by those who felt empowered by his example to do whatever they wanted and manipulate people. As the third Jamgön Kongtrül explained in a teaching given to students of Chögyam Trungpa, "You shouldn't imitate or judge the behavior of your teacher, Chögyam Trungpa Rinpoche, unless you can imitate his mind." The way in which certain Western teachers use their spiritual authority for egotistical purposes is contrary to what Chögyam Trungpa did.

This misunderstanding of the meaning of freedom from convention in tantra even led to an event that really shook his students. In 1979, he proclaimed the "Big No," to denounce those students who acted only in response to their desires without respecting the people around them. He himself recounted the circumstances around this event and its meaning in a talk that he gave shortly afterward: "When the Big No came out, I found that everyone was indulging in their world too much. I had to say No. So I crashed my arm and fist down on my coffee table, and I broke it. I put a dent in it. Then I painted a giant picture of the Big No in the entrance hall of my house: BIG NO. There was ink everywhere after that proclamation. The message was: From now onward, it's NO. . . . That No is that you don't give in to things that indulge your reality. There is no special reality beyond reality. That is the Big No, as opposed to the regular no."[21] If Chögyam Trungpa succeeded in transmitting the dharma in the West, it is because, whatever his behavior, he was deeply open, deeply himself, hiding nothing.

Over the course of interviews with different journalists or during discussions at seminars that I have taught, for a while I tried to present traditional explanations and historic precedents in an effort to better understand the reasons for Chögyam Trungpa's behavior. Even if such explanations have their use, I came to the conclusion that it was unnecessary to hold on to them.

No doubt Chögyam Trungpa would not have accepted such arguments; he rejected the language of authority. Whatever one might say, there are aspects in the life of Chögyam Trungpa that are shocking, and his relationship to alcohol remains one of them.

This question was posed to his student Pema Chödrön, well known for the depth of her teaching. We should stress that Pema Chödrön is a nun and that Chögyam Trungpa is the founder of a very strict monastery that follows the letter of the vinaya rules. The journalist asked her: "Would you say that the intention behind his unconventional behavior, including his sexual exploits and his drinking, was to help others?"

Pema replied: "As the years went on, I felt everything he did was to help others. But I would also say now that maybe my understanding has gone even deeper, and it feels more to the point to say I don't know. I don't know what he was doing. I know he changed my life. I know I love him.

21. *Great Eastern Sun*, p. 141.

But I don't know who he was."[22] I should acknowledge that while I was writing this work, meeting his close students, and consulting the archives, it sometimes happened that I was shocked, to the point where once or twice I asked myself if I would be able to continue this work. It is one thing to notice such excess in the lives of masters of the past; it is quite another to see it in a contemporary.

This shocking character is not an innocuous element, unrelated to the teaching of such a master. Chögyam Trungpa was constantly trying to avert any tendency among his students to worship him in a theistic and somewhat idolatrous way. He wanted people to take into account that he was not a god, and rely on their own intelligence.

The teaching of the Buddha, as Chögyam Trungpa explained throughout his work, is a lesson in relaxing into insecurity and the absence of a stable ground. It is necessary not to fear chaos, but to learn how to connect to it.

Obstacles should not be seen as threats to be fought off, because then, instead of trying to establish contact with them, we spend our time warding them off as though they were evil and antagonistic to the teaching. On the contrary, it is necessary to work with negativity and try to use it as an "adornment."[23] We must learn to establish a link with our pain and distress, which are integral parts of the path. As Chögyam Trungpa wrote: "Basic negativity is very revealing, sharp, and accurate. If we leave it as basic negativity rather than overlaying it with conceptualized ideas, we see the nature of its intelligence, which is very precise as well as energetic."[24] So the problem is not negativity itself, but our reaction to it—or, as Chögyam Trungpa put it, "negative negativity."

Like chaos, negativity actually offers a distinct opportunity to experience enlightenment. From the time he arrived in the United States, Chögyam Trungpa paid a great deal of attention to what went on at the parties held by his students. One aspect of this was that he was connecting him-

---

22. Pema Chödrön, "No Right No Wrong," *Tricycle*, Fall 1993, p. 17.

23. *Crazy Wisdom*, p. 160.

24. Chögyam Trungpa, *Garuda II: Working with Negativity* (Tail of the Tiger, Barnet, VT, and Karma Dzong, Boulder), Spring 1972, p. 39.

self to these young hippies' lives without discouraging them or attempting to direct what was going on. He also often allowed confusion to develop further. For the Dorje Loppön, Lodrö Dorje, one of Chögyam Trungpa's most senior students, this was the first manifestation of the notion of *feast* as it is practiced in tantra. As the Loppön explained: "The point of offering a party is to recognize our confusion, instead of hiding things under the carpet, in a civilized way, with a nicely policed ego."

For a master of crazy wisdom, the more intense the confusion, the greater the chances of entering into a relationship with this open space, without any major preconception. In such a situation, the ego's insanity is thoroughly exposed. It is not possible to follow the path without first getting a slap in the face of ego, which paradoxically is also the source of real relief, because it puts a stop to one's illusions.

Chaos shows us that we are not solid and fixed, nor is the world: "Chaos has an order by virtue of which it isn't really chaos. But when there's no chaos, no confusion, there's luxury, comfort. Comfort and luxury lead you more into samsara because you are in a position to create more kinds of luxurious possibilities, psychologically, philosophically, physically.... But strangely enough ... creating more luxurious situations adds further to your collection of chaos."[25] Embracing chaos is thus the only way to break completely with spiritual materialism.

Only in a context of complete absence of hope can chaos become a creative force. Chögyam Trungpa taught this approach on numerous occasions, using the word *hopelessness* to distinguish it from despair. When we expect nothing, it becomes possible to see things as they are, with an "intelligent uncertainty—sharp, inquisitive."[26]

To be in the company of Chögyam Trungpa was to be constantly exposed and naked. It was impossible to take a moment's rest. His presence was marked by a deep intensity. And it was even more intense for the practitioner who knew, through his or her practice, how to enter into contact with the teacher.

---

25. Chögyam Trungpa, in Herbert V. Guenther and Chögyam Trungpa, *The Dawn of Tantra*, p. 88.

26. *Crazy Wisdom*, p. 171.

The chaos caused by such encounters with the teacher is traditional in the lineage of Chögyam Trungpa. Naropa, one of the greatest teachers of the Kagyü lineage, realized one day how limited his own apprenticeship was, even though he was the head of one of the most prestigious Buddhist universities in India at the time. So he decided to leave his post to search for and study with Tilopa, a true master, who lived a very simple yogic life. But Naropa was then put to the test for twelve years by his teacher. For example, Tilopa told him: "Go and fetch me some soup from the kitchen; then maybe I'll teach you." So Naropa went to steal some soup and was beaten by the cooks. He returned bloodied but happy. Tilopa then told him: "I want another bowl. Go and get some more." He went back to get more soup, was caught, and this time returned half dead. This kind of thing happened over and over again, always with a point: to dispel Naropa's pride or his misapprehension of reality.

When you were traveling on an airplane with Chögyam Trungpa, he might ask you to go tell the pilot that he was the king of Bhutan and suggest that this should be announced to all the passengers, or that the pilot should check to see if there was a special party waiting at the gate to receive "the king." If you were driving him in your car in certain circumstances, he might tell you to go faster. In that situation you might be concerned about safety or about getting a ticket, but a little voice in the back seat would keep firmly but gently insisting: "Faster." You have a sense of being right on the edge of what you can handle. You don't know what to do. Your mind goes crazy. As he explained: "The student of tantra should be in a constant state of panic. That panic is electric and should be regarded as worthwhile. Panic serves two purposes: it overcomes our sense of smugness and self-satisfaction, and it sharpens our clarity enormously. It has been said by Padma Karpo and other great tantric teachers that studying tantra is like riding on a razor blade. . . . Sudden panic creates an enormous sense of fresh air, and that quality of openness is exactly what tantra should create. If we are good tantra students, we open ourselves each moment. We panic a thousand times a day, 108 times an hour."[27]

---

27. *Journey without Goal*, pp. 55–56.

During the end of the 1984 Vajradhatu Seminary and the 1984 Kalapa Assembly, one of the seminars devoted to the vision of Shambhala and open only to his most senior students, Chögyam Trungpa began his talks at about three o'clock in the morning and kept his students up all night. Then after a few days, he started his talks at six o'clock and finished at eleven. In this way, night became day, and day became night. At seven in the evening, it was time to organize breakfast. The students were thus led to abandon their usual points of reference. Other such reference points might dissolve at the same time, such as the idea of knowing whom you liked and whom you disliked. When the situation becomes topsy-turvy and extreme, everyone discovers that they are carrying a useless burden, which, however, is possible to abandon in order to have a more naked experience of reality.

These situations of chaos that Chögyam Trungpa continually created were a golden opportunity to face up directly to one's own confusion and the wisdom it contains. More than being a tantric teacher, Chögyam Trungpa *manifested* tantra, constantly creating uncomfortable but magnetizing situations of chaos and panic, which cut through hypocrisy and can liberate in unexpected ways.

Chapter Eight

Maitri

OPENING OUT TO THE MANIFESTATIONS OF SPACE

The creation of Maitri, a Buddhist community working in a semiclinical situation with Western neurosis, is a landmark in the growth of Tibetan Buddhist teachings in America. It marks a practical and potentially valuable application of the insights of vajrayana Buddhism to emotional disorder.[1]

—CHÖGYAM TRUNGPA

CHÖGYAM TRUNGPA CONTINUALLY invented new ways of presenting the teachings we have just examined. One of the constants of his work was his ability to give a profound explanation of the path without using the usual Buddhist terms. He taught psychology, theater, and art, but the underlying approach was the same. Without allowing any concepts to impinge, he plunged his students into the nakedness of experiencing their own unfiltered reality.

---

1. Chögyam Trungpa, "Space Therapy and the Maitri Community" (March 1974), in *The Collected Works of Chögyam Trungpa*, vol. 2 (Boston: Shambhala Publications, 2003), pp. 566–575.

One of the finest examples of this talent is the creation of Maitri Space Awareness practice. Buddhism is sometimes compared to therapy, and its relationship with Western psychology has often been studied. Indeed, both fields take a very pragmatic approach toward suffering, and neither has recourse to external solutions for solving people's problems.

But what was unique about Chögyam Trungpa's approach was the way he joined a *practical* therapeutic technique to the Buddhist description of the workings of the mind and confusion. This is Maitri, one of the most striking of Chögyam Trungpa's contributions, but also one of the least well known, whose potential for development has not yet been fully explored.

1. From an Experimental Therapeutic Community to the Development of Contemplative Psychology

The origins of Maitri go back to meetings that took place between Chögyam Trungpa and Shunryu Suzuki Roshi in May 1971 at the Zen Center in San Francisco. While discussing their problems in presenting the Buddhist tradition in the West, they observed that dharma centers were attracting a certain number of people with serious psychological problems. For example, a young man who had never recovered from an acid trip had lived at Tail of the Tiger for a few weeks. The community had had a lot of trouble trying to help him and include him in their way of life.

For other people with severe emotional difficulties, the practice of meditation is not much use. Suzuki Roshi suggested to Chögyam Trungpa that they set up a community for people suffering from serious problems. But Suzuki Roshi died later in 1971, before it had been decided what form this community would take. Chögyam Trungpa was taken with the idea and decided to put the project into action.

He set up an "experimental community," just like many others at the time. He considered that having people live together while taking into account the details of daily life would be a good way to help them: "I had the idea of quite possibly not using any form of therapies at all, just purely creating a living situation on the model of our community living situation, which brings up a lot of shit and all kinds of things."[2] This is one of the main points in his teaching, which he and Shunryu Suzuki shared: the importance of meditation in action.

The creation of Maitri rooms

Setting up a community is relatively easy, but how then to present your specific vision? It was a great challenge.

> I feel that presenting meditation techniques or any particular techniques are not appropriate. We shouldn't present them at all. We should just purely be very discreet. Staff members there will practice and sit together, meditate, the patients or audience or guests, can take part in purely domestic matters, handling that. Something is lacking there I discovered. Only the judgment to rate how well they wash their dishes, how well they put a nail into wood and how well they brush their teeth. When you do that well then you are cured. . . . I felt something is inadequate. I felt my own vision is challenged. Something is not quite right. In fact I found it slightly pathetic. We wanted to do something heroic and we ended up just purely doing grandma's job. . .[3]

These remarks allow us to see how Chögyam Trungpa thought and how he tried to find a form that corresponded to his vision.

So how to begin? Tibet had no psychiatric hospitals or specialized institutions that could have been used as a model. Instead, Chögyam Trungpa set about analyzing his own education and some of the retreats

---

2. Chögyam Trungpa, from an unpublished talk at the Second Maitri Conference, Boulder, February 1973. These talks were given to those people working with the Maitri approach and helping to formulate plans for the therapeutic community.

3. Ibid.

he had done, such as the bardo retreat, during which the practitioners remain in entirely sealed rooms.[4]

In December 1972, during the "Crazy Wisdom" seminary at the Snow Lion Inn in Jackson Hole, Wyoming, he had the idea of constructing a series of different rooms in which different postures would be taken. He thus came up with a new approach, even if it was still anchored in the most esoteric and traditional teachings of tantric Buddhism.

He explained the idea as follows:

> I have been tossing around all kinds of ideas and approaches. . . . Little J. M. was dancing and singing his Tahiti [hula dance], and he wanted all of us to sing and dance, and nobody would cooperate with him. I felt very uncomfortable at the time because somebody might complain downstairs, the lady trying to fall asleep, and there was a neighbor next door, and there was a world outside and above us. I felt that there would be a complaint coming from above and below and all quarters. . . . I felt very claustrophobic, and at the same time I enjoyed his company and his beauty. Suddenly I realized myself in a box. All those complaints and paranoid ideas and everything. . . . I felt it's a square world that you're living in and there is an exit of some kind. I suddenly remembered the bardo retreat techniques for relating with space. Relating with the light dawned on me.[5]

He then dictated the following lines:

> People with parental problems need a four-windowed house.
> People with drug problems need a long tunnel with windows.

---

4. See Chögyam Trungpa's commentary in *The Tibetan Book of the Dead: The Great Liberation Through Hearing in the Bardo*, where, among other things, he says: "One of the most highly advanced and dangerous forms of practice is the bardo retreat, which consists of seven weeks of meditation in utter darkness" (p. 11).

5. Chögyam Trungpa, unpublished talk at the Second Maitri Conference, Boulder, February 1973.

People with spiritual problems need underground windows.
People with suicidal problems need a tower with windows.
People with intellectual problems need a room without
   windows.

What we experience as psychological problems are in fact false relationships with space. From a conventional viewpoint, we consider our egos to be solid and the surrounding space as shifting and navigable. But from the Buddhist perspective, we are open and fluid while space is solid and indestructible. This is a threat to the ego. Chögyam Trungpa explained: "You cannot destroy space, but at the same time, space is very accommodating, nevertheless. Space also kills you, it is very uncompassionate—but at the same time, it is very accommodating, nevertheless."[6]

In other words, if we open ourselves to space, we destroy our egos and work at the root of our emotional problems. Our relationship with space is fundamental to our being. Such is the practice of Maitri, which Chögyam Trungpa decided to call "space therapy." By entering these different rooms, we discover different aspects of space, different ways of connecting with the world.

2. The Practice of Space Therapy

So how does this practice work?

You go into a room measuring about seven by seven, or forty-nine feet square. There are five different types of rooms: blue, yellow, red, green, and white. In each room, the carpet and walls are the same color. The shapes of the windows are each different and allow in colored light. In the green room the window is square and on the ceiling, but in the blue room large rectangles have been cut into two of the walls.

In each of these rooms, you adopt a specific posture, which you keep for about three-quarters of an hour. For example, in the yellow room you

---

6. Chögyam Trungpa, *Glimpses of Space: The Feminine Principle and Evam* (Halifax: Vajradhatu Publications, 1999), p. 50.

lie on your back with your arms open wide and your legs apart. The backs of the hands are placed on the floor, with the fingers open, thus causing a slight tension in the muscles, which must be maintained throughout the posture.

The practice quite simply consists in being open to everything that happens. Adopting a specific posture in a particular room profoundly changes our state of mind, though not by adding anything new. Instead it clearly brings out the particular characteristics of who we are.

Maitri

The aim of the practice can be seen in the name that Chögyam Trungpa gave to it—Maitri, a traditional Buddhist term that means "love," or, in Chögyam Trungpa's preferred translation, "loving-kindness." Marvin Casper, who was in charge of Maitri at the Naropa Institute, explained: "At first that might sound very sweet, or maybe too sweet. Depending upon how cynical you are. Or how much Buddhism you have studied. But it is not sweetness in the sense of being nice, or being a good, socially minded citizen. It's much bolder than that. It's basically being open. Extremely open. Open first to your own energy, and to your own neurosis, and then as well to others."[7]

Loving-kindness comes from a benevolent attitude toward everything that happens to us. It is thus linked to an absence of judgment regarding all of our experiences.[8] It is a feeling of natural gentleness and friendship that frees us from the continual aggression that penetrates all we do. It arises from a dimension that is profoundly sane, open, intelligent, and warm, and which exists in everyone.

As opposed to the traditional medical approach, which aims at curing a problem, this sort of Buddhist approach is based on the conviction that

---

7. Marvin Casper, "Introduction to Maitri Theory and Practice," August 20, 1978.

8. "Whenever there is aggression and disliking in any aspect of the environment as you are growing up, that is the ground of insanity, from the Buddhist point of view." Chögyam Trungpa, "Creating an Environment of Sanity," *Naropa Institute Journal of Psychology* 2 (1983). Reprinted in *The Collected Works of Chögyam Trungpa*, vol. 2.

no matter what the suffering person may be going through, their basic sanity is always at work. In other words, the approach is to work on the mind of the patient instead of concentrating on their problems: "A fundamental shift in allegiance away from fascination or intoxication with illness, toward sanity, can take place. It is a gentle recovery, a recovery based on the inspiration to develop oneself—to live and learn and work in the world and be useful to others."[9] It is not a matter of avoiding problems, but instead having the courage to dig down to their roots.

The tantric perspective: The five buddha families

These rooms reflect the principles of tantra, which distinguishes five main energies, called buddha families. Enlightenment is not uniform, but instead has a great diversity of appearances: "We are not, as we might imagine, expected to be uniform and regimented, to be ideally enlightened and absolutely cool and kind and wise," explained Chögyam Trungpa.[10] The five buddha families are expressions of fundamental sanity, which can be combined in numerous ways.

The buddha families are not limited to our personal psychology but also describe a particular *atmosphere* that can be found in all things: the seasons, the emotions, the five elements, and so on. This distinguishes them from the sort of psychological classifications that we have in the West.

The first family, associated with the color white, is called *buddha*. It is associated with the element of space, the primary openness of all experience. This openness is basic intelligence that is not limited by the ego. It can also become closed under the influence of doubt and insecurity, of anxiety and ignorance.

The second family is *vajra* and is connected with the color blue and the element of water. It is the clarity of pure, sharp vision. This wisdom is like a mirror because it reflects everything. When confused, it becomes aggressive.

---

9. Maitri Psychological Services brochure, no date.

10. *The Lion's Roar*, p. 165.

The next family is *ratna*, "the jewel," and is connected with the color yellow. The sense of richness that is associated with ratna can manifest as an ability to cope with anything. Ratna is linked to the element of earth. But when trust has been lost in this feeling of basic fullness, this energy turns into a sensation of constant poverty, of insufficiency and dissatisfaction, or else of stifling pride.

The next family is connected with the color red and is *padma*, the lotus—the flower that is born in mud, yet manifests a pure, delicate beauty. It is linked to the element of fire, which magnetizes those who look at it. It is the wisdom of discrimination. This knowledge derived from uniting with what we examine can take the appearance of compassion or else of fickle and wild seduction.

The fifth family, associated with the color green, is *karma*, action. It is linked to the wind, which has the quality of being active yet always goes in only one direction at a time. This all-accomplishing wisdom can be either highly effective or else a violent, aggressive competitiveness that can take the form of jealousy.[11] Inseparable from wisdom, therefore, is confusion. Through the development of a benevolent attitude toward ourselves, we discover that wisdom and confusion are coemergent—that we can't reject anything of what we are. We need to learn to transform the mud of our confusion into the gold of wisdom, to open ourselves to things as they are.

3. The Maitri Center

Judith Lief, a senior student of Chögyam Trungpa's who studied Maitri teachings with him in the early 1970s, remembers that in Boulder in 1972, when people wanted to study with Chögyam Trungpa, they were given a choice. They were asked if they wanted to join the Mudra theater group

---

11. In the context of this book, it is impossible to examine the five buddha families in greater depth. They should be studied and contemplated during a Maitri seminar. The families are discussed in depth in *The Essential Chögyam Trungpa*, *The Path Is the Goal*, and *Cutting Through Spiritual Materialism*. See also n. 17.

or the Maitri psychology group, which were then the main streams of Chögyam Trungpa's teaching. While not all students joined one group or the other, many did.

When the Maitri group was founded, it had a dual purpose: understanding the workings of one's own mind, and more specifically the structure of one's ego; and founding a community capable of helping those with severe psychological problems. With this in mind, Chögyam Trungpa presented teachings on the six realms and the bardos. These are ways of understanding different psychological states and the contrasts between fundamental sanity and the confusion that conceals it.[12]

The activities of the Maitri group led to a conference in December 1973. Chögyam Trungpa gave an intensive presentation of the five buddha families. He also put the finishing touches on the design of the Maitri rooms, as they still exist today. He discussed at length the therapeutic angle of what he wanted to do in the project, especially emphasizing the possibility of applying the intuitions of Buddhist psychology to the various problems people suffer from in the modern Western world.

In 1973 some of Chögyam Trungpa's students moved into a farmhouse in Elizabethtown, New York, to set up the Maitri Center. It was directed first by Thomas F. Rich (who would later become Chögyam Trungpa's regent), and then by Charles (Chuck) Lief. In the spring of 1974, the project moved to a twelve-acre site donated by a rich benefactor in Wingdale, on the Connecticut border.

The idea was to live together in the community while working on the technique of "space therapy." When the community environment had been created, based on a minimal hierarchy, it allowed conventional roles to be cut through and in particular the usual therapeutic relationships.

---

12. Based on direct observation of various mental structures, these teachings provide a clear, precise view of the mind. The traditional Buddhist structure of six realms—gods, jealous gods, human beings, animals, hungry ghosts, and hell beings—is sometimes understood as a literal description of possible modes of being. But in many seminars given by Chögyam Trungpa, these six spheres were used to describe the six worlds that we create as the logical outcomes of the powerful emotional states of pride, envy, desire, ignorance, greed, and anger. The six worlds or realms are the context for experiencing the bardos, which arise as intensified experiences of the worlds. See *Transcending Madness*.

Everyone in the community had to work. The routine that was thus put in place provided a ground for relating directly to neuroses.

The rooms were built in 1974, but the Maitri community never grew very large and had only a few patients. Overall, the sangha was not ready, and it was difficult to find funding for a project that was so ahead of its time.

As a result, there was neither enough money nor enough expertise to allow such a program to be developed. But, as with other Chögyam Trungpa projects, abandoning it did not mean that it was a failure. In retrospect, it is clear that the perspective it opened remains very much alive and a constant source of inspiration.

Sometimes, years later, like a seed that has awaited the right moment to sprout, a project that had apparently been long forgotten is reborn thanks to its striking coherence and accuracy.[13] This is another sign of Chögyam Trungpa's profound genius and the depth of his teachings, which continue to bear fruit years after his death.[14]

In 1976 the land was sold and the money paid over to the Naropa Institute for capital development and to support the new master's degree program in Buddhist and Western psychology. Maitri practice had been presented at the Institute since 1974, and it developed considerably, becoming a specific training course for therapists. As part of their studies, students went into a group retreat for as long as twelve weeks to practice shamatha-vipashyana meditation and the various postures in the Maitri rooms.

In this way, the practice of Maitri became part of the training of psychologists, who can thus study how the ego is constructed and how it

---

13. In the United States, the Greyston Foundation in Yonkers, New York, which deals with the social rehabilitation of people in difficulty, has adopted many of the main points of this vision. Its director, Chuck Lief, was one of the people who founded Elizabethtown. In Europe, the establishment in 1998 of Karuna, a training program in Buddhist psychology based on Maitri, is also part of this heritage.

14. This leads us to think that everything Chögyam Trungpa did was meaningful, that nothing was accidental. In some respects, his various projects lead their own lives. They sometimes have to wait for the right conditions before revealing themselves. The numerous changes he made to his work rarely constitute an abandonment. Rather, the opposite

gives rise to a horde of kleshas or, in the language of psychology, neuroses. Basically, neuroses are linked to the way we solidify ourselves, the world, and the space between us and others. In therapeutic terms, the practice of Maitri allows us to understand the link between wisdom and confusion. It also provides a way to help patients who come to be freed of their neuroses. A Maitri-trained practitioner can help patients to enter into close contact with who they are and the logic of their confusion.

Furthermore, contemplative psychology is a therapeutic approach that unites the interpersonal discipline of psychotherapy with the personal discipline of working on oneself by practicing meditation. In this context, helping others can become an integral part of one's own path, and in return provide a profound existential solidity to one's clinical work.

A degree-granting program in contemplative psychology was started at Naropa in 1976.[15] A review, *Journal of Contemplative Psychotherapy*, was also launched to present the work of the team of teachers. Chögyam Trungpa himself contributed a number of articles. In this way, hundreds of students have received training in contemplative psychotherapy.

Edward M. Podvoll (1936–2003)—a psychiatrist who received his M.D. at New York University, completed his residency at Stanford, and went on to become the head of the Institute's psychology department in 1978—wanted to go back to Chögyam Trungpa's original inspiration and use this practice to help those with psychological problems. In 1981, he started Maitri Psychological Services. The therapists use the Maitri rooms with their clients, either individually or in groups.

For over ten years, the discipline of Maitri was practiced only at the Naropa Institute and was largely confined to the psychology program. Although this practice was not a major focus for the rest of the community, Chögyam Trungpa continued teaching the principles of the five buddha families on various occasions and always in an entirely new way.

---

applies. Chögyam Trungpa was like a geographer studying unknown territory, creating numerous roads and cities. If some of them are unfinished, his plans still allow his successors to complete them.

15. The Naropa M.A. program in Psychology: Contemplative Psychotherapy.

4. The Development of Maitri

Strangely enough, after a period of limited development, Maitri finally took off. First, after the late 1980s a large number of classes on the campus of the Naropa Institute featured this practice. Examples include "Teaching and Learning Styles" (Richard Brown), "Maitri Space Awareness: An Approach to Art Therapy" (Bernie Marek), and "Joining Heaven and Earth through Speech: A Meditation and Poetic Workshop" (Gary Allen). This list shows that Maitri was no longer oriented toward psychology alone, but now opened out to many other disciplines. Maitri practice allows students to enter into the world of qualities that reflect each experience or, in Buddhist terms, link us with the luminosity of all phenomena. This field is not encumbered by mental constructs but is very lively and personal. It is thus particularly suited to artistic practice: "By working with the five buddha families, we are trying to develop some basic understanding of how to see things in their ultimate essence, their own innate nature. We can use this knowledge with regard to painting or poetry or arranging flowers or making films or composing music. . . . The five buddha family principles seem to cover a whole new dimension of perception. They are very important at all levels of perception and in all creative situations."[16]

While Chögyam Trungpa was presenting the five buddha families to the Maitri group in 1973, he also presented them to the Mudra group, as well as during a seminar devoted to the film he was making about Milarepa. In any artistic or psychological field, attention to the five buddha families opens up a new range of experience and fields to be explored.

Thanks to this new lease on life and to the deep experience of a number of teachers, Maitri practice moved beyond the Naropa Institute, which had long been the guardian of the practice. In the late 1980s, Ernst Liebhart, a psychology professor, had Maitri rooms built at his own expense and organized shorter programs in his native Germany, which were open to everyone. It was a huge success. It was observed that this practice could be of real help to its practitioners, even over a short period, and whether they were interested in psychology or not.

---

16. *Dharma Art*, p. 80.

Other rooms were built at Karmê Chöling in Vermont and at Dechen Chöling in France, thus making it possible to organize a variety of different programs.

In 1993, Allyn Lyon, who was one of the main teachers of Maitri at Naropa, started to teach Maitri programs in Europe, with glasses that provide a glimpse of the practice when it is not possible to build rooms. The practitioner adopts the posture while wearing colored glasses. It has thus become possible to make Chögyam Trungpa's wish come true and allow everyone to have a personal relationship with the five buddha families, even during a very short time such as a weekend.

Why did Chögyam Trungpa devote so many teachings to the five buddha families?[17]

They were at the heart of his teaching approach. As he never stopped explaining, the dharma is not religious: "We do not have to relate to teaching only in the religious context. We also have to read the symbolism connected with our situation. What we live, where we live, how we live—all these living situations also have a basic message that we can read, that we can work with."[18]

---

17. This list contains references to some of the public teachings that Chögyam Trungpa gave on the subject. It is far from exhaustive but gives an idea of their importance for Chögyam Trungpa.

Cutting Through Spiritual Materialism (Boston: Shambhala Publications, 1973), "The Six Realms," pp. 138–148, and "Tantra," pp. 224–230.

Journey without Goal (Boston: Shambhala Publications, 1981), "Mandala Principle," pp. 31–38, and "Five Buddha Families," pp. 77–85.

The Tibetan Book of the Dead (Boston: Shambhala Publications, 1975), "Commentary," pp. 1–29.

The Myth of Freedom (Boston: Shambhala Publications, 1976), "Styles of imprisonment," pp. 19–40, and "Mandala," pp. 152–156.

Orderly Chaos: The Mandala Principle (Boston: Shambhala Publications, 1991).

Transcending Madness: The Experience of the Six Bardos (Boston: Shambhala Publications, 1992).

The Lion's Roar (Boston: Shambhala Publications, 1992), "The Five Buddha Families and Mahamudra," pp. 161–175.

18. *The Lion's Roar*, p. 163.

Mahamudra, the "great symbol," consists in bringing out the indivisibility of samsara and nirvana while listening to all the basic messages of our existence. It means entering into a relationship with the details of our daily lives, as they truly are. It is a genuinely personal experience. The five buddha families allow us to make contact with the texture of our existence and to experience the various styles that are at work all around us. The path is no longer based on fantasy but becomes real and anchored in our lives at their most intimate. Maitri practice teaches us to distinguish between times when we experience phenomena directly and those moments, all too frequent, when we are overly centered on ourselves and no longer perceive anything. The instant when we become separated from the reality of things as they are is the birth of conflicting emotions (kleshas), and it is then that we shut ourselves off from energy.

To take an example: you are driving, then suddenly become conscious of yourself and so lose your sense of oneness with the situation; maybe you have an accident. We do this sort of quick check all the time, again and again. You are talking with someone, and you suddenly wonder if the person likes you or not, whether you matter to them, whether what you're saying is clever enough. Automatically, you become separated from the person and the real situation. This is precisely how the ego works.

Everything you then do to reestablish your relationship with the person—ask them if they like you, try to make them tell, and so on—only deepens the initial duality. It is not possible to rediscover space by working from your ego.

So how to become more sane? The saner you want to be, the more neurotic you become, because it's the separation that creates the problem. Maitri practice does not aim to liberate the student, as Chögyam Trungpa stated: "Let me explain to you another principle connected with this space therapy. We are not particularly trying to cure them. Do you see that? We are trying to get them to relate with the intensity of what they are."[19] Maitri practice leads to a process of abandoning our will to control everything, or the ambition to be perfect and avoid all suffering.

---

19. Chögyam Trungpa, unpublished talk at the Second Maitri Conference, Boulder, February 1973.

If the discipline of sitting practice teaches us how to be with our experience as it is, the practice of Maitri, like that of tantra, makes what we experience more intense. When we maintain the posture in one of the rooms and accept whatever comes into our minds, incredibly embarrassing or painful experiences can arise. Neurotic states that we have not always fully recognized seem to float up to the surface. We accept looking directly at who we really are, both our wisdom and the extent of our confusion. Quite simply, we remain open to what is, without drawing any conclusions: "The postures exaggerate psychological space in that they highlight it. It's like putting a spotlight on something that you had regular lighting on previously. It is a highlight in the sense of [experiencing] a pure type [buddha family]. You are doing [experiencing or expressing] a pure type. You are refining your perception. As you get experience recognizing the exaggeration, you begin to perceive subtlety. So we are refining perception, and at the same time, the room is bringing up that type. There is more vividness, so there is more to see."[20]

For example, if we experience great anger on going into a room, we experience that emotion in a very direct way. The things that become obvious in this context are far less clear in our daily lives, when we tend to be angry *about* something rather than just being in a state of anger.

It is difficult to present the depth of a practice with such varied ramifications.

Maitri is an approach based on the Buddhist principles of loving-kindness and compassion. It allows people's psychological problems to be worked with, and so takes its place in the overall work of Chögyam Trungpa in displaying the relevance of the Buddhist approach in confronting the difficulties of our times. For experienced practitioners, it becomes a means to communicate their experience and wisdom to the world and to help others by using a language everyone can understand.

It provides an access to the sacred dimension of existence by showing that the world is a free play of energies.

It is also an entrance into the nondualistic experience of tantra and

---

20. Ibid.

thus allows wisdom and neurosis to be linked together in their basic unity.

This practice allows us to see ourselves as we are; it is like a microscope that opens a perspective on each aspect of our minds.

Maitri has developed in many different directions. For instance, in her book *Enlightened by Design*, Helen Berliner has shown how knowledge of the five buddha families allows us to understand our environment and to transform it by adding peace, clarity, richness, warmth, and energy. By coordinating our homes according to the five basic energies, we enlighten our lives profoundly.[21]

Maitri is helpful to practitioners of the sadhanas, who are trying to connect with the energies of the various mandala deities. Buddhist deities are the representatives of the buddha families and reveal the great wisdom of the emotions. Maitri is thus a useful practice that provides a sacred perspective of the world while entering the very heart of our own experiences.

---

21. Helen Berliner, *Enlightened by Design* (Boston: Shambhala Publications, 1999).

Chapter Nine

MUDRA

SPACE AWARENESS

HRIH!
From the space of unerring auspicious coincidence
Now as a hundred luminous rays of kindness stream
    forth,
To the festival which hosts the three worlds as guests
We perform the drama of fearless mercy.
May this benefit and joy spread to beings in the three
    worlds.[1]

—CHÖGYAM TRUNGPA

IN 1972, CHÖGYAM TRUNGPA started work on a new project, which he called Mudra Space Awareness, aimed at all those interested in the theater arts, whether drama, performance, or music. In this project, Chögyam Trungpa presented teachings and above all practices that are so advanced and so nonconceptual that we are only now beginning to understand their true importance.

The Mudra theater group existed for approximately ten or twelve years, mounting all of the plays written by Chögyam Trungpa and teaching many of his students. The group formally disbanded when it became clear that numerous projects in the sangha were taking precedence, and this gave the impression that the Mudra practices virtually vanished from the community for many years. However, Lee Worley, one of the

---

1. Chögyam Trungpa composed this unpublished invocation for the Mudra group.

few professional actors in the Mudra group, began to weave her understanding into her acting training at Naropa Institute (now University), and some Mudra groups remained active in Europe. During the 1990s Mudra began to spark renewed curiosity.[2]

So it was that Craig Smith, one of Chögyam Trungpa's students who first encountered the Mudra discipline in the mid-1970s, after a nineteen-year break began to present the practice of Mudra at various meditation centers connected with Chögyam Trungpa's work. Andy Karr told me in an interview that after being the director of the Mudra group in Boulder in the 1970s, it took him twenty-five years to begin to understand the true scope and meaning of these teachings.

So why this strange destiny, which is strikingly similar to that of Maitri?

Mudra is a very direct way of presenting the heart of the contemplative experience. During the period between 1975 and 1995, Chögyam Trungpa's students tried to understand the Buddhist tradition, which he had explained in such a precise and extensive way, and thus turned away from these practices. Later, the astonishing depth of these practices appeared to them in a new light.

1. The Birth of Full Mudra Space Awareness

In 1972, the Boulder theater group was formed by some of Chögyam Trungpa's students who had already studied or worked in the theater. Some wanted to make it their career. Chögyam Trungpa encouraged them and told them about the monastic dances he had practiced with great interest in Tibet. As part of his studies at Surmang, he had devoted himself completely to monastic dance for three months in order to learn all of the movements required for a series of dances he had to lead at the

---

2. It is impossible in this chapter to present all of the practices that have been developed. I have chosen those that seemed to be the most important. It should also be noted that, as he did with Maitri, Ernst Liebhart in Germany was the first to organize weekends and seminars devoted to the practice of Mudra that were open to all. He thus played an essential role in seeing to it that the precious nature of these teachings was understood.

end of this period. Surmang is well known for its specific cycle of dances associated with the deity Chakrasamvara.

As he explained in *Born in Tibet*: "According to monastic rules, secular dancing is not permitted, but the Buddhist dancing is a spiritual exercise in awareness. The Lord Buddha is portrayed in sculpture and painting making different gestures (Skt. *mudra*), each of which has its own special significance. And so it is with our dancing; each step and each movement of the hands, arms, and head has its own symbolical meaning and brings an increase of understanding both to dancers and spectators."[3]

From these monastic dances Chögyam Trungpa experienced the heart of a contemplative tradition that uses a series of fixed ritual movements to create an atmosphere of basic sanity and to provide an open space of clarity in the minds of both the performers and the audience.

Chögyam Trungpa was convinced that it was possible to create theater based on such an idea of presence. Using this discipline, it becomes possible to transform both the people on the stage and those who are watching them. Such a project coincided with a trend in contemporary theater to transform the audience instead of just entertaining it. There was much work being done on breaking down the barrier between performer and spectator. Some artists, such as Meredith Monk and Robert Wilson, destroyed the audience's typical expectations by presenting a series of nonconceptual sounds, images, and movements.

The creation of Mudra, the sound and perception cycles

One of the first programs given at Rocky Mountain Dharma Center in Colorado during the summer of 1972 was an encounter with the recently created theater group. The initial project was to develop Buddhist theater in America without Chögyam Trungpa's direct help.

During Chögyam Trungpa's three-month retreat at this time in Massachusetts, he wrote several plays, including *The Kingdom of Philosophy*, a philosophical tragedy based on the idea of a country governed entirely by

---

3. *Born in Tibet*, 4th ed. (2000), p. 92.

high-level philosophers who have power because of their philosophical discoveries; however, they pay little attention to the country's politics or economy.

At the same time, Chögyam Trungpa wrote his *Sound Cycles*, a series of pieces organized by the association of the syllables and vowels of English and Sanskrit words.[4] The Sound Cycles heighten the attention paid to words. With no involvement in psychological implications or the meaning of what is being said, the only requirement is to make the sounds of the words resonate and to make contact with their power: "These Sound Cycles are a means of relating to the space in which your vocal projection takes place."[5]

The theater group that Chögyam Trungpa had organized worked on this cycle, adding movements to the sounds. He began to become very intimately involved in the group and, using this cycle, presented several exercises on perception and the exploration of objects in space using the five buddha families. According to those working with him at the time, Chögyam Trungpa was like the sun radiating its beams in all directions. His brilliance was inspiring. For example, he precisely described how people enter into a relationship with reality, while guiding them through a very simple action, such as being in contact with a piece of wood. In this approach, you begin by making contact with the object visually, by "visual radiation," then by sound, which is space's perceptible aspect (and which surpasses our usual idea of sound, then by its smell—which Chögyam Trungpa said was like swimming in solid space and thus entering into relationship with the quality of things—and finally by touch, which he described as a deliberate action linked to a gesture of letting go (we can hold objects without really touching them). Even if this is an organic process that we usually do unconsciously, it is important to be aware of the various steps.

"In order to perform, we have to relate to reality. This is asking a lot, I suppose, but if we are going to give an enlightened performance, we have

---

4. This set of five texts, each one associated with one of the five buddha families, was published in the appendix of *Timely Rain*, pp. 203ff.

5. Chögyam Trungpa, "Sound Cycles," February 19, 1973, p. 1, unpublished.

to do it."[6] He invited his students to explore their way of connecting with reality with more curiosity. He told them that it did not matter whether they danced marvelously or acted brilliantly. The main point was to learn to be correctly in touch with things. It was necessary to return to a direct experience of the world that transcends our usual assumptions regarding reality. By using these exercises, Chögyam Trungpa could directly point to the moment when the mind unwinds into genuine, pure experience.

2. The Mudra Theater Meeting

In February 1973, Jean-Claude van Itallie and Chögyam Trungpa organized a large conference. Jean-Claude, a well-known American playwright and director, had first met Chögyam Trungpa in England around 1968. Together they had spent many hours discussing theater, and Jean-Claude had introduced Chögyam Trungpa to a number of avant-garde theater people in New York, beginning with Chögyam Trungpa's first visit to the city in 1970. Jean-Claude had arranged for Rinpoche to meet Peter Brook at some point as well. Thanks to grants they had received from the board of Theater Communications Group and the Theater Panel of the National Endowment for the Arts, groups with which Jean-Claude was affiliated, they invited several experimental theater companies, including the Open Theater, the Manhattan Project, the Byrd Hoffman School of Byrds, the Magic Theater of Berkeley, and the Provisional Open Theater of Los Angeles. Each company presented work representative of its theatrical approach with the idea of exploring the meeting points between various forms of the avant-garde and Chögyam Trungpa's meditative approach.

Chögyam Trungpa was very appreciative of the work of many of the groups that attended the conference. However, he did not at all like the work of the Iowa Theater Lab. He considered it based on a series of manipulations. This led to a somewhat confrontational discussion, after which the Iowa Theater Lab people left the Mudra conference.

---

6. Chögyam Trungpa, "Theater Meeting," February 8, 1973, unpublished.

The highlight of the meeting was the show put on by Robert Wilson and his company, the Byrd Hoffman School of Byrds, which surprised everybody.[7] The actors, holding candles, led the audience into a room full of oranges and apples. The oranges continuously rolled around the floor, creating a very slow visual effect. By emphasizing visual plasticity, he thus developed a living picture that was both immobile and in continuous, irresistible evolution. The young Buddhists did not understand what was happening and became irritated. They started to behave raucously and to eat the oranges, thus deflecting Robert Wilson's performance from its normal course.

Initially Chögyam Trungpa tried to stop them, but when he realized there was no hope of doing so, he also picked up an orange and ate it, as David Rome remembers.

This incident had an effect that could be viewed as shocking, negative, or provocative, depending on one's point of view. Some of the theater people were shocked by the attitude of the Buddhists, apparently even more so than Robert Wilson himself.

In the subsequent discussion, Chögyam Trungpa apologized somewhat on behalf of his students and tried to pacify the situation. Nonetheless, several companies decided to withdraw. Before they went, however, Chögyam Trungpa gave a talk on the ego of artists. Without the slightest fear or embarrassment about what had happened the day before, he used the situation and transformed it into teaching. He was unconcerned about how the participants would react or what they would say about him. Chögyam Trungpa never looked for anybody's approval, and this gave him the greatest liberty. At a moment of chaos, he taught about egolessness.

Because of their behavior the day before, most of the Buddhist students felt embarrassed. The historic meeting between the director Robert Wilson, one of the greatest artists of his day, and Chögyam Trungpa and

---

7. At the beginning of his career Robert Wilson had already directed *The Life and Times of Sigmund Freud* (1969) and *Deafman Glance* (1970). He became renowned in Europe after his success at the historic festival of Nancy (1971). That same year he directed *Overture* with Madeleine Renaud; in its French version, the show lasted seven days, twelve hours per day, from noon to midnight.

his sangha did not lead to future collaboration. Whether due to the naiveté of the students or to a difference between the approaches of the two men, each went his own way after the conference. But Chögyam Trungpa was not deterred by the problems that arose. Without regrets, he pressed onward.

When Chögyam Trungpa's students presented their work, they set up a huge installation of several rooms composed completely of newspapers. Each room was devoted to one of the five buddha families. In the center, representing the buddha family, Chögyam Trungpa sat on a chair with an empty seat in front of him so that participants could sit down and ask him questions. At this event, Chögyam Trungpa also asked two of his students, David Rome and Ruth Astor, to present the Sound Cycles with the movements that had been associated with them.

3. The Intensification Exercises

The day after this theater meeting, Chögyam Trungpa presented a series of new exercises to his own theater students. Although the meeting had been only a partial success, it was now a catalyst for making progress. A new page of Mudra theater was turned.

The exercises he presented were based on his conviction that all actors must develop a presence born of their physical and psychological way of being in relation with space. For space is, in effect, the backdrop of all performances and accommodates all activities. Thus, one of the key points of the dzogchen teachings—the vajrayana appreciation of space—assumes a particularly pragmatic aspect when applied to the theater.

As he explained: "As I see it, the study of acting doesn't seem particularly to be the training of one's body or voice to develop some highly skilled technical ability. The problem in acting is not being able to relate with the space which surrounds the body. In other words, the problem is in the relationship between the projector (which is the actor in this case) and the projections (which is the audience). Unless we are able to develop a sense of sympathy with ourselves and a sense of sympathy with space, there is a tendency to become hostile and feel a need to impress the audience. Or we become self-conscious, which automatically creates a solid, frozen space where it is difficult to move or speak, and we find ourselves imprisoned in this solid space."[8]

To allow us to comprehend the confused way we connect with space, within the context of presenting the Mudra exercises, Chögyam Trungpa posited that, contrary to what is generally thought, space is full and solid. Instead of focusing on what is happening inside us, he asked everyone doing the Mudra exercises to look outside, into space, and to experience how its richness seems about to crush us.

In these exercises the view that is adopted is that what we think of as our bodies is in fact space, and what we consider to be empty space, outside our bodies, is in fact mind.

To bring this across, he presented several series of exercises that intensify our bodies and the space around them in an increasingly solid way. This is how he presented the first one:

> In order to learn to relate with space, we have to learn to intensify the body and build intensive situations as much as possible. Can you just try to feel the space around your body? Pull your muscles as if space is crowding in on you. Clench your teeth and your toes.... Very strange to say, in order to learn how to relax, you have to develop really solid tenseness. You can breathe out and breathe in, but don't rest your breath, just develop complete intensification. Then you begin to feel that space is closing in on you. In order to relate with space, you have to relate with tension.[9]

This notion of intensification is quite unusual. It is a metaphor for an indescribable experience. When Chögyam Trungpa presented this practice, nobody knew how to interpret what was happening. Although there was a confusing element to it, especially at the beginning, the students' devotion and trust in their teacher generally led them to follow the discipline he suggested.

---

8. Chögyam Trungpa, unpublished talk to theater group, no date.

9. Ibid.

The first series of exercises produces an intensification of space, of the limbs, then of the torso, heart, and head. As he himself put it, it is a way of working with the principles of shamatha meditation and the development of peace, in other words, connecting with space while intensifying our attention on something precise.

The second series of intensification exercises included three exercises: learning to stand, a walking practice, and an exercise based on monastic dancing. This series corresponds to the principles of vipashyana meditation. This is a logical succession: "Having been born, so to speak, now you can try to stand and then we'll begin to walk and then we'll introduce the monastic dance which I studied in Tibet."

These exercises are extremely difficult. Participants take turns guiding the practitioners and encouraging them to intensify more and more. That leader is called the shadow. Fenja Heupers, who took part in this group, explains her surprise the first time she tried the exercises. Although she had been learning to release her body for some years, using a variety of different techniques, in this case it was necessary to make extremely intense physical efforts to strengthen all of the body's muscles. She did not understand the point of what she was doing, but as it constantly intrigued her, she carried on. She then learned how to synchronize her body and mind and to develop a feeling of presence in the world.

This practice can utterly alter one's understanding of experience. Normally, we pay no attention to space. All of our attention is fixed on the thing or person we are making contact with. We notice a good-looking person going by in the street, or the glass of water we are going to drink, and not the space itself. Through intensification, our attention changes direction. The central idea is that the moment of intensification should lead to basic release. Learning this is a passport to open space and a radical way of cutting through samsara: "This becomes extremely irritating and painful, but at the same time it provides some basic sanity in that you are forced to relate to the space."[10]

The experience of intensification that Chögyam Trungpa highlighted in the Mudra exercises was not the only arena in which he created

---

10. Ibid.

intensification for his students. These guided exercises in intensification had a strong kinship to what students felt in the presence of Rinpoche himself. He could create a sense of very solid and claustrophobic space around himself or a sense of vast and open space with no boundaries. The point of Mudra practice—like other practices he developed or emphasized, and like being in his presence altogether—was to learn to cultivate a sense of basic existence that does not depend on any reference point. Chögyam Trungpa intensified many situations rather than making them more relaxed.

4. Mudra, Dzogchen, and Mahamudra

Chögyam Trungpa pointed out that the intensification exercises that he had presented were not his own inventions, but in fact derived directly from the dzogchen tradition, the ultimate teachings of the Tibetan tradition. Although he did not emphasize this aspect, instead preferring that his students simply perform the exercises, he explained on a number of occasions how they fit into the tradition: "A lot of the exercises are sort of maha ati yoga practices. They are what's known as the Four Torches. Actually, the maha ati doesn't talk about space; it talks about wind or air. The first one, the wind of karma, is related with muscles and intensification of limbs. So, in other words, your limbs are related as kinds of tools to grab things with, which is connected with karma's volitional action. If you relate with the wind of karma, which is that creation of space within your muscles, you relate with the space or the air which is contained within the muscles. The second one is related with creating space through the eyes and has to do with the wind of emotions or kleshas. The third one is the wind of body. It is connected to the earth and the four elements. The last one is called inner luminosity. It is connected with brain and heart together, which is something very subtle."[11]

---

11. "Intensification Exercises," February 24, 1973, unpublished. The three winds (elements) are derived from the three kayas. In the context of Mudra, Chögyam Trungpa presented dharmakaya and sambhogakaya practices.

Relating to space, which is crucial to dzogchen, was explored using the first three exercises in the first Mudra series that he presented. Chögyam Trungpa then introduced some of the symbols of mahamudra, which he did by presenting more advanced movements. These were derived from heruka dances, dances of male deities in the vajrayana.[12] Chögyam Trungpa spoke little about the significance of the exercises he gave. Instead, he emphasized the practice itself and encouraged naked experience, free from any concept. Again and again, he taught how to be—quite simply and ultimately, to be.

5. The Mudra Group

After the presentation of the intensification exercises following the conference, a Mudra theater group was officially set up, meeting as often as three times a week. Thirty people took part in the group on a regular basis in Boulder.[13] Chögyam Trungpa asked that a roll call be conducted before every session, and those who were absent too often were no longer permitted to participate. He wanted genuine commitment.

Chögyam Trungpa often attended these group sessions, observing how everyone performed the various exercises. He often pushed the students to intensify their efforts even more, then afterward answered their questions.

The exercises can have an extremely profound effect. They are so direct that they create a highly emotional atmosphere. Andy Karr was struck several years later, when he started his formal tantric practice, to find the atmosphere quite similar. There is an extreme or heightened clarity that makes the slightest klesha, or conflictual emotion, very sharp.

---

12. Unlike many other teachers, Chögyam Trungpa always presented dzogchen as superior to mahamudra, while insisting on their complementary nature.

13. Other groups were started in New York and in Berkeley, California.

6. The Second Meeting: Being and Projecting in Space

For the second Mudra meeting, in 1976, Chögyam Trungpa invited only members of the community, and he introduced several new exercises.

One of these is called "Being," which, in contrast with most of those described in this chapter, has been extensively practiced in various centers ever since.

Standing in a circle, the participants become aware of the space around them, of the earth beneath and the vastness of space above. They remain standing, looking in front of them, but not at anything in particular. They thus develop a panoramic awareness. They *are*.

"First you work with the sense of existence. You are standing and you are there. Feel that basic sense of being. Then, in order to prove that existence, you have to do something, to project out. Finally, you begin to feel some sort of play back and forth, as the projector and the projection relate together. So in the practice, you go slowly through the threefold process of perception: the sense of being, the sense of doing, and the sense of linking together."[14]

Then someone starts moving, slowly enters the circle, turns around the person to their left, passes behind, then goes back to the center of the circle, walks toward the next person, and then continues in the same way until they return to their place. At that moment, the person to their left starts walking in the same way. Meanwhile, the others simply remain still, feeling the way space is modified when someone passes by them and then moves away. But this attention is not psychological; it is directed at the very nature of space.

Many of the later Mudra exercises require the use of long bamboo sticks, which Chögyam Trungpa had seen Peter Brook use when they met in New York. In one of them, two rows of people are face to face. They walk forward and meet while holding sticks vertically, then horizontally. The stick is an extension of the self and allows us to understand that our awareness extends farther than we realize. When presenting this exercise, Chögyam Trungpa used to tell how, when he was a child, he often held a

---

14. "Being and Projecting," in *Dharma Art*, p. 56.

mirror to direct the sun's beams toward the peak of a mountain. Just as these beams can touch distant objects, our awareness can spread in a precise fashion. We simply have to learn to project our feeling of presence.

7. The Plays

Chögyam Trungpa's work led to staging plays, which were often written by him or else by his students during workshops. The main point for him was to show the essence of a theatrical experience and how it can help us become genuinely human.

As in the theater, where what happens on the stage is instantly realized, the content of one of Chögyam Trungpa's talks might be forgotten, but the way he spoke, answered questions, played with his fan, or drank his glass of water struck those who came to see him. Such is true theater: a way of making a particular moment surge up instantly.

Chögyam Trungpa insisted on the point that being on stage meant being natural: being an actor or dancer first meant learning how to be simply and fully on stage. This sense of presence can only be developed if a sane relationship is established with the space around us.

Chögyam Trungpa warned his students against the ambition that pushes people to look for success along a well-worn track. Actors, like all artists, lose their dignity and vision if they strive to please their audience. Attention should not be focused on the spectators.

In this way, there is a clear link between acting on stage and living out our lives. There is no fundamental difference. We are always playing parts and can at all moments pay full attention to them. Art is an extension of our normal lives: "Our goal is not to reach Broadway-Nirvana particularly. Anyway, Broadway is not my idea of Nirvana. We are more interested in changing people's perceptions about theater."[15]

Chögyam Trungpa's vision was to have the Mudra group become a full-time theater company, with the actors living together in an intentional community, so that their work would become a kind of sadhana,

---

15. "Theater Meeting," February 15, 1973, unpublished.

or spiritual practice. His idea was to produce Western plays, especially those of Shakespeare and Samuel Beckett, and to study the Japanese Noh plays and Kabuki, while creating new forms of theater. Once again, Chögyam Trungpa proved his incredible ability to show how the dharma can bring the most genuine and lively forces into all areas of life. I have already mentioned how he met many of the important artists of his day, from Robert Wilson to Peter Brook and Meredith Monk. He was deeply inspired by them, while he communicated to them the ancestral wisdom he had inherited. Even though the Mudra group ceased to be a major focus for students at the end of the 1970s, the teachings behind it have continued to inspire many people and helped to train entire generations of actors and dancers at Naropa University. Mudra both casts a bright light on what theater really is and makes its magic inherent.

Mudra also offers a path toward a deep understanding of Buddhism's highest teaching. Leaving aside the backdrop of the theater, where they were devised, such practices allow us to discover the nature of the unconditional space in which we live without being fully aware of it.

A parallel can be drawn with Maitri Space Awareness. In both cases, extremely profound teachings were presented in a particular context: one psychology, and the other the theater. Today, it has been understood that these practices can be of great help to practitioners, and the context in which they were first presented—the theater or psychology—is secondary. Their depth is limitless.

Finally, they can teach the most vital contemplative truths to a large number of people who do not necessarily know all the subtleties of Buddhist thought. They are an exceptionally practical means of transmitting contemplative experience beyond intellectual understanding.

Chapter Ten

PRESENTING THE SHAMBHALA TEACHINGS

STUDENT: *Could you talk about the Tibetan legends concerning the Kingdom of Shambhala?*

CHÖGYAM TRUNGPA: *Shambhala was an enlightened society that manifested nonagression. Its geographical location was in the middle of Asia, in the middle, or the heart, of the Orient. The Shambhala society was able to transmute aggression into love. Consequently, everybody in Shambhala attained enlightenment. So they no longer needed to domesticate their animals, and they no longer needed to fight wars. Finally, the whole society, the whole country—including all the buildings—ceased to exist on the earthly plane. That is the story of Shambhala.*

STUDENT: *Do you think the Kingdom of Shambhala will manifest again on a worldwide scale as a Golden or Enlightened Age?*

CHÖGYAM TRUNGPA: *You bet.*

STUDENT: *Do you have any time frame for that, say a hundred years or two hundred years from now?*

CHÖGYAM TRUNGPA: *Right now. It is possible.*

STUDENT: *Many lamas have said it may happen within a hundred or two hundred years.*

CHÖGYAM TRUNGPA: *That's speculation. It happens right now.*[1]

---

1. *Great Eastern Sun*, p. 193–194.

*The Buddha said that when buddhadharma degenerates
in the world, the Shambhala tradition will revitalize it.*[2]
—THRANGU RINPOCHE

CHÖGYAM TRUNGPA'S VISION was based not only on Buddhism but
also on the inspiration to establish the Kingdom of Shambhala. But in
North America it was not until 1976 that he publicly referred to this
source.[3]

1. The Vision of the Kingdom of Shambhala

On the Silk Route, there were many legends and mythical or historic tales
concerning the existence of a peaceful, prosperous kingdom, called
Shambhala. Its inhabitants lived in dignity and in profound harmony
with one another.

This land was a source of inspiration for the cultural, artistic, political, and military traditions throughout much of Asia:[4] "Shambhala is a

---

2. Thrangu Rinpoche, in *Vajradhatu Sun*, June/July 1980, p. 4.

3. In many respects, this chapter deals with the deepest and most secret heart of Chögyam
Trungpa's teachings. After a great deal of hesitation and despite my limited abilities, it
seemed necessary to make this attempt at explaining the teachings in their most intimate
depth; otherwise the rest of Chögyam Trungpa's work could not be explored in full. But it
must be stated right from the start of this chapter that its contents are at the limit of my own
understanding, and I ask the reader not to forget that a proper presentation of the Shambhala teachings would require several volumes. I also acknowledge my debt to David Rome,
who gave so much help in this endeavor with astonishing depth and liberty, and to Carolyn
Gimian, whose observations were crucial.

4. "That particular vision broke down into the Taoist tradition and the Bön tradition of
Tibet, the Islamic tradition of the Middle East, and whatever tradition Russia might have."
Chögyam Trungpa, "Introduction to the Principle of the Shambhala Tradition," Naropa In-
stitute, Summer 1979.

Central Asian culture, which is neither Aryan nor Mongolian. It is a unified tradition, one which we have long forgotten altogether."[5]

Among the Tibetans, there is a popular belief that this kingdom still exists, hidden in some distant valleys of the Himalayas, perhaps even in Afghanistan. In many respects it is like our Atlantis. There are spiritual works, such as the *Great Commentary on Kalachakra* by Mipham Rinpoche, that would allow an explorer to retrace its location, just as Heinrich Schliemann used the *Iliad* to find the ruins of Troy.

The Kingdom of Shambhala is said to be surrounded by iron mountains. From the outside, its shape is circular, and it is circled by snowy mountains. Inside, it is shaped like a blooming lotus with eight petals. Between each of these petals flows a wide stream that separates them. From a distance it looks like a small town, but once the traveler is inside, it so vast that its limits are measureless.[6]

Shambhala is supposed to be located to the north of India and the Himalayas, beyond the river Sita, in what is now eastern Turkestan. But fundamentally, as Chögyam Trungpa explained, it is to be found "in the middle of Asia, in the middle, or the heart, of the Orient."[7] It is the physical and spiritual axis of this region of the world. The people enjoy excellent harvests, great wealth, happiness, and freedom from illness. All the inhabitants devote their time to meditation.

The path leading to Shambhala is above all a spiritual one. If ordinary persons went there, all they would see would be an uninhabited dusty valley surrounded by daunting mountains. It is only by purifying their

---

5. Ibid.

6. "According to the *Great Commentary on the Kalacakra* by the renowned nineteenth-century Buddhist teacher Mipham, the land of Shambhala is north of the river Sita, and the country is divided by eight mountain ranges. The palace of the Rigdens, the imperial rulers of Shambhala, is built on top of a circular mountain in the center of the country. This mountain, Mipham tells us, is named Kailasa. The palace, which is called the palace of Kalapa, comprises many square miles." *Shambhala: The Sacred Path of the Warrior* (Shambhala Library, 2003), p. 6.

7. Chögyam Trungpa, "A Question of Heart," public talk, Vancouver, July 29, 1982, in *Great Eastern Sun*, p. 193.

hearts and setting them right that travelers can reach it. The kingdom is liberated by correct intention.

The main point for Chögyam Trungpa was just this inspiration. There is no contradiction in the answers to questions such as: Does the Kingdom of Shambhala really exist? Is it somewhere on earth? Is it hidden in another dimension of reality? These questions demonstrate the human aspiration to live in a true community. Such a deep desire requires recognition. Instead of causing us to waste our time over projects we would like to carry out in the future, it inspires us to open to our present moment. It is an invitation for us to manifest our own dignity in all its greatness.

The Shambhala vision displays the basic unity that exists between the spiritual perspective and social life. In the words of Chögyam Trungpa: "The kingdom of Shambhala could be said to be a mythical kingdom or a real kingdom. . . . Spirituality was secularized, meaning that day-to-day living situations were handled properly. Life was not based on the worship of a deity or on vigorous religious practice, as such. Rather, that wonderful world of Shambhala was based on actually relating with your life, your body, your food, your household, your marital situation, your breath, your environment, your atmosphere."[8]

While Buddhist teachings emphasize the need for renunciation from civil society—as in the example of the Buddha himself, who reached enlightenment after giving up his throne and leaving home—the Shambhala vision invites all of us to work at building the kingdom: "Many religions have encouraged individuals to become monks or nuns. Although monasticism is very natural, in some sense, it's also a heightened or rarefied level of existence. In the Shambhala teachings our main concern is working with society. We want to develop an enlightened society that will be based on the idea of pure letting go."[9]

Some Eastern traditions encourage those who aspire to a truly spiri-

---

8. Chögyam Trungpa, "The Kingdom, the Cocoon, the Great Eastern Sun," public talk, Boston, March 27, 1980, in *Great Eastern Sun*, p. 6.

9. *Great Eastern Sun*, p. 45.

tual life to free themselves from normal social ties. They ask their adepts to give up family life, jobs, and any form of amusement. They instruct their followers to beg for what they need rather than buy and sell (and thus work for a living).

By asking his own students to marry and get jobs, Chögyam Trungpa was not renouncing part of the authentic Tradition. He was not watering it down, nor was he adapting it. Instead he was bringing out its ultimate purpose. He was asking his students to see all appearances, everything that we perceive, from a viewpoint of awareness (*rikpa*), and so develop a sacred vision that would allow them to understand the primordial purity of all phenomena.

Shambhala teachings do not ask us to abandon the world of relative truth (*kundzop*) for that of ultimate truth (*döndam*), because they are intrinsically one. In this way, these teachings are basically coherent with all those given by Chögyam Trungpa. For example, the title of his first book, *Meditation in Action*, affirms at once that it is in the heat of ordinary action that spiritual fulfillment should take place.

2. Discovering in Our Hearts a Sense of Genuine Initiation

In this era, we are totally alienated from ourselves, and we have lost the connection with initiation, or transmission of spiritual influence or traditional teachings. This is what is generally called the spiritual crisis of the West.

The various forms of transmission no longer touch us. They seem so far removed and abstract that no one knows how to incorporate them into their lives. Their capacity to transform the existences of those who receive them has been considerably reduced. The traditional chain of initiation has been broken.

Shambhala teachings offer the possibility of rediscovering a spiritual path that does not rely on any dogmas, even though it is profoundly rooted in the most ancient Tradition. Although such teachings may be

Traditional, they are not religious.[10] Instead, they invite all of us to discover the path *in ourselves*. In this way, the statement that the Kingdom of Shambhala really exists in each person's heart is not just a simple image, but describes accurately everybody's deepest aspiration.

In the "holy night" that has fallen on the West, which is spoken of by Hölderlin,[11] genuine spirituality is no longer commonplace. There then exist several possibilities. You can invent new paths to suit yourself by listening to your "inner voice" (while running the risk of reducing this opening to an individual psychological process unsupported by any real discipline); you can adopt the dogmas of a religion and so acquire the reference points you need to be sure you are on the right path; or else, inside yourself, you can discover the path of a totally different Tradition.

It is this last possibility that Chögyam Trungpa offered in such a striking way in his Shambhala teachings. Over and above all morality, all norms of behavior, everyone must find their own intimate path home, which involves rediscovering their own heart. Such a discovery is inseparable from any true discipline, and it can only be done by renouncing our own frivolousness. But this apprenticeship solves no problems. Instead, by opening the way, it pushes us to a deeper exploration of our relationship with ourselves and the world. Thus, such a path does not protect us from the harshness of reality and the distress of our era; it actually draws us inside them more completely.

Basic goodness

The human heart is the "invariable middle" where the kingdom can be found. It cannot be sullied or stained. Whenever we encounter it in its fundamental nakedness, we experience what Chögyam Trungpa called

---

10. It would be useful here to refer to the distinction between religion and initiation as it appears in the work of René Guénon, who considered that "religion views being only as an individual human state and has absolutely no aim to remove it from this situation, but instead aims to guarantee the most favorable conditions in its present state." *Aperçus sur l'initiation* (Perspectives on Initiation) (Paris: Éditions Traditionnelles, 1992), p. 27.

11. In the poem "Brot und Wein" (Bread and Wine), Friedrich Hölderlin describes the situation of humanity after the departure of the gods.

basic goodness.[12] This expression is one of the central notions of this teaching. We must now try to understand it, because it is the ground in which we can plant the seed of an enlightened society.

Basic goodness is the purity inherent in *all* experience, the openness that is present in every situation. Thus it cannot be conditioned by the circumstances we find ourselves in. This primordial state is free of any stains, in other words, of any doubts or concepts that distance it from spontaneous direct experience. Even if the basic opening has been covered over, like the sky with clouds, it can never be altered, just as clouds never damage the sky.

Basic goodness manifests itself in every instant of pure presence. Even if they are fleeting, such instants form a continuity in our experience that puts us in touch with something beyond all measure.

The important word in this expression is *basic*, because it indicates the *primordial aspect of experience*, independent of any circumstances. At first sight, there seems to be a clear paradox: how can basic goodness indicate an *experience* that is so radical if, by definition, experience is of the greatest fragility? For the philosopher Kant, what is independent of all experience is precisely what creates the very possibility of experience! In this sense, basic goodness is the precondition of all experience.

It is possible to become enlightened through the unconditional.

As for the word *goodness*, it comes across as surprising, even irritating, given all the evil, deception, cowardice, and hypocrisy we constantly see in ourselves and in the world. But this is not a moral term. It is not the expression of Chögyam Trungpa's personal opinion to say that we are all good—that would be incredibly naive; instead the point is to make us aware of our tendency not to see the openness, both basic and good, that constitutes us. For we do not recognize this openness when it manifests

---

12. "In Tibetan, basic goodness is known as kadak." Chögyam Trungpa, *1983 Seminary Transcripts: Vajrayana* (Boulder: Vajradhatu Publications), p. 71. *Kadak* is the ultimate point of the maha ati, or dzogchen, the main doctrine of the Nyingma school. It is a teaching of ultimate or primordial purity. This teaching is considered by its adepts to be the final and most secret message of the lessons of the Buddha, because of the radical way it explains the ultimate nature of the mind and reality.

itself. We find such experiences too harsh and vivid, and we prefer to ignore them.

The word *goodness* accentuates the term *basic* to make us sense its true resonance. The word functions more as a teaching device than as an expression of theory. It is not an affirmation concerning reality—Chögyam Trungpa was not a philosopher—but instead an invitation to let the primordial space of our own nature unravel in all its fullness. When we relax into what is basic, its "goodness" appears, even if the tender heart itself is, properly speaking, neither good nor bad. It simply is what it is. Chögyam Trungpa used the term *goodness* with extraordinary accuracy, for etymologically it means "without fault." Basic goodness is faultless because it is unborn, and so cannot die. It is unconditional; it depends on nothing. In an interview in 1985, Chögyam Trungpa affirmed: "Usually, religion is connected with punishing yourself. People still tend to take original sin seriously. They should let go of that. Maybe basic goodness will replace original sin!"[13] Before any judgment, before any doctrine, it is possible to make contact with our own intelligence, as we can with true reality, and discover the resources it contains.

Whatever our situation, our confusion, our resources or psychological state, basically nothing can threaten our richness and dignity.

However, to realize this and remain in the experience of basic goodness, we must look directly at who we are. In our society, the idea of stopping and simply encountering our own experience, or the situation as it is, seems almost absurd. We are constantly running around and scattering our energies through any number of activities. Once again, the practice of meditation provides the opportunity to slow down. It is not a technique that aims to produce an effect, but a means to rest in the most elementary nature of our own hearts.

By making contact with our hearts, we realize that a state of primordial enlightenment exists inside us. For example, at the same time that we see the purple color of the tablecloth in the kitchen, the white wall,

---

13. Chögyam Trungpa, "Pragmatism and Practice: An Interview with Vajracharya the Ven. Trungpa Rinpoche," *Vajradhatu Sun*, June/July 1985, pp. 1 and 8. Reprinted in *The Collected Works of Chögyam Trungpa*, vol. 8.

a chair, a tree, a passerby, we know that we are seeing. Even when we are asleep, our basic intelligence still exists: we are awake. In other words, we have the ability to pay *attention* to our bodies, our feelings, our states of mind.

Another aspect of this state of enlightenment, this opening that constitutes a human being, is gentleness and sensitivity. Whatever our culture, race, or education, humans are born with this basic tenderness, this capacity to be touched by the world, to feel sad and to cry, to feel joyful. These are extremely simple qualities (which we may or may not recognize and cultivate). When we are genuine, we appreciate the world. This can be as simple as the way the bark curves on a tree, a mangy dog biting its tail, clouds crossing the sky and announcing snow, the fact of missing a train that pulls away at the very moment you arrive on the platform, or a particularly well-performed piece of music. Suddenly, we are moved. This is the germ of an opening that can be termed the experience of basic goodness.

So this phrase means a state of presence and naked awareness, the tenderness and gentleness of an open heart, and the ultimate experience of enlightenment with its benevolence toward others. In such moments, the world appears sharper and simpler: "When things become so wretched and so poor, the appreciation of simplicity has completely gone wrong. Therefore we have to introduce some dignity and goodness into the situation. Human beings have lost their strength; they have become feeble."[14] In this way, spontaneously emerging sense perceptions are all opportunities to connect with basic goodness.

Basic goodness is at the heart of the Shambhala teachings. For many people, it is a veritable koan[15] whose true resonance can only be reached in the practice of meditation. It is both the ground of the path and its

---

14. Chögyam Trungpa, *1981 Kalapa Assembly Transcripts* (Boulder: Vajradhatu Publications), p. 19.

15. In Zen, a koan is a paradoxical sentence that makes no logical or rational sense. Its "solution" requires a sudden change in the level of understanding. Zen students are given koans on which they then meditate, until they perceive an ultimate reality beyond all contradictions or dualistic ideas.

fruition. After this apprenticeship in learning to recognize, again and again, each moment of our singular experience, we discover the unconditional possibility of trusting our own hearts. Such is the beginning of what Chögyam Trungpa called the "path of the warrior": learning to recognize the manifestations of basic goodness in the living present while remaining in its primordial state in an ever more constant way.

Fear

Shambhala: The Sacred Path of the Warrior opens with a mythical evocation like so many found in spiritual traditions: evoking a treasure that has been lost or hidden.[16] In this case, it is the complete allegiance of human society to basic goodness:

> From the great cosmic mirror
> Without beginning and without end,
> Human society became manifest.
> At that time liberation and confusion arose.
> When fear and doubt occurred
> Towards the confidence which is primordially free,
> Countless multitudes of cowards arose.
> When the confidence which is primordially free
> Was followed and delighted in,
> Countless multitudes of warriors arose.[17]

---

16. "It is well known that in nearly all traditions, allusion is made to something that is hidden or has disappeared, which, however, is symbolized and always has the same basic meaning, or even meanings, because, as in all symbolism, there are many, but they are always tightly linked together. In reality, it is always a matter of spiritual obscurity, in terms of the law of cycles, that arrives in the history of humanity; thus it is above all a loss of the primordial state, and, as a direct consequence, also the loss of the corresponding tradition, because it is one with the very knowledge that is essentially implied in the possession of such a state." René Guénon, *Parole perdue et mots substitués* in *Etudes sur le Franc-Maçonnerie et le compagnonnage*, vol. 2 (Paris: Études Traditionnelles, 1984), p. 26.

17. *Shambhala: The Sacred Path of the Warrior* (Shambhala Library, 2003), p. 3. It is interesting to compare this fall with the one René Guénon describes: "When man was separated

To Chögyam Trungpa's mind, the reason for this loss of confidence in basic goodness, which obscures humanity's primary nature to the point of making it inhumane, is neither unbridled passion nor original sin, nor even materialism, language, the market economy, or technology, but . . . *fear* (or, to be even more precise, our fear of fear).

This separation did not happen at a moment in time; it occurs constantly. Chögyam Trungpa interpreted this as both a mythical origin and something we experience all the time. At each moment, we have the choice between confronting our fear and running away from it. The openness of basic goodness and its nakedness are frightening.

In this context, fear does not mean being scared of something in particular that may or may not happen, such as thunderstorms or spiders. Instead, it stands for a kind of anxiety, a sensation of basic inadequacy that darkens everything we do. The threat in such fear lies nowhere; it is completely indeterminate.

Fear itself is not an obstacle. It is a sign of contact with the brilliance of the opening. But its denial, being "afraid of fear," shuts the door of our heart. By thus running away, we manipulate our experience and turn away from ourselves. There are countless strategies that can be used to take our minds off things and amuse ourselves, but this only succeeds in chasing away all those fleeting moments of presence that strip us naked.

Generally, we do not even recognize the sort of experience of fear that Chögyam Trungpa defined. All we see are the reactions we have in order to avoid it. In this way we weave a sort of cocoon to shield ourselves from all the sharp and jagged aspects of the real world. This cocoon is the reason basic goodness and the Kingdom of Shambhala have been stifled and obscured. The fear of fear that Chögyam Trungpa described is a matter of wrapping our hearts, in the hope of finding security, under layers of protection that make us less and less sensitive.

Adopting a pose, fidgeting, chatting about nothing, or drowning ourselves in our habitual thoughts are all examples of ways in which we stop

---

from his primordial center, and was thus shut up in the temporal sphere, he could no longer reach the unique point whence all things can be contemplated in their aspect . . . of being primordial." *Le Roi du Monde* (*The Lord of the World*) (Paris: Gallimard, 1958).

anything sharp or real from happening to us. We are running away from our hearts. We prefer "to hide in our personal jungles and caves. When we hide from the world in this way, we feel secure. We may think we have quieted our fear, but we are actually making ourselves numb with fear."[18]

Once again, the problem is not with fear but with the cowardice that makes us incapable of bearing it: "In order to experience fearlessness, it is necessary to experience fear."[19] Cowardice "is to embed ourselves in this cocoon, in which we perpetuate our habitual patterns. When we are constantly re-creating our basic patterns of behavior and thought, we never have to leap into fresh air or onto fresh ground."[20]

The warrior

Courage is the quality that the warrior develops. In this case, the word *warrior* does not mean someone who manifests aggression and violence like a stock character in a Hollywood war movie, but rather a sort of knight from the Middle Ages, or a Japanese samurai, who fights against the desire for personal victory. The Tibetan term *pawo* means "those who are valiant," who are entirely loyal to the brilliance of basic goodness, the ground from which everything emerges.

If you are a warrior, what matters is not to affirm or impose yourself on others, but instead to be faithful to your own heart. This courage consists in allowing your heart to be open and vulnerable. In the words of Jeremy Hayward: "When you stay in tune with your own heart and feel its quality without judging it or impulsively reacting to it, you will discover beneath all the emotional highlights a deeper, tender, more constant feeling. At the core of the heart is a sense of profound, unwavering sadness and joy that comes from being truly open to the world and responding deeply to it."[21]

---

18. *Shambhala: The Sacred Path of the Warrior* (Shambhala Library, 2003), pp. 52–53.

19. Ibid., p. 34.

20. Ibid., p. 53.

21. Jeremy Hayward, *Sacred World: A Guide to Shambhala Warriorship in Daily Life* (New York: Bantam New Age, 1995), p. 124.

Normally, we are afraid of the depth of such a feeling that strips us bare. The true warrior, says Chögyam Trungpa, should be "sad and tender, and because of that, the warrior can be very brave as well. Without that heartfelt sadness, bravery is brittle, like a china cup. If you drop it, it will break or chip."[22]

At a time when everyone seeks pleasure and personal comfort, and when this is even the declared purpose of many pseudospiritual paths and therapeutic techniques, Chögyam Trungpa showed that cultivating "heartfelt sadness" is the true path. We should not immunize ourselves against the world, but instead open ourselves to it if we want to be fully human. "What man, while fleeing sadness, can ever be touched by a living breath?" wrote Martin Heidegger.[23]

This is another example of Chögyam Trungpa's attention to language. The word *sad* comes from the Latin *satis*, which means "enough." We thus find a sense of fullness and richness in the term that also appears in the word *satisfaction*. So sadness has nothing to do with the common conception that sees it as a form of depression. In fact it is the natural quality of the human heart that is both tender and full. This impartial experience of plenitude draws everything together into a profound unity.

The warrior who confronts his existence and fear produces a powerful form of dignity—*wangthang*, a Tibetan term that literally means "field of power," but Chögyam Trungpa preferred to translate it as "authentic presence." Such a feeling of power provides profound confidence that radiates and puts us in direct contact with reality. It is the life force manifested at its peak.

Such a power cannot confirm our existence, or else it will change into poison; instead it is a wind of joy that strips us bare: "The personal experience of this wind comes as a feeling of being completely and powerfully in the present."[24] So there is no reason to be afraid of this power, even if

---

22. *Shambhala: The Sacred Path of the Warrior* (Shambhala Library, 2003), p. 38.

23. Martin Heidegger, *L'expérience de la pensée*, question 3, trans. André Préau (Paris: Gallimard, 1966), p. 27.

24. *Shambhala: The Sacred Path of the Warrior* (Shambhala Library, 2003), p. 124.

our society generally reduces such displays of brilliance and vigor to a uniform level.

Chögyam Trungpa taught his students specific practices designed to rouse this force and even to ride it.

3. The Shambhala Teachings: A Complete Cycle of Termas

While still young, Chögyam Trungpa had shown a great interest in this vision of Shambhala and in the teachings or popular stories associated with it. He heard some of them from his mother. Chögyam Trungpa's relationship with her is extremely moving. He protected her so that she could stay close to his monastery and regularly visited her. He wanted contact with her and her story:

"People in our village were often shy if somebody asked them their family name," he wrote. "Once I asked my mother, when I was about four or five, before I started my education:

> "Mother, what is our name?"
>
> She was very shy. She said, "What do you mean by *our*? You know that your name is Trungpa Rinpoche."
>
> But I insisted. . . .
>
> She said, "Well, you should forget that. It's a very humble name, and you might be ashamed of it." . . .
>
> I kept asking and finally she said, "Mukpo, Mukpo of course."
>
> And I distinctly remember asking her whether I was her son who came out of her body, and at first she said, "Yes."[25]

In the context of the Shambhala teachings, Chögyam Trungpa later decided to use the family name Mukpo. His Shambhala title was Dorje Dradül of Mukpo. *Dorje Dradül* means "Indestructible Warrior," and this is the name he used when he signed the texts he wrote about the

---

25. Ibid., pp. 93–94.

Shambhala teachings. He thus affirmed the importance of his family heritage.

This refusal to push his mother out of his spiritual world is both a celebration of his family heritage and a way of honoring feminine energy, which he himself qualified as "threefold: unborn, unceasing, and its nature is like that of space, or sky. So the question of unborn, in this case, is that the basic ground has manifested itself. It is taking a direction towards reality, through a sense of love, compassion and warmth."[26]

These two aspects, family lineage and feminine energy, are crucial to any understanding of the Shambhala teachings. They are a way of making us appreciate the wealth that lies hidden in our own culture, and they place feminine energy at the heart of the path.

Chögyam Trungpa knew from his family that he was descended from Gesar of Ling, a famous warrior in an epic poem that was recited by all the bards of Tibet: "He's part of my ancestry already. He is part of my blood and flesh. If you actually relate with the notion that you have dignity which comes from your family lineage, then there is a general sense of appreciation of all your demeanor."[27]

This is how he explained these two forms of lineage: one, family; the other, spiritual: "They both exist simultaneously in order to protect each other."[28] The Shambhala teachings are also there to teach us to connect with the wisdom of our family lineage (but in a larger sense that is not dependent on birthright).

As a young man, Chögyam Trungpa witnessed the invasion of Tibet by the Chinese, but this did not discourage him: "The minute the Communist troops began to march through our property in the Surmang Monastery, I thought that a greater society of buddhadharma could be created, that a greater vision could be executed properly. Since then, and continuously, my Shambhala vision has never diminished."[29]

---

26. Chögyam Trungpa, *Glimpses of Shunyata* (Halifax: Vajradhatu Publications, 1999), p. 9.

27. Chögyam Trungpa, *1978 Kalapa Assembly Transcripts* (Boulder: Vajradhatu Publications), p. 176.

28. Ibid., p. 177.

29. Ibid., p. 198.

In the midst of this confusion and panic, many wondered if they should flee, and turned to Chögyam Trungpa for advice. At this difficult moment, he decided to go into retreat. (He also needed to go into hiding because there was a price on his head and the Chinese were looking for him.) He devoted this retreat to connecting with the Shambhala vision, as Lady Künchok, a young nun who went with him, remembers. During this time, he wrote a text of over a thousand pages that was "an allegory of the Kingdom of Shambhala and its sovereign who freed humanity after the dark ages."[30] Unfortunately, this text was lost when Chögyam Trungpa fled to India.

In India, Chögyam Trungpa kept thinking about how to present such teachings. Thrangu Rinpoche, who had also received many teachings from Jamgön Kongtrul of Sechen, remembers a conversation they had together. When asked what he wanted to do now, Chögyam Trungpa replied: "Well, I'm not staying around here long. I want to go to the West and particularly to America. I saw . . . that I could find Shambhala there."[31]

In England, he wrote a short text, *The Golden Dot,* in which he jotted down what he could remember of his lost book. It describes a realm of pure light that transcends the world of confusion, and how our world emerges from that universe—a world that is in fact the Kingdom of Shambhala.

His wife, Diana Mukpo, remembers that, from the earliest days, he often spoke to her about his vision of the Kingdom of Shambhala and his desire to establish it on earth. In 1973, after the first Seminary, he even told her that life would have no more meaning for him if he could not transmit these teachings. It seemed increasingly clear to him that our world was in desperate need of them.

Yet it was only in 1976 that he finally opened his heart: "I have tried to restrain myself because I felt that if I spoke too early it might not be understood; and if I spoke too late it might have become out of date and not

---

30. *Born in Tibet,* 4th ed. (2000), pp. 179–180.

31. Quoted by Thrangu Rinpoche in "Remembering the Vidhyadhara," an interview by Carolyn Gimian and Larry Mermelstein, *Vajradhatu Sun,* December 1990/January 1991, p. 24.

have any effect. So I waited for the right occasion to break this particular ice and tell you the truth of Shambhala, which is my heart blood, the very essence of myself."[32]

Receiving the termas

In order to present these teachings, Chögyam Trungpa entered into direct contact with the kingdom. In 1968, he confided to James George, then the Canadian High Commissioner in India, that he could see Shambhala in his mirror every time he entered into deep meditation. James George even witnessed a scene when Chögyam Trungpa gave a detailed description of the kingdom while holding a mirror. This is what he remembers: "After looking intently into it for some time, he began to describe what he saw. Within a vast circle of high snowcapped mountains lay a green valley and a beautiful city, in the center of which rose a terraced hill with a small palace or temple on top of it. Around this hill was a square, walled enclosure, and around this again were other enclosures containing temples, gardens and sacred monuments. The most singular thing about the inhabitants of the city was that they were of all faiths, races and nations and appeared to come from the four corners of the earth."[33]

Strange as such tales of communication with other beings or other planes of reality may seem to us now, they are found in all cultures in which people are in touch with the divine. In the West, we think more of poets listening to the Muses or the Hebrew tradition of prophets. Such communication gives humanity a new home, a fresh configuration of the world. In Tibet, this is the role of the tertöns, or finders of treasure.

The tertön, poet, and prophet may appear totally different from one another, but they all reestablish a link with the divine in the context of the period in which they live.

---

32. Chögyam Trungpa, *1978 Kalapa Assembly Transcripts* (Boulder: Vajradhatu Publications), p. 183.

33. James George, "Searching for Shambhala," in *Search: Journey on the Inner Path* (New York: Harper & Row, 1979), p. 14.

Tertöns play a particularly important role in the Nyingma school. Even if it is the most ancient school in Tibet, most of the teachings its adepts study are only a few centuries old, and in some cases even more recent. These texts, or termas, answer the specific needs of the time when they were received. They can then often have a long life.

However, while there are many tertöns in Tibet, few have ever discovered a complete cycle of teachings, like the one Chögyam Trungpa received. The entire cycle of termas distills the essence of the teachings and presents the entire path in a living way. From a traditional point of view, receiving such a cycle marks Chögyam Trungpa as one of the truly great spiritual teachers.

In the history of Shambhala and its presentation in our era, the turning point came in the fall of 1976, during the three-month-long Buddhist Seminary, which was being held in a hotel called the King's Gate. There, Chögyam Trungpa received two termas directly from the Rigdens, or kings of Shambhala.

For some time, Chögyam Trungpa had been telling certain close students that he was looking for the symbol that would express enlightenment. All he knew was that it was black and monolithic. Then, during the night of October 25, he received the primordial stroke (*ashe*), the heart of the Shambhala teachings.

That evening, he invited several students to join him and organized a Japanese tea ceremony for them. According to a memoir written by Carolyn Gimian about this evening, they then listened to several different pieces of music for rather a long time, including a recording of Japanese koto music. When the Dorje Dradül heard a particular note sounded on the koto, a high, slightly dissonant note that was piercing and sad, he said: "That's the sound of enlightenment."

Then, during the night, he listened to Handel's *Water Music* again and again. The atmosphere changed and became more and more intense, as if there was going to be an explosion.

As dawn approached, the Dorje Dradül asked for a brush, ink, and paper. He then produced a stroke of quite extraordinary power. He realized that something crucial was happening. Around nine in the morning, he asked for his private secretary, David Rome, to join him. The Dorje Dradül showed the stroke to David, and then he dictated the first descriptions of the stroke of Ashe, in a poem entitled "Tung Shi," which literally means "East/West." The spark that had emerged from the stroke was a spark linking the spirit of the East and that of the West.

Where did this tangible symbol of enlightenment come from?

From the vastness of space, which is always present but which cannot be captured by our conventional minds. It is like heaven. Nothing can corrupt it. It could be called absolute Ashe. We experience it at the very moment we see ourselves drift off into our daydreams or chatter, or else when a sudden event brings us back to the present.

From this limitless opening, relative Ashe is born, which lives in everyone's heart and is its essential nature.

The Ashe that can be drawn with brush and ink allows a link to be made to both the relative and absolute Ashes. This practice is the principle of all action.

In this context, the idea of action takes on a particular meaning. In Buddhism, the notion of karma, or action, shows the involvement of all beings in samsara. Each action sets off a progressive phenomenon that matures and will, sooner or later, inevitably lead to a fruit, the consequence of this action. Here, karma becomes a positive force, because an enlightened action is sanctified by its ability to help others.

In *Sacred World: A Guide to Shambhala Warriorship in Daily Life*, Jeremy Hayward, a close student of Chögyam Trungpa's who served for a long period as the director of Shambhala Training International, describes the practice of Ashe, the principle of all action:

> It is outwardly very simple: standing or kneeling in front of white calligraphy paper, with a bowl of black ink and a calligraphy brush, the warrior makes one stroke down on the paper. . . . The stroke of Ashe is the warrior's weapon—a two-edged sword that cuts all aggression and hatred and, at the same time, cuts itself so that no sense of self-importance or self-righteousness remains, no idea that you are a victor over something or someone. When you

do the stroke wholeheartedly, you have no separate sense of self. The stroke cuts through your conceptual thoughts and cloudy emotions, joining your mind and body.[34]

This gesture of primordial confidence is not an exercise in calligraphy or traditional Chinese painting; instead it is a way to make contact with the magic of all experience. Drawing the Ashe teaches us to synchronize our heart and our actions, to join heaven and earth. Heaven is the first inspiration, the largest possible welcome for all that is, while earth is the basis that supports us: "Traditionally, heaven is the realm of the gods, the most sacred space. So, symbolically, the principle of heaven represents any lofty ideal or experience of vastness and sacredness. The grandeur and vision of heaven are what inspire human greatness and creativity. Earth, on the other hand, symbolizes practicality and receptivity. It is the ground that supports and promotes life. . . . When humans combine the freedom of heaven and the practicality of earth, they can live in a good human society with one another."[35]

The great blade of the Ashe cuts through all confusion, fear, and hesitation, and so liberates the warrior instantly. Such a gesture radiates with basic goodness and the qualities of enlightenment that it contains. Bearing such brilliance requires a heroism that the warrior must learn to develop.

The process that liberates the energy of basic goodness is the ultimate purpose of the invocation of windhorse (lungta), a pre-Buddhist notion represented by the horse depicted at the center of prayer flags (rectangles of colored, printed cloth that are hung in garlands all over Tibet on the roofs of temples and houses or on stone poles at the peaks of mountains). As an animal, the horse symbolizes mobility, the energy of movement.

---

34. Jeremy Hayward, Sacred World, pp. 199–200. I present here an outline of this practice so that the reader can form an idea of the meaning of the stroke of Ashe and the coherence of the cycle of termas that the Dorje Dradül received. But this highly precise discipline must be transmitted by a qualified person in an appropriate context.

35. Shambhala: The Sacred Path of the Warrior (Shambhala Library, 2003), pp. 145–146.

When the principle of the horse is present, the pure energy of the wind can be mastered.

Invoking windhorse implies seeing the Great Eastern Sun: "You realize that you can uplift yourself, that you can appreciate your existence as a human being."[36]

By placing such a strong emphasis on action in the world, the Shambhala teachings speak an immediate, concrete language. Each "tool" we use—a pen, a brush—can allow us to raise or invoke the energy of windhorse and work for the creation of an enlightened society, the Kingdom of Shambhala on earth. A tool becomes a weapon that allows us to display our courage.

Chögyam Trungpa explained this basic principle as follows:

> When a rose has good thorns, it proves to be a good rose, a healthy rose. A thornless rose does not blossom so well, and it is too reachable to the flower picker's hand. Such a castrated rose becomes colorless. Likewise, if the warrior does not have a sword, he lacks color. . . . Even the Chinese emperor has no eunuch roses in his garden. The sword is regarded as one of man's most treasurable dignities. [We can cherish the inherent power in the weapons we hold, overcome our own hesitation and fear, and stop being intimidated by the power of the wind.] The weapon that the warrior wears is the central magical focus by means of which we can actually connect ourselves together properly. A fan could be that weapon, or for that matter, a tank could be that weapon. There's no difference between the two: a fan is a tank if you like; a brush is a sword, and so on.[37]

Holding this weapon allows us to manifest the gentleness of the maternal lineage and the dignity of fearlessness found in the paternal lineage, which, when united, sharpen our intelligence.

---

36. Ibid., p. 45.

37. Chögyam Trungpa, *1978 Kalapa Assembly Transcripts* (Boulder: Vajradhatu Publications), p. 117.

If we use these weapons to manifest as authentic warriors, then we become the weapons of the Rigden kings, as it is proclaimed in "The Supplication to the Rigden Father," which the Dorje Dradül wrote: "We are your arrows adorned with garuda's feathers."[38]

The practice of Ashe and the invocation of windhorse allow us to rouse primordial dignity within us and so become the weapons of space. We thus rediscover the paradox that states that Shambhala is a path entire in itself that exposes us to the ultimate teachings, while not aiming for our own personal enlightenment, but instead for the creation of the kingdom for everyone's good.

The king joins heaven and earth

In the first place, such a vision of joining heaven and earth does not open a purely individual path, but instead aims at establishing a just society in which human relationships are harmonious, rather like in Chinese Confucianism.[39] As in the perspective of mahayana Buddhism, in which properly speaking no one can be enlightened before all beings have been freed from the cycle of suffering, according to the Shambhala approach the work will be finished only when the kingdom has been realized. And such work cannot be undertaken without a king:

---

38. *Timely Rain*, p. 179.

39. René Alleau noted concerning China: "The emperor's main function is to ensure the balance of the cosmos itself, to watch over the regular coming of the seasons, to accord the designations of the macrocosm to those of the microcosm and to maintain good relationships between the 'ten thousand beings.' The notion of Justice thus appears as the essential, basic attribute of the old imperial power. An unjust emperor exposed the entire empire to the worst physical and material dangers. Harvests would be lost, cattle would die, trade would collapse, monsters would be born, 'Heaven' and 'Earth' would manifest their anger in endless disasters. This is why all of the Chinese secret societies that aimed to overthrow a sovereign power had the same rallying cry: 'Struggle for Justice,' which should clearly not be interpreted as an ethical affirmation. That would be a complete misunderstanding. In reality, the Chinese peasants and merchants immediately grasped what this demand for a return to balance meant in practical terms: better harvest, better business and appeasement of the manes." *Aspect de l'alchimie traditionnelle* (Paris: Éditions de Minuit, 1953), p. 81.

> To join heaven and earth
> In order to establish a human society
> Man must have his King.

This verse comes from the terma text that the Dorje Dradül wrote down a few days after receiving the stroke of Ashe. As opposed to the intense experience of the night of October 25, this event was not so strange or powerful. The Dorje Dradül was wearing a dressing gown and talking with some students when he suddenly stopped and started writing in Tibetan on some notecards. As he completed them, he placed them on a table behind him. A few hours later, he had finished. He had just transcribed *The Golden Sun of the Great East*, a root text.[40] There were certain problems correctly ordering the various cards, which he had not numbered.[41] He explained that, strictly speaking, he had not written them; all he had done was to copy down what the kings of Shambhala, the Rigdens, had dictated to him. He said that it sometimes felt like writing down a text that had appeared before him, as though on a screen.

The Golden Sun of the Great East shows how the stroke of Ashe allows the kingdom to be realized and permits us to become the weapon, or the agents, of the Rigden kings. The text starts with a chronological description of a primordial time when the first king joined heaven and earth by performing the stroke of Ashe, in order to create a golden age. This model provides an example of how we can do so too.

Joining heaven and earth means bringing together the spiritual, unconditional world and the concrete dimension of existence.

---

40. It is studied during an advanced residential program connected with Shambhala Training called Warrior's Assembly.

41. Chögyam Trungpa received *The Golden Sun of the Great East* during the Vajrayana Seminary of 1976, at Land O'Lakes, Wisconsin, two or three days after having received the stroke of black Ashe on October 25, 1976. On January 15, 1978, he received *The Letter of the Black Ashe*. Finally, he received *The Letter of the Golden Key Which Fulfills Desire* on October 5, 1978. Study of these three termas lies at the heart of the "sacred path" of the warrior, the second cycle of teachings within Shambhala Training, and is thus addressed to students who already have some knowledge of the principles of the art of the warrior as presented above.

In *Great Eastern Sun*, his second book on the Shambhala teachings and the path of the warrior, Chögyam Trungpa points out that there are three sorts of kings or rulers. The first is someone who tries to subjugate others, even turn them into slaves. The second devotes himself to governing all living beings in a more or less just way. Finally, the third tries to bring out the royalty that is inherent in each being.

Chögyam Trungpa wrote: "I am the third type of lord. We are all lords or ladies, one way or another."[42] So, by drawing the stroke of Ashe, we learn to become the king or queen of our own world. This remark clarifies the meaning of the Shambhala teachings, which aim to help all human beings recover their intrinsic dignity. Maintaining this inner dignity at all times and recognizing it in everyone else is a constant celebration of all existence.

On January 15, 1978 the Dorje Dradül received another terma: *The Letter of the Black Ashe*—which, despite its title, does not discuss the black Ashe. While *The Golden Sun of the Great East* describes the movement that can establish the kingdom, *The Letter of the Black Ashe* shows how human beings are faced with a choice, based on the primordial nature of everything that exists. They can live like a group of cowards or else set up a society of warriors. The text presents how to cultivate the qualities that allow choosing the latter possibility. In one section, *The Letter of the Black Ashe* uses the metaphor of bringing up children, who become adolescents and then adults, and so learn to sharpen their bravery. We are presented with a path that involves developing four dignities: meek, perky, outrageous, and inscrutable. As Chögyam Trungpa explained, for the warrior "there is a developmental process for deepening and furthering authentic presence. This process is called the warrior's path of the *four dignities*. This path is connected with how to incorporate more and more space into your world, so that ultimately you can achieve the realization of the universal monarch. As your world becomes more and more vast, obviously, any notion of self-centered, egotistical existence becomes increasingly remote."[43]

---

42. *Great Eastern Sun*, p. 118.

43. *Shambhala: The Sacred Path of the Warrior* (Shambhala Library, 2003), pp. 185–186.

We have already mentioned how prayer flags are found all over Tibet, with a windhorse in the middle. In their four corners are found four animals: a tiger, a lion, a garuda, and a dragon. They incarnate the four dignities.[44]

The tiger pays attention as it moves through the jungle; it is the image of *meekness*—but not in the sense that realizing this dignity would make us timid or timorous; instead, the basic goodness that exists in us and in all the world will be recognized and celebrated in each of our actions.

The snow lion leaps from peak to peak enjoying the invigorating air. It symbolizes the qualities of *perky* warriors, who have unflagging curiosity. Their discipline allows them to go beyond all doubts that may arise and cause them to lose confidence in their own experience.

The garuda, a mythical winged animal that never needs to touch the ground, incarnates the *outrageousness* of a total liberty that no longer needs any reference points to measure itself against.

The dragon, which joins heaven and earth, allows us to understand the dignity of the *inscrutable*. This state of being, without hesitation, is expressed by a deep inner solidity. Inscrutability implies a generosity that frees us of all inhibitions; it is a form of confidence that does not try to explain itself at length.

The journey from meekness to inscrutability takes us farther and farther beyond emotional and conceptual reference points.

These four dignities are also qualities of the egolessness that the warrior learns to manifest. They are all aspects of relative Ashe, the nature of life itself. The path does not consist in creating them, but in encountering them and then cultivating them.

---

44. The same four animals can also be found in the Chinese tradition (although the snow lion, the emblem of Tibet, is generally replaced by a tortoise); see, for example, Bill Porter, *Road to Heaven: Encounters with Chinese Hermits* (San Francisco: Mercury House, 1993). These animals also represent the four directions and the four elements. In Tibet they are found as well in the Bön tradition (see Samten G. Karmay, "L'apparition de petit homme tête-noire," Paris, *Journal Asiatique*, 1986). As is often the case, Chögyam Trungpa's approach surpasses anthropological and cultural biases to reveal the universality of such principles, which come alive here and now.

On October 5, 1978, the Dorje Dradül received a third terma: *The Letter of the Golden Key Which Fulfills Desire*. This terma presents another possible way to join heaven and earth: by connecting ourselves with the richness of our world (which is not financial but a state of mind), we are invited to "plunge into the golden ocean" with a deep intensity while raising our own dignity through our recognition of the sacred order.[45]

Chögyam Trungpa emphasized that this terma is all the more important now, at a time when people often pay no attention to how they dress or what they eat. Their relationship with themselves and with the world is impoverished.

4. How to Enter into Relationship with the Dralas

Thus, steeped in Shambhala vision, Chögyam Trungpa received a set of termas. This complete cycle of teachings responds to a historical context in the West: in this current era, human beings have lost their *dignity* and their self-confidence. Without these qualities, an ascetic lifestyle becomes a meaningless exercise, or even a way to punish ourselves. For this reason, it is vital to be involved in the world.

In other words, the Shambhala teachings do not in fact offer a path of initiation for those who are willing to leave the world, such as many religions propose. Rather, these teachings respond fully to people in the world, to our current situation, and to the difficulties that compromise any authentic spiritual approach.

Thrangu Rinpoche remembers meeting with Chögyam Trungpa, who explained the thinking behind his approach: "He told me that America in general is a very developed country, in many ways. But there was a problem because there's been so much destruction of the land, so many big roads had been built and the land has been wasted and destroyed. Also, most of the people . . . don't have any particular native tradition or culture. So, although externally it was a highly developed country, the peo-

---

45. This sacred order is represented by the principles of lha, nyen, and lu, which will be dealt with in chapter 15, "A Buddhism for the West."

ple suffer inwardly from diminished or depressed life energy, or *yang*, and diminished or damaged *drala*."[46]

We have lost our spiritual perspective, both in terms of our own minds, emotions, and bodies and in terms of our relationship with the world, which has been reduced to a simple set of objects we can use when we want. Our relationship with it is becoming increasingly technological. Thus, a river is simply seen as a reserve of energy that a dam can exploit fully, and animals as matter we can exploit as efficiently as possible.

Given this situation, the Shambhala teachings can be described as an apprenticeship that shows us how to connect with the world and the dralas that inhabit it. The word *dra* literally means "enemy," in other words, all the obstacles—external or internal—that threaten our own dignity. *La* means "above," "superior." So "*drala* is the unconditional wisdom and power of the world that are beyond any dualism."[47] Dralas have a tangible existence in the relative world in which we live. They can almost be looked on as gods or deities—even if they are not creators of the world, nor objects of belief or worship.[48]

The word *deity* is in fact of considerable interest. It comes from the Indo-European radical *dei*, which means "to shine." A deity is thus something that is bright as day (Latin *dies*) but which does not blind us. The most striking form of this shining is beauty. The divine is indeed basically beautiful—but not because it meets standards of beauty; instead, as something that stands out more than the rest.

Such deities will not save us; instead they are the very face of the phenomenal world: "Drala could almost be called an entity. It is not quite on the level of a god or gods, but it is an individual strength that does exist. Therefore, we not only speak of drala principle, but we speak of

---

46. Thrangu Rinpoche, "Remembering the Vidhyadhara," an interview by Carolyn Rose Gimian and Larry Mermelstein, *Vajradhatu Sun*, December 1990/January 1991, p. 24.

47. *Shambhala: The Sacred Path of the Warrior* (Shambhala Library, 2003), pp. 108–109.

48. There is an understandable resistance to translating *drala* as "deity," because dralas are egoless. As they have no intrinsic being, they are not subject to the cycle of rebirths. But for many reasons, I still think that this translation is preferable. See Fabrice Midal, *Mythe et dieux tibétains* (Paris: Éditions du Seuil, 2000).

meeting the 'dralas.' The dralas are the elements of reality—water of water, fire of fire, earth of earth—anything that connects you with the elemental quality of reality, anything that reminds you of the depth of perception. There are dralas in the rocks or the trees or the mountains or a snowflake or a clod of dirt. Whatever is there, whatever you come across in your life, those are the dralas of reality."[49]

Although the word *drala* designates a specific kind of deity in Tibet, the Dorje Dradül used it to describe the intrinsic quality of all gods, in all cultures. Chögyam Trungpa wanted to help people recover a living relationship with their own deities, because such a relationship is an essential part of all human life, as the Greek philosopher Heraclitus put it: "Man is man because he lives in the proximity of gods (*daimon*)."

Has there been a culture other than ours in the long history of humanity that has had no such relationship? Chögyam Trungpa was constantly astonished by this disappearance of divinity—or, as he put it, loss of connection to the sacred—that marks the West.

During his stay in England, he visited the Roman spa town of Bath. There, he was struck by the fact that the Europeans had lost all connection with their own gods, which they now saw as just vestiges. Yet he himself experienced their presence by looking at those fragmentary architectural remains. As he explained: "Nowadays we make fun of the Greek gods or the Roman gods. We think they're funny; we think they're just a story."[50] While teaching in the United States and Canada, he asked his students to look into their own traditions in order to rediscover the meaning of the sacred, or deity.

To act as an example, Chögyam Trungpa presented to his students specific gods—especially the ones associated with the epic of Gesar of Ling, with which he had such strong ties. He thus invited them to share his own experience.

At every level of this teaching, one finds these two aspects: first, Shambhala is a path that presents the source of all authentic spiritual

---

49. *Shambhala: The Sacred Path of the Warrior* (Shambhala Library, 2003), pp. 111–112.

50. Chögyam Trungpa, *1979 Kalapa Assembly Transcripts* (Boulder: Vajradhatu Publications), p. 33.

traditions, that precedes any specific beliefs and lies at the heart of our hearts; second, Shambhala is a traditional lineage transmitted from teacher to disciple, and it thus contains a specific teaching bearing its own magic.

If we want to open ourselves to the presence of the dralas, we need a path that allows us to recognize them as simply and deeply as possible. A relationship with the dralas depends not on belief but on an openness that accepts whatever occurs.

So how can we make contact with the dralas?

The simplest and most profound way is the practice of meditation, which teaches us to open our minds. We thus let our minds rest in their primordial emptiness. There we have the possibility of letting ourselves be watched by the bright flash of all things. This entirely open space from which the dralas emerge is the *cosmic mirror*, the situation before thought appeared and communication was born. It is a nonexistent world, yet at the same time it contains everything, just as the sky contains all the clouds. Chögyam Trungpa explained: "This unconditional state is likened to a primordial *mirror* because, like a mirror, it is willing to reflect anything, from the gross level up to the refined level, and it still remains as it is."[51] A mirror reflects indiscriminately.

As the practice of meditation helps us to develop a sense of the largest presence, our perceptions become more precise and we can discover the sacred world of the dralas.

By establishing a link with gentleness, courage, and intelligence, this discipline opens up the path of the four dignities, which the warrior follows up to his highest accomplishment. He learns to be meek and to appreciate himself; to be perky and to explore the world; to be outrageous and no longer frightened of making mistakes; to be inscrutable and so experience a general feeling of plenitude. Windhorse is the fuel that drives our relationship with the four dignities.

Finally, in order to help his close students to invoke the dralas in their lives, Chögyam Trungpa composed the Werma sadhana. In this practice, whose form is based on the tradition of tantric Buddhism, practitioners

---

51. *Shambhala: The Sacred Path of the Warrior* (Shambhala Library, 2003), p. 105.

learn to identify themselves more closely and more deeply with the Rigden king and so see the world from his viewpoint.

It is necessary to be prepared in order to achieve such a change in perspective. To do so, practitioners must have studied and contemplated *The Golden Sun of the Great East, The Letter of the Black Ashe,* and *The Letter of the Golden Key Which Fulfills Desire.* They will have thus learned to create a sense of inner dignity, to recognize basic goodness, to transcend their fear, and to appreciate the golden ocean of the world.

Once familiar with such a vision, they can receive an abhisheka (initiation), which consists in entering the Kingdom during a Kalapa Assembly. Through this initiation, warriors receive the power to practice the invocation of Werma sadhana to enter the world of Shambhala and remain there.

Chapter Eleven

FROM SHAMBHALA
TEACHINGS TO
SHAMBHALA TRAINING

Shambhala Training is designed and developed on the basis of training and discipline, uplifting and civilizing ourselves. . . . How we can actually be a decent, dignified, and awake human being. How to conduct ourselves properly in this society without laying trips on others or ourselves and treating our children better, our husbands better, our wives better. . . . So the idea is quite a practical one in the sense that we should learn how to conduct ourselves properly to what is known as the Great Eastern Sun vision, which is the notion of perpetually looking ahead, forward.[1]

—CHÖGYAM TRUNGPA

1. A Weekend of Shambhala Training

Shambhala Training[2] began as a series of seminars on meditation, organized according to the vision of the Kingdom of Shambhala and the various termas that Chögyam Trungpa had received. It is one of the best-known aspects of Chögyam Trungpa's legacy; he even called it his most vital contribution. Each year, around three hundred weekend courses take place in locations throughout the world, or about six a week.

---

1. Shambhala Training, Level Five, November 16, 1979.

2. For this chapter, I am greatly indebted to an unpublished article by David Schneider, "Enlightened Society," which was of great assistance in encouraging my attempts at writing a tentative history of the creation of Shambhala Training.

Like so many of the study and practice programs set up by Chögyam Trungpa in every sphere of his activity, Shambhala Training places
emphasis on the direct, personal experience of sitting meditation. This
practice allows the practitioners to approach their lives in a fresh way
and to discover that it is possible to cut through confusion and
hesitation.

During the day, practice periods alternate with individual meditation
interviews with the director or an assistant and with discussion groups.
Lunch breaks and teatimes enable everyone to get acquainted. In the
evenings, the director presents some aspect of the Shambhala teachings
in a lecture format that also includes questions and answers.

A Shambhala Training program creates a situation in which everyone
can get in touch with their own hearts. Many find such an experience
threatening. It may be the first time they have had the opportunity to
connect with themselves in such a direct way, without any filter. Thus,
the atmosphere must be disciplined and structured as well as relaxed
and welcoming. An aura of dignity and gentleness sets the tone for
Shambhala Training. Without it, no one would have the courage to un-
dergo the experience. The external environment is an important part of
communicating the teachings in a Shambhala Training weekend. Flags,
banners, flower arrangements (ikebana), and carefully chosen furniture
all help to create this atmosphere. The dignities that a warrior cultivates
must be felt in the very space where the program takes place.

The first level of Shambhala Training, originally called "Ordinary
Magic" and now "The Art of Being Human," is the entrance into the
teachings. Every Shambhala center organizes several of these introductory programs each year. During this first weekend of intensive meditation, the participants discover moments of basic goodness and, at the
same time, confront their habitual patterns of thought and behavior.
Thus, right from the first session of meditation, practitioners experience
the contrast between the freshness of basic goodness and their own egos'
stifling cocoons. As they progress, their concrete shells begin to crack and
break into pieces, and people begin to feel that they are manifesting genuinely, sometimes for the first time in their lives.

2. The Creation of Shambhala Training

There is a historical paradox about the birth of Shambhala Training. Originally, the intention behind the program was not to introduce the Shambhala teachings but instead to present the practice of meditation simply and directly to as many people as possible.

One of the key moments was the visit that Werner Erhard paid to Chögyam Trungpa in 1976 and the great impression he made. At the time, Werner Erhard (who had changed his name from John Paul Rosenberg) was at the peak of his dazzling rise as the director of est (Erhard Seminars Training), a system of "group awareness training" that he had founded in 1971. (The organization still exists, now under the name "The Forum.") According to Erhard, people were unhappy because their minds had been incorrectly "programmed" by destructive conditioning. As a result of this discovery, he set up a system of training to help participants transform their own consciousness so as to allow them to get what they want out of life. The seminars that he organized toward this end were extremely intense. Participants were locked in a room and not permitted to leave for the duration of the seminar. The aim was to make everyone take stock of themselves with complete honesty. At the end of the weekend, people reported feeling very different. Their defenses had been broken down. They had become more sensitive, more open, and a little closer to who they really were. Needless to say, est methods appeared to be quite forced.

Werner Erhard had arranged an audience with the Karmapa, who encouraged him in his desire to help people and suggested that he should meet Chögyam Trungpa. So, with a few of his assistants, Werner Erhard traveled to Rocky Mountain Dharma Center during a seminar given there in the summer of 1976. He arrived late for Chögyam Trungpa's talk, in a white limousine. After the talk, he was invited to Rinpoche's residence—a little trailer (near the site of what is now the Great Stupa of Dharmakaya, dedicated to Chögyam Trungpa's memory). Werner Erhard handed out Cuban cigars all around, which was a sign of great wealth at the time, given the U.S. embargo. He was trying to make his presence felt.

A number of Rinpoche's students were also at the meeting. He had asked one of them, Karl Springer (then head of external affairs for Vajra-dhatu) to pose a few questions to Erhard and sound him out. Meanwhile, Chögyam Trungpa observed in silence. During the visit, which lasted about three quarters of an hour, Werner Erhard explained that his work was like that of Chögyam Trungpa, except that he had discovered a quicker path to enlightenment!

Soon after his departure, Chögyam Trungpa said, "We could do better than that! We should get the people who go to est, put them in a room, then just quite simply make them sit down until their discursive chatter-ing dissolves."

The meeting with Werner Erhard evidently gave Chögyam Trungpa the idea that it would be a good thing to make the basic practice and in-sights of meditation available to a wider audience. He realized that there was a larger potential to address people who are involved in society and who are not willing to give up their family or professional lives. For many the Buddhist path might seem too demanding and alien to their culture. Its religious character and its ritualistic side might scare them and put them off.

Thus, around this time, discussions were first held about how to launch an introductory program of meditation that did not rely on presenting Buddhist concepts. A few months later, Chögyam Trungpa received *The Golden Sun of the Great East*, the first Shambhala terma text, and began presenting many of the Shambhala teachings to his closest students. By the next year, the suggestion was made to organize a large project combining the presentation of the Shambhala teachings with the practice of medita-tion to the broadest possible audience. To carry out this project, Chögyam Trungpa endorsed the idea presented by his board of directors to organize a large advertising campaign, with a view to attracting as many people as possible. There were plans to conduct these practice sessions in cities throughout North America, and people were throwing around astronom-ical figures about the growth of the community. Some people thought that the sangha could grow by twelve million in the following five years.[3]

---

3. See Ellen Lieberson, "Early Days," in *Kiki Soso*, no. 11, Shambhala Training Publication, Halifax, Summer 1997, p. 3.

In the fall of 1976, the first public seminar was held, called Weekend Intensive Meditation Program. Others were to follow. An advertising campaign was launched and large lecture halls were rented, but very few people came to the early programs.

Joshua Zim, first editor of the *Vajradhatu Sun* and communications officer of Vajradhatu, pointed out that the acronym of the Weekend Intensive Meditation Program, WIMP, was rather unfortunate. He suggested several others to the Vajradhatu's board of directors, which eventually chose SIT, or Shambhala Intensive Training. Chögyam Trungpa agreed, even though he disliked the word *training*. Soon it took the form it has kept ever since: Shambhala Training.

In March 1977, Chögyam Trungpa left on a nine-month retreat in Rowe, Massachusetts (at a farm referred to as Charlemont). He entrusted several of his students with the task of setting up Shambhala Training. But nobody really knew how to go about it.

Some of the students who started to direct the training seemed to think that their role was to be authoritarian or even haughty with others. They tried to project an overwhelming charisma and heavy-handed confidence, as though it were necessary to impress the public. Not understanding what was being asked of them, people often became arrogant when they directed Shambhala Training. They were very proud of being the disciples of a true teacher and thus able to follow an authentic spiritual path.

Chögyam Trungpa chose two extremely energetic young people, Peter Lieberson and Ellen Kearney, to present Shambhala Training throughout North America. Forty thousand dollars was spent on an aggressive campaign and paid to a public relations expert in Chicago. But after a time they had to admit that the concept they were supposed to present was unclear to them, and they didn't know what to do.

On November 9, 1977, Chögyam Trungpa became aware of the problems that had developed during his absence and the lack of understanding of the principles of the Shambhala vision. He wrote a letter to Joshua Zim, which was in fact addressed to the Shambhala Training directors. It caused a profound shock and shook up these students. In it, he said, "there seems to be very little understanding of Shambhala Training among those who are involved. It is somewhat shocking: these people have studied with me for a long time and yet they haven't developed a general understanding of Shambhala dignity, the dignity that we are trying to express in a style beyond that of Buddhism alone."[4]

Chögyam Trungpa understood that arrogance was toxic to the genuine presentation of the teachings—whether Buddhist or Shambhala. Of course, it was necessary for the teachers to display a feeling of confidence, but that did not mean artificially mimicking it and pretending to be other than they really were—and thus risk being like the frog in Aesop's fable who tried to puff himself up to be as big as an ox and ended up bursting. Nobody seemed to grasp the true meaning of confidence and dignity or to understand that they had the means to radiate these qualities within themselves—there was no need for pretense.

One of the themes of Chögyam Trungpa's teaching had always been, from the time of his arrival in North America in 1970, a total rejection of any form of hypocrisy in which one conceals oneself behind the mask of convention. However, this was not intended to encourage his students to pretend to be someone else or to parody spiritual attainment. In the realm of the Shambhala teachings, confidence is associated with gentleness and has nothing "macho" about it.

On returning from his long retreat, the Dorje Dradül presented his older students with a series of some twelve lectures given over a period of several months, the first set of what were then called the Shambhala Training Director Talks,[5] in which he emphasized recognition of basic goodness, as well as the development of gentleness and loving-kindness. For the first time, Chögyam Trungpa spoke of "basic goodness" and "cocoon." At the end of the set of talks, he gave his first public Shambhala Training lecture, which was held in an auditorium at the University of Colorado on March 12, 1978. Around a thousand or more attended this talk. For many of his students, the Director Talks were a revelation. They realized that gentleness could be just as toxic to the ego and its manipulations as cyni-

---

4. Unpublished letter to Joshua Zim, p. 1. Used by permission of Diana J. Mukpo.

5. Also known as the "Meek Series," these teachings were given in Boulder in January 1978.

cism. In these talks, Chögyam Trungpa presented a groundbreaking description of the Shambhala way of gentleness and tenderness, showing how these qualities manifest themselves naturally if we are able to make genuine contact with our hearts. This notion of a tender heart is not just a quality of sentiment or emotion; it also contains a primordial aspect, a fundamental openness at its core. In one of his talks from this series, entitled "Spark of Confidence," Chögyam Trungpa stated: "The idea of confidence comes from nowhere. It just arises. It just comes up. It's a sudden flash that has a very healthy note. When that kind of spark begins to happen, begins to project out, then there is no problem. But people are not going to be inspired by your being heavy-handed. That's one of the key points we have to be careful of. It seems that our training process altogether is based on tuning in to this spark of confidence. All the principles we have are included in this spark, which is one flash, one basic flash. It is spiritual as well as secular, all in one. That's the key point."

3. The Five Levels of Shambhala Training

During a meeting of the Vajradhatu Board of Directors in June 1977, while Chögyam Trungpa was away on his long retreat, Karl Springer expressed concern about the future of Shambhala Training. Chögyam Trungpa had explained that one of the problems with est was that it provided just a workshop, then left the participants without any tools to work with or a path to follow. Jeremy Hayward, who for some years had been the member of the board of directors who worked with Naropa Institute and various other educational ventures, then asked, "What will the participants do after the initial program?" Then, in a moment of inspiration, the Vajra Regent, Chögyam Trungpa's dharma heir, declared, "We'll offer a series of five weekends. During the fourth one, they'll meet me, then at Level Five they'll see the Dorje Dradül."[6] In this way the idea of presenting the Shambhala Training program in five levels came about. But at the time,

---

6. The first time levels Four and Five of the Shambhala Training were conducted was, respectively, in February and November 1979 in Boulder.

the Regent had no idea what each level would contain, as most of the Shambhala teachings that made up the cycle had not yet been presented.

When he returned to Boulder at the end of his long retreat, Chögyam Trungpa appointed Lila Rich the international head of Shambhala Training. She was the Regent's wife and manifested great maternal gentleness. This was an important decision. At the time, Chögyam Trungpa was starting to give women an increasingly vital role in all his activities. This choice was also connected with the change of tone that Chögyam Trungpa wanted to see in the presentation of the dharma, and the emphasis he was now to place on gentleness and tenderness.

One of Lila Rich's primary tasks was to educate the directors of Shambhala Training in the threefold logic of each of the five levels. With the precise outline and the logic of the levels created by the Dorje Dradül, the various program directors could understand the material and present it according to their own experience.

Learning to use threefold logic is an essential part of the training of teachers in the Tibetan tradition. There are a number of different versions of threefold logic. One common approach is that a fact or situation is envisaged in terms of first its source or starting point, then the path it takes, and finally its fruition, or the result reached by the path.

Chögyam Trungpa often trained his students in the Buddhist and Shambhala teachings by asking them to describe the threefold logic of a particular subject that he would come up with on the spot. For example, he might ask a student to present the threefold logic of fire. There are not necessarily right answers in such an exercise, but there may be mistakes. If necessary, he corrected his students' understanding with affection and humor. Working with threefold logic is an excellent way to build confidence and understanding of a topic.

Jeremy Hayward recalls that when he asked Chögyam Trungpa what should be presented at each level, the simple reply was: "Just talk about your own experience; that's what I do!" The solution was abrupt but clear: teachers should show themselves as they are and reveal how the teachings have affected their own lives.

Little by little, thanks to the vision and patience of Chögyam Trungpa, the first cycle of Shambhala Training took shape. Its success is due to the fact that, in five levels, everyone can discover the genuinely profound sense of the contemplative approach without any previous preparation. As the participants follow the cycle, they familiarize themselves with the practices of mindfulness and awareness (shamatha and vipashyana) and find out how the practice can become a part of their entire experience and lives. The Dorje Dradül managed to coin a new vocabulary that speaks directly to people's hearts while presenting vast, profound experiences.

4. Presenting the Shambhala Teachings beyond the First Cycle

In Snowmass, Colorado, from October 7 to November 2, 1978, the Dorje Dradül taught a new program to his close students, called Kalapa Assembly, in which he introduced a number of Shambhala teachings. He presented and explained the Shambhala terma texts he had received—*The Golden Sun of the Great East*, *The Letter of the Black Ashe*, and *The Letter of the Golden Key*.

At the end of this Assembly, his students asked him how they should present what they had received to those who had not been able to attend. Thus was born the idea of a "Shambhala education" program, which would continue after the first five levels. One evening per week, the study of the Shambhala texts was presented to Buddhist students who had attended the Vajradhatu Seminary.

The first Level Five Shambhala Training program was presented by the Dorje Dradül in November 1979. Within the next two years, several hundred people completed Level Five with Chögyam Trungpa. Many, but not all, of these participants were the Buddhist students of Chögyam Trungpa who were hungry for this new approach to the teachings. The Dorje Dradül felt once again concerned about the notion of a Shambhala path, and wondered what the students—especially those who were not Buddhists—would do after Level Five. It was then decided that Level Five graduates would be invited to attend the teachings of the Shambhala education program. Thus another cycle of weekends, the "graduate program," was initiated. This program was identified by letters rather than numbers, consisting of levels A through F. Chögyam Trungpa himself presented the stroke of Ashe and the practice of lungta (windhorse) in Level F. David Rome was usually called upon to present many of the details of these practices, and he, Lila Rich, Jeremy Hayward, and a few others often assisted Chögyam Trungpa when he taught a level.

Although it had been quick and easy to organize the first five levels, the curriculum for the rest of the Shambhala Training program proved complicated and difficult to organize into a coherent program. Over the next fifteen years, the program was modified often.

The Dorje Dradül gave his students much of the responsibility for working out the details of presenting the teachings in the later levels. These teachings had been meant for Westerners, and Rinpoche's Western students became the guardians of the teachings. In fact, he was often hesitant to present some of these teachings to other Tibetan teachers, feeling that they might appropriate them without a real appreciation of how he wanted them presented.

Finally, after years of consideration and revision, the program now seems to present the Shambhala path in a coherent form: those students who have completed the first cycle can now stop, or even go back to their own spiritual tradition if they have one—because the first five levels provide a complete presentation of the path of meditation and the voice of the heart.

Or else they can continue by taking the sacred path of the warrior, which introduces them to the study of the various termas that the Dorje Dradül received. This advanced cycle presents the path of initiation that is unique to the Shambhala teachings.

5. Buddhism and Shambhala

Affirming the independence of the Shambhala teachings

When first introduced by Chögyam Trungpa, Shambhala Training answered the need for a jargon-free presentation of the general principles of meditation. But the Shambhala teachings soon came to include a complete, specific path based on the terma texts and the practices received by the Dorje Dradül.

Some of Chögyam Trungpa's students were enthusiastic about the Shambhala teachings, because they immediately understood how magical these teachings are and how they speak to our deepest aspirations. But others felt that the Shambhala teachings were too secular and watered down or limited. In particular, some people felt that the emphasis on basic goodness was too "lovey and lighty" (to use one of Rinpoche's expressions) and in direct contradiction to their understanding of the first noble truth.

As they had embarked on the path of Buddhism many years before, and were now quite committed to their practice, they did not want to undertake another approach. Some people questioned whether the Shambhala path was not just a different way of presenting the same Buddhist teachings to more people.

There were disagreements on this point. Some new students were drawn to Shambhala Training but had no interest in becoming Buddhists. A number of people from other religious traditions came to the Shambhala Training program and found that it answered their need for a contemplative component of their spiritual life. Many new students stated how original the teachings they had received were. These were important growing pains in the community around Chögyam Trungpa. Clearly, Shambhala Training showed itself to be a vehicle for an authentic, profound path.

At the Naropa Institute, there was one young student who had been profoundly affected by his encounter with Chögyam Trungpa's teachings, but he still felt himself to be a Christian. He didn't know what to do. Some Buddhist students at Naropa ridiculed him as a "stupid theist." After a great deal of hesitation, he requested a personal interview with Chögyam Trungpa. He was very nervous but managed to explain his desire to study the Christian tradition more deeply. Chögyam Trungpa told him, "You must promise me something"—which made the student all the more nervous. Before he had had time to reply, Chögyam Trungpa went on, "You must promise me that you'll never become a Buddhist. I'd like you to pursue your Christian studies and then come back and teach at the Naropa Institute."

Chögyam Trungpa really meant what he said, for the aim of the Shambhala environment that he had created was not just to protect the buddhadharma in this age of spiritual materialism; it was to protect and nourish all authentic forms of discipline.

A vaster vision

While the Dorje Dradül did not want all his Shambhala students to become Buddhists, he did want all his Buddhist students to take Shambhala Training. Egolessness, in the vision developed by Shambhala, is more direct, and, as he explained, one is actually much more exposed.[7] In the way that Buddhism was being presented in the 1970s, it was still possible to protect the ego by excluding certain aspects of one's life from the reach of Buddhist practice. One might have precision and mindfulness in one's sitting practice, yet still feel that it was acceptable to leave one's clothes in a pile on the floor. But genuine egolessness demands that there be no space untouched—no private aspect left. Shambhala practitioners must show themselves as they are in every situation. Everything is included in such a vision: how to wash the dishes, iron your shirt, go to the supermarket, direct a company, write a computer program, sell a product, sit on a chair, pour a cup of tea, rear children, and so on.

Whereas Siddhartha Gautama gave up his kingdom to become the Buddha, in order to help others, the king of Shambhala remained on his throne. For Chögyam Trungpa, this was a vital point: in our time in history, an authentic spirituality would take root in a secular context, within society rather than apart from it. It must mark out a place where it can develop. In the West, Freemasonry perhaps provides an example of a similar desire to work toward bettering humanity in a context that brings together both a social dimension and initiation. In both cases, the aim is not to attain enlightenment for oneself, but to create an enlightened society

---

7. Chögyam Trungpa, *1978 Kalapa Assembly Transcripts* (Boulder: Vajradhatu Publications), p. 5.

that will be a continual source of inspiration for all people. Chögyam Trungpa even borrowed the Masonic term *lodge* to describe working situations that brought together students who had completed Shambhala Training and attended Kalapa Assembly. In these Shambhala Lodges, students could emulate an enlightened society and in that way work on creating the Kingdom of Shambhala.

Chögyam Trungpa was fully aware that this approach was running against the view of Buddhism as a monastic or yogic practice. It was the opposite of the sentiment expressed in the traditional notion of becoming a "foster-child of the mountains," wearing the mist as clothing, and surviving on wild plants. But, as he explained:

> The prophecy of Padmasambhava tells us that at the end of twenty-five hundred years of the dark age, when human beings become savages and eat bad food and wear clothes of rags, at that point the teachings of the imperial yana will return with the golden umbrella. The prophecy also says that after twenty-five hundred years, there will be an introduction of mind lineage [the ultimate transmission of teachings, which presents enlightenment without any external ornament]. So the dharma should return, but at this point, the dharma should come back as the imperial yana. That doesn't necessarily mean that the teachers are going to be kings and queens and countesses and dukes and duchesses, as such. But what is actually emphasized here is that we have to take a different point of view altogether. When things become so wretched and so poor, the appreciation of simplicity has completely gone wrong. Therefore we have to introduce some dignity and goodness into the situation.[8]

---

8. Chögyam Trungpa, *1981 Kalapa Assembly Transcripts* (Boulder: Vajradhatu Publications), p. 19.

Chapter Twelve

Rethinking
Education

We would like to rethink the educational system altogether and to present a better, further educational system, starting from the elementary level up to university level.[1]
—CHÖGYAM TRUNGPA

1. The Naropa Institute

The project

Many of Chögyam Trungpa's early students had just left college and were often unhappy with the education they had received. It seemed to have no real connection with their true aspirations and their desire to change their lives. In 1973, two of them, John Baker and Marvin Casper, the editors of *Cutting Through Spiritual Materialism* and *The Myth of Freedom*, had several discussions with Chögyam Trungpa about their idea of setting up a university based on the principles he had taught them: "Pointing his finger like a pistol, Chögyam Trungpa said: 'I'm pulling the trigger on the

---

1. Chögyam Trungpa, Alumni dinner, Naropa Institute, August 5, 1980, unpublished.

Naropa Institute.'"[2] As with many other projects, the original idea was not, strictly speaking, Chögyam Trungpa's, but the atmosphere he created encouraged others to take this kind of initiative.

Naropa Institute, as it was then called, started out as a summer school. A group of Rinpoche's students worked tirelessly for months to prepare for the first session. Between two and three hundred students were expected, but a few months before Naropa opened, it became clear that a much larger group was planning to attend. In fact, to everyone's surprise, one thousand eight hundred enrolled. So, with very little warning, it was necessary to find more housing, enough teachers, rooms to hold classes, and so on. The situation was extremely chaotic:

"A month before classes were to begin, when chaos was the rule rather than the exception, Trungpa Rinpoche left for a vacation in the Caribbean. He called Baker and asked how things were going. 'I feel that this is a wild animal and I'm just trying to hold on to its back and not fall off,' Baker replied.

'You know, my whole life has been like that,' Trungpa Rinpoche said."[3]

The Nalanda heritage

Chögyam Trungpa quickly explained his vision: he wanted to found a Buddhist university in North America, modeled on Nalanda, which had been an important center for learning in India in the eleventh century, welcoming scholars from all over Asia. Not only Buddhist texts and doctrine were studied there, but also the arts and sciences. Chögyam Trungpa suggested that they call their new university Nalanda.

Some students found the name presumptuous. They feared that scholars would make fun of them and not take the project seriously. So Chögyam Trungpa suggested that they call the school the Naropa Institute, after the Indian yogi Naropa, one of the greatest teachers of the

---

2. Quoted by Stephen Foehr in "Where East Meets West and Sparks Fly," *Shambhala Sun*, January 2000, p. 44.

3. Ibid., p 46.

Kagyü school. Before becoming an itinerant yogi, he had been one of the abbots of Nalanda, where he was appreciated and renowned for his scholarship. But at some point Naropa came to understand the limits of an education that does not forge a strong enough link between theory and contemplative practice. Because of this lack of discipline, he had not been able to understand fully the teachings of Buddhism. Over and above the intellectual comprehension of a phenomenon, there also existed a more authentic spiritual reality that was missing at Nalanda. So Naropa left to study with a genuine teacher who transmitted the heart of the teachings to him and allowed him to go "beyond the technical, theoretical, prajna [knowledge] level."[4]

Giving such a name to a university implied that this would be a school that Naropa would not have left. Chögyam Trungpa wanted it to be even better than Nalanda! He was aware that he was undertaking a huge and highly ambitious enterprise. Such a project did not just concern the next few years, as he explained, but the following century as well.

As with many other projects, Chögyam Trungpa began by clearly outlining as vast a vision as possible. Once that had been done, a direction was set that allowed everyone to orient themselves.

To fully understand Chögyam Trungpa's interest in such a project, it is important to remember his constant desire to transform society from within. In much the same way that Harvard was founded by the Christian church to train and educate the "gentlemen" of the next generation, Naropa Institute was established as a training ground for the new generation. It was designed to present an education based on a nontheistic spiritual model that would train men and women in a totally new way.

Naropa Institute was not intended as a sectarian organization, nor even a Buddhist university, in the sense that there are Christian universities that teach theology in order to train clergy. Chögyam Trungpa wanted Naropa Institute to be a place where many traditions could all present their own wisdom. By means of provoking such encounters, sparks would certainly fly, which would help all of society.

---

4. *Illusion's Game*, p. 94.

Basically, he did not approach Buddhism as a body of doctrine that must be learned. It was neither a religion nor a philosophy but a complete approach to life—one that could allow us to rediscover the roots of our own culture and our own heart. The most varied disciplines would be taught there: art, poetry, dance, psychology, and studies of Buddhism and of the other great spiritual traditions.

The importance of meditation

One of the first principles of the institute was to give a central role to meditation. It was one of the key points in Chögyam Trungpa's vision of education.

Meditation is not a religious exercise but a way of learning how to work with our minds and emotions. Although Chögyam Trungpa gave courses on Buddhist meditation at Naropa, he wanted it to be taught without reliance on Buddhist jargon: instructors should transmit their own personal understanding of it directly.

Meditation is not belief-based. It is a discipline that allows us to join heart and mind, and it is thus a way to make the discoveries of our intellects part of our personal paths. It thus ensures that teachings are not pure theory. Since its founding in 1974, Naropa Institute has created a new approach to higher education. It makes meditative and contemplative practice a key part of the curriculum. No other institution in the United States has explored the relationship between meditation and teaching in such depth or for so long.

Meditation is an apprenticeship that allows us to be present in what we are doing. Chögyam Trungpa even claimed that many great artists and thinkers, who had not followed any specific form of practice, had discovered their own discipline of meditation.

But the vast majority of men and women who devote their lives to the mind lack this base. Most people experience a fundamental dualism between their daily lives and their intellectual or artistic work. Their lives lack real coherence because of the absence of this practice. This is one of the reasons for the dramatic existence of some artists and intellectuals outside their specialized field; they are disoriented and lost. As Chögyam

Trungpa explained: "When study is combined with meditation practice, it has a different flavor. Where direct experience is lacking, study tends to be mainly memorizing terms and definitions and trying to convince oneself of their validity. When balanced with meditative discipline, study takes on much more life and reality. It develops clarity about how the mind works and how that knowledge can be expressed. In this way, study and practice help one another enormously, and each becomes more real and satisfying. It is like eating a sandwich—because of the bread, you appreciate the meat much more."[5]

A contemplative education

Thanks to meditation, what students learn there is not separate from their own experiences and lives. They can identify with the knowledge and analyses that are presented to them and scrutinize them personally. The main obstacle is a lingering idea that training means accumulating information about a given subject. To be well educated should mean something quite different from simply having a particular expertise.

The idea of Naropa Institute was to approach education with an open mind, based on egolessness and an absence of spiritual materialism. Learning cannot be divorced from work on the self. Chögyam Trungpa often expressed this as: "The question is the answer." He wanted this sentence to be written in capital letters on the Golden Gate Bridge in San Francisco. When you ask a question, you recognize that you don't know, and thus demonstrate a certain curiosity. When you no longer feel that you have something to learn, there can be no intelligence. Not hurrying to get an answer is to recognize that basic space in which intelligence can appear. For this reason, one of his mottoes was "The love of wisdom puts you on the spot all the time."

Unlearning is as important as learning. Education should be based on each person's inherent wisdom and thus must begin by pruning away our

---

5. Chögyam Trungpa, "The Meeting of Buddhist and Western Psychology," *Journal of Contemplative Psychotherapy* 4 (Boulder: Naropa Institute, 1987), p. 7. Reprinted in *The Collected Works of Chögyam Trungpa*, vol. 2.

habitual patterns of thought. Judy Lief, who was for a long time head of the institute, explains: "A part of this educational process is the removing of preconceptions so that our perceptions are more direct. Mind freed from such preconceptions is very accurate and true. The process of 'unlearning' makes it possible to see things in a very fresh way—without the usual baggage of fixed categories and presuppositions of all sorts."[6]

For the first graduation ceremony, in August 1977, Chögyam Trungpa wrote a poem, entitled "Lion's Roar," that presents the heart of his vision:[7]

> Genuine people bring genuine intellect,
> Genuine mind brings genuine discipline,
> Genuine teacher and student bring true wisdom;
> Naropa the great siddha brought the spotless discipline
>   of the Practice Lineage.
> Theory is empty head without brains,
> Chatting logicians are the parrot flock,
> Clever psychologists swallowing their own tongues,
> Chic artists manufacturing garbage collages—
> At this illustrious Institute we are free from confusion.
> Let us celebrate in the name of sanity,
> Let us proclaim the true discipline,
> Let us rejoice:
> The eternally rising sun is everpresent.
> In the name of the lineage, I rejoice.

A brief history of the Naropa Institute

During the first session of 1974, Ram Dass, author of a best-selling book, *Be Here Now* (and, as Richard Alpert, once a very popular professor at Harvard), agreed to be the main speaker along with Chögyam

---

6. Judy Lief, "The Naropa Institute," *Vajradhatu Sun*, June/July 1988, p. 22.

7. From *First Thought Best Thought*, by Chögyam Trungpa, p. 119. © 1989 by Diana J. Mukpo. Reprinted by arrangement with Shambhala Publications, Inc., Boston, www.shambhala.com. Reprinted with permission of Diana J. Mukpo.

Trungpa. They took turns teaching throughout each week. During that first summer, Chögyam Trungpa taught "The Tibetan Buddhist Path" and "Tibetan Buddhist Meditation," while Ram Dass presented "The Yoga of the *Bhagavad Gita.*" During the second session of this summer school, Chögyam Trungpa gave the first public presentation of tantric Buddhism in a series of lectures that were subsequently published in the book *Journey without Goal.*

Meanwhile, many other seminars and workshops were held, led by teachers from a variety of different backgrounds.

The first summer of Naropa Institute delivered a shock to the Buddhist community that had grown up around Chögyam Trungpa in Boulder. All at once, hundreds of new students arrived, many of whom decided to stay in Boulder to study with Rinpoche. The closeness and intimacy of a small community suddenly disappeared. Chögyam Trungpa, who now had to take charge of a far larger group of students, was less available to others. A new phase in his life and work had begun.

The following year, Chögyam Trungpa taught "The Three Yanas of Tibetan Buddhism" and "Iconography." Courses in Theravada Buddhism, which greatly interested Chögyam Trungpa, were taught by Joseph Goldstein and Jack Kornfield, among others. Karma Thinley Rinpoche was also present, as was the Rongae family, who taught the art of thangka painting, and Rabbi Zalman Schachter, a leader of Jewish renewal.

The poetry department was an important part of Naropa from the beginning and became one of the university's main attractions. Chögyam Trungpa asked Allen Ginsberg to head up the department, which Allen named the Jack Kerouac School of Disembodied Poetics. In addition to Ginsberg, William Burroughs, Anne Waldman, Gregory Corso, Ed Sanders, and Diane di Prima, among others, taught there in 1975.

In 1976, the first B.A. and M.A. programs in Buddhist studies were launched, as well as a bachelor and master of fine arts in thangka painting. Arts certificates were offered in dance, poetry, and theater.

By 1980, Naropa offered five bachelor's programs: Buddhist studies, Buddhist and Western psychology, dance, theater, and poetry. Two master's degrees were available in Buddhist studies and psychology.

The M.A. in psychology, which included the practice of Maitri Space

Awareness, discussed in chapter 8, was a big success. It begins with the study and understanding of the human mind through an analysis of confusion and wisdom as conceived in Buddhism. Such an approach, whose accuracy seems unequaled, opened new perspectives in psychology. It also enabled many Buddhists to enter occupations in the field of psychology while following their own spiritual path.

Official recognition

As early as 1976, Naropa Institute began to seek accreditation as an institution of higher learning, which would give its degrees official standing. A long process then began, since the institute was still in its infancy. After years of effort and two unsuccessful bids, the institute became fully accredited in 1985.[8] An important step had just been taken. As Chancellor Barbara Dilley put it at the time: "The accreditation means that we are going to become available to a larger group of people, and the students receiving a degree from the Institute will be able to further their studies in many other institutions of higher learning. For the Institute itself, I think that accreditation means we are taking ourselves a lot more seriously. We are finding our way in bringing our heritage and our inspiration of Buddhist psychology and philosophy into the mainstream of American education. That's the banner that is being raised at this point. The dharma as it is known in the traditions of the East could begin to mingle and both refresh and provoke the wisdom that is present in the West."[9]

Today the official name of the school is Naropa University.

---

8. Naropa Institute obtained full academic accreditation from the North Central Association of Colleges and Schools on August 22, 1985. Current areas of B.A. study being offered include contemplative psychology, early childhood education, environmental studies, inter-arts studies, religious studies, and the visual arts. Graduate programs include Buddhist studies, contemplative psychotherapy, somatic psychology, transpersonal psychology, and writing and poetics. The annual Summer Institute provides a variety of courses and workshops for both degree and nondegree students.

9. Barbara Dilley, "The Naropa Institute Receives Full Accreditation," *Vajradhatu Sun*, October/November 1986, p. 11.

2. The Schools

When some of Chögyam Trungpa's students expressed an interest in starting a preschool and later an elementary school, to give their children an education based on Buddhism and Shambhala, Chögyam Trungpa encouraged them.[10] Such projects corresponded to the vision he was trying to implement: integrating the teachings he was presenting into everyone's daily lives. Taking care of children and fully integrating them into the community was vital if the dharma was really going to take root.

In a talk given in 1980, he explained the vision he wanted to implement:

> At Naropa Institute we approach the whole educational system according to the principles of buddhadharma. We would like to present a traditional approach, similar to the Victorian style of education or other European approaches. Recently, education in America has been based on entertainment. That is to say, the professors and teachers have become more and more cowardly. They don't want to push their students to follow their instructions or the traditional educational format. In the schooling of young children in preparatory schools or elementary schools, we begin to find more that children are told to use their toys to learn with. We are not going to push you to do anything drastic. You don't have to memorize; you don't have to think, even. Just play nicely with the toys we provide, and you will learn something about our history, our mathematics, our alphabet, and our grammar. That is the idea of education that seems to have been created by the present generation, which had a terrible time with their schooling. Now they are in power, so they have invented a system of entertainment-as-education, so that children won't have to go through terrible

---

10. In 1974 he set up the Nalanda Foundation, devoted to education. Its main body is the Naropa Institute, but it also stands as an umbrella structure able to take in other organizations, such as the various schools.

education situations. That approach is actually based on good intentions, excellent, maybe. But, on the other hand, it could mean the destruction of the educational system altogether. We have to push our children and ourselves to relate properly with the principles of education, which means discipline, respecting our elders, that is to say our teachers, and putting ourselves through a certain amount of painful situations.[11]

This perspective is an alternative to the current situation in education, in which the view of the humanities, which has nourished so many generations, has disappeared—not only in the United States but in Europe too.

In the name of a supposedly open, anti-elitist approach to teaching, students no longer have the opportunity to receive a real education. To this ideological abandonment of traditional culture has been added a stifling requirement that education lead to profitability. Students are now supposed to learn techniques that will be useful in their working lives; they are no longer taught how to cultivate themselves and develop as human beings. Education has thus been reduced to a way of learning to be efficient and earn a living.

Nor would a return to the methods of the past be an answer. Discipline as it was presented then now seems to us arbitrary and harsh. Chögyam Trungpa had the courage to show that a real education requires a difficult and sometimes painful apprenticeship, which is an inseparable part of any genuine opening.

He also believed in education without punishment, however: "Shambhala education is education without punishment, absolutely. Many people have tried that approach but find it quite difficult. They often end up punishing people anyway. It's tricky, but I think it's quite possible. We can be free from the mentality of praise and blame."[12] Discipline should not be imposed externally, but instead be recognized as what allows people to grow and develop.

---

11. Chögyam Trungpa, "Hearty Discipline" (1980), in *The Collected Works of Chögyam Trungpa*, vol. 2, pp. 624–626.

12. *Great Eastern Sun*, p. 91.

Alaya, a preschool for children between two and five

Beginning in 1976, there was discussion about starting a preschool for the children of Buddhist parents in Boulder. The school opened two years later in Boulder, at 3340 Nineteenth Street. It was attended mainly by children of Buddhist parents in the community but was also open to pupils from any other background. It was located in a large ranch-style house, with several rooms and attractive play areas covering a little over an acre.

Chögyam Trungpa chose to call his preschool Alaya. This Sanskrit term means "the fundamental unbiased ground of mind." Such a place would be devoted to appreciating the inherent basic goodness in everyone.

Chögyam Trungpa often said that this school should not be "a parking lot for children." He criticized the attitude of parents who primarily consider their offspring to be obstacles in their path and so want to get rid of them during the day. Chögyam Trungpa taught that even when children cannot yet eat properly, or dress themselves, or walk, we should still consider them full human beings and open our world to them. School should be an expression of our concern and affection for them. Expressing a view that accords with both mahayana and Shambhala teachings, Chögyam Trungpa said: "We are developing some kind of mutual confidence so that our children are no longer regarded as underdeveloped apes but as fully developed embryonic beings."[13]

Vidya, an elementary school

A few years after the Alaya preschool came into being, an elementary and high school was started in Boulder by students of Chögyam Trungpa. The name given to this school was Vidya, "intuition or intellect" in Sanskrit. Chögyam Trungpa chose this name to show that the most important point at this age is to help children to develop and recognize their intelligence.

Children at Vidya were taught using both the Buddhist and Shambhala teachings as a basis. They were encouraged to view themselves as warriors

---

13. Chögyam Trungpa, "Opening Talk: Alaya Preschool," March 1978, unpublished.

in the world; in other words, to have the confidence to trust their own hearts and their own freedom. With this in mind, they were told the life stories of great teachers of the Buddhist lineage and great warriors from the Eastern and Western traditions, with the aim of inspiring them. They were also taught various contemplative arts, such as kyudo (archery) and ikebana (flower arranging). These disciplines allowed them to begin studying the principles of "heaven, earth, and man," which were then extended in haikus, painting, and observation of the phenomenal world. The idea behind this approach was that children could grasp these principles directly and would thus be equipped with guidelines to help them act wisely in their daily lives.

Chögyam Trungpa also wanted the students to learn about their own Western culture. There was never any feeling that Tibetan or even Asian culture should dominate their education. Instead, there was an understanding that Buddhist wisdom is not intrinsically tied to one cultural tradition. Therefore, the emphasis was on discovering the source of the dignity that resides in all people. As he said during a talk on education, "If children can't experience and appreciate literature properly, there is no possibility of their experiencing sanity—which requires more sophistication than purely appreciating a peanut butter and jelly sandwich on the spot."[14]

Chögyam Trungpa sometimes dropped in to see the students, give an ikebana presentation or an elocution lesson, or present a Buddhist teaching. On one occasion he told them that while they had several toys, their minds were more important, because you can lose your toys but not your mind.

In the approach that was pioneered at Vidya, the development of the individual is founded on the recognition of basic goodness. Thus, the children's chaos, fears, shyness, and confusion were welcomed just as much as their gentleness and curiosity. The aim of education is of course to nourish the latter qualities, but at the same time the former must not

---

14. Chögyam Trungpa, "The Alaya Principle and Children," Karma Dzong, Boulder, August 31, 1976, unpublished.

be rejected. Fear, agitation, and undisciplined behavior are recognized as stepping-stones for future progress; they can be gone beyond.

The students who attended these schools when they opened are now young adults. It changed their lives so much that they recall their experiences with great emotion. What struck them more than anything was the prevailing atmosphere. Everything was oriented toward the appreciation of each person's unique personal qualities. But the chief challenges these schools had to face were to educate the children of Chögyam Trungpa's Buddhist students in a way that stayed true to their convictions, did not isolate them from the rest of the world, and respected the children's personalities. These concrete difficulties made many members of the community more humble, because it showed that a vision of an enlightened society required constant fieldwork.

Chapter Thirteen

PORTRAIT OF CHÖGYAM
TRUNGPA AS AN ARTIST

I don't think particularly in terms of being an artist. I regard myself as just a day-to-day person. Just like everyone else. I dress myself, I brush my teeth. I just do all those details of life expansively.[1]

—CHÖGYAM TRUNGPA

IN ORDER TO APPRECIATE Chögyam Trungpa's world, it is important to consider its artistic dimension and the decisive role that art played for him. Chögyam Trungpa loved to create forms and engage with the symbolic character of the world. His interest in numerous artistic disciplines, such as ikebana (flower arrangement), calligraphy, photography, and poetry, was extremely strong.

Beyond his desire to present the dharma freely, Chögyam Trungpa was an artist, even if he did not want to embark on producing a complete body of artistic work. For him, art was a part of daily life. As his secretary, David Rome, explains: "The 'sacred world' expressed through art is not in opposition to a profane world. Samsara and nirvana are

---

1. Chögyam Trungpa, "Dharma Art Is Collective Work, Enlightened Vision," *Vajradhatu Sun*, February/March 1981. Reprinted in *The Collected Works of Chögyam Trungpa*, vol. 7, as "Art of Simplicity: 'Discovering Elegance.'"

nondual. This basic view, so different in its thrust from the mainstream of Western spiritual and artistic tradition, sees 'Art' as part of a continuous spectrum that includes every kind of creativity in one's life even, as Rinpoche was fond of saying, how we brush our teeth and wear our clothes. While not separate from everyday life, art nonetheless represents a heightening of experience, what Trungpa Rinpoche refers to as 'extending the mind through the sense perceptions.' It is the apprehension and the expression of what he calls 'basic beauty,' beauty that transcends the dualities of beautiful versus ugly."[2]

1. The Theater

Chögyam Trungpa wrote and directed plays from the early 1970s onward. In the context of the artistic renewal then in full swing, these works allowed him to present the experience of enlightenment without any theoretical explanations.

He wrote three important plays: *Prajna*, *Water Festival*, and *Kingdom of Philosophy*, to which can be added some shorter pieces such as *Sandcastles* and *Proclamation*.

Prajna, whose title means "the basic intelligence that sees things as they are," is based on a recitation of the *Heart Sutra*, a classic Buddhist text.[3] It was performed for the first time on August 11, 1974. A group of men and women in brown robes form a sort of chorus "who serve as uncompromising spokesmen for the teachings. Their behavior cuts through the neurotic trips of the people they confront; their actions arise spontaneously without reference to passion, aggression, or confusion. Their gestures become statements that are straightforward, but do not follow any pre-

---

2. David I. Rome, introduction to Chögyam Trungpa, *The Art of Calligraphy: Joining Heaven and Earth* (Boston: Shambhala Publications, 1994), p. 1.

3. *Prajna* premiered at the Naropa Institute in Boulder, performed by the Mudra theater group directed by Andy Karr. It was published in *Loka I: A Journal from Naropa Institute* (Garden City, NY: Anchor Press/Doubleday, 1975), pp. 139–143, and is reprinted in *The Collected Works of Chögyam Trungpa*, vol. 7.

dictable social pattern. There is no chance to argue or reason with them."[4] The action of the play reproduces that of the ritual found in all scriptural texts (or sadhana), where, to make a sacred space, the troublesome spirits who symbolize the confusion in us and the world are chased away. Chögyam Trungpa's personal style comes across in this play: a mix of humor, intimidation, and a sharp precision that seeks to transmit the nature of space and egolessness.

Water Festival, which was produced two years later, is a humorous, even sarcastic play that contains nothing overtly Buddhist. One of the characters speaks of his intense thirst that nothing can quench. Chögyam Trungpa was playing with a paradox: the script constantly alludes to water, and yet the thirst increases. The intensity of the desire becomes ridiculous and grotesque. The main character, who is called Parkinson, wears a cubic hat with a chin strap. All the other characters wear turquoise silk costumes.

The curtain opens on Parkinson alone. "The Thirsty Man" then launches into a monologue to explain how thirsty he is. He's drying up. He's cracking. He's on fire. The play's other main character is an Old Lady. She wakes up in a foreign country whose language is unknown to her. Everything, from the costumes to the chorus, seems unreal. With its Mudra exercises, this play is more about developing a sense of presence than telling a story.

Kingdom of Philosophy is the longest of all Chögyam Trungpa's plays; it lasts almost three hours. It was performed for the first and only time on July 15, 1979. As Chögyam Trungpa explained in the epilogue to the unpublished play, *Kingdom of Philosophy* "is not entirely unfamiliar to us. The world of this play is ruled by a technocratic scientific mentality. This mentality regards its world as a philosophical world because it regards its truths as the truths about reality. But its technocrat rulers pay very little attention to the understanding of human relationships, in which lies the essence of politics."

The various characters—the Chief, the Secretary, the General, the Poet, the Student Leader, and his Wife—are so naive that they destroy their

4. Andy Karr, in *Loka I*, p. 139.

kingdom. However, no reference points allow the audience to understand what is happening. The characters are not linked to their actions. Several striking scenes reveal each character's false confidence, as when the Chief is incapable of choosing between the pleasure of having a cup of tea or smoking a cigar. The play thus swings from farcical comedy to high seriousness. As the journalist Joshua Zim wrote: "Unlike conventional drama in which the audience is told why a situation is serious and how it might be viewed ironically, *Kingdom of Philosophy* just lets fly. There is no explanation for solemnity, no preparation for humor. They just occur, out of nowhere, and they occur so quickly that the audience cannot register what it is feeling at any given moment. In this respect, the Vajracharya [Chögyam Trungpa] defeats every attempt by the audience to declare emotional or conceptual territory over the play. The ground falls away."[5]

Robin Kornman remembers a reading of *Kingdom of Philosophy* in Chögyam Trungpa's bedroom: "It was a confusing play, and at the end I said, 'I keep on changing my mind about who was right. It was confusing.' Rinpoche smiled and said that that was exactly what he was aiming for."

Ashley Howes, who participated in *Water Festival* and *Kingdom of Philosophy*, considers that these two plays had a highly theatrical, artificial effect that was reminiscent of Japanese Noh theater, with a sprinkling of vaudeville. The characters are more symbolic than real. They are not fixed by an ego, but instead create themselves constantly. It would be impossible to guess that these plays had been written by a meditation teacher, because they contain no allusions to the practice or to Buddhism. In both the action takes place in a foreign country that is not described physically and is purely imaginary. If wisdom and confusion are one (or not-two), the same could be said of wisdom and the absurd. These two plays are studies of sacred absurdity, or perhaps absurd sacredness.

To celebrate the summer solstice of 1980, Chögyam Trungpa wrote *Proclamation*. Here he returned to the search for forms for a typically Buddhist theater, as he had done with *Prajna*. This play, which has nothing sarcastic about it, is an opportunity to celebrate the unity of the com-

---

5. Joshua Zim, "Theater of Groundlessness," *Nalanda News* (Boulder, August/September 1979), p. 27.

munity. It takes the form of a ritual that establishes victory over the ego and invites the dralas (deities that represent local elemental energies) to join the festivities. Thus it revisits, in simpler terms, the principles of the monastic dances performed on important occasions.

2. Photography and Cinema

Chögyam Trungpa had always been interested in photography. This interest had begun in Tibet when he set up a darkroom in the library of the monastery of Surmang. In the isolated region where he then lived, he sometimes had to wait six months to obtain the necessary chemicals, but he was very enthusiastic nonetheless. He was thus able to photograph his guru.

In the United States, he devoted himself more fully to this discipline. Westerners have been able to appreciate his photographs perhaps more fully than his Tibetan calligraphy or his ikebana, since the camera is after all an instrument familiar to Western technology. Michael Wood, a professional photographer, remembers the first time he saw Chögyam Trungpa's photos. They were to change his work and the way he thought about his art:

> In 1979, I was fortunate enough to take part in a course in Toronto called "Iconography." The material for this course included some of Trungpa Rinpoche's photographs. Some of these were slides of different works of art that Rinpoche felt expressed the principles of Dharma Art, and some were just of things he saw—those were the ones that really caught my attention.
>
> When I saw them, my professional photographer half began doing a critique: his exposures weren't perfect, and his focus wasn't precise, and his compositions did not fall within any formula I had been taught, and so on. There was a lot of professional arrogance on my part.
>
> My other half was speechless and dumbfounded. I had never seen anything so fresh and startling. Actually, I was quite astounded

—I had never seen any photographs like these before. I had no idea where these images came from, so I was left intrigued but bewildered.

For me, the most astonishing aspect of Trungpa Rinpoche's photographs is how awake they are. There is no storyline or attempt to manipulate the audience.

Seeing them, one's mind is stopped and the experience of wakefulness is transmitted.[6]

Chögyam Trungpa believed that photography is by nature a sharp and precise art, and he sought to explore this dimension in his photographs. They are neither complex nor narrative. Chögyam Trungpa had no favorite subjects or themes that he tried to depict. For him, photography was an experience of great precision. For example, when he photographed blades of grass, he made each blade appear as it was.

At the same time, he did not photograph particular objects so much as the clarity of space itself. In this way, something totally unexpected yet obvious is revealed. Instead of a blade of grass, what we see is a moment of reality. Thus did Chögyam Trungpa photograph a feather in front of the sun, the fragments of signposts against a blue sky—all apparently "uninteresting" subjects.

But his way of looking turned banality into a heightened experience.

---

6. In 1984, Michael Wood and John McQuade founded the Miksang Society for Contemplative Photography in Toronto, offering a cycle of photographic practice based on principles developed by Chögyam Trungpa. *Miksang* is a Tibetan word that means "good eye." Miksang consists in synchronizing the eye and the mind in order to give rise to pure, direct perception. The Vajra Regent Ösel Tendzin was closely involved in the founding and development of Miksang.

As Michael Wood explained in an article in the *Vajradhatu Sun* (December 1986/January 1987): "The path of contemplative photography is a discipline of perception. The student learns how to work through the obstacles to clear seeing, which in turn can be given expression with appropriate photographic technique. Students very often have the notion or preconception that the nature of beauty can only be found in the beauty of nature. Contemplative photography, however, recognizes beauty as the inherent quality of the first flash of perception, which is experienced before the conceptual distinctions between this and that, beautiful and ugly, like and dislike, worth photographing and not worth photographing."

Commenting on one of his photographs of tree branches, he wrote: "We could view the trees as cracks in the sky, like cracks in glasses. We could adopt that change of perspective. The space that exists around you could be solid—and you could be only a hollow in the middle of that solid space."[7]

From these remarks, we can see that Chögyam Trungpa was not interested in the aesthetic aspect of an image, but rather in how it might provoke a profound experience. In a 1972 seminar, he explained: "Where there is grass growing, is that solid grass, or is it hollow grass in the midst of concrete space? . . . The grass is the space, and around the grass is the solidity."[8] This basic teaching, which completely inverts our habitual thoughts and is at the heart of his Mudra "intensification" exercises, is here made visible.

To my knowledge, no real exhibition of Chögyam Trungpa's photographs has ever been organized. However, a number of his photographs are reproduced in the book *Dharma Art*.

The Milarepa film project

When Chögyam Trungpa discovered the existence in Stockholm of nineteen thangkas devoted to the life of Milarepa, one of the most important figures in Tibetan Buddhism, he decided to make a film about him. Milarepa was an example of the wisdom and outrageousness of Tibetan Buddhism, which Chögyam Trungpa felt he had inherited, and the idea for the film seemed to him to be a good opportunity to evoke this spiritual tradition.

In spring 1972, he described his project in a seminar that he led on the art of filmmaking. It was an occasion to think about movies and their meaning in Buddhist terms. He presented the principle of the five energies (or five buddha families) by using natural images, the details of various thangkas, and assorted sounds. He tried to arouse the greatest possible attention in his students to the texture, length, and rhythm of the images.

---

7. *Dharma Art*, caption to photo between pp. 48 and 49.

8. *Orderly Chaos*, p. 9.

The film he started to make was to be neither narrative nor literary, but extremely visual. The chronology of Milarepa's life supplied the film's structure: his unhappy childhood, the period when he practiced black magic, his years of solitary meditation that culminated in his enlightenment, and the teachings he then proclaimed in his spiritual songs. But all of this would be presented by allusion. The audience would be free to become involved in Milarepa's path rather than see it as something external to them: "Implication is more important than what you actually said,"[9] as Chögyam Trungpa explained. "I was hoping that we could present everything in such a way that the audience has to take part in the film. This means that we need lots of space, absolutely lots of space; and lots of speed, as well as lots of richness. These three principles seem to work with each other in such a way that the audience begins to take part in the presence. In other words, they give birth to each vision as they watch the screen, rather than having the sense that we are making the film. This would depend largely on editing."[10]

He insisted on the need to include moments of silence to express Milarepa's profound solitude and give an impression of the space it created: "I think space is the most important thing. Space and silence—you don't play music while you are presenting space. It is desolate. You begin to value objects much more."[11]

Chögyam Trungpa never made the slightest compromise when it came to his vision. For example, he did not want to make a popular feature film in the hope of presenting the dharma to as many people as possible. Such an idea seemed to him to be against the teachings he held, which were based on the desire to be completely authentic. For this reason, Chögyam Trungpa saw art as something quite opposed to entertainment, which he viewed as anything that distracts people from what is

9. Milarepa Film Workshop, 1972, unpublished transcript, p. 5. An article based on the Milarepa Film Workshop, entitled "Visual Dharma: Film Workshop on the Tibetan Buddhist View of Aesthetics and Filmmaking," appears in *The Collected Works of Chögyam Trungpa*, vol. 7.

10. Ibid., p. 4.

11. Ibid.

essential. Thus, to his mind, some movies that are regarded as intellectual are in fact just as much entertainments as feature films whose only purpose is to please the crowd and make a lot of money. Some may be more elaborate or sophisticated than commercial films, but they are all just as distant from genuine art, which should deal with the serious matter of existence in absolute terms—even if this can be done in a light way. Art is naturally sacred.[12]

Although a trip to Stockholm was organized and about three quarters of the project was shot, the film devoted to Milarepa was unfortunately never finished.[13] But there remains the transcription of the seminar devoted to it, which gave birth to the idea of "Visual Dharma" and would lead Chögyam Trungpa and his students to return to the reflections about art that they had begun on this occasion.

3. Poetry

Dohas and haikus

Chögyam Trungpa was a regular composer of poetry and creator of calligraphy. In particular, he had loved poetry since childhood.

In India there is a traditional form of spontaneous song known as the doha. These poetic texts are inspired by the practitioner's mystical experience and are the expression of the poet's spiritual accomplishment. Dohas are improvised and sung during a ganachakra, a feast organized by a group of practitioners on a propitious occasion. In this practice, which

---

12. At a time when traditional sacred artists remain faithful to their ancestral canons and modernist artists have no relationship with the sacred, Chögyam Trungpa's thought is of considerable importance in examining the greatest artists of the twentieth century, who tried to find a possibility of art other than a sacred one. See Fabrice Midal, "Qu'est-ce qu'un art sacré aujourd'hui?" Ph.D. thesis, Université Paris I, Panthéon-Sorbonne, 2000.

13. This film was never shown, as it was not shot properly. A problem with the camera lens caused the film to go out of focus some of the time, and this could not be corrected at the time. The footage eventually made its way into the Shambhala Archives; perhaps in the future it will be resurrected with modern technology.

Chögyam Trungpa planned two other films, one devoted to the *Tibetan Book of the Dead*, the other to "Battle of Ego." Neither was ever made.

is part of the tantric teachings, sensory desires and perceptions become a source of celebration, as the practitioner recognizes their sacred nature. Marpa the Tibetan guru introduced them to his students in Tibet, and his disciple Milarepa was especially well known for his talent in this field. Many practitioners from all schools know Milarepa's *Hundred Thousand Songs* by heart.

When studying with his guru, Jamgön Kongtrül of Sechen, Chögyam Trungpa learned this tradition and started to write prolifically. He then gave his poems to his teacher. One day, he asked the guru for his opinion. Jamgön Kongtrül told him that he wrote with too much deliberate intention. He decided to show him what to do. For three hours, they worked together: Jamgön Kongtrül wrote a line, then Chögyam Trungpa composed the next one, trying to do his best. When the poem was finished, Jamgön Kongtrül read it out. It sounded as if he had written the entire text.

Chögyam Trungpa continued his apprenticeship enthusiastically: "I began to write poems all over the place. I wouldn't write simple notes for people. I always wrote formal poetry."[14] He started to appreciate the Tibetan meter, with its lines of six or eighteen syllables.

Sometime later, Jamgön Kongtrül saw him again and told him his verse was still not free enough. Chögyam Trungpa's poems need not imitate his guru's; he should find his own voice. As Jamgön Kongtrül was aware of how interested Chögyam Trungpa was in this exercise, whenever a great poet came to the monastery, he sent a messenger asking Chögyam Trungpa to join them. During these meetings, he asked him to write a poem or compose one orally. It was an excellent apprenticeship.

In addition to traditional dohas, which Jamgön Kongtrul taught him to master, Chögyam Trungpa learned about Japanese poetry during his stay in India. He particularly liked the haiku, a short poem of three lines with respectively five, seven, and five syllables, and subsequently often had his students practice them.

Haikus are composed according to a threefold logic that Chögyam Trungpa cherished. You begin with the first thought. This is the overall idea that gives the poem its tone. The second phrase develops this initial

---

14. "Jamgön Kongtrül," Boulder, December 1974, fifth talk, unpublished.

theme. Finally, the last movement is a sort of reversal or upturning of what has been said so far. Chögyam Trungpa, the master of outrage, excelled at this exercise. The new direction he gave his poems never failed to surprise his audience, while also sounding exactly right. Here is one example that illustrates these principles:

> His parents are having tea
> With his new girlfriend—
> Like a general inspecting the troops.[15]

Encounters with Allen Ginsberg

In 1970, while Chögyam Trungpa, Diana Mukpo, and Kunga, one of his students, were getting into a taxi, a man came up to them and said, "My father is ill—may I take your cab?" Kunga recognized the man as Allen Ginsberg, the famous Beat poet and emblem of American counterculture. He introduced him to Chögyam Trungpa.

In fact, Allen Ginsberg had already met Chögyam Trungpa in India, while the latter was at the Young Lamas School, but neither of them remembered that encounter. It was only after Chögyam Trungpa's death that Allen Ginsberg found a photo of himself with a young monk who had shown him the region around the school, and realized that the monk was none other than Chögyam Trungpa.

In any case, after this second meeting in New York, a sincere friendship began between the two. While Chögyam Trungpa introduced Allen Ginsberg to the Buddhist discipline of meditation, Ginsberg introduced him to the poetry of the Beat Generation, such as Jack Kerouac's *Mexico City Blues*. He also explained the very idea behind modern poetry since

---

15. From *Timely Rain*, by Chögyam Trungpa, p. 55. © 1972, 1983, 1998 by Diana J. Mukpo. Reprinted by arrangement with Shambhala Publications, Inc., Boston, www.shambhala.com. Reprinted with permission of Diana J. Mukpo.

Here is an example by Basho, one of the most famous Japanese masters of haiku:

> It happens that clouds
> Provide a restful change
> For moon admirers

Rimbaud and Apollinaire: poets had adopted a very free attitude toward language, as in the famous line of William Carlos Williams: "No ideas but in things,"[16] which is an invitation to pay attention above all to the words themselves. From this viewpoint, Ginsberg criticized certain turns of phrase in Chögyam Trungpa's poetry, such as the use of conventional metaphors like "galloping on a white horse." He explained that without concrete reality, it was merely an image. Symbolism should be more lively and anchored in an experience of the power of words themselves. Rinpoche started to introduce these more contemporary ideas into his poetry and to pay more attention to the poetic dimension itself. This change is particularly striking between *Mudra*, published in 1972, and the collection *First Thought Best Thought*, which appeared eleven years later.

Here is an excerpt from a poem written in 1959:

> The yogin who lives only in the hour
> Is the favoured one of all kingdoms;
> And since there is no need to reckon gifts and honour,
> Sever me from the appearance of devotees![17]

And here is one written in 1976:

> Chögyam is alive;
> No hope for the death of Chögyie
> With hot warm towels
> Breakfast in bed
> Chamber pots in their proper places
> Serving Chögyie as the precious jewel who may not
>   stay with us—

---

16. Declared on two occasions, in 1944, in *A Sort of a Song* and in 1946, in *Paterson I*.

17. From *Mudra*, by Chögyam Trungpa, p. 29. © 1972 by Diana J. Mukpo. Reprinted by arrangement with Shambhala Publications, Inc., Boston, www.shambhala.com. Reprinted with permission of Diana J. Mukpo.

All take part in the platitude of serving Chögyie as a
dying person![18]

David Rome, who edited Chögyam Trungpa's poetry, thinks that it
was in about 1974 that Chögyam Trungpa found his own voice and produced his best work. It is sharp, brilliant, seizing on the slightest details
of our confusion. In the preface to a collection of poems, Allen Ginsberg
explained this quite specific quality: "The dramatic situation of someone who has realized the World as pure mind, & gone beyond attachment to ego to return to the world & work with universal ignorance,
confront the spiritual-materialist daydream of Western world—and tell
it in modernist poetry—provides the historic excitement this book puts
in our laps."[19]

It is necessary to emphasize the singular character of a poetry that
sought to employ the modern revolution we have already discussed. Generally, when spiritual teachers produce works of art, they try to follow the
canons of their tradition. Like his photographs, Chögyam Trungpa's
poems present the quintessence of the Buddhist experience but without
using any of the usual techniques of the masters of the past. He found a
new way to transmit the thought of buddhadharma.

Ginsberg added: "This book is evidence of a Buddha-natured child
taking first verbal steps age 35, in totally other language direction than he
spoke age 10, talking side of mouth slang: redneck, hippie, chamber of
commerce, good citizen, Oxfordian aesthete slang, like a dream Bodhisattva with thousand eyes & mouths talking turkey."[20]

In his poems, Chögyam Trungpa set about unseating the reader. His
texts begin by captivating or seducing us. Then the logic that has been
installed collapses. A sudden glimpse of immense space, beyond our

---

18. From *First Thought Best Thought*, by Chögyam Trungpa, p. 106. © 1989 by Diana J.
Mukpo. Reprinted by arrangement with Shambhala Publications, Inc., Boston, www.sham-
bhala.com. Reprinted with permission of Diana J. Mukpo.

19. Allen Ginsberg, introduction to *First Thought Best Thought*, p. xiii.

20. Ibid., p. xiv.

habitual thoughts, appears. Consider, for example, this text entitled "Samsara and Nirvana":

> A crow is black
> Because the lotus is white.
> Ants run fast
> Because the elephant is slow.
> Buddha was profound;
> Sentient beings are confused.[21]

These words play with our habitual use of logic. The repetition of *because* creates an illusion of meaning. Ants do not run faster than elephants, but because they are small, they appear to. On the other hand, the final affirmation sounds true, but in this context, it must remain questionable. Are human beings really confused and Buddha enlightened? We are not so sure anymore.

Improvisation

Chögyam Trungpa advised Allen Ginsberg on several points. First, he raised doubts about the sincerity of his political commitments. At the time, Ginsberg was actively opposed to nuclear power and to American involvement in the Vietnam War and was also fighting for gay rights. Chögyam Trungpa sometimes found such activities naive. To his mind, they could conceal deep resentment beneath a veil of generosity.

Furthermore, Chögyam Trungpa encouraged Ginsberg to alter the nature of the readings that he was then giving regularly across the United States. Instead of just reading out texts he had already written, he advised him to improvise.

It was in the spring of 1971, in Berkeley, that this change was to happen:

---

21. From *Timely Rain*, by Chögyam Trungpa, p. 46. © 1972, 1983, 1998 by Diana J. Mukpo. Reprinted by arrangement with Shambhala Publications, Inc., Boston, www.shambhala.com. Reprinted with permission of Diana J. Mukpo.

During his talk with Trungpa at the hotel, Allen had complained that he was fatigued by the endless cross-country poetry readings and the extended air travel. "That's because you don't like your poetry," said Trungpa.

"What do you know about poetry?" exclaimed Allen, struck but amused.

"Why do you need to depend on a piece of paper when you recite your poetry?" continued Trungpa. "Don't you trust your own mind? Why don't you do like the great poets, like Milarepa—improvise spontaneously on the spot."

That evening, at the Trungpa lecture, Allen improvised a silly ditty, rhyming "moon" and "June," "beer" and "dear"; it was surprisingly easy. His father's example and all Allen's youthful years of writing rhymed couplets came to fruition.[22]

The next evening, Allen had to give a public reading. Following Chögyam Trungpa's suggestion, he did not bring any books with him. "It was the first time I ever got onstage without a text, and had to improvise it out of the whole cloth of what I was thinking at the moment. And it was really awkward and unfinished, but it was so profound . . . and so liberating when I realized I didn't have to worry if I lost a poem any more, because I was the poet, I could just make it up."[23]

Chögyam Trungpa often asked his students to write a poem spontaneously. If they were feeling highly self-conscious and tense in his presence, such a request could terrify them. Even if you were feeling relaxed about being around him, the prospect of revealing your state of mind through a spontaneous poem was daunting. But he then explained that they should not be ashamed about sharing their state of mind, no matter how uncomfortable such an experience might be. Our habitual tendency is to avoid anything unpleasant about ourselves. But here, what really

---

22. Barry Miles, *Ginsberg: A Biography* (New York: Harper, 1989), p. 441.

23. Allen Ginsberg in Barry Miles, *Ginsberg*, pp. 441ff.

mattered was to forge a moment of authenticity in the present, and not necessarily to be brilliant.

Whereas Western art aims at the perfection of form, Chögyam Trungpa's poetry is marked by improvisation. His poetry is not an exercise in writing but a way of instantly living out an experience.

When he wanted to write a poem, he called for his secretary or one of his assistants and dictated it. David Rome explains the process:

> At the end of a long day of scheduled business—administrative meetings, individual or group audiences, perhaps a visit to a fledgling business venture, followed in the evening by a public talk or a community ceremony—late into the evening or even in the early hours of morning, Ven. Trungpa Rinpoche, just when his loyal but weary attendants think they are about to be released, declares, "Let's write a poem." Pen and paper are made ready. Then perhaps with a few moments of silent thought, more likely with no pause at all, he commences to dictate. The dictation is unhesitating, at a rate as fast and upon occasion faster (alas!) than the scribe can record. At the conclusion of dictation, Rinpoche asks, "Are there any problems?" This leads to a quick review of any unclear or grammatically inconsistent passages. Perhaps a few changes, such as bringing persons or tenses into agreement, are made, rarely anything of substance—though in the process Rinpoche himself may be inspired to interject a new couplet or stanza. Then a title—often a title and subtitle—are supplied by the poet, and the scribe is called upon to read the newborn poem, in a strong voice and with good enunciation, to the small audience which typically is present on these occasions. More often than not, further poems reiterating this sequence of events will follow over the course of another hour or two, or three.[24]

---

24. David I. Rome, editor's preface to *First Thought Best Thought*, p. xxiv.

Poetry as personal experience

From the day Chögyam Trungpa decided to cast off his monk's robes, he also decided to give up keeping the slightest "secret garden." His poetry is a particularly moving example of the way he shared his heart and mind with his audiences and readers.

In the course of this book, I have never tried to describe Chögyam Trungpa's experience; how is it possible to know what such a man thought or felt? But his poetry is an invitation into his inner self.

We must once again follow David Rome, who, in his afterword to the collection *Timely Rain*, which he edited, describes the specific nature of Chögyam Trungpa's poetry. He shows that it is "perhaps the only place where he is able to step out of all the roles and self-inventions and speak truthfully from—and to—his own heart."[25]

David Rome emphasized the importance of the theme of solitude, which Chögyam Trungpa often returned to, adopting a variety of tones depending on his situation. But such solitude is never tinged with the slightest poverty. It is linked to a profound nakedness, an absolute stripping away, which lies behind all existences, but which he was able to take on to a quite exceptional degree.

This excerpt from one of his poems is particularly eloquent on this point:

> Fatherless, always dwelling in foreign lands,
> Motherless, not hearing the speech of my own country,
> Friendless, tears not quenching my thirst,
> Remembering the warriors of the father and mother
>   lineages,
> I live alone in the sole blessing
> Of the only father guru and the Great Eastern Sun.[26]

---

25. David I. Rome, afterword to *Timely Rain*, p. 193.

26. From *The Rain of Wisdom*, by Chögyam Trungpa, p. 289. © 1980 by Diana J. Mukpo. Reprinted by arrangement with Shambhala Publications, Inc., Boston, www.shambhala.com. Reprinted with permission of Diana J. Mukpo.

Chögyam Trungpa's poems open the door of his heart for us: "By turns thorny and tender-hearted—like Trungpa Rinpoche himself— these poems are passionate transmutations of loneliness that invite us to taste the raw and real stuff of life."[27]

4. Painting and Calligraphy

When still a child, Chögyam Trungpa became interested in painting. As an adolescent, he visited the monastery of Karma, the third most important monastery of the Karma Kagyü school. The entire region around it, called Karma Geru, was famous for its art. The monastery's artists traveled throughout Tibet to honor commissions they had received. But Chögyam Trungpa noted the decline in their tradition, which he understood when he looked at the life-size sculptures of the various incarnations of the Gyalwa Karmapa, the supreme lama of the order. He observed that the artistic quality was perfect up until the portrait of the eighth incarnation, but that the workmanship declined in the next seven. He spoke of this disappointment in Born in Tibet, adding: "This point struck me and I felt that it might be possible for me to do something to revive Tibetan art."[28] Although Communist oppression put an end to this project, he was to remain faithful to this ambition all his life. So how to cut through conformity and rediscover a truly spiritual art?

Chögyam Trungpa's artistic taste matured very quickly. He was immediately able to distinguish between conventional art and work that possessed a genuine sacred dimension. The difficulty in making such judgments is one of the clearest signs of the artistic decadence of our era, which also affects all of our spiritual traditions. Works that follow the traditional canons are generally lifeless imitations. In a sense, Chögyam Trungpa's work was an answer to the crisis in sacred art today.

In Tibet, Chögyam Trungpa had learned the techniques of traditional

---

27. David I. Rome, afterword to Timely Rain, p. 199.

28. Born in Tibet, 4th ed. (2000), p. 87.

painting, and during his stay in India, he made some drawings and paintings that have been preserved.[29] He learned calligraphy in England and worked on it later in the United States. The advantage of calligraphy is that it is produced instantaneously and with great freedom. This choice can perhaps be explained by the shock he experienced when confronted with the Japanese tradition. It was a source of renewal for his vision.

When he decided to produce some calligraphy, an atmosphere of profound calm intensity reigned around him. His slow, precise movements created an immense space for all who were present. The motion of his arm above the sheet of paper was extremely sensual. Sarah Coleman describes the experience thus: "His joy was so radiant and clear, you felt like you could eat it. Watching him work was a great moment of happiness."

His early calligraphy is precise. The care he put into trying to capture the shape of the letters is manifest. Later, it became increasingly free when compared with traditional norms.

Furthermore, Chögyam Trungpa enriched the Tibetan tradition with Japanese techniques, which he learned from masters such as Soen Roshi and Edo Roshi. In this way, he united two Asian traditions. Tibetan calligraphy is generally carried out with a bamboo pen, thus resulting in letters with sharp angles and abrupt transitions between upstrokes and downstrokes. In contrast, the brush used in Japanese and Chinese calligraphy produces sinuous lines and subtle changes of direction. Chögyam Trungpa also tried to produce calligraphy in English, but the Roman alphabet offered him fewer possibilities.

David Rome described the general order in which Chögyam Trungpa worked: "Typically, the initial one or two strokes of a calligraphy by

---

29. For example, after a vision of Guru Rinpoche, he painted a thangka of this teacher. It is in the form of Guru Nangsi Silnön, "the guru who is the power of all apparent phenomena and of all existence." In contrast to conventional thangkas, there is no sketch of a landscape in the background. The vision is suspended in the middle of the sky. Guru Rinpoche is thus depicted on a cloud and seems to be moving toward the viewer. Chögyam Trungpa also painted a thangka of Yeshe Tsogyal, Guru Rinpoche's female spiritual partner; three paintings of different protectors, in which he painted only their faces; and a magnificent interpretation of the dream of Milarepa. This final work is in the spirit of Chinese landscape art, with a central pillar on which a vulture has made its nest.

Trungpa Rinpoche have a gentle deliberateness, evoking a sense of mindfulness and precision; then there is a crescendo, expressed in greater speed of execution and a sense of leap or abrupt sword stroke; finally, a 'follow through' stroke both completes the gesture and lets go of it."[30]

Chögyam Trungpa never kept his work; he gave it away. He considered that the commercialization of art created a situation of corruption both for the artist and for the public. He produced his calligraphy for particular events, such as the opening of a meditation center or the birthday of one of his students. In Boulder, this led to a joke: How can you tell if a house belongs to a Buddhist? You just have to look through the window and see if there is any calligraphy hanging on the wall.[31]

5. Ikebana

Chögyam Trungpa studied ikebana in England with Stella Coe, one of the finest English teachers in the Sogetsu school of Japanese flower arrangement: "My meeting with my teacher provided me with a tremendous shock and surprise that such a new dimension of working with reality could be expressed by means of that particular arrangement. . . . in fact the whole thing is like the Buddhist teaching."[32] Chögyam Trungpa appreciated this artistic form, which allowed him to work with the moment and share his vision with those around him, for he loved working in a group.

This discipline goes back to the sixth century CE, when offerings of flowers were made to the Buddha. A contemplative tradition then developed from these early bouquets. As Stella Coe writes: "Ikebana was recognized along with other arts, as a means of calming and purifying the

---

30. David I. Rome, introduction to *The Art of Calligraphy,* p. 10.

31. *The Art of Calligraphy: Joining Heaven and Earth,* a book reproducing some of Chögyam Trungpa's calligraphies, was published by Shambhala Publications in 1994. The excellent introduction by David Rome provides a detailed description of Chögyam Trungpa's working methods, which I have followed here.

32. Chögyam Trungpa, *Kalapa Ikebana Newsletter,* Winter 1984, p. 1.

mind; it was therefore adapted to the training needs of the samurai and practiced by them as a means of composing their minds in order to be at one with nature, to experience neither hesitation, nor fear."[33]

The state of mind that presides over the creation of an arrangement is vital. The way of working, Chögyam Trungpa explained, is more important than the final result, as opposed to the attitude of most practitioners today, who become lost in the technique rather than allowing the exercise to transform them: "The arrangements are dismantled after a few hours, and nobody regards them as monumental works of art. It is just a one-shot deal."[34]

Chögyam Trungpa's arrangements were often spectacular. Whenever he could, he liked to select a main branch that was as large as an entire tree.

6. A Complete Artist

We have looked at some of the aspects of Chögyam Trungpa's artistic activities. But more than being a painter, photographer, theater director, or filmmaker, Chögyam Trungpa was an artist who used different disciplines. For him, there was no difference between making a film, serving dinner, getting dressed, holding a conversation, opening a door, signing his name, smoking a cigarette, or giving a talk. He paid attention to the slightest details while having a clear vision of what he wanted to convey. For him, everything was a moment to celebrate life.

Nietzsche gave an excellent description of this position:

> We must consider in this production of creative beings the indescribable malaise that they so often spread around themselves, when we evaluate the joy and ennoblement that humanity owes to

33. Stella Coe, *Ikebana: A Practical and Philosophical Guide to Japanese Flower Arrangement* (New York: Woodstock, 1984), p. 24.

34. Chögyam Trungpa, *1980 Seminary Transcripts: Hinayana-Mahayana* (Boulder: Vajradhatu Publications), p. 23.

their works. Their inability to dominate themselves, their jealousy, their ill-will and their uncertain characters mean that there are as often wrong-doers for humanity, where they would be its benefactors. In particular, the behavior of one genius to another is one of history's darkest pages. Veneration of genius has often been an unconscious form of devil worship. We should calculate how many men have corrupted their character and taste by frequenting geniuses. We have perhaps more need of great men without works than great works for which such a heavy price has to be paid in terms of human souls. But at present we barely understand what a great man without works might be.[35]

Chögyam Trungpa is an example of a great man without great works. Instead of carefully producing remarkable work or making masterpieces, he preferred to see artistic work as a celebration of the present. In a calligraphy, an ikebana arrangement, or a photograph, the result did not matter to him so much as the moment of production. All his works were improvisations. For him, the end never justifies the means. What matters is "how." His work contains no notion of aggression, power grabbing, or ambition. He wanted to preserve the freshness of true freedom. He did not think that artists have anything special about them that put them above society. Once a work is finished, he asserted, then the artist is just one more spectator among others.

---

35. Friedrich Nietzsche, *Dawn of Day*.

Chapter Fourteen

THE KARMAPA'S VISIT AND THE INTRODUCTION OF FORMALITIES MANIFESTING ENLIGHTENMENT

In working with students in the Western world, I have been presenting a twofold message: first, how to overcome psychological and spiritual materialism; second, how to overcome physical materialism. The first message is designed to help people become genuine practitioners in the Buddhist world. The second message is to help people overcome actual physical materialism by practicing the disciplines of body, speech, and mind, so that they become warriors in the enlightened world of Shambhala.[1]

—CHÖGYAM TRUNGPA

1. Establishing a Set of Formalities

If we were to try to understand Chögyam Trungpa only from the content of his talks, we would miss out on a profound part of his vision. For the formalities he created and adopted were just as powerful a vehicle as his oral and written teachings. They helped to communicate enlightenment. As he put it: "Atmosphere answers ninety percent of the questions. Words are just a confirmation, and give something to hang on to."[2]

His way of being an artist, in everything he did, appears all the more startling in the way he taught his students to dress, to behave when

---

1. *Great Eastern Sun*, p. 37.

2. Chögyam Trungpa, talk to Level Two team of Shambhala Training, October 9, 1978, unpublished.

teaching, to arrange meditation centers, or to organize Seminary and cycles of Shambhala Training. All of these sorts of behavior or "formalities" were ways for him to transmit his spirit and vision. By such means, Chögyam Trungpa remains alive. Going to one of his centers is not like going anywhere else, for it means entering the world dedicated to enlightenment that he established. We receive a deep and direct transmission of a moment of enlightenment, which involves our minds just as much as our senses and emotions.

Why formalities?

Although Chögyam Trungpa constantly emphasized formalities, it is the part of his teachings that people find the most disturbing.

Some consider that the world created by Chögyam Trungpa degenerates into uniformity, especially when his students imitate him too closely. It is certainly true that many of them, especially early on, copied his teaching style, or the way he moved his hands when he spoke, or the habit of beginning talks with "There seems to be . . . ," a favorite expression of his for a time.

Many of his students' apartments were furnished like his in imitation of what they thought they had understood of the Shambhala teachings. At one time, one could find the same living room with a light-colored couch (white or beige), an attractive piece of calligraphy in black India ink—very often a present from Chögyam Trungpa—hung on the wall in a nice sober frame, plus a few items of Japanese decoration to round off an austere yet comfortable interior. Was that the project of Chögyam Trungpa? Should Shambhala culture lead to such uniformity?

In even more radical terms, some wonder if the flags on the walls and the other graphic designs that go with them, the wearing of a navy blue blazer to a lecture, afternoon tea, and the endless cocktail parties—all of which can indeed be found in some of the centers founded by Chögyam Trungpa—are really a necessary part of the teachings.

Why should wearing a tie, as Chögyam Trungpa encouraged his male students to do, bring us any closer to the dharma? Doesn't this interfere with our freedom, and bring us into line with middle-class conformity?

Aren't all these formalities now dated and, the Europeans might ask, only appropriate in an American context? Wouldn't Chögyam Trungpa have done things differently if he had lived elsewhere or been addressing a different generation? Such questions deserve careful analysis.

To follow these formalities in a blind or servile way, or else to reject them in the name of individualism, is to miss the point. Chögyam Trungpa attempted by a variety of means to show that a different relationship with formality is possible.

Such an effort is admittedly irritating. By asking his students to pay attention to their lifestyle, Chögyam Trungpa ran counter to the "casual" character of American life, which is daily becoming ever more the norm.

The so-called freedom from rules that characterizes our time leads people to a uniformity that was unknown before. Everyone in Paris, Berlin, New York, San Francisco, and Tokyo tends to be dressed the same way, eat the same fast food, and drink the same beverages.

It is one of the strangest paradoxes about our society. Never has individuality been talked about so much, yet it is uniformity that clearly dominates. The same people who criticize and condemn rituals as things of the past blindly obey the dictates of consumer society. As the philosopher and jurist Pierre Legendre put it: "Management preaches for transparent, rational and benevolent power, it chases away the darkness of mythology, it believes in the uselessness of ceremonies."[3] But, as Pierre Legendre explained, to renounce ritual would mean giving up what makes us human.

Formalities are what constitute our lifestyles. Unlike animals, human beings don't have the singular capacity of naturally being human.[4] We

---

3. Pierre Legendre, *La Fabrique de l'homme occidental* (Paris: Mille et une nuits, 1996), p. 7. In the English word *management*, we find the Old French word *masnage* or *mesnage*, meaning "household." Management is the economic order that is limited to the domestic sphere, while the political order applies to community life. When the economic order becomes public there is no more real community life.

4. Being human requires a strange kind of "effort." For example, a cat is always feline, whatever it does. But a person can easily be "inhuman"; humanity is not given to us once and for all. The path described by Chögyam Trungpa is not so much spiritual as a way to attain to our own humanity.

can be polite or rude, direct or underhanded, have ulterior motives or speak from the heart, and so on.

Chögyam Trungpa was constantly taking part in rituals and elaborating forms of behavior. As Herbert Guenther explained: "We need not be mystified by the idea of ritual. An example of ritual is the custom of a man's removing his hat when he meets a lady. It is a kind of formalized gesture. It is also a way of going about a human relationship."[5] Chögyam Trungpa showed that all the gestures that make up human relationships can be expressions of our dignity, transmit basic goodness, and express our openness to others. Attention to formalities was the deepest way to make the teachings incarnate in everyone's life through concrete discipline.

Here, the word *formality* is not being used in its weak sense, or to stand for arbitrary politeness. Instead, it designates the idea of "giving form," in other words, in its full sense of framing a typically human way of life, which is no longer "natural." We all live in a web of rituals. This is the primary meaning of culture.[6]

Thus it should be understood that Chögyam Trungpa's idea was to invent formalities not for their own sake, but only so that they would help us open out to the pure presence of nowness. Chögyam Trungpa often explained that *now* is the only thing that matters: "When corruption enters a culture, it is because that culture ceases to be *now*; it becomes past and

---

5. Herbert V. Guenther, in Herbert V. Guenther and Chögyam Trungpa, *The Dawn of Tantra*, p. 2.

6. Note that nothing is strictly natural or cultural for human beings. These two orders are so closely interwoven that any distinction is extremely limited. Maurice de Merleau-Ponty, in *Phénoménologie de la perception* (Paris: Gallimard, Collection Tel, 1952), pp. 220–221, had this to say on the subject:

"It is no more natural or less conventional to cry out in anger, to kiss a loved one, or to call a table a table. Feelings and passionate behavior have been invented just like words. Even ones such as paternity, which seem inscribed in the human body, are in reality institutions.

"It is impossible to fix an initial layer of behavior in man which we could call 'natural,' followed by an artificial spiritual or cultural world. In man, everything is artificial and everything is natural, to put it another way there is not a single word or behavior that does not owe something to our biological selves, but which does not at the same time escape from the simplicity of animal existence, or alter the meaning of vital functions, by a sort of sleight of hand or genius for ambiguity which could stand as a definition of mankind."

future. Periods in history when great art was created, when learning advanced or peace spread, were all *now*. These situations happened at the very moment of their *now*. But after *now* happened, then those cultures lost their *now*."[7] This quality can be seen, for example, when we compare a sculpture that makes the space around it alive and vitalizes our vision, or an overwhelming monument. Based on this understanding, Chögyam Trungpa instituted new rituals, then dropped them or altered them if they seemed to him to lose this quality.

In other words, Chögyam Trungpa tried to give his disoriented students the chance to rediscover a genuine culture.

2. The Karmapa's Visit: A Turning Point

How formalities allow a "sacred vision" to be manifested

When we recall how Chögyam Trungpa and his students lived in the youth culture of the early 1970s, such an insistence on formality may seem surprising. The crucial moment of change was the first visit of Rangjung Rikpe Dorje, His Holiness the sixteenth Karmapa, to America in 1974. This occasion would bring with it a totally unfamiliar series of ceremonies, formalities, and etiquette, all displaying a striking dignity. This was a historic opportunity for Chögyam Trungpa to expose his students to the greatness of the Kagyü lineage and to introduce them to the Tibetan formalities that made up the tradition. But what mattered was not so much to maintain the Tibetan character of formalities as to demonstrate the way that formality can create an environment that transforms everyone's state of mind.

On this occasion, Chögyam Trungpa wrote an inscription in the book called *Empowerment*, which was published in celebration of the Karmapa's visit: "Many American students have wanted to reject their own traditions and seek something more colorful elsewhere, but the message of nonaggression and compassion presented by buddhadharma has brought them to appreciate America as their true homeground.

---

7. *Shambhala: The Sacred Path of the Warrior* (Shambhala Library, 2003), p. 101.

Accordingly, I would like to dedicate this volume to the land and the people of the United States of America: for providing accommodations and openness to His Holiness, and in honor of the Bicentennial of America's freedom."[8]

Such a visit was a pivotal historic event, which put an official seal on Chögyam Trungpa's attempts to establish the dharma in the West, not as a foreign entity, but as a genuine path available to anyone seeking to reconnect with their heart and the root of their innate wisdom.

Given that the Karmapa is the spiritual head of the Karma Kagyü lineage, and one of the highest Buddhist dignitaries, his visit was a great event. As Chögyam Trungpa wrote: "The visit to the United States of His Holiness the sixteenth Gyalwa Karmapa was a landmark historical event, from the point of view of both the orient and the occident. For American spiritual seekers especially, it made the powerful statement that a living embodiment of enlightenment could manifest himself quite apart from political or cultural demonstrations."[9]

Press releases were sent out in all major cities, and there was extensive media coverage of the event. Although Tibet had been discussed publicly before, one might say that this was the first time that Americans had seen the "official face" of Tibetan Buddhism. (His Holiness the Dalai Lama did not come to the United States for the first time until 1976.) The Karmapa had a very regal presence, and people with no connection to Tibetan Buddhism were deeply affected by just seeing him. Chögyam Trungpa and his students set up receptions in major cities and in Boulder for the Karmapa to meet with civic leaders, politicians, artists, university professors, and others. With a group of monks, Gyalwa Karmapa traveled across the United States, visiting towns and carrying out several ceremonies and empowerment rituals both in front of large audiences and for small groups of practitioners.

---

8. *Empowerment* (Boulder: Vajradhatu Publications, 1976), p. 7.

9. Ibid.

An intense period of preparation

Well before his arrival, there was an intense period of preparation. To receive the Karmapa properly, Chögyam Trungpa carried out an amount of work that surpasses anything we can imagine. He organized groups of his students in every city where His Holiness would be visiting and told them how to transform the environments that he would be living and teaching in. Chögyam Trungpa himself was completely involved in these preparations, rarely rested, and slept only a few hours a night. He seemed to be everywhere. He wanted to deal with the slightest detail himself. He showed everyone what to do. He wanted to receive the Karmapa in grand style.

It came as a shock to see their teacher work so intensely. He was quite capable at three o'clock in the morning of explaining in his soft voice how to iron the satin cloth used to cover the seat on which His Holiness would sit at Karma Dzong, the chief center in Boulder. It was the first time that most of his students had ever seen a traditional Tibetan throne, which Rinpoche insisted should be constructed in every city where the Karmapa would teach. Rinpoche would personally check to see that the students working on preparing the Karmapa's residence had enough to eat; he toured every venue and would personally explain the significance of the particular decorations he wanted in each room where the Karmapa was going to give an initiation, meet people, and so on. Early on, he sent one of his students to Japan to buy the finest brocades for His Holiness's thrones and other uses. Then, once the brocades were received, he would meet with the seamstresses to discuss how to sew them and would personally visit them to see how the work was coming. He consulted with carpenters, painters, cooks, drivers, and others.

Whenever the students felt that the preparations were complete, Chögyam Trungpa would appear wanting more to be done, more details to be attended to. He wanted more candles, more colors, more decorations....

In this way, he introduced the formalities that expressed the Karmapa's absolute dignity—but which also implied recognition of our own dignity too: "We are not purely devotees who will kneel in the dirt and receive blessings, but we are elegant people, worthy of receiving the teachings."[10] Chögyam Trungpa encouraged his students, many of whom were rather disheveled at the time, to bone up on their Western etiquette, to work on their posture and polish their table manners, to press their best suit, or buy one, to find an elegant but modest dress, and to cut their hair and beards in some cases. At the same time, he gave intensive lessons in Tibetan culture and etiquette. He wanted his students to be as relaxed with and knowledgeable about the convention of making and serving Tibetan butter tea as they were with creating an English tea party or brewing and serving a good cup of coffee. To provide appropriate security and drivers for His Holiness, Rinpoche asked a group of his students to serve as guards. Their essential job was to create an appropriate environment to receive the Karmapa. (Discussion of the guards known as the Dorje Kasung appears in chapter 21.)

A moving meeting

To understand fully the importance of the meeting between Chögyam Trungpa and the Karmapa, it must be remembered that he was Chögyam Trungpa's spiritual superior and had recognized him as the eleventh Trungpa.[11]

But, as surprising as it might seem today with hindsight when we know about the exemplary work the Karmapa carried out in the world, and the attitude of intense, unhesitating devotion that Chögyam Trungpa had for him, before this first visit the Dorje Dradül was not 100 percent enthusiastic about the visit of the Karmapa. He felt that it was important to make all these preparations, yet he explained quite honestly that he was

---

10. Chögyam Trungpa, "His Holiness Karmapa's Funeral," Boulder, December 1981, unpublished.

11. After the death of the tenth Trungpa in 1938, the monks of Surmang sent a messenger to the Karmapa to inform him of their teacher's passing and ask for indications as to where they could find his new incarnation. A few months later, he visited the monastery of Palpung, which was then run by Jamgön Kongtrül, who had been a disciple of the tenth Trungpa, and who once again asked him whether he had found the eleventh Trungpa. He succeeded in doing so by writing two letters describing some visions he had had. When the child was found, the Karmapa enthroned him during a later trip to the region.

above all receiving the holder of the lineage. He was not sure of the Karmapa's personal attainment. He spoke about problems that some of the highest lamas encountered in trying to get sufficient education. Sometimes they were expected to "perform" as spiritual leaders at such a young age that there was not sufficient time given to their actual accomplishment of the teachings.

Thus by officially inviting and receiving the Karmapa, Chögyam Trungpa was principally inviting the lineage holder to bless the dharmic situation in the West. This was of capital importance, but he didn't know what to expect in terms of the Karmapa's personal level of attainment. What was extraordinary about Chögyam Trungpa's attitude is the way he exposed his thinking on this matter to his students so openly. It ran against usual diplomatic rules and provides another example of the qualities that allowed Chögyam Trungpa to plant Buddhism so deeply in the West: he never hid behind conventions. He completely trusted his students. Because of his honesty, everything he said was taken seriously. One might also note that Chögyam Trungpa had been outside of the Tibetan "fold" since his marriage and departure from England in 1970. Reports sent to India about his behavior by his Tibetan colleagues in England portrayed Rinpoche as a troubled lama, not a great spiritual pioneer. So both the Karmapa and Chögyam Trungpa were unsure of how they would feel about one another.

When the Karmapa first arrived in North America, Chögyam Trungpa welcomed him as he got off the plane in New York. As soon as he saw him, he was deeply struck and moved. Their meeting was incredibly intense. Chögyam Trungpa walked beside him, sobbing without the slightest reserve.

When he returned to Boulder to complete the preparations for His Holiness's visit there, he gathered all his students together. Sarah Coleman remembers the extremely serious atmosphere that reigned. Chögyam Trungpa explained to them that the Karmapa was truly accomplished, and they should forget everything he had said before: "There's no doubt about it. I don't have a single one. He's really the true holder of the lineage. He understands everything. It's true. There isn't the slightest problem between us. I'm telling you. I'm pleased and relieved you can see him. Now

prepare to meet someone who's completely enlightened." He wept. Everyone was surprised because Chögyam Trungpa had never spoken of anyone, or at least no living person, in this way.

What is impressive in this story is that Chögyam Trungpa had no
qualms about sharing with his students his doubts concerning what was
in fact a sensitive subject. One of the reasons that Chögyam Trungpa was
criticized by other Tibetans was that he absolutely refused to keep any
secrets from his students, including being open about the politics going
on in the Tibetan world. He shared his heart with them, in complete
honesty, with no regard for political convention. Thanks to this attitude,
when he himself witnessed the authentic presence of His Holiness
Karmapa, it was even more powerful for his students. Clearly, there was
no pretense. He displayed the authentic meaning of the devotion and
truth of the teachings that the Karmapa manifested. For devotion has
nothing to do with some conventional beatific admiration, nor even respect for a hierarchical superior; it is the recognition of the unique truth
of spiritual realization.

During the entire visit, Chögyam Trungpa manifested his emotion, for
example, prostrating at the Karmapa's feet with no concern for the fact
that his paralysis meant that he could not get up again. His students had
to help him rise. Chögyam Trungpa did not find this humiliating. His
love for the Karmapa overflowed at all times.

Such behavior sent an electric shock through the sangha. As Eric
Spiegel, then present, says: "We were submerged in the intensity of the
devotion he constantly manifested." Tibetan Buddhism, and especially
the Kagyü school, is famous for its fearless devotion and overall for the
acceptance of emotions when they are an ardent expression of a desire
for enlightenment. Buddhism includes all of our being, in a unity, without the Western dichotomy between sense and sensibility. The greater
our devotion, the nearer we are to the mind of the teacher and of the
buddhas.

The high point of the Karmapa's visit was incontestably the vajra
crown ceremony, which he performed a number of times during his visit
to the United States, and for the first time in America on September 21,
1974, at the New York Dharmadhatu. During each of these events, which

he alone can perform, he enters into the manifestation of Chenrezik (Avalokiteshvara), the Bodhisattva of Compassion. His expression transformed, the Karmapa then puts the sacred crown on his head and holds it with his right hand while reciting the mantra of Chenrezik (OM MANI PADME HUM) 108 times. The force of the presence that radiates from him, his intense radiance, the austere music of the trumpets and cymbals make this ritual one of the most unforgettable there is. His intent gaze, looking out toward the infinite, takes on a cosmic profundity. It seems as if his mind, transcending all limits, extends well beyond what for us is his bodily form. For those who are ready to recognize it, he reveals the unity underlying the limitless variety of appearances. Each one has a pure and direct experience of enlightenment, an inexhaustible energy of compassion toward all beings mixed with emptiness, which has become distinctly tangible.

These ceremonies were public, but those who worked intensely to create such an environment lived the event in a heightened way. The constant attention to the forms, which had required so much effort and precision, had also opened in them an enhanced receptivity, allowing the master to manifest more completely. From such an expression of their respect, each person found him- or herself humbler, more vulnerable, more in keeping with this dignity.

This visit was also a turning point in how Chögyam Trungpa was viewed by the Tibetan world. Until then, many considered him to be a maverick, a renegade. What was being said in Tibetan circles was: "He has abandoned Buddhism for the religion of the West"; "He is not teaching the dharma."[12] He had abandoned his monk's robes, he had married a Westerner, he had not seen his gurus again, and so on.

But the Karmapa was struck by what he discovered about Chögyam Trungpa's work in the United States and by Chögyam Trungpa himself. On September 29, 1974, the thirteenth day of the eighth month of the Year of the Wood Tiger, according to the Tibetan calendar, the Karmapa made a solemn proclamation:

---

12. As quoted by Thrangu Rinpoche, who was always close to Chögyam Trungpa, in the *Vajradhatu Sun,* October/November 1990, p. 19.

Chökyi Gyamtso Trungpa Rinpoche, supreme incarnate being, has magnificently carried out the vajra holder's discipline in the land of America, bringing about the liberation of students and ripening them in the dharma. This wonderful truth is clearly manifest.

Accordingly, I empower Chögyam Trungpa Vajra Holder and Possessor of the Victory Banner of the Practice Lineage of the Karma Kagyü. Let this be recognized by all people of both elevated and ordinary station.

By this declaration, the Karmapa recognized the importance of the work accomplished by Chögyam Trungpa, who now was publicly recognized as one of the greatest teachers of Tibetan Buddhism. Even if his approach was still shocking to many other Tibetan teachers, he had now become an example rather than a renegade. What he had accomplished was now recognized. It was no longer possible to discount the potential of Westerners to hear the complete and authentic dharma. His students displayed a real understanding of Buddhism, and the way they looked after the Karmapa and his large suite of important dignitaries and monks impressed everybody.

The sacred vision

Having once been anticonformist hippies, most of Chögyam Trungpa's students had until now rejected all sorts of formality, which they considered superficial or artificial. For many of them, being Buddhist meant belonging to a rather eccentric elite. It was out of the question for them to obey rules and end up being like their parents' generation, whom they regarded as prisoners of middle-class conventionality.

The Karmapa's visit was a revelation of Buddhism's royal, dignified aspect, which was now also a Western inheritance. In this way, formalities could be a way for them to experience "sacred outlook, or *tag nang* in Tibetan, [which] literally means 'pure perception,'"[13] instead of accepting an alienating conformity.

---

13. *The Heart of the Buddha*, p. 142.

In vajrayana Buddhism, the approach to the sacred is not "a matter of things being big and enormous and beyond the measure of one's thought; rather it has to do with things being so true, so real, so direct. We know a fire burns. We know the earth carries us. We know that space accommodates us. All these are *real* facts, and so obvious. Obviousness becomes sacredness from the point of view of vajrayana. It is not that things are sacred because they are beyond our imagination, but because they are so obvious."[14]

The Karmapa himself was struck by the dignity he found embodied in Chögyam Trungpa's students. He asked in astonishment: "How on earth did you manage to make them not slouch like in Europe, and to look at the vajra crown properly, fully?"[15] The posture of keeping the head up and the shoulders straight, and the discipline Chögyam Trungpa's students displayed, were all sure signs of their attainment.

After the Karmapa's visit, a sense of ceremony and formality henceforth became an integral part of community life. For example, Chögyam Trungpa's students began to address him with more formality and to stand when he entered a room to give a talk. They no longer felt comfortable leaning against the wall or even lying down when he was giving a lecture, and people began to think about what they wore to an interview with him or to a talk he was giving. The world was no longer seen as unconnected with the spiritual path and undeserving of attention. On the contrary, it was the place where an authentic spirituality could express itself. Hence the vital importance of decorum, which "occurs at every point where mind touches the phenomenal world. That is why we stand when a person of rank enters the space, or bow when we first enter the shrine room. We are not performing these actions because they are prescribed in a code. Decorum exists because such actions, properly executed, express natural hierarchy and sacred world on the spot."[16]

However, remaining faithful to his vision, Chögyam Trungpa refused

---

14. *Illusion's Game,* p. 133.

15. Quoted by Chögyam Trungpa, "His Holiness Karmapa's Funeral," Boulder, December 1981, unpublished.

16. Chögyam Trungpa, "The Decorum of Shambhala," Shambhala Lodge, Boulder, 1986, p. 4.

whenever his students suggested that he should follow Tibetan custom and sit on a throne when he taught, that brocade should be placed on the seat of any chair he might occupy, or that everyone should prostrate three times to begin each meeting with him. Some of these formalities did begin to be introduced in special contexts, such as his presentation of advanced vajrayana teachings, but he never allowed them to become the everyday protocol. He did not want to simply reproduce Tibetan customs, but rather to create new ones that would be more accessible and relevant to the Western world, while conveying the same sense of dignity. Another step in his presentation of Buddhism had been taken.

He wanted the approach of seeing the world as sacred to infiltrate our way of seeing the secular world: "You may be living in a very difficult situation. Maybe your apartment is purely plastic, flimsy, and artificial, built by the setting-sun people. You don't have to live in a palace all the time. Wherever you are, it is a palace."[17]

The difficulty in such a vision, which in fact institutes a new culture, is that it immediately rubs up against our opposition to any formality of ritual. We assume that it is a purely arbitrary formality with no relationship to our hearts.

Chögyam Trungpa fully realized this difficulty, which is symptomatic of the profound crisis of the West: "the humanistic view of good manners and dignity [is] merely [a] conventional [game] remote from the actuality of the situation."[18]

However, "the point of good behavior is to communicate our respect for others. So we should be concerned with how we behave. When someone enters a room, we should say hello, or stand up and greet them with a handshake. Those rituals are connected with how to have more consideration for others."[19]

After the Karmapa's visit, Chögyam Trungpa constantly presented the reason behind these formalities. He familiarized his students with the natural dignity that can exist in them.

---

17. *Great Eastern Sun*, p. 43.

18. *The Heart of the Buddha*, p. 176.

19. *Shambhala: The Sacred Path of the Warrior* (Shambhala Library, 2003), pp. 127–128.

Chapter Fifteen

A BUDDHISM
FOR THE WEST

FOUNDING A NEW CULTURE

My students are learning to develop some sense of culture and society . . . through proper households, table manners, and decorum of all kinds: how to dress, how to eat, how to be—all these principles.[1]

—CHÖGYAM TRUNGPA

PRESENTING THE BUDDHADHARMA through purely Tibetan forms and rituals would probably reduce it to mere folklore, distant from the problems each of us encounter in our daily lives and the political and social questions we are confronted with. Chögyam Trungpa was aware of this stumbling block and so abandoned a large part of the references to his own culture, the better to present the true heart of the Buddhist vision.

He tried to present Buddhism in such a way that it could be seen not as something foreign to the West, but as a way of entering into the heart of the wisdom each culture contains.

---

1. Chögyam Trungpa, "Tenth Anniversary Dharma Celebration," *Vajradhatu Sun*, February/March 1981, p. 28.

Buddhism has an intrinsically universal potential and has moved into the most varied countries and civilizations. For instance, the way it is practiced in Tibet is very different from what happens in Japan. Chögyam Trungpa thought it vital to discover forms that could become part of our culture and so allow a Western Buddhism to grow—which would also be colored by the Shambhala vision and teachings.

Chögyam Trungpa emphasized that it was not a question of his students becoming Tibetan. Their karma was American, as he explained in 1974 during a seminar entitled "Tibetan Buddhism and American Karma."

This culture would offer an opportunity to enter into a relationship with others and to put into action the vision of the bodhisattva in the creation of an enlightened society. It would teach us how to be in direct contact with reality as it is, to feel comfortable in all kinds of social situations, to know what we must do in the presence of the Karmapa or our boss, in a city life or with our children.

To create such a culture, Chögyam Trungpa mined three major traditions: those of England, Japan, and Tibet. These three worlds, however different they may seem, have a common sense of ceremony that is highly developed and that, from the perspective of founding an enlightened society, could take on a new meaning.

1. The Sources of a New Culture: England, Japan, and Tibet

England and the West

Chögyam Trungpa saw England as an example of courtesy and dignity that could serve as a model for his American students. Over the centuries, Great Britain has developed an extremely subtle formal language, which has in turn nourished the rest of the world. By borrowing from many of its forms, Chögyam Trungpa helped his students to rediscover their own roots.

Ties, suits, and uniforms

During the Karmapa's visit, the word went around: if you were a man, you had to wear a tie. To understand the meaning of this request and avoid trivializing it, it is necessary to study Chögyam Trungpa's own relationship with clothing. This will allow us to grasp the importance of the apparently banal fact of being well dressed.

During the first years of his stay in England, Chögyam Trungpa wore the traditional robes of a monk, before abandoning them after his car accident. When he arrived in the United States, he dressed in a casual way as his students did, in the hippie fashion. He took a liking to certain kinds of ethnic clothing. He traveled to Mexico a few months after his arrival in the United States and bought several Mexican shirts that he wore quite frequently during the early seventies. When he taught at the Vajradhatu Seminary in Jackson Hole, Wyoming, in 1973, he sometimes wore cowboy shirts and occasionally a cowboy hat as well. He was in the West and so appropriated its culture.

After the first visit of His Holiness the Karmapa in 1974, Chögyam Trungpa wore a suit and tie for almost all public occasions. For the Karmapa's visit, he had hesitated over what he should wear as a mark of respect. He did not want to return to his monk's robes, because he had broken his vows. Part of the time, he wore a chuba, the Tibetan layman's dress. But much of the time he wore a suit and tie.

His choice of wearing a suit and tie came from his appreciation of English manners. He encouraged his male students to wear them as well, because it was an opportunity to work with real discipline. Each religious practitioner wears a sort of uniform, which represents the discipline he or she is attempting to follow: male Orthodox Jews wear skullcaps or hats and a *talis katan*, a small fringed prayer shawl, under their clothing. In the Catholic Church, until recently, priests wore dark clothing, black robes, and a cross, and nuns wore habits as well. But today we are suspicious of such distinctive dress. Some priests have started wearing jeans, and we consider anyone sporting monastic robes to be isolated or out of touch with the real world, rather than the bearer of a dignity that we should honor.

So, by choosing to wear lay dress, which has no religious connotation but which displays a sense of dignity, Chögyam Trungpa was trying to present the dharma in today's world. This conveys one of the main principles of the Shambhala vision: the need to take into account the riches of our own culture and traditions and to celebrate them.

As he explained: "You might laugh at us because we recommend that you wear a tie over your shirt, and a jacket on top of that. You might laugh because we say that you should comb your hair and present yourselves as ladies and gentlemen. That advice could be a shocking message, in some sense, but it was shocking to the Buddha. Suppose he were here right now, and he saw that you were dressed in accordance with your local culture, your local discipline. He would probably say that wearing a shirt and tie and jacket was part of the twentieth vinaya."[2] Chögyam Trungpa was insisting once again on the importance of a living discipline. One of his students, David Sable, remembers the first time he wore a suit. Chögyam Trungpa beckoned him over, touched the cloth, and asked: "Is it polyester?" He recalls that the way these words were pronounced was so crushing, and at the same time so full of love, that he was deeply moved.

Chögyam Trungpa insisted that his students wear good-quality clothes. He encouraged them to be elegant—a word that had disappeared from the vocabulary of this generation of hippies. The way we dress, he explained to them, should express the confidence we have in ourselves and in others. It is part of our responsibility to society.

When he found out that three-piece pinstriped suits were generally worn by bankers, and that politicians preferred plain two-piece suits, Chögyam Trungpa chose the latter. For him, dress was a precise vocabulary and grammar.

Dressing badly is not only linked to laziness and depression; it is also a sign that we are hiding by closing in on ourselves. By emphasizing the care we take about the way we look, Chögyam Trungpa was asking us to project our meditative presence and awareness into the world. The confi-

---

2. Chögyam Trungpa, *1980 Seminary Transcripts: Hinayana-Mahayana* (Boulder: Vajradhatu Publications), p. 76. The vinaya is the code of disciplinary rules for Buddhist monks and nuns.

dence we feel when we are well dressed should radiate around us. Chögyam Trungpa would sometimes take his students into stores to show
them how to choose their clothes. With astonishing accuracy, he immediately picked out the finest garments that contained what he called *yün*,
or a natural sense of richness.[3]

For example, when buying a tie, he generally chose one with a striking,
clearly delineated pattern. When teaching, he preferred to wear large designs that could be seen from a distance.

However, Chögyam Trungpa should not be identified with a suit. Depending on the situation, he also wore Japanese clothes, especially beginning in 1976 when he presented the Shambhala teachings, Tibetan chubas,
and clothing from the various countries he visited.

During the last years of his life, Chögyam Trungpa liked wearing military uniforms, which he had made to order by an English tailor. He gave
each of them a specific name. During certain talks, he sometimes asked
for the meaning of each item of his uniform to be described.

All of these clothes were different ways of manifesting various sorts of
energy, according to his audience or a particular context.

He had a precise way of putting on his clothes, which was related to the
principles he was trying to reveal to his students. In this way, those who
helped him dress often received a powerful transmission. As Walter Fordham explained: "When he put on a shirt, he would button the top button
first and then work down from there. In the early days, he usually did this
by himself with deft movements of his good hand. But toward the end of
his life, the Kusung [the attendant who was helping him] would often button his shirt for him. Sometimes this top button would be extremely tight,
and the Kusung had to work very hard to get it buttoned at all. At these
moments, we would sometimes try to talk him out of wearing that partic-

---

3. Chögyam Trungpa, *1978 Kalapa Assembly Transcripts* (Boulder: Vajradhatu Publications),
pp. 58ff. "The essence of richness is called yün in Tibetan. (That particular term is actually
a sort of traditional Bön term.) . . . When you buy clothes, you find the yün in the situation,
the particular power spot you want to draw in. In eating good food, drinking wine, or buying jewelry, there is a certain particular spot which hits you. It hits you in the first thought,
the basic thought. At the same time, you find that if you see a gold coin, suddenly a particular aspect of that gold coin hits you as richness, which is called yün."

ular shirt. 'Wouldn't you like to try a shirt with a larger collar, Sir?' But he would usually tell us to just go ahead and button it. 'It seems fine,' he would say. And he would wear the tight collar throughout the day, never showing any sign of discomfort.... He said that that tightness around his collar was his reminder of his discipline when he was wearing Western clothes. When he wore Japanese clothes, the reminder of discipline was the obi, or the tightness, around the hara. He was very particular about how he put his ties on. He would never turn his collar up, which is the way most people do it, because his collars were starched, and if you turn the collar up it breaks the line of the starch, so that when you turn it back down again, it doesn't have a nice crisp, clean crease to it. So he would work the tie under the collar without turning the collar up. The Kusung would help do that, and then he would tie the tie."[4]

The way we dress is related to an extremely profound aspect of the teachings. Truly elegant manifestations of the body, speech, and mind can create gaps that instantly dissolve doubt, depression, and discouragement. In the language of Shambhala, elegance is a way to connect ourselves to our internal dralas and through them to the ultimate or secret dralas—in other words, "provoke tremendous wakefulness, tremendous nowness in your state of mind."[5] Sense perceptions can touch our hearts directly and so allow us to enter into contact with the forces of the phenomenal world.

This idea of dressing with dignity seems out of place in a regimen of meditation and spiritual study. For most men today, wearing a suit and tie is an obligation imposed by their work, and it impinges on their freedom. Fortunately there is always the weekend, and now even casual Fridays, when American workers can dress more freely.

But for Chögyam Trungpa, dressing can be a way to connect with a sacred vision and learn to display a warrior's dignity. He gave an extremely precise description of the importance of a certain strictness:

4. Walter Fordham, interview, *The Iron Wheel*, Winter 1998, pp. 28ff.

5. *Shambhala: The Sacred Path of the Warrior* (Shambhala Library, 2003), p. 123.

"Sometimes if your clothes fit you well, you feel that they are too tight. ... The occasional irritation coming from your neck, the crotch of your pants, or your waist is usually a good sign. It means that your clothes fit you well, but your neurosis doesn't fit your clothes. The modern approach is often free and casual. That is the attraction of polyester leisure suits. You feel stiff if you are dressed up. You are tempted to take off your tie or your jacket or your shoes. Then you can hang out and put your feet on the table and act freely, hoping that your mind will act freely at the same time. But at that point your mind begins to dribble. It begins to leak, and garbage of all kinds comes out of your mind. That version of relaxation does not provide real freedom at all. Therefore, for the warrior, wearing well-fit clothing is regarded as wearing a suit of armor."[6]

The image of a suit of armor is extremely potent. Chögyam Trungpa provided a practical view and gave his students skillful means to help manifest the openness that is part of all meditative experience. If a warrior has neither weapons nor armor to remind him of his discipline, he cannot open himself up and so transcend fear.

Savoir-vivre and table manners

In 1976, Mrs. Pybus, Chögyam Trungpa's mother-in-law, arrived in Boulder from England to spend Christmas with one of her daughters, Chögyam Trungpa's sister-in-law. She was completely alienated from Chögyam Trungpa and his wife, Diana, her other daughter. She had been extremely angry with this dark-skinned man who had married her daughter at the age of sixteen without the mother's permission. Rinpoche decided to visit her while she was in town. He showed up for Christmas dinner and begged her forgiveness for "stealing" her daughter. It was the first time they had seen each other in years. After this meeting, she accepted an invitation to dinner at Rinpoche's home. Chögyam Trungpa had an extremely elaborate meal prepared in her honor. What a surprise it was for that high-society lady to see a former Tibetan monk organizing an

---

6. Ibid., p. 121.

impeccable dinner using the best silver service. She was impressed. The former hippies around Chögyam Trungpa had become distinguished.

Six months later, Mrs. Pybus moved to Boulder.

Apart from his clothes and the emphasis on good table manners, Chögyam Trungpa taught his students a method of elocution based on an Oxonian, or Oxford, accent. He himself had learned to speak this way when he attended Oxford University. In the evolution of the Dorje Kasung, a path of service based on the practice of "guarding," Rinpoche decided to adopt elements of the British military, including aspects of the Kasung uniforms and the British style of saluting and marching. In this way, England provided Chögyam Trungpa with elements of a highly developed culture, even though he was quite aware that British culture was declining and that decorum there was often kept up in a lifeless way.

Japan

In his efforts to introduce new formalities into the community, Chögyam Trungpa also turned toward Japanese culture, with the help of some of his students, and in particular Mipham Halpern, who had been a student of Suzuki Roshi's at Zen Center. Chögyam Trungpa's interest in Japan is surprising, because, although both countries are Buddhist, the Tibetan and Japanese worlds are very different.

As early as his stay in India in 1959, Chögyam Trungpa was exposed to this culture and found it very impressive. He first discovered the Japanese haiku tradition, a discipline that allowed the essence of buddhadharma to be manifested instantly through poetry: "It's a question of writing your own mind on a piece of paper. Through poetry, you could find your own state of mind. That's precisely the concept of haiku: writing your mind."[7]

Chögyam Trungpa sometimes asked his students to compose sponta-

---

7. "Pragmatism and Practice: An Interview with Vajracharya the Ven. Trungpa Rinpoche," *Vajradhatu Sun*, June/July 1985, p. 8. Reprinted in *The Collected Works of Chögyam Trungpa*, vol. 8.

neous haikus. It was a way of learning to penetrate the present in an un-expected and spontaneous manner. Although it comes as a surprise for Westerners, such a form of expression is not psychological, yet it still re-veals a tangibly affective state. As Patricia Donegan, a poet and student of Chögyam Trungpa's, says: "For the Japanese, a poem isn't judged by how great is the idea being expressed or how fancy the language is or how the words are put together. The main thing is, does it move the reader? Did it move the poet in the first place? Did the poet communi-cate his feeling? The closest word I can think of would be 'poignancy,' al-though that doesn't exactly say it either. In Japan they say *koroko*. *Koroko* means 'heart-mind' in Japanese. In Japanese, like Chinese and Korean, they have one word for 'heart' and 'mind' together. It has a lot to do with vulnerability."[8]

Haikus have the extraordinary ability to reveal a sort of objective sen-timent, beyond subjective introspection. This comes from the poet's abil-ity to penetrate to the root of an experience. To succeed, you must open the space of an empty heart—a characteristic of the perspective of ma-hayana, the great vehicle.

Ikebana

In England, as we have already said, Chögyam Trungpa learned the art of Japanese flower arranging. In the United States, he soon understood the important contribution this tradition could bring to the culture he was putting together.

Ikebana students learn an extremely profound discipline that pro-vides a way of familiarizing themselves with the meaning of formality, which is not seen as mere strictness, but as a way of releasing beauty. When studying with a qualified teacher, you do not learn to master a form, but instead to compose a flower arrangement. It becomes an ex-tremely direct, concrete experience. The right form is natural. There is the paradox, as Shunryu Suzuki explained: "There is a big misunder-standing about the idea of naturalness. Most people who come to us

8. Patricia Donegan, "Haiku," *Kalapa Ikebana*, Summer 1984, p. 2.

believe in some freedom or naturalness, but their understanding is what we call *jinen ken gedo*, or heretical naturalness. *Jinen ken gedo* means that there is no need to be formal—just a kind of "let-alone" policy or sloppiness. That is naturalness for most people. But that is not the naturalness we mean."[9]

What is truly natural is free from all reference points and our habitual patterns of thought or behavior. Being natural means doing what we do simply and completely. A flower arrangement, for example, allows us to discover something genuinely natural and free. The discipline is a mirror that allows us to see ourselves accurately.

In 1982 Chögyam Trungpa founded a specialized school of ikebana, Kalapa Ikebana, and published a newsletter. In it, he explained: "In the Western world flower arranging is regarded as something only ladies do and it's just decorative. . . . It's just purely beautifying. But in this case it's practice and we have to think in those terms."[10]

Chögyam Trungpa transmitted his knowledge and encouraged his students who lived far away to practice this discipline in the school of their choice. Meanwhile he conducted several seminars in which he showed how composing an ikebana arrangement can mean creating a sacred environment, transforming the room where it is placed, giving it a density and presence that opens the hearts of those who enter. It can transform any place, because it is a powerful weapon that can cut through the setting-sun world of depression.

Kobun Chino Roshi and Kanjuro Shibata Sensei

In the United States, Chögyam Trungpa met a large number of teachers of the Zen tradition. After the death of Shunryu Suzuki, he kept up friendly relations with one of Suzuki Roshi's co-teachers at Zen Center, Kobun Chino Roshi, a Japanese living in California, who regularly came to see Chögyam Trungpa. One day, he asked Kobun Chino if he knew a warrior teacher in Japan. Kobun Chino told him about Kanjuro Shibata

---

9. Shunryu Suzuki, *Zen Mind, Beginner's Mind* (New York: Weatherhill, 1970), p. 107.

10. Chögyam Trungpa, *Kalapa Ikebana*, Spring 1983, p. 2.

Sensei, his own teacher of kyudo, the ancestral Japanese art of archery. He was the twentieth holder of the lineage of master archers and bowmakers (*onyumishi*) for the emperor of Japan.

Chögyam Trungpa sent two of his students, Nick Sabrocca and Mipham (also known as Robert) Halpern, to Japan in order to invite him, on Rinpoche's behalf, to come and teach in the United States. Shibata Sensei came for the first time in 1980 with his son-in-law, Nobohiro. He did not yet know Chögyam Trungpa personally.

The first time that any of Chögyam Trungpa's students saw Shibata Sensei present the art of kyudo was at the 1980 Midsummer's Day (a celebration discussed later in this chapter). At one of the opening ceremonies, Shibata Sensei performed the ancient ceremony of shihobarai, which he had performed many times for the Japanese imperial family. It involves establishing the sacred space of the four directions and then shooting two arrows to command the sacred energies of the situation. From that moment on, Chögyam Trungpa and his students were aware that Shibata Sensei was not just an "archery teacher," but someone with real presence and connection to the energies of drala. At the beginning of their relationship, Shibata Sensei was very surprised by Chögyam Trungpa's unorthodox behavior. But Sensei soon realized that his ability to go beyond formalities with such freedom showed that he was a real king.

The Japanese were no longer interested in kyudo. He explained how they now saw it as a sport aimed at a purely personal attainment, not as one of the highest moral and spiritual disciplines. When Chögyam Trungpa asked him to teach the art of the true warrior, which consists in cutting through the ego, Shibata Sensei realized that he had found somewhere to present the true tradition he had inherited. In an interview given in 1991, he described his first meeting with Chögyam Trungpa: "He told me that his grandfather had been a bowmaker in Tibet, just as mine had been in Japan. We spoke about the way that, almost everywhere in the world, the use of bow and arrow has been reduced to sports competitions or else the killing of animals for food. In both cases, the person who shoots is hoping only for victory. Rinpoche told me that his grandfather had taught him how, from a Buddhist point of view, there should be no hope involved in shooting an arrow, and it should not be based on hitting the target, on victory or fame. At the time, I didn't know Chögyam Trungpa and was unaware of the depth of his understanding. So I was surprised to hear him speak of the absence of hope, because it was exactly what my grandfather had taught me in a transmission concerning the depth of kyudo as a meditative practice. Our two grandfathers had spoken to their grandsons, at different times, of this use of bow and arrow without any idea of gain. This is how kyudo differs from the usual approach to archery. In kyudo, there is no hope. Hope is not the question. The question lies in the fact that, after a long and authentic practice, your human dignity is revealed. This natural dignity is already within us, but it is blocked by a number of obstacles. Dissipating them allows our natural dignity to radiate."[11]

If Chögyam Trungpa's students were not very skilled, and even rather clumsy, they were still driven by a serious motivation, which appealed to Shibata Sensei. He became an inspiring and living example of a warrior for the entire community.

On December 29, 1981, Chögyam Trungpa wrote a poem, "Golden Sun," in homage to Shibata Sensei on his birthday:

> In the land of kami-no-yama, I still miss you.
> We are all longing for your wisdom.
> As you know, we have lost our leader the
>   Karmapa,
> But it is comforting to have you as good friend
>   and teacher.
> The mirror has never stopped reflecting,
> The kiku has never stopped blossoming.
> Yumi still twangs,
> Ya still fly.
> Our students constantly practice and look forward
>   to your further teaching.

---

11. Shibata Sensei, in *Cheval du Vent* (Paris: Centre Shambhala de Paris), no. 2, December 2000, p. 1.

I, your friend, am getting old and sick,
But still my heart's blood turns into liquid iron.[12]

Shibata Sensei and his wife spent more and more time in America.
Mrs. Kiyoko Shibata taught the tea ceremony in Boulder beginning in the
early eighties. Chögyam Trungpa encouraged some of his students to
study with her and founded Kalapa Cha, an association devoted to the
study and practice of this path. He took part in several of its meetings and
gave instructions to his students on how to hold the utensils and objects
used in such a ceremony. A teahouse was constructed in the garden of the
Kalapa Court in Boulder, where Mrs. Shibata taught most of her classes.
When Chögyam Trungpa moved to Nova Scotia and sold the Court, the
teahouse was given to the Naropa Institute, so that the study of tea could
continue there. Following Mrs. Shibata's death, a special tea ceremony
honoring her was held during the Magyal Pomra Encampment summer
program at Rocky Mountain Dharma Center, and a small wooden post
was placed as a memorial on the encampment grounds in a ceremony
conducted by Chögyam Trungpa. The study of tea has continued and expanded. Today, there are active groups in Boulder, Nova Scotia, New York
City, and other locations.

Oryoki

Oryoki is the way meals are eaten in Japanese monasteries.[13] It was practiced within the Buddhist community established by Chögyam Trungpa
for the first time at the Magyal Pomra Encampment at Rocky Mountain Dharma Center in 1979; and after the 1980 Seminary, where it was

---

12. From *First Thought Best Thought*, by Chögyam Trungpa, p. 191. © 1989 by Diana J.
Mukpo. Reprinted by arrangement with Shambhala Publications, Inc., Boston, www.sham-
bhala.com. Reprinted with permission of Diana J. Mukpo. This poem also appears in *Timely
Rain*, p. 161, © 1972, 1983, 1998 by Diana J. Mukpo.

13. Oryoki belongs to the Soto Zen lineage developed by Dogen, who wrote a famous work
entitled *Tenzo Kyokun*, or "Instructions for the Head Cook."

introduced to all the participants, it was introduced as a regular practice for residential meditation programs throughout the entire sangha.
It was another essential part of the culture that Chögyam Trungpa was
creating.

The practice of oryoki was transmitted to Chögyam Trungpa and his
students by Kobun Chino Roshi: "It was a big decision to make. Oryoki is
a very traditional practice of meal bowls and utensils. In Japan unless you
are ordained or participating in meditation for many years, usually you
cannot receive those."[14]

But, knowing the respect Chögyam Trungpa had for this practice and
the great attention to the slightest detail that it requires from students,
Kobun Chino Roshi accepted his request. Thanks to this discipline, the
often chaotic mealtimes at practice programs in Chögyam Trungpa's
community were now integrated with their meditation practice.

It is a practice of great clarity and deep rigor. To give a superficial idea
of the precision it requires, this is what must be done in order to receive
the food you will eat during the oryoki meal. Each student has an oryoki
set consisting of three bowls to hold the food, a napkin, chopsticks, a
spoon, and a cleaning implement, all wrapped up in a cloth that becomes
like a place mat on which all of these objects are unwrapped and arranged.
After everyone has unwrapped their sets, slowly and in concert, servers
come around with food. To receive food in the first bowl, which is also
called the Buddha bowl, the section of four people being served bow to the
server in unison. Then you wait with your hands together in anjali, the
mudra of bowing. As the server comes to you, you raise the Buddha bowl
and use the wooden spoon to help receive the food from the server; you indicate when you have enough by raising the hand that is holding the
spoon, then hold the bowl in both hands and wait for the entire group of
four to be served; then all exchange a bow with the server before he or she
moves on to the next group. Communication is silent, made purely by gesture. During this entire process, you are sitting in meditation posture, and
you eat in that same posture, silently and with mindful attention. Before

---

14. Kobun Chino Roshi, "Way Seeking Mind," *Vajrahatu Sun*, February/March 1988, p. 3.

eating, the entire assembly chants together, and there are also chants at the end of the meal. There is also a ritual for cleaning the bowls and rewrapping the set.

Through thoroughly learning a ritual form such as oryoki, we can learn to give ourselves over to it fully and connect with a pure perception that is, as already stated, the gateway to the experience of sacred world. We thus learn to transform our confusion into wisdom by reaching a point at which we taste our food without wondering whether we like it or not.

The practice of oryoki, like all traditional Japanese ways, seems initially very limiting because of all the rules that must be followed. But, little by little, it begins to help us relax and appreciate the food even more.

As Chögyam Trungpa explained with his characteristic humor, oryoki also allows us to work on a difficulty found in all communities: "I would like to make a basic statement, if you would care to hear it, about the food neurosis that exists in Western culture—or, rather, I wouldn't say exactly Western culture, but unbuddhist culture. Food neurosis is quite horrendous. People have such cultural hang-ups and cultural fascinations about food. If they don't have pancakes for breakfast, or fried eggs and bacon, they feel bad until they go to bed."[15] When we eat oryoki style, we develop an attitude of acceptance. At the time of Buddha, when a monk received food from a benefactor, he made no distinction between what he liked and disliked, between what is good and bad. He received what he was given with a spirit of gratitude and did not refuse any gift just because he did not like the dish he was presented with. At the same time, the donor always tried to give what was best. So the relationship between giver and receiver was based on mutual appreciation.

Thus the practice of oryoki makes for a change in the atmosphere of a meditation center: cooking recovers the central place it has in Zen where the cook is one of the monastery's most accomplished teachers and respected as such.

---

15. Chögyam Trungpa, *1980 Seminary Transcripts: Hinayana-Mahayana* (Boulder: Vajradhatu Publications), p. 13.

Rituals

In the early days, when Chögyam Trungpa gave a lecture, he simply walked into the room and sat down at the front. Within a few years, audiences rose when he entered the room, and he was usually accompanied by at least one attendant who would help him with his microphone and so on. However, beginning in the early eighties, a formal procession was added to his entrances and exits from formal teaching situations among his close students, such as at the Vajradhatu Seminary or Kalapa Assembly. Chögyam Trungpa adopted numerous Japanese elements in the procession. He modified the age-old tradition of Shinto ceremonies, to which he added elements from the traditions of Zen Buddhism and Shingon.

The procession began with the incense bearer, or osenko. He is followed by the kaishaku bearer, who carries two wood blocks that are struck together, which serves to awaken the mind. The kaishaku was followed by a traditional drum, which Chögyam Trungpa later replaced by a gandhi, a set of wooden sticks belonging to the Tibetan tradition, whose sound is less clear and crisp than the kaishaku.

Preceded by fragrance and sound, Chögyam Trungpa entered, followed by his nyoi, or scepter, carried by one of the most senior students. *Nyoi* in Japanese (*jue* in Chinese) is the character than means "to be completely relaxed." As Chögyam Trungpa explained, "Being fully at rest means that you are not self-conscious anymore about being a king and a leader. So when you hold the nyoi, you are no longer embarrassed and you are upright; you are right there."[16]

Behind the bearer of the nyoi came a student carrying Chögyam Trungpa's notes for the talk or dharma texts, usually in a brocade pouch. In Tibet, dharma texts, whether they are sutras, shastras, or termas, are carried in this manner and treated with the greatest respect.

Next, someone, usually a female student, came behind carrying the suehiro, Chögyam Trungpa's fan, which he used in a quite remarkable way while teaching.

---

16. Chögyam Trungpa, *1982 Seminary Transcripts: Vajrayana* (Boulder: Vajradhatu Publications), p. 64.

The procession ended with the bearer of the inkin, or ceremonial gong, which was sounded in a pattern with the kaishaku and gandhi.

Japanese culture unites the tradition of the samurai, or authentic warrior, with great attention and respect for the kamis, or local deities. The kamis are natural, personalized forces such as the sun, the moon, and the typhoon, as well as anything that seems mysterious or dangerous, such as mountains, seas, rivers, rocks, winds, wild animals, trees, or strangely shaped or unknown objects. In the same way some men and animals, living or dead, can be considered to be a kami. Chögyam Trungpa appreciated this approach, which has similarities with the Shambhala vision, for the kamis are rather like the notion of drala. Establishing a relationship with them is a way to understand sacred world and to connect in an extraordinary manner with the energy of the most basic things.

This use of Japanese traditions seemed especially appropriate to the profane situation Chögyam Trungpa found in the West. Japanese tradition, more than any other, has developed highly subtle rituals that are not limited to the monastic life.

Tibet

Chögyam Trungpa took from Tibet its taste for pomp, gilding, and brocades. In tantra, as it is practiced in Tibet, the phenomenal world is celebrated in its most colorful and lively aspects. In this culture, there is no hesitation about the strength of emotions, as can be seen in the iconography, with its vividly colored deities in extravagant postures. Chögyam Trungpa retained a taste for bright colors and was interested in how they can affect the mind.

In addition to this great richness, Tibetan culture is marked by an earthy, basic, almost crude character, which Chögyam Trungpa united with British and Japanese elegance. This characteristic comes out in an anecdote told by Chögyam Trungpa, about when he was an adolescent and was speaking with his mother while playing with the little pickled radishes that were fed to horses: "I was picking up these little pickled radishes off the floor outside the monastery kitchen. Tülkus are not supposed to eat them, but I was chewing on one. . . . I was about to bite into another pickled radish, which was dirty. . . . I'm afraid I did bite it, and I remember chewing it. It was very crunchy and tasted something like a *tsukemono*, a kind of Japanese pickle, and I liked it very much."[17] Chögyam Trungpa always kept this liking for great simplicity.

In his attempts to create a lay culture, Chögyam Trungpa paid attention to Tibetan rituals and especially local traditions such as Bön. In this way, he introduced the ceremony of lhasang, whose purpose is to purify the environment and attract the blessings of the dralas to all those who are present. In Tibet, this is done whenever an important event is to take place or some action must be carried out. In a lhasang, juniper branches are burned to produce white smoke, which is offered to attract the energy of drala. Everyone present chants an invocation to the dralas, and the person presiding over the lhasang adds milk, barley, and other offerings to the fire. The participants circle the fire pit and sometimes may bring articles that they would like to have blessed from the smoke of the lhasang. At important ceremonial lhasangs to open programs such as Kalapa Assembly, a number of senior students would carry flags around the lhasang, waving them over the smoke. For the participants, there often was a feeling of a wind of energy arising as they circled the fire while chanting.

Chögyam Trungpa also presented the Tibetan principles of lha, nyen, and lu to his students. These three elements describe the way in which humans can integrate themselves into the fabric of basic reality. They constitute a very profound way of understanding the logic of all true actions. Chögyam Trungpa described them as the principles of natural hierarchy.

Lha means "divine" or "deity," and refers to the highest places on earth, such as the snowy peaks of mountains. It also represents the first or primordial glimpse of enlightenment.

Nyen means "friend." It begins on the slopes of the great mountains and includes forests, jungles, and plains. It corresponds to solidity and bravery.

---

17. *Shambhala: The Sacred Path of the Warrior* (Shambhala Library, 2003), pp. 96–97.

Finally, *lu* literally means "water being," and is associated with lakes and rivers and the lowlands. It corresponds to the richness of water.

If our actions are to be just and appropriate to a given situation, then they must be linked to these three principles: they must contain a vision (lha) of the energy (nyen) and an attention to details (lu); in other words, awareness of how things are organized.

Walter Fordham, who managed Chögyam Trungpa's house for seven years, is an important witness to how Chögyam Trungpa applied such principles: "In terms of his personal effects, everything was always arranged according to the principle of lha, nyen, and lu. Medals and jewelry were in the top drawer of his bureau, underwear and socks in his bottom drawer, sweaters and shirts in the middle drawers. He taught the Kusung [attendants], housekeepers, servers, and others who were around him the proper way to handle things. These instructions always related to the lha, nyen, and lu of an object. For example, he demonstrated that holding a water glass near the rim was a sign of arrogance— of not respecting the body of the glass. If you offer the glass to somebody, you should relate to the lu aspect of the glass by holding it near the bottom. But if you are drinking from the glass yourself, you should express a nyen relationship to the glass by holding it slightly below the middle."[18]

Chögyam Trungpa was generally very scrupulous about following Buddhist rituals in their Tibetan form. For example, the way he gave initiations (abhisheka) was perhaps more traditional and detailed than that used by any other Tibetan teacher in the West. He also spent a lot of time making sure that the students understood each element of the ritual.

2. The World of Shambhala

By drawing on English, Japanese, and Tibetan traditions, Chögyam Trungpa created a particular culture.

---

18. Walter Fordham, interview, *The Iron Wheel*, Halifax, Winter 1998, p. 28.

The meditation room

Whichever Shambhala Center you go to, you will find that the walls of the meditation room are generally painted white, while the door, pillars, windows, and moldings are bright blue and orange. These colors reflect a sense of the richness of Tibet.

Chögyam Trungpa also liked to use very stylized symbols, such as the flaming jewels that represent the Buddhist teachings, the vajra (the scepter held by tantric deities), and the knot of eternity, representing emptiness. Remaining faithful to the Japanese tradition he appreciated so much, he saw to it that the whole atmosphere was still spacious.

Banners that he designed himself and traditional Tibetan scroll paintings (thangkas) are hung on the walls of the meditation room. On the floor, red and yellow rectangular meditation cushions, called *gomden*, are arranged in rows. Chögyam Trungpa created the gomden and introduced it around 1981, replacing the zafu, the round Japanese meditation cushion he had used when he first came to North America.[19] The colors of the gomdens are typically Tibetan, but their shape is unique. Plumper than Tibetan cushions, they are better suited to Western physiques.

Publications and posters

The strength and unity of Chögyam Trungpa's vision can be seen clearly in the publications he worked on. In the early issues of the review *Garuda,* which were published between 1971 and 1977, the main principles of his aesthetics were already at work.

Great importance was given to the graphics. Meticulous attention was paid to the form of the review and its layout. Chögyam Trungpa con-

---

19. The zafu needs to be fluffed into shape before each session, and students found various ways and postures to adopt while sitting on it. Chögyam Trungpa did not like this lack of precision, which led his students to develop their own idiosyncratic styles of meditation. At first, he insisted on the importance of sitting in the middle of the zafu, then he decided to devise another cushion for people to sit on in a simple way. In Zen, the way to use the zafu is much more clearly defined.

stantly insisted that each element of the graphics should express the spirit of enlightenment.

He saw to it that the relationship between text and image was surprising and often tinged with a humor that some might find irritating. The vital point for him was to create a slight shock, or a breach in the mind that was reading the text. As he explained: "There is some kind of a shock so that the person will be invited to read what it says on the poster. So there is a kind of flash, and then there is inquisitiveness, so people will pay attention to it."[20] Some pages of the review were left almost blank, such as page 55 of *Garuda III*, which contains a black spot and a tiny reproduction of Bodhidharma, the Zen patriarch, in the bottom corner.

Gina Stick, who worked with Chögyam Trungpa on many design projects, explained that when they needed to produce a poster announcing a program of devotion, they did not provide much information about the subject, but instead sought to embody its particular energy in graphic form. Chögyam Trungpa showed a surprising freedom and curiosity about this sort of work, which he greatly appreciated. His aim was not to be purely aesthetic but to wake up the reader.

When he had a new project, he started by designing a logo, a symbolic form that manifested its meaning.

His students often found some of his ideas ugly, such as the brochure he produced to announce Shambhala Training in 1980. It is true that no attempt was made to be attractive. Chögyam Trungpa used a daring arrangement of colors—a khaki green surrounding a golden yellow sun, in which was written, in red letters: "How to Accomplish Living in the Challenge." Instead of being aesthetically pleasing, it had an uncompromising energy. He was being faithful to his rejection of all spiritual materialism: the dharma will not save you, but it will make you honest and encourage you to face up to who you are. It is a true challenge, displayed in this simple yet surprising play of colors, which transmits a force that almost makes us ill at ease. The path is not rosy, but instead pushes us ever farther into reality. This is what this illustration is saying. It is transmitting

---

20. Chögyam Trungpa, interview by Pat Patterson, San Francisco, 20 September 1980.

the entire Shambhala vision on a preconceptual level, through careful use of a graphic vocabulary.

Pins and flags

After the suit and tie (or, for women, the dress), the second sign of being one of Chögyam Trungpa's students was a pin on the left lapel, near the heart. Particularly in connection with the Shambhala teachings, Chögyam Trungpa designed a large number of pins for different activities and organizations and gave them to his students as a sign of participation in a sphere of his work. He created pins for practitioners of ikebana and kyudo and for those who completed Shambhala Training. People who worked in various departments at Vajradhatu received a pin connected with their work, and he even had pins for members of his family. For him, these pins were more than just symbols of identification; they were like seed sylla-bles,[21] which contain the essence of a teaching's power and magic.

During a yearlong retreat at Charlemont in Rowe, Massachusetts, in 1977, he devoted a lot of time to devising graphics for the entirety of his mandala. He designed flags, banners, pins, and medals that transmitted his teaching on a symbolic level.

The best-known flag, designed in 1977, has a white rectangular background, which depicts basic goodness, and in the center is a yellow sun, representing the Great Eastern Sun. At one end of the flag, there are four vertical lines colored white, orange, red, and blue that represent the four qualities of warriorship, or the four dignities (meek, perky, outrageous, and inscrutable). This is also the flag of Shambhala, and it is found in all the centers. It depicts the fulfillment of the Shambhala vision, which each has to accomplish.

---

21. A seed syllable is a single syllable, generally in Sanskrit, that represents the essential reality of a particular deity.

Symbolism and the magic of colors

Chögyam Trungpa paid a lot of attention to the meanings of colors and their symbolic effect, and even more to their intrinsic magic.

During a talk in which he mentioned his childhood in Tibet, he told a story that displays his interest in colors, and in particular the four he would later use so often in connection with the presentation of the Shambhala teachings: "At the age of thirteen, I was made the local governor of Surmang. There were processions, enthronements, presentations of seals, and everything. It was very interesting. My mother had a black brocade chuba to wear in order to take part in those ceremonies, and she changed her style of wearing her hair. She adopted the local style of Surmang rather than the style of our birthplace. . . . She combed her hair back, and she developed two locks of hair. She came to me and said, 'This celebration is very important, but I don't have any tassels to wear on the end of my pigtail.' So I unlocked my secret box, in which I tried to keep little things in case my mother needed something or in case I had to give a present to somebody. We opened the lock, and—this is no joke—I found four tassels for her to wear. One was white, another one was orange, another one was red, and the fourth one was blue. I asked her which one she would like to wear. All of them were very small tassels that she could braid into her hair. She was ready to fix her hair, and she said, 'Maybe I should take the orange one. It looks nice; it goes with my chuba,' which was deep blue with griffin and dragon designs on it. And I said, 'Why don't you use all of them?' And she said, 'Don't you think that would be too sensational? Nobody does such a thing at all.' And I said, 'No. We can undo some of the complicated knots so that they look natural in your hair.' And she said, 'I don't know how to do that.' At that moment my sister came along. She just walked in, and she watched the whole thing. I gave the tassels to my sister and asked her to braid my mother's hair in white, orange, red and blue tassels on the day of my coronation. My mother wore them, and it came out beautifully."[22]

---

22. Chögyam Trungpa, *1979 Kalapa Assembly Transcripts* (Boulder: Vajradhatu Publications), p. 17.

Chögyam Trungpa used these colors in many contexts. He also made use of the combination of five colors (white, blue, yellow, red, and green) representing the five buddha families in the tantric tradition of Buddhism.

This attention to color went in a variety of directions. Having grown up in a culture where it is possible to strike camp, roll up the thangkas and mats, and then move and set up an elegant, sacred space quickly and easily, Chögyam Trungpa tried to transfer this nomadic culture to a Western context. He conceived a series of banners and standards, decorated with calligraphy, that could transported quickly and easily and could be hung in all of his centers. It was a way to present his teachings anywhere. Thus, a barn in a small village in France or a large hotel reserved for the teacher's visit could rapidly be transformed into a sacred space, the Kingdom of Shambhala.

Ceremonies

Chögyam Trungpa created a specific culture, not only based on formalities and discipline, but also by introducing ceremonies to bring together the entire community. These events, especially those that mark the passing of the seasons, are called "nyida days," from the Tibetan *nyima* (sun) and *dawa* (moon). Nyida days take place at the equinoxes and solstices. These four days are a celebration of the family.

The summer solstice, on June 21, is celebrated as Midsummer's Day, while the winter solstice is devoted to Children's Day. The autumnal equinox is also the time to celebrate the Rite of Passage for eight-year-old children. A lhasang is organized during each of these festivities. The most important of them is Midsummer's Day.

Midsummer's Day

Chögyam Trungpa organized the first Midsummer's Day festival in 1978, after his retreat in Massachusetts where he had given much thought to how he could bring out the social and community angle essential to the Shambhala teachings. Midsummer's Day offered an opportunity for him to introduce the pomp and ritual splendor that are part of traditional Tibetan festivals. The celebration of Midsummer's Day generally included dance, theater, music, and sports competitions.

The linchpin is a parade. Various groups within the community would parade, some in costumes, holding banners. Among others, there was Alaya preschool, Vidya primary school, the Naropa Institute, the Nālandā Translation Committee, the Board of Directors of Vajradhatu/Nalanda, Kalapa Ikebana, Mudra Theater, the Dorje Kasung, the Ratna Business Society, the Nalanda Gagaku Society, and so on. Chögyam Trungpa and Diana Mukpo would be the first to parade in, sometimes on horseback. One year His Holiness the Karmapa attended Midsummer's Day and reviewed the parade from the canopy at the center of the parade grounds.

One of Chögyam Trungpa's plays was often produced on this occasion. Once he even wrote a play especially for the event. Concerts were also organized. As mentioned earlier, Shibata Sensei's first introduction to the community took place at Midsummer's Day.

This event included children, whom Chögyam Trungpa wanted to be part of community life. He taught that they should not be considered obstacles on their parents' spiritual paths, but rather as an opportunity. There were games and competitions for the children, and they were also invited to march in the parade.

The meaning of such an event is to celebrate your own existence and that of all humans—which does not mean avoiding serious matters, but instead is a profound way of being Buddhist. It was also an event filled with humor and joy.

In 1972, Sara Kapp had been living for some time at Karmê Chöling without daring to ask to speak to Chögyam Trungpa. But when a New York modeling agency wanted to sign her as a model, she decided to ask his advice. Posing in front of the camera all day did not seem appropriate for someone who was trying to cut through her ego.

Chögyam Trungpa asked her why she wanted to become a model. She explained how she had experienced some difficulty in sticking to any one thing after finishing college. So she thought that maybe picking out something for a few years might be beneficial.

If that is the reason, he replied, then there's no problem. He encouraged her to follow her career, and as she continued to hesitate, he told her: "The only obstacle I can see is if you do this work hoping to earn lots of money or to be on the cover of *Vogue*. That would be sad, because you'd be losing yourself in the future. It's a real shame when people regret not having enough money, or having missed a career opportunity, because they are then fixing themselves in the past. It's very, very sad." Then, staring into her eyes, he repeated: "It's very, very, very sad because that way we miss out on the present, and the present is marvelous." She went on to become one of the best-known runway models of her day. For a period of time, one could find mannequins of Sara Kapp in Saks and other expensive department stores throughout the United States. Her last major modeling contract was as the first Princess Borghese for Revlon. She now works behind the scenes in the fashion industry in Milan.

Shambhala Day

During the same retreat in 1977, Chögyam Trungpa decided to inaugurate the celebration of Shambhala Day, which corresponds to the Tibetan New Year. By 1979, he had introduced the new festivity to the entire community. Depending on the lunar calendar, it generally takes place in February.

During this ceremony, the community in Boulder gathered together at dawn, and Chögyam Trungpa then made a speech to the entire sangha. Thanks to a telephone hookup, all of his students in all his centers could hear it directly. The rest of the day was devoted to various festivities that took place in different people's homes. Then the sangha met up again at the end of the afternoon to practice *The Sadhana of Mahamudra*, which was followed by dinner and a ball.

Sometimes, in 1979 for example, Chögyam Trungpa invited children aged between eight and fifteen to tea in his house, out of a desire to include the entire community.

The whole day was a constant celebration, but not in order to escape the routine or "let yourself go." Instead it was a means of enjoying existence, which implies real discipline.

In Boulder, Chögyam Trungpa and his family would invite about seventy-five people to have breakfast at his house following the dawn address. The breakfast was usually a huge Chinese dim sum meal. Then people would retire to various parts of the house to play board games and to drink and chat. A second large meal, usually a roast with various accompaniments, was served early in the evening. Other members of the community would be having banquets and celebrating together in their homes. Then people would reassemble for a meeting of the Shambhala Lodge in the evening. It was an enormous and exhausting celebration, which in later years expanded to a two-day feast.

Chögyam Trungpa's birthday

Chögyam Trungpa's birthday was another important holiday during the year, and it was one of the earliest community celebrations. One of the very first parties that Rinpoche gave after his arrival in Boulder was the celebration of his birthday in February 1971. The first parties were informal gatherings of the community in Boulder. Some of the parties were rather wild. At one, Trungpa wore a cowboy hat, and everyone sang "For He's a Jolly Good Fellow." Often, his birthday was also an opportunity for Chögyam Trungpa to present a special teaching for all the community. He often talked about his own remarks as "his gift."

Beginning around 1974, the celebration took place at various rented halls, such as the Elks Lodge in Boulder. The grandest celebrations in the early eighties took place in the ballroom at the Hilton Hotel in Denver. By this time, the atmosphere had become formal, and the event no longer concerned the Boulder sangha alone. The international community was invited to send birthday wishes, which were read at the celebration. Rinpoche's birthday was an opportunity for students to show their love for and connection with him, which they often did by presenting him with a special gift. One year, for example, a Japanese brocade hanging of a snow lion was presented to him. This was a woven tapestry that he had been admiring for a number of years when he visited a particular store in Japan Town in San Francisco. He was very excited and surprised when he received this. Another time, a Japanese suit of armor was presented to him, which he kept on the Shambhala shrine at his house and later transferred to the main shrine room in Halifax, Nova Scotia. A series of Chinese paintings of the disciples of the Buddha, the lohans, was a gift another year. At the Hilton, there were ice sculptures in the form of Japanese warriors decorating the entrance to the hall where the party was held. An enormous cake, beautifully decorated with the symbols of the four dignities, was presented to Rinpoche at one point during the evening, and the event usually ended with waltzing. Due to his paralysis, Rinpoche did not waltz, but it was a form of dance he loved, and his wife often opened the dancing, sometimes having the first dance with Rinpoche's dharma heir, the Vajra Regent Ösel Tendzin. The men wore tuxedos and the women long ball gowns and white gloves.

Marriages

In addition to these annual events that structured the year, Chögyam Trungpa established ceremonies for the important moments in our lives: the birth of children, their passage into adulthood, weddings, and funerals.

In the Buddhist tradition, marriages are not an especially important event, and monks in Tibet did not participate directly in performing weddings. But Rinpoche quickly realized the importance of marriage and weddings in the West, and they become important when trying to create a new culture.

The first weddings Chögyam Trungpa conducted were held in his small house in Four Mile Canyon, outside of Boulder. The living room could hold a dozen people. The ceremony he developed was related to the mahayana tradition. He would always make opening remarks, explaining how sharing your life with someone is a way of learning to open up to another person and to put them before yourself, thus cutting through our habitual egocentrism.

The ceremony consists of the wedding couple making six different offerings representing the six paramitas, or transcendent virtues: food for generosity, perfume for discipline, incense for patience, flowers for effort, light for meditation, and a musical instrument for transcendent knowledge. By giving such symbols, the couple commit themselves to cultivating these virtues.

As the Shambhala teachings started to develop, Chögyam Trungpa devised more elaborate Shambhala wedding ceremonies. The first one was conducted for his private secretary, the Kasung Kyi Khyap, David Rome, and his wife, Martha Rome. It evoked the true importance of joining the masculine and feminine lineages in the vision of the Kingdom of Shambhala.

Chögyam Trungpa involved himself deeply in preparing for this ceremony, which took place at dawn so that the sun rose during his speech. The bride, dressed in a Japanese wedding kimono, wore a white veil over her face. Chögyam Trungpa wrote a special text for this Shambhala wedding ceremony, including verses for the instant the veil was removed, as well as several invocations and rituals that have been practiced regularly since. The invocation of the Rigden Fathers, which he wrote for this particular occasion, has become a standard chant in some Shambhala Training programs.

What must not be forgotten about this dense and complete series of rituals, ceremonies, and formalities is that during their years of training, all his students learned to use them and so manifest sacredness in any context. Ceremonies or other events can be organized quite freely once the vocabulary of the formalities has been understood. This allows dignity and confidence to declare themselves in any situation.

Paradoxically, this freedom arises from a knowledge of precisely described formalities. It is necessary to avoid both the absence of discipline and the blind or repetitive adherence to customs. Chögyam Trungpa constantly steered clear of both stumbling blocks. He created extremely precise and complex rituals. But as soon as one of them crystallized, he altered it. He even deliberately created difficulties for those students who became too attached to a particular formality or began to follow it mechanically, forgetting its real significance.

By setting up what might be called a culture of nowness, Chögyam Trungpa showed his students how to keep it alive.

Although he did have his students draft a series of manuals that describe the rituals he devised so that they could be conserved, his main concern was to explain the rationales behind their conception. He showed us all how to respond to a given situation. For instance, one of his students might be called on to teach in a dark barn. But he would now know how to transform it into a place that manifested the dignity and awake quality of the Great Eastern Sun. Any location could be transformed and become the Kingdom of Shambhala, thus radiating its presence and spirit in a tangible way. Learning how to celebrate the present moment by entering into its depths is the true meaning of all ceremonies. Human beings can then enjoy their existence if they can confront themselves honestly: "Reality is very unpleasant sometimes, but if you get into reality properly, thoroughly, then it is blissful. And it is pleasant. This is so because reality speaks genuineness."[23]

It is possible to enjoy ourselves in a dignified and serene way if we are not fixated on *personal* pleasure: "Looking for a boyfriend or girlfriend or going to restaurants or cinemas doesn't help. You need your dralas to connect with the situation. It is not superstition. It usually works in your life. So please don't try to substitute the setting-sun world for the Great Eastern Sun world."

Chögyam Trungpa set up a new culture, oriented toward a celebration and invocation of the dralas, which manifest the inherent dignity of each situation. Such was one of his most important legacies for future generations. These formalities are all ways of helping Westerners to rely on their own lives when progressing along a spiritual path and helping others.

As he explained on Midsummer's Day 1981:[24] "At this point, it is not so important to maintain Vajradhatu, Nālandā, or the Naropa Institute as is, as organizations alone; what we really need is to propagate our sense of helping others. The bodhisattva ideal of working with others, dealing with others, is absolutely important. Please think of that."

---

23. Chögyam Trungpa, "What Is Ngeton?" *Vajradhatu Sun*, April/May 1983, p. 5.

24. That year the ceremony took place at Hogan Ranch outside Boulder with 750 participants.

Chapter Sixteen

FORMS ASSOCIATED WITH SPEECH

Language is language. If there were no human beings, there wouldn't be language. Each word that we speak should be regarded as a gem. When we speak or talk, we should regard words as tangible rather than pure sound.[1]

—CHÖGYAM TRUNGPA

1. Teaching Elocution: Recognizing the Importance of Speech

In 1983, Chögyam Trungpa decided to work on forms associated with speech. He had long observed the difficulties his students had in speaking the English language, especially in terms of articulation—Americans have a tendency to talk very fast and to swallow their words, which can make them hard to understand. Such inattention to what one says reflects a lack of understanding of the inherent dignity of speech and of the way to coordinate body and mind.

---

1. Chögyam Trungpa, "Community Talk and Birthday Celebration," *Vajradhatu Sun*, February/March 1984, p. 19.

For many years, Chögyam Trungpa thought about how to establish a discipline that could address this situation. During the retreat at Charlemont in 1977, he tried to introduce some of his visiting students to an educated mid-Atlantic accent as is spoken in some parts of New England. He especially worked on this approach with one particular student, Jane Condon.[2]

In 1983, he started dictating a book of fictional memoirs written by a high official to the king of Shambhala, in the mythical kingdom. While he was working on the first few chapters in Boulder, he would dictate material and then ask that it be read back to him aloud many times. He was very attentive to how the text was being read.

Shortly afterward, he left to give a series of talks in Philadelphia, on his way to a month-long retreat in New Hampshire. Marty Janowitz remembers how, one evening in the car, Chögyam Trungpa leaned forward and asked him, "Do you think I'm losing my English accent?" Marty replied, "I haven't thought of you as having an English accent for ages."

That very evening, at the home of Dan and Meera Meade, then the Vajradhatu ambassadors to Philadelphia, Chögyam Trungpa asked Marty Janowitz to read aloud the first chapter of the Shambhala memoirs in an English accent. Marty put on an accent that made everyone laugh. But Chögyam Trungpa did not want a parody. He began ruthlessly correcting Marty's accent and soon turned to others who were present that evening, encouraging them to speak as though they had been trained at Oxford.

With the help of everyone there that evening, Chögyam Trungpa wrote a poem that became his first elocution exercise. Each person contributed a line. Then Chögyam Trungpa immediately had them recite it back using an Oxonian accent. This became a new form of practice, on the spot.

That day he had visited the Liberty Bell, an icon of American history

---

2. In Tibet, he had already developed a great interest in languages. With his guru in Sechen, he decided to learn other languages and began with the Amdo dialect, which has a different pronunciation from Tibetan and uses words that have fallen out of use elsewhere.

that greatly impressed him. It figured into the elocution exercise composed that evening, which follows below.

How to Speak the English Language and
How Not to Speak Americanism

Spider is black,
Sky is blue,
How tantalizing this world.

Kathy's hair is black,
Her complexion is white,
Her attention is like a bowstring.

More than monumental,
More than tattered,
More than dying,
The Liberty Bell is more than antique.

Conglomerate's garden party
Is full of the vicissitudes of life.
I feel sorry for the Queen of England.

A tug of war,
Smell fish like the Japanese,
How gorgeous to be a mountain deer.

Be a tiger,
A roamlike tiger.
How fabulous I am.[3]

He then wrote around ten different elocution exercises, which become progressively more difficult.

Thus a new era opened. For the next year, Chögyam Trungpa took

---

3. Chögyam Trungpa, May 4, 1983, Strafford, Pennsylvania. Published by Vajradhatu Publications in the "Elocution Home Study Course" (1983).

every opportunity to devote himself to sharing elocution lessons with his students. After his stay in Philadelphia, he proceeded to his month-long retreat in Fasnacloich, New Hampshire, with the Vajra Regent Ösel Tendzin. This retreat was part of the continuing training of the Regent that Chögyam Trungpa carried out over a number of years.

To everyone's surprise, the retreat was not devoted to Chögyam Trungpa's giving esoteric teachings but was largely given over to the composition of the Shambhala memoirs, writing haiku about the four seasons, and the practice of elocution. Chögyam Trungpa corrected the speech of all the retreatants with great precision and passion. In addition to the Vajra Regent, some of the members of Vajradhatu's Board of Directors spent time with Rinpoche at this retreat. His eldest son, Ösel Mukpo, now Sakyong Mipham Rinpoche, also visited for several weeks.

Carolyn Gimian, who was there as a member of Rinpoche's staff and was finishing the manuscript of *Shambhala: The Sacred Path of the Warrior*, was selected by Rinpoche, much to her dismay, to become his prime elocution student. Looking back at the retreat, she remembers how he asked all the visitors to Fasnacloich to adopt this new practice. When correcting their readings, Chögyam Trungpa was not looking for a perfect accent, nor even the correct intonation, but rather a pronunciation linked to the spirit and power of the word. To achieve this, it is necessary to enter into contact with both the precision and the power of speech. The form—speaking with an Oxonian accent—is only the beginning. Ultimately, the point is connecting with the nowness of language and communication. This is not purely a question of imitation; anyone can take elocution lessons and learn a received, upper-class English accent, but this would not communicate Chögyam Trungpa's purpose.

During this retreat, David Rome visited Chögyam Trungpa. David was one of Chögyam Trungpa's editors, in addition to other roles he played on his staff. He had worked with him on the editing and production of several of his plays, and he had edited most of Chögyam Trungpa's poetry written in America. David often read Chögyam Trungpa's poetry aloud in public—at readings with other poets, at Buddhist seminars, and in other contexts. However, he had never taken part in an elocution exercise. He was rather resistant to the idea of reading with an English accent; however, Chögyam Trungpa insisted that he read the first elocution exercise, printed on page 341. Carolyn Gimian remembers how he read it. He did not adopt an English accent, but the emphasis he placed on words and his intonation and rhythm were exactly like the way Chögyam Trungpa himself read this exercise. It was clear that, although he had not studied elocution, he had learned how to connect with language in precisely the way that Chögyam Trungpa was hoping to convey to his other students. This was an important lesson for Carolyn. Elocution is an important first step in learning to communicate, but not from a technical point of view, like eager executives adopting a method to increase profits. Instead, the success of elocution comes from discovering the links between our minds and speech.

These exercises can allow someone to experience the meaning and sound of a word as precious and tangible. Following the retreat at Fasnacloich, elocution became a regular part of spending time with Chögyam Trungpa, over the next few years. During the 1984 and 1985 Seminaries, after giving his talks—which rarely began before the middle of the night—Chögyam Trungpa almost always gave an elocution lesson.

The threefold logic of elocution

This work on elocution is based on a training process similar to that used in the other disciplines introduced by Chögyam Trungpa, such as service at the Court or the practices of ikebana and oryoki. You start by learning a rather rigid form, which requires enormous discipline. This is the hinayana approach, which is extremely strict and rigorous. In this case, it is a matter of transforming our habitual way of speaking by making the effort to adopt an Oxonian accent.

In the practice of elocution as developed by Chögyam Trungpa, the starting point is to work on the elocution exercises, imitating an Oxonian English accent, regardless of one's normal way of speaking. The student must remain highly attentive and try to mimic not only the proper pronunciation but also the inflections of the words. As Chögyam Trungpa put it, making such an effort "is like imitating the Buddha by sitting under a tree and meditating at the hinayana level."[4]

Then there is a second step, in which a feeling of relaxation comes into the discipline. You continue to follow the method, but you can use it in a more natural way. Chögyam Trungpa referred to this as the mahayana approach or stage of elocution.

Finally, the last step is to return to your habitual way of speaking, while remembering this discipline. This is the vajrayana step. The power of speech is then revealed: "The point is to have awareness of the consonants and vowels and to pay respect to the language with which you were brought up."[5] Through the discipline of elocution, Chögyam Trungpa also presented the principle of speech as mantra, or sacred word. This sacredness comes not from the fact that some words have a supernatural power, but simply from the speaker's direct engagement with the symbolism and inherent vigor of speech. Through this discipline, the practitioner joins heaven and earth, or mind and body, in a real situation. The vowels are space, or heaven, to which are joined the consonants that represent the earth.[6]

2. The Qualities Game

During the same period that Chögyam Trungpa began to present elocution, he also introduced a parlor game that he shared with his students. Beginning with the retreat at Fasnacloich, he became very keen on the Qualities Game, which he played at the end of many evening meals in 1983 and 1984. One of the characteristics of all of these group activities was that they served to create formality in the space around him all the time. It was no longer possible to "hang out" talking to others at a dinner, reception, or cocktail party at which Chögyam Trungpa was present. If he

---

4. Chögyam Trungpa, *1984 Seminary Transcripts: Hinayana-Mahayana* (Boulder: Vajradhatu Publications), pp. 56–57.

5. Ibid., p. 25.

6. Ibid., p. 8.

was there, elocution and the Qualities Game were sure to make an appearance shortly. He introduced these activities to small and very large groups, from people around the dining room table to an audience of several hundred.

The Qualities Game is played as follows. Someone who is "it" leaves the room, while the others choose the name of a famous person, thing, or place. The person can be living or dead. Sometimes a philosophical principle might be chosen, such as "communism." Once the choice has been made, the person who is "it" comes back and asks questions about the qualities of the thing to be discovered. For example, you can ask: "If this were a tree, what kind of tree would it be?" The answer might be "an old tree growing on a rock" or "an apple tree blooming in an orchard on a spring day." By asking these questions, the person has to find the answer. After some time, Chögyam Trungpa decided to change the rules of the game. He would now choose the thing that all the others would guess. His answers were sometimes quite subtle, and the game could go on for hours. There was a lot of humor to these sessions, and students would compete to find the answer.

Chögyam Trungpa had transformed a simple amusement into a way to share his mind and way of looking at things.

The game often ended up lasting several hours before someone discovered the mystery solution. Sometimes two or three rounds of the game would be played in an evening. Chögyam Trungpa had favorites in this game, and while he never used the same answer twice in one night, it was not uncommon for Gesar of Ling or the Taj Mahal to be the answer to the Qualities Game. Interestingly, even when he used the same answer many times, he always took a fresh approach to the subject, so it was never that easy to guess the answer.

3. The Shambhala Anthem and Other Songs

In April 1977, during the early part of his yearlong retreat at Charlemont in Massachusetts, Chögyam Trungpa composed a song that he called the Shambhala Anthem. He wrote the lyrics first in Tibetan and translated them with the assistance of David Rome and others visiting him on retreat. He put the anthem to music, selecting as the tune "Let Erin Remember the Day of Old," taken from an Irish march. "Let Erin Remember" is part of the March Past in the ceremony of Trooping the Colour, the Queen of England's Birthday Parade, which was a favorite album of Chögyam Trungpa's. Words to the original song "Let Erin Remember" were written by Thomas Moore in the eighteenth century.

The Shambhala Anthem was sung on many occasions earlier, but it really came into its own, becoming a focus of attention, beginning with the Fasnacloich retreat in 1983. Following a rousing evening of reading the memoirs, doing elocution, and perhaps playing the Qualities Game a few times, Chögyam Trungpa would end the formal evening's activities at Fasnacloich with thirty or sixty minutes of singing the Shambhala Anthem over and over. He went through a period in which he adopted a Scottish accent while singing the song, which he encouraged his students to mimic. While there was something serious about all this activity, there was something very humorous about it at the same time. Chögyam Trungpa himself sang the anthem as a duet in his strange high voice at the end of most of his public appearances from 1983 on. Following the duet (usually with a female volunteer from the audience), he would typically invite the entire audience to sing the anthem together. His accident in England in 1969, which had paralyzed his left side, damaged his voice, giving it a strange tonality. Chögyam Trungpa thought, or at least said that he thought, that singing in as high a range as possible was good for exercising and developing the vocal cords. Depending on the occasion and one's predisposition, hearing him sing in his high falsetto could be an utterly moving or else unsettling experience, for his voice was unlike anything one had heard before.

Chögyam Trungpa composed the lyrics to several other songs, using as melodies other music from Trooping the Colour or several English folk songs, such as "The Minstrel Boy." As Carolyn Gimian wrote in the liner notes for a CD of his songs: "For Buddhism to take root and flourish in North America, it must be transmitted from one generation of Westerners to the next within their own families and customs, rather than continuing to come only from outside, or 'foreign' sources. Only as intimate family lore would Buddhism and the Shambhala tradition become like flesh and bones to future practitioners. The songs . . . are one of the ways that he found to further that transmission. They are meant to be passed down from generation to generation within the families and clans of Shambhala; to be sung on holidays; as lullabies at weddings, funerals, and other rites of passage; in short, whenever an opportunity presents itself. The more we sing them, the more these powerful incantations can help to bring forth the world of Shambhala."[7]

The anthem and other songs, like the flag of the Kingdom of Shambhala or the pins that Chögyam Trungpa designed, were ways to evoke the dignity and greatness of the teachings.

The retreat at Fasnacloich ushered in a new era in Chögyam Trungpa's teaching and presentation. In a sense, this was the gateway into the last era of his life, one characterized by a much less conceptual but nevertheless demanding approach. From this time on, when students were invited to have dinner with him, Chögyam Trungpa asked them to improvise haiku about the four seasons or other topics and take part in elocution exercises. For his guests' enjoyment, he would often include a reading of some chapters from the Shambhala memoirs he was continuing to write. After all of that, they might play a few rounds of the Qualities Game before finally singing the Shambhala Anthem, sometimes more than twenty times in a row.

The order of these elements in an evening, which often lasted until dawn, sometimes varied, but generally most of them were present. All of these disciplines celebrate some aspect of speech, which in the Buddhist perspective allows the body and mind to synchronize. This makes for genuine communication in the deepest sense,

---

7. Carolyn Rose Gimian, in *Dragon's Thunder: Songs of Chögyam Trungpa, Dorje Dradül of Mukpo* (Halifax: Vajradhatu Publications, 2000), liner notes, p. 1. On this CD of the main songs that Chögyam Trungpa wrote, he can be heard singing the anthem of the Kingdom of Shambhala in his unusual voice. Thanks to the magic of technology, it is possible to experience this extraordinary voice that defied all conventions and so receive a transmission of his ultimate inscrutability.

Chapter Seventeen

THE CREATION
OF THE COURT

The Kalapa Court is the place where the most sanity is displayed. It is not a question of relaxing into a particularly luxurious situation, but of maintaining sanity in one's daily life. This is the demand of Kalapa Court. It is expected that one work with one's mind to a point of sanity.[1]

—DIANA MUKPO

BEGINNING IN 1976 with the creation of the Kalapa Court, Chögyam Trungpa's home became the place where the culture inspired by the Buddhist vision could manifest itself. His house was a kind of palace, not because of its luxuriousness but because of the sacred vision that touched everything that occurred there and the constant radiance of Chögyam Trungpa's presence. While many masters live a quiet, retiring, private life after their obligations have been fulfilled, Chögyam Trungpa remained constantly open and available to one and all. There was not a single moment when he was not teaching. As the sangha continued to greatly expand, a large number of students were invited to share his world, or even to contribute to it in various ways.

---

1. Diana J. Mukpo, "Kalapa Court," *Vajradhatu Sun*, December 1978, p. 3.

1. Daily Life with Chögyam Trungpa

Four Mile Canyon

When he arrived in the Boulder area in 1970, Chögyam Trungpa set up home in a cabin called "Gunung Mas" in the mountains near Gold Hill. Then, a few months later, he moved to Four Mile Canyon, to a little, modern two-story house by a stream in a canyon outside Boulder. On the first floor were the living quarters for Chögyam Trungpa and his family. Here there was also a dining room, where Chögyam Trungpa sometimes held parties. On the second floor was a living room that initially was used as a meditation hall. After a meditation center was opened elsewhere, it reverted to a living room that could seat about ten people. It was here that Rinpoche gave his first "tantra groups," presenting teachings on the nature of the mind and preliminary practice (*ngöndro*) to some of his closest students in early 1974. These groups continued at other locations until 1976.

From 1970 to 1976, Chögyam Trungpa lived very informally. His wife often cooked for him, and he occasionally prepared his own meals or asked a student to help make him something. But his wife remembers how he already paid attention to the slightest detail. If they were short of money, for example, they might drink a bottle of cheap wine, but in elegant glasses.

It was such an open house that Diana Mukpo had very little private life with Rinpoche: "Our domestic situation . . . was really a nightmare. In the early days, we would wake up and there would be somebody meditating in our bedroom. And I would say, 'You've got to get these people out, they're driving me crazy.' I remember one day I completely got to the brink of insanity. It was Easter Day, and I said, 'There's an Easter egg hunt.' They all went outside, and I locked all the doors and windows so that I could be alone with Rinpoche."[2]

In 1974, David Rome became Chögyam Trungpa's secretary and also took care of him in other ways. David woke him up, made him tea and something to eat—generally Japanese noodles—helped him get dressed, and drove him to his office. He stayed with him all day and went every-

---

2. Diana J. Mukpo, "Stories That Need Telling," *Shambhala News,* September 2000, p. 16.

where with him, to teachings, meetings, specific ceremonies, and other events. On the way back, they often stopped at a Mexican restaurant. Chögyam Trungpa went through phases of always eating the same meals. For instance, he might order the same pizza for several weeks.

After dinner, David drove him back home around midnight, then returned the next morning.

Aurora 7

In the summer of 1976, having lived in several residences on the outskirts of Boulder, Chögyam Trungpa moved into town, to the corner of Seventh Street and Aurora Street. This was a famous address, because it had been the home of astronaut Scott Carpenter, who had named his space capsule *Aurora 7*.[3]

It was the first time that Chögyam Trungpa had lived in the center of town. Before, he was sheltered from all the people who constantly wanted to see him, ask his advice, or visit a Tibetan "guru." He now began to consider how to make himself available to people in an appropriate way. Thus arose the idea of organizing his domestic situation as a focal point where students could participate in his life and have contact with him beyond the lecture hall or the hallways of the office. Chögyam Trungpa was keen on this idea because it allowed him to put into daily practice some of the forms of service he had introduced to the community from the time of His Holiness the Karmapa's first visit to America in 1974. They could now be applied to his own domestic situation, rather than purely to hosting other important teachers.

His cook was then Max King, an American of Chinese origin, who made excellent Asian dishes. Max cooked breakfast and dinner for Chögyam Trungpa, and every evening a dozen or more people were invited to dinner.

---

3. Scott Carpenter was chosen on April 9, 1959, as a member of the Mercury 7 team. He was the copilot of the first manned American orbital space flight. On May 24, 1962, Carpenter became the second American to orbit the earth, flying his ship, *Aurora 7*, which performed three orbits.

In the spring of 1976, Dilgo Khyentse Rinpoche came to the United States for the first time, followed shortly afterward by the Karmapa's second visit. To help receive them, Chögyam Trungpa invited one of his students, John Perks, an Englishman with quite varied work experience, including some time as a butler, to work with him. Together, they began creating an approach to protocol and service that reflected elements of English service as well as some Tibetan qualities and uniquely "Shambhalian" practices as well.

John Perks was a charismatic man who invested a great deal of discipline and humor in this project. At the beginning, as recalled by Ronald Stubbert, one of the members of the Vajradhatu Board of Directors, it all seemed highly eccentric, often more like a TV caricature than a genuine royal court. As with many other aspects of Chögyam Trungpa's life and teaching, for some time no one was quite sure if this was all a farce or to be taken very seriously.

550 Mapleton Avenue

In the fall of 1976, Chögyam Trungpa moved into a larger house, where he decided to live with his family—his wife and his sons, the Sawang, Taggie, and Gesar—as well as the family of the Regent, who had been officially appointed a few months before. Life became more formal. John Perks began as the butler. Then he became master of the household, Walter Fordham was the butler, and Robert Vogler became master of the household for the Regent. The residence was called Kalapa Court in reference to the Kingdom of Shambhala, whose capital is Kalapa. Roles such as butler and master of the household were a bit different from the way they are traditionally conceived. The people in these positions were expected to exert leadership as much as members of the board of directors or meditation teachers in the community. Rinpoche talked at length to people working in his household about the need to radiate gentleness and genuineness. It was a training ground for people, and they were also expected to help train others.

Eleventh and Cascade Streets

In the fall of 1978, Chögyam Trungpa moved to Eleventh Street, to the house that he would keep until his death. The entire house was arranged in a specific way for the establishment of the Court. A specially adapted kitchen was built so that service could be done easily.

Chögyam Trungpa invested a lot of energy in decorating his new home. He had an extremely precise idea of what he wanted, even designing his own rugs. He asked several students to work with him. Robert Rader remembers the day when Chögyam Trungpa asked him to find some gilded hangings to put on the walls. But each time Robert brought another sample, Rinpoche said that it was not what he was looking for, even if it was of good quality. He explained that he wanted a color like gold coins that are slightly tarnished. When the right cloth was at last found, it made a tonic, dignified contrast with the white carpet, which Robert Rader would never have dared choose, but which he liked very much.

This attention to every aspect of Court life was not limited to the residence in Boulder. Henceforth, the atmosphere of the Court was to be re-created wherever Chögyam Trungpa went. When he visited the various centers, it was necessary to choose where he would stay and then transform the location before receiving him. The whole community was involved. Some of these experiments took place before Chögyam Trungpa even moved into his official "Court" in Colorado.

For example, in the spring of 1976, Rinpoche experimented with formal service and other elements of Court etiquette when he traveled to New York and California to host Dilgo Khyentse Rinpoche. Carolyn Gimian, who was then living in Berkeley, California, remembers the radical change that resulted from this new approach:

We had invited Chögyam Trungpa to teach for one month in the Bay Area, which includes Berkeley, San Francisco, Palo Alto, and as far south as Santa Cruz. In the past, when Rinpoche had visited, he had been put up in very simple surroundings. The Dharmadhatu, our local meditation center, would rent a house somewhere in a decent neighborhood, and he would move in with one cook or attendant, something like that. Or he might bring Lady Diana and his children, but still it was a fairly simple scene. However, when he was coming this time, he sent an advance party of the Regent and Michael Root to prepare for his visit. They also came out ahead because His Holiness Dilgo Khyentse Rinpoche was going to be in the Bay Area during this time. When the Regent and Michael saw the house that we had rented for Rinpoche in the Berkeley Hills (a nice area), they were appalled at the furnishings, which were kind of "hippie-dippie." We thought they were fine. They insisted that we rent a complete suite of living room furniture and that we rent or borrow good china, linens, and so forth, for the dining room. I remember going shopping with them for silver candelabras, crystal glasses, and other things. It was quite an outrageous change. Then they suggested that we introduce dinner servers, and we started training people how to serve and clear at dinner. I was fairly intimately involved in all this because I was with Rinpoche's cook, Max King, at this time. We had lived together for many years, so the two of us were invited to live in Rinpoche's household while he was in town. We were very involved with setting up the house and running it. I used to train the dinner servers. Many of them got a half-hour lesson before they had to actually bring out the food. I remember one fellow whose hands couldn't stop shaking through the whole meal. It really stood everything on its head, and many people were a bit freaked out by the style.

In Asia, it would be quite normal to establish a dignified and elegant environment to receive great teachers. Such is the situation in Tibetan monasteries, where special attention is always paid to a rinpoche. What is astonishing about the way Chögyam Trungpa introduced these formalities to his students is that he did not teach them ancestral Tibetan customs. Instead he created a new culture from scratch, which was based on the principles of Buddhism and the Shambhala teachings, but also included Western traditions.

In addition to Chögyam Trungpa and his family and the Vajra Regent and his family, John Perks moved into the basement of the Court with his wife and children. Then, at the end of 1979, Walter Fordham and his family joined them. During a certain period, Mrs. Pybus, Rinpoche's mother-in-law, also lived in the Kalapa Court.

Each day had its precise rituals, even though nothing was predictable with Chögyam Trungpa. He could quite easily get up at two in the afternoon, or else go to bed at that time. So I shall simply present a "typical" day, although such a day probably never existed.

On waking up, Chögyam Trungpa would ask his personal attendant, or Kusung, to bring the tea offering to him in his bedroom. He would add hot water to the various teacups for the various shrines in the house, which included a personal shrine in the sitting room off his bedroom, as well as the kitchen shrine and the shrine in the meditation room of the house. These were traditional tea offerings to the dharmapalas, or the protectors. [4]

After that, Chögyam Trungpa drank his own tea. For many years, he drank green tea, often gunpowder, with a drop of milk. He often drank from an Oriental-style cup, although he might also use an elegant Western cup and saucer. He then had breakfast. This was rarely before eleven or noon. His habit of rising late led to the joke that Chögyam Trungpa had never taken into account the different time zones and had remained on Tibetan time.

After Max King left the position in 1978, Chögyam Trungpa had a number of cooks during his years in America. Rinpoche developed a strong "culinary" relationship with Shari Vogler, who was his head cook, or machen, for many years. For several years, when Shari took a maternity leave, Joann Carmin was the machen for Rinpoche. There were also a number of guest cooks who enjoyed making dinner one night a month at the Kalapa Court or volunteered to cook for Rinpoche when he traveled. The relationship between Chögyam Trungpa and these cooks was

---

4. In Buddhism, the nature of the various divinities and protectors is extremely subtle. While having a certain reality, they have no more of an independent existence than any other being. The protectors' mission is to guard practitioners against all the obstacles they might meet on their path, such as a lack of attention, a sudden panic attack, etc.

intimate, and he had a great deal of respect and affection for his "cook-ies," as he sometimes called them.

Each morning, Rinpoche's cook for the day, usually Shari, would meet with him to find out what he wanted for breakfast and what his food plans for the rest of the day would be. Depending on the season and his mood, he might stay in his bedroom for breakfast or sit in the kitchen or on the outdoor patio leading to the garden. There he met with his cook to discuss the day's program and the various menus to be put together, in-cluding a discussion of the guests for dinner that evening.[5]

He really enjoyed cooking on occasion. One of his favorite dishes con-sisted of a pan of boiled lamb, to which he added eggs, blue cheese, and Japanese plums.

Going back to his early years in the United States, he liked improvis-ing recipes. His cook at Tail of the Tiger, Chuck Lief, remembers that Chögyam Trungpa particularly savored strange culinary experiments. For instance, he would prepare momos (traditional Tibetan dumplings), which he stuffed with ox tongue that had been marinated in sake and soy sauce. He was amused by people's reactions to his various experiments. He took mischievous delight in stuffing a duck with a leg of lamb, then roasting it. This dish was called "Ducklam."

On his return from a trip to Mexico, in October 1981, based on the food he had there, he decided to eat on a regular basis a dish he had in-vented himself, which he called *carne yarave* after a Mexican Indian princess. It consisted of beef or lamb cut into fine strips, then braised in soy sauce, diced tomatoes, green peppers, bacon, and fresh cilantro, to which he added large quantities of a seasoning he loved, MSG (mono-sodium glutamate).

He also liked a dish made of tripe in white sauce, with pasta and cau-liflower, which was thus entirely white.

With a particular attention to symbolism, Chögyam Trungpa insisted that the right utensils be used for the right meal. For Indian food, he pre-ferred using a chapati (flat unleavened bread) and the fingers of his right

---

5. During the first eight years she worked for Chögyam Trungpa, Shari Vogler met him every morning. Then he let her organize things as she wished.

hand, the traditional way to eat Indian food, while for East Asian dishes he used chopsticks. He soon acquired several different services corresponding to the various sorts of cooking that were served.

After breakfast, he usually met with his private secretary or the person designated as his attaché for the day, to go over his schedule. Then he showered and dressed, assisted by his Kusung. In addition to the Kusung, there was often a Kusung-in-training at the Court, as well as other servers who were called Shabdu. Then there would be people working in the kitchen, people attending to the housecleaning and answering mail that came to the house, as well as people helping with the children, and Dorje Kasung serving as "house guards," as drivers, and in other capacities. So on any day, at any time, there might be a dozen or more people all at the Kalapa Court, ostensibly to serve Rinpoche and his family. In fact, although they did provide a lot of help, they were really there because they wanted to spend time around him and valued that experience, as well as the specific training they received in various disciplines of meditation in action. Everything was done with incredible precision.

A few years after Rinpoche's death, his closest Kusung met in order to write down the highly precise and specific procedures they followed when helping him shower. To their surprise, they realized that the choreography was different for each of them. So how had he managed to remember each one so perfectly?

In the afternoon, after breakfast, he often had meetings, for example with the Nālandā Translation Committee, the board of directors, or members of any number of groups in the sangha, or privately with individual members of the community.

In the 1970s the heart of the community was at Karma Dzong, the meditation center in Boulder. During this period, Rinpoche went to the office almost every day when he was in town, but in the late seventies and in the eighties his residence became the focal point of his activities. Some people came to practice the tea ceremony in the little teahouse he had had specially built for that purpose in the garden; others came for an audience. In the summer, he invited hundreds of people to garden parties or other major festivities.

On a typical evening, he went out to give teachings or perform a ceremony, or he might invite people to his house for a meeting. Then he often
invited a few students to dinner, which could be served any time between
midnight and six in the morning. He never ate before teaching because,
as he explained to Shari Vogler, he was connected to the celestial level of
lha and did not want to create interferences by having to digest at the
same time.[6] Shari Vogler, who lived with him as his cook, remembers the
intense joy that reigned at the Kalapa Court during the late seventies and
early eighties. Everyone was expecting the unexpected, which never failed
to materialize and open everyone's hearts.

In 1981, John Perks moved to Nova Scotia, so Walter Fordham was put
in charge of service. Then, in 1985, following a long retreat at Mill Village
in Nova Scotia, Chögyam Trungpa started eating more often in his room
and saw fewer people, presumably because of failing health. But at least
until 1986, he would still organize sumptuous banquets, either in his
house or in the various Dharmadhatus he visited.

2. The Creation of a Mandala, or Court

Within a few years, the environment created by Chögyam Trungpa had
acquired a different aspect: according to the Shambhala teachings, it was
a royal Court; but according to tantric Buddhism, it meant creating a
mandala.

Chögyam Trungpa presented the traditions of Buddhism and Shambhala not as a theoretical body of teachings but as a way of sharing his
own experience with his students, so that the dharma "entered their
blood." Instead of just teaching the principle of the mandala—which he
was also to do—he created one. He conceived situations that put every-

---

6. "Psychologically, lha represents the first wakefulness. It is the experience of tremendous
freshness and freedom from pollution in your state of mind. Lha is what reflects the Great
Eastern Sun for the first time in your being, and it is also the sense of shining out, projecting tremendous goodness. In the body, lha is the head, especially the eyes and forehead, so
it represents physical upliftedness and projecting out as well." *Shambhala: The Sacred Path
of the Warrior* (Shambhala Library, 2003), p. 151.

one in contact with the meaning of the teaching as based on his own experience, not just an intellectual understanding.

Because in a book we have only words to convey what we want to say, we shall now attempt to explain the nature of a mandala.

The mandala as a field of experience

The notion of mandala is very hard to understand, because it is quite different from our habitual thought processes. First, in contrast to the impression created by the iconographic depiction, a mandala does not represent a reality that exists outside ourselves, like an image of the universe. On the contrary, the mandala is above all the whole of our being; it is "a sense of total existence with you in the center."[7]

The word *mandala* literally means a "circle" that incorporates everything, and leaves nothing out. Such an assembly is a profound unity—not as a flattened-out uniformity, but rather as a world where everything can appear in its true size, in its place, with its own current of reality.

While we generally think that our present situation is more or less haphazard, the notion of mandala shows that our relationship with the world and the things around us in fact constitutes our very being. Where we are is the center of the mandala. In other words, there is no "subject" that is related to "objects" outside it. Everything is part of the same reality and is neither pointless nor fortuitous.

Seeing enlightenment in terms of mandala may seem paradoxical, if we naively take enlightenment to be a sort of boundless freedom. On the contrary, Buddhist vajrayana teachings assert that, even in enlightenment there is a space with boundaries, but these are not part of the territory of the ego. The mandala is a *horizon*, the very possibility of visibility.

The three mandalas

In addition to the general principle of mandala, in terms of practice, Buddhism distinguishes between three different mandalas, which are

---

7. *Crazy Wisdom*, p. 46.

also interdependent. They are discussed separately only for teaching purposes and constitute three possibilities of developing a pure vision of the world, in other words, a capacity to recognize the sacred character of existence. The fifteenth Karmapa expressed this as follows: "Whether one is walking, sitting, or lying down, whether one is talking, whatever one does, one should abandon discursive interest in this ordinary world and precisely maintain contemplation on its triple aspect: seeing appearance as the deity, perceiving sound as mantra, and seeing mental activity as pure awareness."[8]

The outer mandala refers to the way we enter into various situations, which are perceived as coherent patterns of interconnected relationships. In other words, as Chögyam Trungpa explained, such a mandala refers simply to moments that are immediate and real, which can be visual, aural, or conceptual, and that are connected with the so-called outside world.[9]

On an inner level, the mandala is related to the degree of naked awareness that we have of our own body and its environment. Our bodies are seen as sacred, allowing us to establish contact with reality: "How we speak, how we look, how we touch our cup, our fork or knife, how we lift things and carry them about—all those things are very deliberate. But such deliberateness is not presented in a manual or book on how to act according to the tantric tradition. The point is there is no such thing as a real tantric diet or proper tantric behavior. Instead, we develop a basic attitude, so that when we begin to extend our arm, we simply do it."[10]

Finally, the secret mandala is recognizing in our own minds a sense of awareness and openness free of any hesitation, which we can invoke at any time.

---

8. Khakhyab Dorje, the fifteenth Karmapa, *Continuelle ondée pour le bien des êtres*, trans. Ken McLeod and François Jaquemart (Toulon-sur-Arroux: Éditions Yiga Tcheu Dzinn, 1980), p. 29.

9. See Chögyam Trungpa, *1982 Seminary Transcripts: Vajrayana* (Boulder: Vajradhatu Publications).

10. *Journey without Goal*, p. 36.

3. Serving Rinpoche

The three dimensions of reality and symbolic language

When the Court was first created, some thought it would only be a passing phase. After returning home from work, they had no desire to serve at the Court and were secretly waiting to be invited to dinner. But others realized that a new era of teaching had begun and that this was an opportunity to be near Chögyam Trungpa. It was like both playing a game and undergoing a powerful experience. Forms can be a language. The way tea is served has its grammar. If you write well, you communicate correctly. When there is real communication, it creates a spacious atmosphere. Serving Chögyam Trungpa was a lesson in communicating in gestures instead of words. To describe what was happening at Kalapa Court, Walter Fordham compared it to the film *Babette's Feast*, which shows how a woman changes the people she lives with by organizing a meal. A top French chef, Babette had to leave France in exile after the 1871 rising. She then goes to Scandinavia, where she serves the members of a Puritan sect. After years of hard work and austerity, she wins ten thousand francs in the lottery and decides to spend all of the money on organizing a sumptuous meal for all the inhabitants of the village. The care she puts into preparing the event is astonishing. Through it, she transforms the entire community.[11] Establishing a particular environment can cause a change in the states of mind of those who enter into direct contact with it. Such was the situation Chögyam Trungpa created.

When you opened the door to Rinpoche's sitting room, anything could happen. He might be completely silent, start talking to you, stay totally still, or pick up a water pistol and shoot at you. You had to respond to the situation at once, however unexpected it was.

In the brilliant context of the Court, everyone's state of mind became utterly exposed. People noticed, often with surprise, the fears they had hidden, their little manipulations to make the world correspond to their desires, and the state of confusion they had tried to conceal.

---

11. *Babette's Feast*, a film by Gabriel Awel released in 1987, was based on a book by Isak Dinesen.

A sense of humor

But serving Chögyam Trungpa was not a stiff or fixed situation; it was full of humor. Humor is a central notion in Chögyam Trungpa's teachings. He often discussed it, and greatly enjoyed witticisms. But his idea of it does not exactly correspond to our habitual definition of the term: it "does not mean telling jokes or being comical or criticizing others and laughing at them. A genuine sense of humor is having a light touch: not beating reality into the ground but appreciating reality with a light touch. The basis of Shambhala vision is rediscovering that perfect and real sense of humor, that light touch of appreciation."[12]

Humor is a particular way to seize the present moment in all its freshness, and a way to ensure that a situation does not remain frozen. When someone served him too stiffly, or was panicked at the idea of making a mistake, he sometimes pinched their behind despite the formal context or did something else to relax the atmosphere.

Chögyam Trungpa also appreciated it when his students played jokes on him. In 1985, he was to give the abhisheka of Vajrayogini. The appointed time for the ceremony approached and passed. He continued to stay put at home, without offering any reason for the delay. Hours passed, and as James Gimian remembers: "We tried everything to coax Rinpoche to come to the shrine hall, with no luck. At a certain point we lost the reference points of ordinary behavior with him. He seemed to both support and enjoy that change in our minds because it let us see the way his mind worked more clearly. So when my mind snapped I got a roll of paper towels, entered his sitting room as if I was entering His Holiness Karmapa's sitting room in Rumtek, Sikkim, with that same religiosity and seriousness that Rinpoche discouraged around himself, I performed three prostrations while mumbling a mantra in fake Tibetan (sort of copying the sounds that the monks make while doing evening pujas, including when they clear their throats and spit). Then after the last prostration I approached Rinpoche, kneeled in front of him with my head bowed, and presented him with the kata made of the roll of paper towels. [It is tradi-

---

12. *Shambhala: The Sacred Path of the Warrior* (Shambhala Library, 2003), p. 15.

tional to present a Tibetan teacher with a kata, or white silk scarf, as an offering.] It seemed to break his mood, and shortly thereafter we left."

Kasung, Kusung, and Shabdu

As mentioned above, the entire community was involved in Court life. There were servants, people who did the household chores, looked after the children, the garden, the Kasung, Kusung, Shabdu. . . .

The complexity of all these functions can seem confusing, but as James Gimian explained: "While all these titles were definitely in existence, often they were just ways for people to get involved. So Rinpoche came up with the titles, and then someone found a reason for this person to be at the Court and made up something for them to do. It wasn't like there was an overall logic and description of what people were supposed to do."[13]

Before starting a shift at the Court, students were expected to practice in the shrine room at the house. In the evening, dinner was served for the entire staff. Often a group of people would have the same shift together for months. For example, one group would always be serving together on the same night of the week, month after month. So people developed strong camaraderie and friendship in this way.

4. The Court and Mandala: A Teaching Situation

In tantric iconography, the mandala is the palace where the deity lives. If you work with a particular practice, if you enter that mandala, you

---

13. The Kasung were responsible for security and the telephone and acted as escorts and drivers for Chögyam Trungpa or visiting teachers. They were introduced for the Karmapa's first visit, in order to take care of him and his safety. Their job was to create the right environment so that everyone could have contact with the teacher in the best possible conditions. The Kasung were trained to face all sorts of crises: fire, medical emergencies, physical or verbal aggression, etc.

The Kusung looked after feeding and dressing Rinpoche. They had a more intimate and personal role.

The Shabdu had a nonmilitary role. They worked for the Kusung, took care of the house, and served Rinpoche.

visualize yourself as the central deity. In daily life, whatever your situation, you still see yourself and your world in that way. Such is the tantric understanding of the sacred, and it is almost claustrophobic. The wealth of the world is so great that it is impossible to avoid it. Every time someone went into Rinpoche's house, this experience became plain; the sacred character of each thing became clearly perceptible, as though the very air were different. Marty Janowitz wrote in 1988:

> Although his Shambhala, Court and Kasung activities were often viewed as the most unorthodox or potentially strange, I would like to suggest that it was exactly those aspects of his teaching that in fact showed him to be the most orthodox and loyal to his vajrayana inheritance.
>
> His presentation of the mandala of the Kalapa Court and the Shambhala Lodge was such an excellent example of his trusting his Western students with the power of a vajrayana view and techniques. He was one of the few masters who felt that his students and this world could truly be transformed, that we could open our minds and that he could share with us the heart, the essence of the vajra world. The Vidyadhara [Chögyam Trungpa] never felt he had to explain or place his actions in context, so that we could feel secure that he knew what he was doing, that he was within the scope of the tradition.
>
> It was somewhat by accident that I realized more clearly what an orthodox vajra master he truly was. A few years ago, I was going to travel in advance of the Vidyadhara in order to prepare the ground of his upcoming tours. He said to me that the focus of his activity was going to be within the household, the Court, as he travelled, and that rather than his giving extended programmatic teaching, he was primarily just going to live in each city for a short time, and people would come along and meet him and experience his world through that household. I was going out a month or so in advance to give talks, seminars, hold organizational meetings etc. with a focus on working with the mandala principle.

In discussions with him, he encouraged me, in addition to reflecting upon my experience and reviewing his extensive teachings here and there on mandala, to work with a book by Herbert Guenther, entitled *Matrix of Mystery*, which was part translation and part commentary on an important Ati root text, the *Guhyagarbha*. . . . I found within it completely literal descriptions of our Court mandala, proposed as the image of natural vivid patterns of unencumbered energy. This view presents the image of a royal household living within a palace as the closest description of enlightened patterns of energy. In the center of the mandala is a majestic quality of energy, which when expressed perfectly appears as a King and Queen and which is surrounded by a subtle arrangement of vassals, ministers, palace guards, etc.

The descriptions were thought provoking to say the least. In subsequent conversations with the Vidyadhara about this text he thought it quite funny that I had presumed he might have invented this imagery. He told me to remember that the Court Mandala was the "real thing, more than Coca-Cola."[14]

A study of different peoples and civilizations shows that all societies have elaborated a set of rituals to structure the relationships people have between themselves and with the world. In this respect, we are living in strange times, which conspire to negate all rituals and forms, in the name of universal clarity.

The Court offers the possibility of a life organized around a series of highly rigorous rituals, but which are not strictly speaking religious. It even constitutes a profane sacred environment, in which we can recognize that each moment of our existence can become sacred. As Chögyam Trungpa often explained: "You have to look at your ordinary domestic reality: your knives, your forks, your plates, your telephone, your dishwasher and your towels—ordinary things. There is nothing mystical or

---

14. Martin Janowitz, "The Kalapa Court: Theory and Practice," *Lodge News* 3, no. 3 (Fall 1988), pp. 2–3.

extraordinary about them, but if there is no connection with ordinary everyday situations, if you don't examine your mundane life, then you will never find any humor or dignity or, ultimately, any reality."[15]

The creation of the Court is an important teaching because it is a response to the fact that so many people nowadays lack a sense of confidence and dignity. Chögyam Trungpa did not want to reintroduce a series of codes that had once existed. He invented new ones according to the situation he found himself in, thus giving fresh life to the dream that *each* human being might be able to invent their own etiquette, without having to follow one that has been imposed externally, or else abandoning all form of discipline. Chögyam Trungpa never hesitated about creating new forms and rituals, while remaining attentive that nothing should become rigid and mechanical. The Court was a space to cultivate and celebrate true Sanity.

Driven by his desire to open the hearts and enlighten the minds of all his students, Chögyam Trungpa used this project to liberate discipline and spontaneity in their inseparability.

---

15. *Shambhala: The Sacred Path of the Warrior* (Shambhala Library, 2003), p. 15.

Chapter Eighteen

DHARMA ART

Poetics also includes one's vision, hearing, and feeling, all together. . . . we are talking about a complete, comprehensive realization of the phenomenal world—seeing things as they are.[1]

　　　　　　　　　　　　　　　—CHÖGYAM TRUNGPA

AS WE HAVE ALREADY seen, Chögyam Trungpa was an artist of the first rank. The singular unity of his vision was manifested in several different media. His son Sakyong Mipham Rinpoche said that living with him often created the impression of taking part in a constant celebration of life. In the foreword to the French edition of *The Heart of the Buddha*, Sakyong Mipham wrote this highly evocative portrait of his father: "When I think of the hours spent in his company, I remember that, even if sometimes there was a lot happening around him, most of the time when we sat together, seemingly nothing much happened. But if I look more closely, I notice that a lot of things happened, My father was always aware of all the details, whether it had to do with the food we ate or the clothes I wore. With him, there wasn't what you would call time off. He

---

1. *The Heart of the Buddha*, p. 200.

was completely involved in all aspects of life, with simplicity and free-dom. It wasn't a question of making a big deal of anything. He taught that the dharma wasn't an exalted or esoteric dogma, but instead had to do with immediate situations." [2]

As emphasized by Sara Kapp, a student of Chögyam Trungpa's, each of his actions was an indication of how we should learn to be. In 1981, he de-cided to go on retreat at Karmê Chöling, and Sara Kapp was invited to join him. The retreat was extremely simple; some time was devoted every day to practicing the texts or liturgies associated with the Shambhala teachings. They often went out shopping and then prepared dinner. One day, noticing that a knife was not sharp enough, Chögyam Trungpa picked up a stone and, with infinite patience, slowly rubbed the blade against it under running water. For at least four hours he stayed in front of the sink, until the knife had been perfectly sharpened. He showed everyone how he had done it. It was so simple and precise.

A few years later, Sara Kapp spent several days with him on a retreat in Nova Scotia. When it was time for her to go, she said, "My only regret is that we didn't have time to sit down together and practice." He look deeply disappointed by what she had said, and replied, "Each minute was practice."

In fact, his entire life was practice. One day, Sara Kapp noticed that he had stopped smoking. She asked why. "Cigarettes have given me up," he said. When she insisted he explain the meaning of such a statement, he added, "I smoked a cigarette without noticing."

Chögyam Trungpa paid attention to everything. In this respect, he was an artist at all times and in everything he did. While he did not value art above other human activities, he was very enthusiastic about artistic dis-ciplines and liked to visit the studios of his students who were artists. Devoting oneself to art did not seem to him to be a waste of time or some-thing secondary that allowed one to avoid the seriousness of formal prac-tice. Instead, it was a way to enter into the heart of life.

It was thus not surprising that he eventually decided to convey the

---

2. Sakyong Mipham, forward to *Le coeur du sujet* (French edition of *The Heart of the Buddha*), (Paris: Éditions du Seuil, 1993), p. 8.

principles of the Buddhist and Shambhala teachings to artists, and convey some principles of art to his Buddhist students.

1. Deliberate Art and Art in Everyday Life

In 1973, during Seminary, Chögyam Trungpa gave a talk on "art in everyday life" in which he distinguished between two conceptions of art. The first aims at producing a painting, poem, or piece of music that will be displayed, read, or performed in public. He called this process *deliberate*, because the artist is trying to master his or her discipline to create works as he or she pleases.

But there is another approach: an "art of meditative experience." The purpose of such art, Chögyam Trungpa explained, is not to be exhibited or broadcast; "instead, it is a perpetually growing process in which we begin to appreciate our surroundings in life, whatever they may be—it doesn't necessarily have to be good, beautiful, and pleasurable at all. The definition of art, from this point of view, is to be able to see the uniqueness of experience. Every moment we might be doing the same things— brushing our teeth every day, combing our hair every day, cooking our dinner every day. But that seeming repetitiveness becomes unique every day. A kind of intimacy takes place with the daily habits that you go through and the art involved in it. That's why it is called art in everyday life."[3] Chögyam Trungpa thus opened another dimension to artistic activity, a dimension that is available to everyone. He himself was the prime example of such mastery. Everything he did was art.

Jerry Granelli, a jazz musician and longtime student, remembers watching him doing calligraphy in the early 1970s. Chögyam Trungpa was writing the names of the students who had decided to take refuge vows. Once his work was finished, he rinsed his brush under the tap so gently that it was as if it were alive. When the brush was completely clean, he put it to his lips to make sure that the hairs were together at the tip. He then carefully cleaned the sink with a sponge.

---

3. *Dharma Art*, p. 27.

Jerry Granelli was struck by the power of Chögyam Trungpa's simple actions and said, "That's art!" Rinpoche replied, "Yes, it is."

Jerry then added, "People have got to see you do that." He thinks this may have had an effect on Chögyam Trungpa. What is certain is that, soon afterward, Chögyam Trungpa developed the idea of "dharma art." The seminars devoted to dharma art were a means of revealing the artistic nature of all our actions and to show how to cultivate such an approach to each moment of our existence.

When asked why dharma art is unique, he explained: "In some sense it is not so much talking about the art itself, the product, but it's training one's perception, how to rearrange your sitting room or what tie to buy, what jacket to buy. Even on that level, there is some sense of perception and also respect, sacredness to everything you do, including how to drink a cup of tea. . . . So that's the basic point, the idea of how to appreciate your life in a very deliberate, mindfulness sense, so that your sense perceptions begin to click into the sacredness of it—which is not necessarily a religious one, but sacred, good."[4]

In dharma art, you learn to see phenomena as phenomena. In this way, there is no longer a subject looking at an object. Instead, the phenomenal world sees itself through our presence—or, to use a tantric image, the phenomenal world makes love to itself.

2. From the Creation of Padma Jong to the Large Installations in Los Angeles and San Francisco

Padma Jong: an artists' community

In 1973, members of a number of the California meditation centers decided to buy some land to set up a retreat center that would also be an artists' community, where craftspeople and artists could live and work in the spirit of the dharma. A large plot of land including several buildings was purchased in March 1974 in northern California. Chögyam Trungpa

---

4. Chögyam Trungpa, interview with Pat Patterson, San Francisco, September 20, 1980. Lightly edited for clarity by Shambhala Publications.

named it Padma Jong. A number of Chögyam Trungpa's students moved there, including Jerry Granelli and his family. It was used for intensive meditation programs, and for four years it served as a meeting place for the California sangha. Chögyam Trungpa gave several seminars there combining the arts with the practice of meditation, including "Art in Everyday Life" in the fall of 1974 and "The Dance of Enlightenment" the following year. The program in 1975 was videotaped, and although the black and white videos are not of good quality, they do provide an opportunity to see some very early presentations on the arts by Chögyam Trungpa. In one session, he created flower arrangements according to the five buddha families, and he also gave several demonstrations of calligraphy. Participants had an opportunity to work with some of the principles that he was presenting, through object arrangements and other exercises.

The programs at Padma Jong, which emphasized the visual arts, were the precursors of a deeper reflection that was soon to come.

During these seminars, he discussed the artist's state of mind and the natural structure of experience by presenting the example of the five buddha families. His explanations were accompanied by the ikebana demonstrations mentioned above.

At the Naropa Institute

Although the teachings at Padma Jong were some of the first examples of Chögyam Trungpa working with the visual arts in America, the programs at Naropa Institute were bigger and more influential. As early as its first summer session in 1974, many courses were devoted to the various arts, in an atmosphere somewhat inspired by Black Mountain College, which had been a vibrant center of experimentation during the 1940s and 1950s.

In a letter written for the first summer program of Naropa Institute, in 1974, Chögyam Trungpa used the expression *dharma art* for the first time, and defined the general idea: "The term *dharma art* does not mean art depicting Buddhist symbols or ideas, such as the Wheel of Life or the story of Gautama Buddha. Rather, dharma art refers to art that springs from a certain state of mind on the part of the artist that could be called a meditative state."[5]

Earlier he had used the expression *visual dharma*. He now opted for the term *dharma art*. "*Dharma* is a Sanskrit word that means 'basic norm.' It's not a particularly religious term. *Dharma* is said to mean 'that which creates harmony,' 'that which makes things workable,' in other words what favors harmony and dignity."[6] The change in name implied a new approach. Chögyam Trungpa shifted the emphasis from the freshness of the perception to the concrete artistic experience.

The study of dharma art

But the real turning point came in 1978, when Chögyam Trungpa decided to give the first dharma art seminar at Naropa Institute. He then proclaimed: "The artist has the huge power to change the world."

While his previous seminars had presented a way of connecting with the world through artistic experience, for the next four years he directly addressed artists. Because of his respect for the power that resides in works of art, Chögyam Trungpa insisted on the responsibility of those who produce them.

The first seminar lasted from July 9 to 14. Chögyam Trungpa gave four evening talks, which were the cornerstone of the event. During the day, participants practiced meditation, took workshops that presented practical exercises in the study of dharma art, and attended a film festival and exhibition.

Chögyam Trungpa had begun to present his Shambhala teachings the year before. Here, in the presentation of dharma art, he used a similar vocabulary to explain a genuine artistic spirit. He taught that art should be the natural expression of our authentic relationship with the world: "Art involves relating with oneself and one's phenomenal world gracefully. In

---

5. *Dharma Art*, p. 1.

6. Chögyam Trungpa, "Dharma Art Stresses Harmony and Elegance," extract from a press conference given on September 9, 1980, in Los Angeles, in *Nalanda News*, August/September 1981, p. 7. Reprinted in *The Collected Works of Chögyam Trungpa*, vol. 7.

this case, the word *gracefully* has the sense of nonaggression, gentleness, and upliftedness; that is a basic attitude of cheerfulness. It is important in becoming artists to make sure that we do not pollute the world."[7]

In developing this approach, artists try to connect with a certain state of wakefulness. This experience, which he called "first thought, best thought," is a state of mind without beginning or end. It is not a case of taking the first thought that comes into your mind, which may be just a reflex, but rather the first authentic thought. It appears suddenly, unexpectedly, in a moment of relaxation. Chögyam Trungpa encouraged this approach. That blank moment, which is sometimes tinged with panic, should not be avoided. On the contrary, it is by not being afraid, by not avoiding it, that the "first thought" may occur. Chögyam Trungpa sometimes asked someone to improvise a poem, even in front of four hundred people. At such times one needs to return to that profound moment of intelligent openness. This is the dharma, "the state before you lay your hand on your brush, your clay, your canvas—very basic, peaceful, cool, free from neurosis."[8] Being an artist means projecting your state of mind and basic openness into your work.

First Thought Best Thought is the title of one of his collections of poems. The term derives from a discussion with Allen Ginsberg, who provided a clear explanation of its meaning: "I was writing a spontaneous chain poem with Chögyam and he said, and we finally agreed, 'First thought is best thought.' That was sort of the formula: first thought, best thought. That is to say, the first thought you had on your mind, the first thought you thought before you thought, yes, you'd have a better thought, before you thought you should have a more formal thought— first thought, best thought. If you stick with first flashes, then you're all right. But the problem is, how do you get to that first thought—that's always the problem. The first thought is always the great elevated, cosmic, noncosmic, shunyata thought. And then, at least according to the Buddhist formulation, after that you begin imposing names and forms

---

7. *Dharma Art*, p. 104.

8. Ibid., p. viii.

and all that. So it's a question of catching yourself at your first open thought."[9]

Using this principle, Chögyam Trungpa presented a piece of threefold logic in order to perceive the world: "the background of the manifestation, the potential of the manifestation, and finally manifesting altogether."[10]

These three principles correspond to "heaven, earth, and man," as part of the Chinese and Japanese traditions, which can be seen, for example, in ikebana, but which can also be applied to any action, even pouring a glass of water.

Heaven, as he explained, is not an empty space but a primordial dimension free of conditions. Heaven has the possibility of descending to earth, thus manifesting itself as a feeling of goodness, gentleness, and balance. An incredible freedom exists within this basic space.

Earth offers a grounding through its ability to accommodate everything.

The principle of "man"—that is, of human beings and human life—joins heaven and earth together.

Chögyam Trungpa did not provide a detailed analysis of these principles in the first talk of the dharma art seminar; instead, as with everything he did, he manifested them. During the initial talk, he did some calligraphy on transparent paper, which the audience could see on an overhead projector. In this way, they could witness the process by which he made heaven, earth, and man visible.

On the second evening, he gave a slide show presenting a selection of Western and Eastern artworks, on which he commented. Where his students generally saw depictions of various subjects, he pointed to another dimension: the sacredness that emerged from each of these works of art.

The next day, he asked his students to look at some films from the point of view of manifesting authentic sanity. The point of the exercise was not to judge whether a movie was interesting or not, but to evaluate

---

9. Allen Ginsberg, teaching given at the Naropa Institute, July 29, 1974, in Carole Tonkinon, *Big Sky Mind: Buddhism and the Beat Generation* (New York: Thorsons, 1995), p. 106.

10. *Dharma Art*, p. 109.

whether it demonstrated basic goodness and authentic openness, or whether it was just entertainment.

In this exercise, Chögyam Trungpa tried to cultivate a critical sensitivity in the participants while making them appreciate the principles of the Great Eastern Sun and the setting sun. The Great Eastern Sun is a vision that tries "to bring us out and to uncover the cosmic elegance that exists in our lives and in our art."[11] It pushes us forward and upward. The setting sun corresponds to an attitude of fear and cowardice. It is based on a set of artificial strategies designed to manipulate an audience.

In this way, Chögyam Trungpa brought out the immense responsibility of each artist.

The following year, he gave another seminar in Boulder, from July 13 to 19, which was specifically devoted to the principles of heaven, earth, and man.[12] It concluded with an exhibition in Denver where he presented some flower arrangements depicting the Shambhala warrior's four dignities. In addition to his own arrangements, some students who had been working with ikebana for several years were also invited to make arrangements that were displayed, and a group of students helped him prepare the exhibit. The joy he showed at each step of the creation of these flower arrangements revealed just how deeply he appreciated the phenomenal world.

Chögyam Trungpa then began to include an exhibition as part of his dharma art seminars. While at first the exhibition focused on the flower arrangements, he began to include the surrounding space and to organize and design the space to hold the arrangements and heighten their power.

A group of assistants helped him prepare for the exhibit. They included artists who had been involved with dharma art for years, as well as students who had recently developed an interest in Chögyam Trungpa's approach to art. This group came to be known as the Explorers of the Phenomenal World, and over time they even developed a uniform. Everyone dressed in khaki clothes, as if going on safari. They often went on field

---

11. Ibid., p. 9.

12. Published in *The Art of Calligraphy: Joining Heaven and Earth.*

trips to gather branches and brush for various arrangements. Chögyam Trungpa himself would always go out with a group of Explorers to find the main branches for the arrangements. He particularly loved to make an arrangement with a pine branch and large white chrysanthemums, and the search for the main pine branch was always a focus of his preparations for the exhibits. These exhibits took place in a number of American cities. Chögyam Trungpa even designed a pin depicting a trident, the symbol of heaven, earth, and man joined together, for the members of this new group. As time went on, the exhibits became installations, which were more complex and involved with the whole space.

From September 19 to 27, 1980, he organized a seminar in Los Angeles entitled "Discovering Elegance," which was followed by an exhibition that combined flower arrangements and an environmental installation at the Institute of Contemporary Art: "The exhibit will comprise a series of about six rooms, each furnished in a combination of Oriental and modern decor and each featuring a flower arrangement appropriate to the activity of the particular room. The first room will be a kitchen, followed by living and dining rooms, a bedroom, a study, a meditation room, a warrior's shrine room, and a chamber in which a large drum will be installed. The rooms will embody art both as everyday life and as one's journey. Beginning with the proverbial knowing how to pour a cup of tea, the point of climax is the beating of the drum, which signifies the proclamation of sanity and dignity to the world."[13]

Each room had its own style. Instead of presenting objects and flower arrangements behind glass, he created an environment that people could walk through and experience directly. Many members of the California sangha contributed to the organization of this event. More than twenty-five thousand dollars was raised to put on the exhibit. However, no entrance fee was charged. Chögyam Trungpa and the Explorers viewed it as a gift to the city of Los Angeles and its residents. About four thousand people visited it during the three days it was open.

---

13. *Nalanda News*, October/November 1980, p. 16. Chögyam Trungpa liked the example of "knowing how to pour a cup of tea" because it displayed the meaning of the most ordinary discipline, which allows us to see our state of mind at once.

The following year, Chögyam Trungpa went to San Francisco to organize another seminar and exhibition. This time, he and his students arranged to borrow some Oriental antiquities of the finest quality. In the center of the exhibit stood a huge sculpture of the third emperor of the Ming dynasty, Yung Lo, whom Chögyam Trungpa greatly respected because of his conversion to Buddhism, which led him to become a valiant and visionary monarch.

A few months after the San Francisco show, Chögyam Trungpa organized an exhibition entitled "Winter Beauty: An Environmental Installation" at the Visual Arts Center, Boulder, from December 26 to 31, 1981, which coincided with a new program presenting dharma art. The exhibition included seven different rooms, each containing different ritual objects and flower arrangements.

Chögyam Trungpa wanted such events to be organized in as many different locations as possible, as a gift from Shambhala to everyone. He felt that all who attended these exhibitions would experience the dignity and confidence of the Kingdom of Shambhala.

3. The Richness of Perception Transcends All Aggression

In dharma art, sensory perceptions are considered to be entranceways into the sacred world. Here, Chögyam Trungpa stands apart from religious traditions that mistrust the senses because they are thought to lead to worldly attachments. But for him, to condemn the senses meant running the risk of losing touch with ourselves. Furthermore, he thought they were a way of connecting with the infinite: "the point is to look properly. See the colors: white, black, blue, yellow, red, green, purple. Look. This is your world! You can't not look. There is no other world. This is your world; it is your feast. You inherited this; you inherited these eyeballs; you inherited this world of color. Look at the greatness of the whole thing. Look! Don't hesitate—look! Open your eyes. Don't blink, and look, look—look further."[14] He taught this both in the Shambhala teachings

---

14. *Shambhala: The Sacred Path of the Warrior* (Shambhala Library, 2003), p. 41.

and throughout his presentation of dharma art. Habitually, our perceptions are conditioned by our responses or reactions to them. Without even realizing it, we make a rapid judgment about what we are seeing. We thus miss the possibility offered by the senses of entering into a direct relationship with the immensity that each perception contains.

Meditation is a way of learning how to let ourselves be touched by the world. We can then learn to be "clairvoyant," in the root sense of clearly perceiving things, as they are, here and now, in truth. This only happens in the moment, on the spot. Language is different from this immediate perception, and it is vital to return to this first contact.

Chögyam Trungpa emphasized the fact that in a nontheistic tradition such as Buddhism, the act of seeing must precede the act of looking. The initial opening of seeing is the dimension through which we can then look at something: "Once I watched a television program on Italian classical art. . . . A point [the presenter] made was that in order to understand art in the Western world, you have to look in order to see. That is the approach of a theistic mystical experience: look in order to see. Seeing is regarded as a discovery; looking is the primary method. It seems obvious: if you want to see, you have to look first. Very sensible, very scientific. Before you draw conclusions, you gather information with the computer. When the computer says thus-and-such and so-and-so is the case, then you begin to see. You look in order to see. But in the nontheistic traditions, such as Buddhism (and at this point, the only nontheistic traditional religion we have in this universe is Buddhism), the idea is to see in order to look."[15]

Thus, perceiving means first seeing the whole as one, before looking at the details.

Perception is only truly sacred if we can make the constant echo of the accompanying commentary disappear—in other words, if we look without needing any mediation. As Herbert Guenther explained, "Every artist knows that he can see in two different ways. The ordinary way is characterized by the fact that perception is always related to accomplishing some

---

15. *The Lion's Roar*, p. 34.

end other than the perception itself. It is treated as a means rather than something in itself. But we can also look at things and enjoy their presence aesthetically."[16]

Going from one type of perception to another requires a profound training that challenges the ego and its desire to centralize.

This approach was shared by many modern artists. For example, Henri Matisse wrote: "Creation begins with a vision. Seeing is already a creative operation that *requires an effort*. All that we see, in our daily lives, is more or less deformed by our acquired habits.... The artist must see everything as if for the first time: he must look at all of life like a child."[17] For Matisse, seeing requires real work, not to structure the way of looking, but to rediscover the authentic, initial brilliance. We need to make a certain effort to remain in the primary openness required for any perception.

From ikebana to arranging objects

One of the practices used by Chögyam Trungpa to convey the ideas of dharma art was ikebana: "It's not just purely a work of art. It is a manifestation of reality which can be presented in a simple but very spacious fashion. Ikebana practice teaches how to go about your life. It requires a great deal of paying attention, nonaggression, and not being speedy."[18] Such a discipline allows us to understand and express the fact that everything is complete in itself, reflecting the order of the universe. Ikebana mirrors this natural hierarchy of the sacred world. Through the choices made, the positions given to the branches and flowers harmonize with heaven, earth, and man. Such a hierarchy has not been fixed once and for all; it has to be reinvented each time one makes an arrangement.

When the arrangement is right, everyone knows it. The relationship

---

16. Herbert V. Guenther, in Herbert V. Guenther and Chögyam Trungpa, *The Dawn of Tantra*, p. 17.

17. Henri Matisse, *Écrits et propos sur art* (Paris: Hermann, 1972), p. 321 (italics added).

18. Chögyam Trungpa, quoted in Karen Hayward, "Grass and Moon: The Way of Flowers," *Vajradhatu Sun*, August/September 1984, p. 16.

between space and the form of the branches and flowers opens into a real presence, which transforms the surroundings.

Chögyam Trungpa often worked with large groups of participants. Quite early on he realized that it would not always be possible to provide everyone with the tools and the education to do ikebana in all of the dharma art seminars he presented. Moreover, he was trying to work with principles that could apply to many artistic enterprises, not just flower arrangement. So Chögyam Trungpa, together with Ludwig Turzanski, an art professor from the University of Colorado who was instrumental in the development of dharma art, came up with the idea of object arrangements: arranging various ordinary objects as an exercise for students attending his seminars on art and dharma. In this practice, someone chooses an object and places it on a tabletop or piece of paper. This is the heaven element, which represents the vastness of the primary manifestation and gives the arrangement its tone.

The person then places another object, which stands for the earth while also entering into relationship with heaven. Finally, the person joins the two by adding a third object. This third element must succeed in providing the arrangement with its own unity. This extremely simple exercise requires no intellectual thinking, but rather arises from a complete, lively presence. It shows how to make a moment of pure presence emerge and stop our minds. This principle "applies to anything you do: making a cup of tea, designing a building, whatever. You have to have the first thought, then the second thought, and the final conclusion and whatever paraphernalia goes with it cosmetically. That makes things complete."[19]

In these programs, Chögyam Trungpa also liked to introduce the practice of calligraphy. In addition to demonstrating calligraphy, he provided exercises for the students. The point was not to aim at excellence in the results—which is impossible to obtain in a few sessions—but to make contact with the principles of heaven, earth, and man by entering into the magic of this discipline.

---

19. Chögyam Trungpa, "Dharma Art Stresses Harmony and Elegance," p. 11. Reprinted in *The Collected Works of Chögyam Trungpa*, vol. 7.

He often started by asking the participants to produce calligraphy without ink, with just water on blank paper, so that nothing visible appeared. It was necessary to stabilize one's mind and connect with the space of the paper, to have the confidence to take up the brush, which is an extension of our being. Calligraphy exercises were also training in how to enter and leave space properly: the brush penetrates the space of the paper, then leaves it.

Polishing the mind

If we try to bring together some of the crucial points of the teachings given in these various programs, what at once springs to our attention is the great insistence with which Chögyam Trungpa asserted that the artwork is never the end of the artist's activity. For him, art was like the traditional practice of archery, or kyudo, in Japan. The aim is not to hit the target with the arrow. If all the gestures are correct, then the arrow will naturally go where it should. Cutting through our attachment to results allows the emphasis to be placed on the discipline, doing what we do as well as possible, at the instant of doing it. To borrow an image from Zen, this offers the possibility of polishing our minds.

Studying the dharma is not a matter of learning things, but of liberating ourselves in the living present. In this respect, it totally transforms our way of being. In the process of working with a specific form—music, dance, painting, video, the tea ceremony—we can work on who we are.

Chögyam Trungpa explained that the teachings of dharma art are connected with the ultimate perspective of the teachings of vajrayana and dzogchen. Dharma art helps to develop a deep appreciation of our environment so that we will not miss out on the present instant.

In this series of teachings, Chögyam Trungpa helped many artists to see the meaning of their work and encouraged them to look more deeply and discover its more basic meaning. In this way, being an artist becomes a spiritual path of infinite depth.

The dharma art path consists of working with our own aggression, which is a real obstacle to any sacred vision. One of the current problems in art is the loss of this sacred vision, which has always animated it. Artists may simply adopt a critical or even cynical attitude to society, which remains extremely limited. Through an involvement that is too strictly social, the artist loses contact with the true magic of art, which alone can transform society.

Chapter Nineteen

THE SOCIAL VISIONARY

*In the past, students have paid very little attention to en-
lightening the world. They have only been involved with
developing themselves. Even then, they have done that
with tremendous complaint and have requested all sorts
of medications. Now at this point we are about to grow
the crops of an enlightened society. It's our mutual effort.*[1]

—CHÖGYAM TRUNGPA

In THE FALL OF 1972, Chögyam Trungpa went on a three-month
retreat in an isolated house near Charlemont, Massachusetts. According
to students who accompanied him on this retreat, he made two important decisions there. First, he decided to place his complete trust in his
students and to transmit to them all the teachings he had received in
Tibet, especially the ultimate teachings of vajrayana. He would keep
nothing secret. Furthermore, he decided that all his teaching activities
should be brought together in one single organization and administration. Chögyam Trungpa had an extraordinary ability to sense the structures and rules that would be required in the future to manage a variety

---

1. Chögyam Trungpa, *1978 Kalapa Assembly Transcripts* (Boulder: Vajradhatu Publications),
pp. 181ff.

of different situations as his organizations expanded. He was especially conscious of the various structures needed to organize any community.[2]

On the one hand, this decision was purely a practical, administrative move: it would create a nonprofit organization that would conform to the various laws governing religious organizations in the United States, and that would unite all of his activities and centers into a single body. At the time, there were two parallel administrations, linked to his two main centers, Tail of the Tiger in Vermont and Karma Dzong in Boulder, which sometimes competed with each other. He put an end to these conflicts by setting up Vajradhatu as the international organization to oversee all of his activities.

The establishment of this legal structure not only led to harmonization in the administration of his organization, but also—somewhat coincidentally and auspiciously—was a link to the more visionary and much more ambitious aspects of his work. The establishment of Vajradhatu reflected his desire to expand his activities and gave him a framework within which this could happen. He wanted to have a real and lasting effect on society. A legal entity such as he helped create has an existence that can survive the death of its founder. By setting up Vajradhatu, Chögyam Trungpa was beginning to look for ways in which his teachings could continue to thrive without his physical presence. He chose an interesting name, for *vajradhatu* means "indestructible or diamondlike space."

The workings of Vajradhatu and its main actors, the members of the board of directors and the various department heads and others who

---

2. There were several possible ways of framing this chapter. A critical and historical approach would have meant comparing Chögyam Trungpa's social vision with the actual workings of his organization and community and then making an assessment. Instead, I have chosen to present Chögyam Trungpa's ideas while trying to get a sense of the range of their application. Obviously some of his ideas were not put into practice, and, while I do not deny this, I have chosen not to dwell on it here, because it seemed so important to understand the unity and coherence of such a vision. I should note that a part of Chögyam Trungpa's teaching consists in providing a pure vision of art, of living as a couple, of bringing up children, and of a human society. Such a pure vision is something that we find first within ourselves. In this sense, it already exists in our hearts, and is not simply an ideal that we must accomplish later. Connecting with this vision allows us to use truth as it exists here and now to guide our lives from that discovery.

played an important role in the organization, are dealt with in chapter 20; here the aim is to study the ideas that motivated Chögyam Trungpa when he founded Vajradhatu.

1. The Need to Unite Spirituality and Politics to Help Others

One might wonder how Chögyam Trungpa came to establish Vajradhatu as one of the largest Buddhist organizations in the West, and why it was that he didn't content himself with the presentation of the Buddhist teachings to a small group of disciples. Chögyam Trungpa was acutely conscious of the power of the teachings that he was bringing to America. Just as Padmasambhava had done in the eighth century in Tibet, he was introducing an important part of the Buddhist tradition into a new world. He did not want just to train a few students to practice during his lifetime, but he wanted the impact of the buddhadharma to be felt in the future. He was in that sense the main architect of a very large project whose time frame surpassed the limits of his own lifetime. To accomplish what he hoped was possible required the establishment of institutions that would survive him and, it was hoped, could transform many aspects of Western spirituality.

Chögyam Trungpa was also aware of the limitations of any teaching that does not penetrate the deepest structures of the mind. Particularly in relationship to his closest students, those he would trust to carry on the tradition he was imparting to them, it was not enough to practice a few minutes a day or follow a few teachings during vacations or weekends. It was not even enough to be driven by an altruistic spirit. He hoped that Buddhism and Shambhala would be incorporated into every aspect of life transforming not only our minds but also the details of how we live, such as the way we dress, how we organize our home life and our work, and most of all, how we relate to others. Ultimately, the kind of discipline he taught was not a matter of obeying rules of behavior; rather, through applying this living vision, we could discover in ourselves a way to exercise our own freedom. Such a far-reaching vision, such a prospect that shakes up our usual beliefs, is linked with the idea of founding a human society oriented toward establishing enlightenment.

Building a political and spiritual community

As early as 1976–78, Chögyam Trungpa started speaking about the vision he had for society. In 1978, during a seminar given to some of his close students, he explained: "The minute the Communist troops began to march through our property in the Surmang Monastery, I thought that a greater society of buddhadharma could be created, that a greater vision could be executed properly. Since then, and continuously, my Shambhala vision has never diminished."[3] Beyond presenting the basic teachings of Buddhism and creating the right conditions for the practice and study of Buddhism and Shambhala, Chögyam Trungpa also had the idea to create a genuine community.

In that sense, he revealed himself as a social visionary and, in the best sense of the term, a politician.

In this way, Vajradhatu was not just the name of an organization of Buddhist centers but the container for a much larger social project. After Chögyam Trungpa's death, his son Sakyong Mipham Rinpoche renamed the umbrella organization Shambhala, which was a logical evolution, since the name Shambhala is so intimately linked to the greater vision that Chögyam Trungpa had. The last great, and perhaps most visionary, project of Chögyam Trungpa's life was to foster the development of enlightened society, which he described in terms of the Kingdom of Shambhala. He wanted to see this not just realized in metaphorical terms but embodied in human society, on earth.

This indeed reveals the unique aspect of Chögyam Trungpa's work. So far as I know, no other Buddhist teacher in the West has attempted such a sweeping project, not even to a far lesser degree. Chögyam Trungpa did not just advise people about how to conduct their lives; he certainly did not want to play the sage; he did not invent a new political theory or dream of a new utopia. Instead he showed how to create a true

---

3. Ibid., p. 185.

society in concrete terms. This is reflected in the society and culture that exist in the communities he started. This project may still be in its infancy, but we can yet observe it "in the flesh." Chögyam Trungpa taught that a "universal" or grand project or vision remains a purely intellectual concept if it is not brought down to earth in a concrete and individual way: "Enlightened society comes from the kitchen sink level, from the bedroom level. Otherwise there's no enlightened society, and everything is purely a hoax."[4]

In other words, Chögyam Trungpa did not see himself as a political philosopher; he was above all a man of action who wanted to transform the world by transforming people's perception and how they lived. However articulate his critique might have been of our society, its main purpose was to change the way we live, in a way that was itself quite radical for the West.

To understand the foundation of Chögyam Trungpa's "political" goals and their intrinsic link with his view of spiritual development, we must return to what motivates the practitioner on the Shambhala path and the Buddhist path of mahayana. The mahayana model of a wise and realized practitioner is the bodhisattva, whose motivation is always to help all beings. From the mahayana perspective, the point of reducing our own confusion is to enable us to work more coherently and effectively for everyone's benefit. As Chögyam Trungpa explained: "The basic mahayana vision is to work for the benefit of others and create a situation that will benefit others. Therefore, you take the attitude that you are willing to dedicate yourself to others. When you take that attitude, you begin to realize that others are more important than yourself."[5] Thanks to this motivation, the practitioner's path becomes real and alive, and far from theoretical. Chögyam Trungpa's social commitment derived from this principle.

Yet we have an ingrained tendency to separate these two domains and consider spirituality as a situation in which, as the political philosopher Hannah Arendt observed, "man renounces action, retires into himself

---

4. *Great Eastern Sun*, p. 33.

5. *Training the Mind and Cultivating Loving-Kindness* (1993), pp. 1–2.

from the world, and flees politics."[6] It is very difficult for us to understand how politics and spirituality can be united. T. S. Eliot demonstrated this tension with great force in his play *Murder in the Cathedral*, in his portrayal of the tragic destiny of Thomas Becket, Archbishop of Canterbury, the archetype of this impossible reconciliation. He was killed because, as his murderer explains, "The moment that Becket, at the King's instance, had been made Archbishop, he resigned the office of Chancellor, he became more priestly than the priests, he ostentatiously and offensively adopted an ascetic manner of life, he affirmed immediately that there was a higher order than that which our King, and he as the King's servant, had for so many years striven to establish; and that—God knows why—the two orders were incompatible."[7]

This tragic dichotomy between spiritual and temporal power is an exclusively Western view, not found in the traditional societies of Asia or in the Islamic world. The separation of powers arose with Christianity and is one of its basic tenets. Ever since Saint Augustine distinguished between the Heavenly and the Earthly Jerusalems—the City of God and the City of Man—the distinction between these two orders underlies much of the political thought in the West.

For Chögyam Trungpa, there was a profound unity between the spiritual and political worlds, to such a degree that dividing them meant losing sight of their primary harmony.[8] His "mystical" project, to adopt the term used by the philosopher Charles Péguy, took this primary unity into

---

6. Hannah Arendt, "La politique a-t-elle finalement encore un sens?" in *Ontologie et Politique: Actes du colloque Hannah Arendt* (Paris: Tierce, 1989), p. 167.

7. T. S. Eliot, *Murder in the Cathedral*, in *The Complete Poems and Plays, 1909–1950* (London: Faber & Faber, 1969), p. 278.

8. Following the French philosopher Charles Péguy, it would perhaps be better to adopt the term *mystical* rather than *political*, in allusion to this passage from the pamphlet *Notre jeunesse*: "Our first rule of conduct or, if you prefer, the first rule of conduct in our actions was thus never to fall into the political, that is to say, when following a line of action, very precisely to challenge ourselves, to distrust ourselves and our action, to be extremely attentive about distinguishing the point of discernment, and once this point has been identified, to retrace our steps to this point of reflection. To such a degree that politics replaces the mystical, devours the mystical, betrays the mystical, and that which releases, abandons, and betrays politics is the sole one that remains faithful to the mystical, what does not betray the

account. Its aim was to incorporate human dignity in one's life in a way that was not limited to spirituality: "People involved with a spiritual discipline have a tendency to want nothing to do with their ordinary life; they regard politics as something secular and undesirable, dirty."[9] But for Chögyam Trungpa, politics was of fundamental importance. He wanted to invent and create an arena in which spirituality and politics were no longer separate.

Founding an "enlightened society"

If the desire not to remain in an "ivory tower" is a key point found in many spiritual paths, how is it possible to unite the need for a genuine inner transformation, a discipline as rigorous as it is profound, with a desire to act in the world and devote our lives to others?

The Beat poet Allen Ginsberg took an active part in demonstrations against the Vietnam War and was involved other political movements that aimed at transforming the world. For example, as an active Buddhist, on June 11, 1978, at the Rocky Flats Nuclear Weapons Plant, he was one of the demonstrators who sat down to meditate on the rail track in order to block the delivery of nuclear materiel to the weapons factory.

Chögyam Trungpa thought there were problems with this sort of political action, which he regarded as often ineffective and limited. In a commentary on the mahayana slogan "When the world is filled with evil,

---

political is also the sole one not to betray the mystical." Charles Péguy, *Notre jeunesse* (1910), in *Oeuvres en prose completes* (Paris: Gallimard, 1992), vol. 3, p. 135.

Our hostility to this primary harmony of the mystic derives from the fact that we confuse it with the Church. As Péguy pointed out "the political forms of the Church have always been against the mystical."

In his desire never to let "politics" dominate, Chögyam Trungpa was always driven by his vision of founding an enlightened society. We can now understand his constant efforts to create forms for a community, while avoiding any solidification, so as to prevent any habits from forming. At all levels of his organization, he did everything he could to ensure that human relationships were simple and lively.

9. Chögyam Trungpa, "A Buddhist Approach to Politics," *Shambhala Review* 5 (Winter 1976), p. 20.

transform all mishaps into the path of bodhi," he remarked: "whatever occurs in your life—environmental problems, political problems, or psychological problems—should be transformed into a part of your wakefulness, or bodhi. . . . You do not blame the environment or the world political situation. Certain people are inspired to write poetry and act in such a way that they would sacrifice their lives for a social cause. We can quite safely say that the Vietnam War produced a lot of poets and philosophers, but their work is not in keeping with this mahayana principle. They were purely reacting against the world being filled with evil; they were not able to transform mishaps into the path of bodhi."[10] And elsewhere he said, "I don't want to play down the colorfulness of the early poems of my friend Allen Ginsberg, but when he made poetry out of his reaction to the Vietnam War and other problems that America faced, he could have been contributing to the problems."[11]

For Chögyam Trungpa, this sort of demonstration often contained an expression of aggression, which cannot lead to true social change. It seemed far more important to him to act on a truly political level.

2. An Enlightened Society

We now come to one of the most complex areas of Chögyam Trungpa's work. When understood with an erroneous or partial view, his vision often provokes resistance and criticism.

One of the main reasons for this is that Chögyam Trungpa touched a sore spot. Many of our beliefs are really just slogans that we repeat to ourselves, never thinking about them in any depth. At the same time, we identify with our preconceptions so completely that we feel very threatened when doubt is cast on our belief system

Shakyamuni Buddha taught the Prajnaparamita, the understanding of the emptiness of self and other, on Vulture Peak Mountain. In this

---

10. *Training the Mind and Cultivating Loving-Kindness* (1993), pp. 72–73.

11. *Great Eastern Sun*, pp. 121–122.

sutra, the noble bodhisattva Avalokiteshvara speaks on behalf of the Buddha, saying: "Form is emptiness; emptiness also is form. . . . There is no birth and no cessation. There is no impurity and no purity. There is no decrease and no increase . . . no suffering, no origin of suffering, no cessation of suffering, no path, no wisdom, no attainment, and no non-attainment."[12] It is said that a large number of the arhats, or disciples of the Buddha, who were present at the teaching had heart attacks and died on the spot when Buddha proclaimed the teaching of emptiness. The Buddha here not only proclaimed that the ego was a collection of false beliefs and tendencies and fundamentally empty but also that the doctrines of Buddhism were themselves empty of ultimate nature. This was radical, shocking news.

Today, we may find the *Prajnaparamita Sutra* much less shocking, largely because of our tendency to segregate spirituality in a separate sphere, far from our everyday lives. We thus can now read the Buddha's fearless proclamation of emptiness without blinking. Yet Chögyam Trungpa was able to shock us, threatening our belief system, when he said, for example, that democracy often does not create either a free or a just human society and that hierarchy may be an essential component of a decent society. Such a view may seem old-fashioned, indeed reactionary, or simply absurd; it certainly touches a nerve.

Facing the distress in our world

Chögyam Trungpa was not trying to shore up Western traditions that were waning or under fire. He was well aware of the crisis gripping the West, and he sought to understand how its social problems could be solved. His interest in politics was a response to the distress of our era. Things had reached such a point and the confusion of our world was so deeply entrenched, he felt, that it would be a mistake to work only on spiritual practice. Chögyam Trungpa discouraged his students from exiling themselves or withdrawing completely from the world, so he did not recommend going into retreat for too long a period of time, although

12. "The Heart Sutra," translated by the Nālandā Translation Committee.

he acknowledged the importance of retreat practice as a means of uncovering confusion and connecting with simplicity as the ground for action.[13]

He saw that contemporary Western culture was not dedicated to encouraging wakefulness or sanity in human beings, but instead that many aspects of Western culture tended to put people to sleep, especially because of the emphasis on more and more material, psychological, and even spiritual comfort. The pursuit of comfort makes human beings incapable of realizing themselves as true human beings, and it makes it impossible to develop genuine discipline, which is the source of true joy. People in our day are no longer exposed to greatness.

The world is dominated by what Chögyam Trungpa called "setting sun," a metaphor for our attempts to avoid reality and provide ourselves with constant pleasure. "The notion of setting sun is that of wanting to go to sleep. You want to go back to your mother's womb, to regress, appreciating that you can hide behind dark clouds. That is to say, there is no bravery; it is complete cowardice. At the same time, there is struggle: you do not want to step out of this world completely; you are still trying to survive, still trying to prevent death. So the setting-sun world is based on a psychological attitude of fear. There is constant fear, and at the same time it is deliberately suicidal."[14]

In the world of the setting sun, the objective is to avoid situations that might put us in contact with anything too brilliant or sharp. We stop cultivating our dignity, which requires too much effort. So we waste our efforts on living in a sort of cocoon in which everything is filtered and diluted.

---

13. During Chögyam Trungpa's stay in Scotland, when some of his students left on a long retreat, he considered that they were simply escaping from their problems. In the United States, he started by encouraging short retreats of a few weeks, then emphasized group discipline by encouraging his students to take a month of group meditation practice (*dathün*).

But it should not be thought that Chögyam Trungpa was against the idea of his students one day undertaking a long retreat, such as the traditional three-year retreat. On the contrary, he tried to open up this possibility, but he wanted to reserve it for students who were already very stable in their practice and not present it as an obligatory step on the path, as he thought was too often the case in Tibet.

14. *Dharma Art*, p. 9.

Beyond individualism and subjectivity: what is a society?

One of the characteristics of the modern world is that it reinforces individualism. In contemporary societies, we tend to think of ourselves as *independent*, which strengthens the boundaries between ourselves and others, whereas the spiritual approach aims at dissolving the barriers between people. Our attempts to become autonomous can make our egos even stronger. After a few years in the West, Chögyam Trungpa realized that this obsessive individualism, based on the cult of each person's subjectivity, was contributing to the creation of a climate of distress and alienation that made it much more difficult to establish a true society.

How can we really live together if we are constantly driven by competition as a way of affirming ourselves?

The basic relaxation that we can experience in meditation practice transforms this struggle for independence. We can stop struggling to affirm subjectivity and begin to trust in the basic nature of what is. This is not a matter of giving up our freedom, but rather of accepting it.

It is on this basis that a genuine society can be established. For Chögyam Trungpa, it would be an "enlightened society." One important aspect of enlightened society that makes it particularly "enlightened" is an ability to live together in a harmonious way. In this situation, the sum—everyone together—surpasses the parts. To describe this notion of a society, Buddhist texts use the analogy of a yak's tail: "There are lots of single hairs that make up the tail, but what you see is a big bundle of hair, which constitutes a yak's tail. You cannot separate each hair out of it."[15]

Building a genuine society is not possible if we start with aggressive individualism; on the contrary, we must start with some yearning toward egolessness. One of the aims of the Buddhist and Shambhala teachings is to make us more aware so that we can acknowledge that "our particular shells are obviously hard, stuffy and smelly, impure, full of shit."[16] Once we acknowledge the problem, there is hope for an end to polluting

---

15. *Orderly Chaos*, p. 125.

16. Chögyam Trungpa, *1978 Kalapa Assembly Transcripts* (Boulder: Vajradhatu Publications), p. 5.

the world. Chögyam Trungpa was no airy dreamer who thought that the doctrine of basic goodness would make everyone miraculously nice to each other. Enlightened society is not a society composed of individuals who have all reached enlightenment, but instead is made up of those who have the courage to work at developing a society in which everyone works on their own sanity and cares for one another. Even then, it is not a simple matter of devoting oneself to other people; one has to be willing to share one's life with other people, which means giving up a great deal of privacy and self-centered views. One has to actually, personally, make a commitment to do this. By setting aside this commitment and dealing with human, social, economic or natural resources only on a conceptual level, as tends to be the case today, we give up the possibility of a real society.

The notion of mandala, discussed in chapter 17, is vital to Chögyam Trungpa's political thought. This term, which means, among other definitions, a "circle" in Sanskrit, symbolizes the integration of all the aspects of life into a single whole. The Tibetan term for mandala is *kyilkhor*. *Kyil* means "center" or "middle," while *khor* means "fringe," "edge", "rim," or "continuation": "It is a way of looking at situations in terms of relativity: if that exists, this exists; if this exists, that exists. Things exist interdependently."[17]

It is quite easy to understand such an image intellectually, and we can even look at and appreciate the wonderful depictions of mandalas done with great refinement and precision in colored sand; but it is far harder to experience the mandala principle personally.

In the social field, such an approach emphasizes the basic unity of society, such that it is impossible to remove the slightest part without affecting the whole. Everyone's place in this world is vital because each person's well-being is connected with society as a whole. As Chögyam Trungpa explained to the leaders of his centers: "The hard workers, the janitors, dishwashers or vacuum cleaners—those people who get their hands dirty have more observations about how things are going on. And that's very impor-

---

17. *Orderly Chaos,* p. 15. This is, as we have seen, a way of conceiving emptiness, the heart of the mahayana teachings, after which tantra can be developed.

tant for us to work with for future reference and for the long term—a long time ago, or to come. In that way we are in contact with the people thoroughly and fully, so that from top to bottom everything is recycled properly. We don't have to pass the buck and say that was the fault of the workers, and that is the fault of the administrators and that is the fault of the teachers. We have the whole thing working together properly and fully. We have meshed ourselves thoroughly in the society."[18]

Everything is our business, and everyone is important and worthy: this is what Chögyam Trungpa taught, which is miles away from our usual situation, in which we are concerned *above all* with our own existence. This is one of the fundamental aspects of his work that attracted many students. Wendy Karr, for example, remembers having looked all her life for a true community in which deep human relationships could take root. As a young woman she had lived for a while on a kibbutz in Israel and later tried living in some hippie communes, but only the fullness of Chögyam Trungpa's vision satisfied her expectations.

3. The Political Project: Propagating Human Dignity

The project of founding a true enlightened society, which would include our family life, our work, and our spiritual aspirations, had to be based on a specific political project. Politics is generally looked down on. Calling someone a politician is hardly flattering and generally implies that he or she is an opportunist, rather than dedicated to the public good. But serving others—that is the true meaning of politics.

As Chögyam Trungpa wrote: "In this world there is politics and there are many political viewpoints. These political viewpoints, however, are concerned with the pragmatics of survival.... Their methods are the only way to organize and maintain the happiness that propagates human dignity to the greatest extent."[19]

---

18. Chögyam Trungpa, "Meeting with Vajradhatu Ambassadors and Emissaries," August 17, 1979, unpublished.

19. Chögyam Trungpa, "Political Treatise," 1972, unpublished.

By failing to realize this, we reduce politics to a struggle for *power*—a notion all the more frightening in that it seems to be a way of affirming our own ego.

For, after the Renaissance, spiritual power dissipated in the West, which in turn profoundly altered the nature of temporal power, and spirituality was no longer seen as a political force. To understand the importance of this, it is enough to remember the anecdote about the meeting between Stalin and Churchill with a view to redrawing the borders of Europe after World War II. Churchill asked if they shouldn't consult the pope. Since he was an Anglican, this was not because of his religious convictions, but was based on the old European idea of the "concert of nations." Stalin's reaction was a modern one: "How many armored divisions does he have?" If the pope had no army, or quantifiable force, then he was considered to be without power.

Furthermore, when power is based on force, it always threatens to turn itself into absolute power.[20] It is just in such a modern perspective that philosophers like Montesquieu conceived the separation of powers, with the results we have now seen.[21] In his own words, power had to be limited by another power.[22]

Such a conception of power is based on the idea that it is a dangerous force.

In Chögyam Trungpa's view, power is different from force. More deeply, it is a natural expression of basic goodness. This allowed Chögyam Trungpa to claim: "The highest in rank do not exert their power from arrogance but from a sense of humbleness, genuineness, and sym-

---

20. As Lord Acton famously said, "Power tends to corrupt, and absolute power corrupts absolutely."

21. Here the reader should consider the basic distinction between power and authority (or "obligation" in Kant). To be legitimate, power must be *authorized* by authority. This distinction was vital in the Roman Empire, as the work of Hannah Arendt has shown. She stressed the fact that "a constant, growingly deep crisis of authority has accompanied the development of the modern world in this century" (*Between Past and Future*, 1954). It is the disappearance of this balance that altered the notion of power.

22. This led to the well-known distinction between the three powers: executive, judicial, and legislative.

pathy."[23] Such power when compared to "armored divisions" can seem laughably insignificant. But this is not necessarily the case.

We generally see gentleness as weakness—what the powerless fall back on. However, in a Buddhist context, gentleness is the antidote to aggression and has real strength. It possesses its own *authority* even if it is far from *authoritarian*. Chögyam Trungpa was a clear incarnation of this.

David Rome remembers once when he was ill and depressed in bed, Chögyam Trungpa came to see him and spoke to him very gently. He told him he was sorry to see him like this, because he had wanted to suggest they go for a walk. The way Chögyam Trungpa spoke to him, accepting the fact that David Rome could not come, aroused his curiosity, and he decided to be courageous and get up.

Such gentleness is never weak or feeble; instead it is precise and so uncompromising that it terrifies some people. Gentleness can cut through the ego—the source of all violence. Contrary to received opinion, which believes that we must be aggressive to win, there is true strength in gentleness: "People feel that they win a victory by being harsh, and they feel overpowered by strong military force or great economic pressure. Nobody thinks gentleness can actually provide *victory*. Nobody actually believes that."[24]

Chögyam Trungpa developed a true friendship with each of his students, or all of the members of his kingdom, which short-circuited or at least mitigated many of the power struggles that generally interfere with human relationships.[25] Friendship in this sense is the recognition of

---

23. *Great Eastern Sun*, p. 103.

24. Chögyam Trungpa, "Lids and Flowers," February 28, 1978, in *Selected Community Talks* (Boulder: Vajradhatu Publications, 1978), p. 132.

25. In his *Nicomachean Ethics*, a work considered to be a moral treatise, Aristotle devoted one and a half chapters to friendship (*philia*). Concern with friendship has lost its meaning in the modern world, where friendship is limited to our private lives; no philosopher would now give it the central place it had for the Greeks. For Aristotle, as for Chögyam Trungpa (although in quite a different way), the borderline between political and personal life is not so clear as it is for us today. This can only be explained by our understanding of the human being as an individual locked in a subjective consciousness.

the dignity and basic goodness that exist in all of us. It is at the heart of politics.

In this respect, Chögyam Trungpa was a great democrat,[26] in the sense that he didn't put up any barriers between himself and others. Absolutely anybody could come to see him and establish direct contact with him. There was nobody who was so "low" or undignified that Chögyam Trungpa would not listen to them attentively. He was a living example of the absolute humility that true power imposes. And such humility, far from being timid or resigned, has a masterful authority.

Enlightened society in the perspective of the Great Eastern Sun

This political vision is related to what Chögyam Trungpa called the perspective of the Great Eastern Sun, one of the central notions of the Shambhala teachings.

The *Sun* shines for all of us, without deciding what it will or will not enlighten. It is all-pervasive vision that illuminates the goodness that exists in all situations. *East* is always the direction that we face and the direction in which we are moving forward. But this is not a geographic orientation. It is constantly in front of us. It is an unconditional East of basic enlightenment, which is present everywhere and with which we can always connect.

Finally, this vision is *Great* because it has power and strength that can rule the world of heaven, earth, and human beings.

As Chögyam Trungpa wrote: "When there is no vision to look forward with, people are confounded by stupidity. When there is no Great Sun shining from the East, human dignity does not exist."[27]

Such an idea broadens the very notion of existence: "Some sense of greater accomplishment can be achieved. We are on our way to establishing a vajra world, the Great Eastern Sun world. People don't just have to

---

26. Chögyam Trungpa defined the vision that drove him as "ultimate democracy." "Lids and Flowers," p. 128.

27. Chögyam Trungpa, *The Tiger Lion Garuda Dragon Glory: The Auto-Commentary on the Text of the Golden Sun of the Great East* (Halifax: Vajradhatu Publications, 2000), p. 15.

think in terms of this little church in Vermont run by the Buddhists. This is much bigger. It goes beyond that. 'Big' is not a good word for this. Probably 'beyond' is a better word. This goes beyond, and it goes very extraordinarily beyond."[28]

The vision of the Great Eastern Sun invites us to extend the habitual limits of our minds. Great Eastern Sun vision is also associated with the capacity constantly to recharge and enliven our inspiration and sense of freedom. In other words, such a vision is "able to inspire people to have the guts to achieve what they set out to achieve, and to have the discipline to regenerate those guts when they feel tired."[29]

This path does not consist purely of overcoming our own confusion in order to reach a state of happiness, joy, or wisdom. In contrast to the pitch of many self-help books and seminars that proliferate today, Chögyam Trungpa never tried to make people's lives easier. His purpose was nothing like the goals promised by various personal development programs. Chögyam Trungpa always returned to this basic point: the way to change the world is not to get people to focus on changing external circumstances or even to modify their own behavior. Rather, they first need to examine how they experience the world.

Chögyam Trungpa's conception of power is not based on setting up political projects or plans. On the contrary. This surprises us because "usually somebody has an idea of ruling the world or of organizing some extraordinary business, and he goes out and collects people."[30] For Chögyam Trungpa, politics was not a matter of defining a plan that should be carried out in the future and be used to convince others to join in. Rather than struggle to establish our dignity later, we have to learn to find it here and now. Chögyam Trungpa constantly stressed the importance of basing any political vision on ourselves, on our experience and

---

28. Chögyam Trungpa, "Community Talk," Karmê Chöling, February 28, 1977, unpublished.

29. "The Great Eastern Sun creates an atmosphere in which you can constantly move forward, recharging energy all the time." *Shambhala: The Sacred Path of the Warrior* (Shambhala Library, 2003), p. 57.

30. Chögyam Trungpa, *1979 Kalapa Assembly Transcripts* (Boulder: Vajradhatu Publications), p. 2.

on the present moment: "There are some problems connected with realizing this vision, of course. Basically, the problems are connected with
our state of mind."[31] We have to work on ourselves. This is one of the
hardest aspects to understand in Chögyam Trungpa's vision, since it is
not based on any theory; for great politicians are those who live out what
they say and embody their vision, rather than those who conceive projects to be carried out later.

Many of the elements we have mentioned in this chapter are surprising, or even shocking, because they do not correspond to our usual ways
of thinking about the politics of change. But they in fact coincide with the
analyses of many of the important thinkers who have tried to define a political destiny for the West and stop the violence amid which we live. However, what Chögyam Trungpa meant by governing cannot be thoroughly
or completely understood from a Western viewpoint. I realized this
when reading his "Political Treatise," a short fragment of what Chögyam
Trungpa intended to be a larger work. He wrote this introductory piece on
politics in Tibetan in England in the 1960s. It made me feel extremely un-
easy. In this case, Chögyam Trungpa's vision has no equivalent in Western
thought. It contains none of the conceptions we find familiar. He speaks of
political action as "the ability to look joyfully into the mirror of mind with
a relaxed mind free from fearful projections and doubt. Therefore, political consciousness is the great confidence that is not afraid to be inspired by
unprejudiced views, and it is the ability not to be swayed by bodily illness
or the mind's sorrows and joys."[32] Here Chögyam Trungpa is talking
about a primordial or absolute level of experience and perception. It is
vital to note that he is talking here about political *consciousness*, not political action per se. From this excerpt we can see that the heart of Chögyam
Trungpa's social vision arises from contact with a primordial purity that is
always available and exists in itself. (This approach exists in other places in
his presentation of the Shambhala teachings, most notably the description
of how drala arises from the cosmic mirror. See the chapter "Discovering

---

31. Ibid., p. 3.

32. Chögyam Trungpa, "Political Treatise," 1972, unpublished.

Magic" in *Shambhala: The Sacred Path of the Warrior*.) Then, in other places in his work, he talks more pragmatically about how to "bring down a whole society into one household."[33] Not that a household is the political model, but we need to translate primordial view into a basic pragmatic level. Everything we do can express the richness of the teachings and the clarity of the mind's mirror. "You can't organize the vision of society purely on the basis of the nation or the world, but you have to study little things, such as how one family works on their situation."[34]

For him, as we see in the quotation above, there is continuity between the levels of nation and family. One has to start on the personal level, having faith in the power of individual sanity as the basis for greater change: "If each person, in his own capacity, contributes a little bit by having a very sane approach, first of all, to his own personal life, which should be straightened out, then his sense of sanity could be developed. It might be just a drop in the ocean, but it would be very valuable."[35]

4. Sacred Order

In addition to addressing the need for sane individual action as the basis for sanity in society, Chögyam Trungpa developed a view of other aspects of how to organize an enlightened society where human beings could live together.

A hierarchical society: a way of taking care of each other and allowing for true transmission

On many occasions, Chögyam Trungpa stressed the importance of hierarchy, by which he meant not just political hierarchy but hierarchy in our

---

33. Chögyam Trungpa, *1979 Kalapa Assembly Transcripts* (Boulder: Vajradhatu Publications), p.9.

34. Ibid.

35. Chögyam Trungpa, "A Buddhist Approach to Politics," *Shambhala Review* 5 (Winter 1976), p. 21.

relationship with the world altogether and with others. In this sense, hierarchy is based on the fact that there is order in reality.

Hierarchy is a word that can provoke instant hostility. Chögyam Trungpa explained that this reaction is based on a narrow view of hierarchy as a vertical power structure, a ladder to be climbed as quickly as possible to reach the top. In this view of hierarchy, there are those above me to whom I must defer and those below me whom I can look down on. Such a conception of hierarchy is extremely limited, even if that is the way it is often experienced because of the corruption that exists in our society. On the one hand, hierarchy is accepted in contemporary society as a necessary component of ego-based competition. The popularity of books on management and being successful in the business world are proof enough of this. To get to the top, according to this view, we must be quite aggressive. On the other hand, we often see this approach to hierarchy denounced as the unenlightened action of authority figures. In other words, if we feel that we are rising on the ladder of power and fame, we embrace it, but when we feel that we are being pushed down by the lid of hierarchy, we criticize and reject it.

As Chögyam Trungpa wrote, the samsaric or degraded experience of hierarchy is "clamping down on the lobsters boiling in the pot. People do feel that way. . . . You are put into the big dungeon and boiled like lobsters, and you work until you die. Isn't that a terrible thing? This is everybody's idea—at least in the world of setting-sun vision or samsaric vision."[36]

The difficulty in conceiving of hierarchy as a positive force is part of the relativism, or even the general derisive attitude that marks our time. Take, for example, a museum in which the intention is to make no distinction between a masterpiece and a nonmasterpiece, because in this way of thinking they are all the same. There are no masterpieces, only different people's criteria for evaluating. Philosophically, this attitude of derision depends on the notion of value. When confronted by an art object,

---

36. Chögyam Trungpa, "Lids and Flowers," p. 128. See also *Shambhala: The Sacred Path of the Warrior* (Shambhala Library, 2003), p. 49: "The analogy for hierarchy in the Great Eastern Sun world is a flowering plant that grows upwards towards the sun. The analogy for setting-sun hierarchy is a lid that flattens you and keeps you in your place."

if we always ask, "What value does it have for me?" we end up doubting any claim of authentic greatness. It is in this sense that the "relative" view is problematic. For instance, what value can an experience have that seems to awaken us from a long numbness when we open ourselves to it? None at all.

Buddhism constantly affirms the possibility of seeing the world as it really is, beyond the distortions of ego. Chögyam Trungpa stated that there is a natural order. Nature operates according to this order, the world is revealed through it, and reality is structured in accord with it. "So the sense of hierarchy, or order, in the Great Eastern Sun world is not connected with imposing arbitrary boundaries or divisions. Great Eastern Sun hierarchy comes from seeing life as a natural process and tuning in to the uncontrived order that exists in the world."[37] Refusal to acknowledge the existence of just such an order opens the door to all forms of arbitrary domination, which are all the more violent because they hide behind deceptive slogans.

One of Chögyam Trungpa's favorite examples of hierarchy is the procession of the four seasons. The seasons exemplify an order that we cannot change. It is something we must learn to respect. The hierarchy of the seasons is not trying to keep us in our place; it is not vertical but horizontal. As Chögyam Trungpa explained: "Cold winter turns into inviting spring, which brings luscious summer, which gives us the productive autumn, which then goes back to winter. The discipline of winter gives way again to the beautiful unfolding process of spring. The spring melts the snow, bringing the exposed earth of summer. Then again, the possibilities of summer cannot last throughout the whole year. So the discipline of autumn occurs . . . that is natural hierarchy."[38]

Chögyam Trungpa did not see the political dimension as an area separate from our everyday lives or the natural order of the world—which makes his thought often difficult to grasp intellectually even if it does point to a set of phenomena all of us can recognize. For example, he

---

37. *Shambhala: The Sacred Path of the Warrior* (Shambhala Library, 2003), pp. 48–49.

38. *Great Eastern Sun*, p. 169.

specified that, in the case of the four seasons, it is basic goodness that governs each situation: "When we talk about a monarch here, we are talking about that which rules the world in the form of basic goodness. From this point of view, we regard basic goodness as the king or queen. It is almost an entity in itself, not just a metaphysical concept or an abstract theory of natural order. Another way of putting this is that what joins heaven and earth together is the king or queen, and therefore it is basic goodness. In other words, if there is natural law and order, the principle of royalty, or the principle of the monarch, already exists. Because the principle of the universal monarch joins heaven, earth, and human beings together, therefore, we can join our body and mind together as well. We can synchronize mind and body together in order to manifest as Shambhala warriors."[39]

Such a hierarchy is thus quite different from the one we generally experience. Its source derives from a different form of thought. Order in this case is not something that rigidly guarantees security; it is not opposed to the notion of chaos, but instead attempts to recognize the order that drives it. Such order does not free us from chaos but has us recognize its inevitable reality. In other words, "It is orderly, because it comes in a pattern; it is chaos, because it is confusing to work with that order."[40]

A hierarchy with neither superiors or inferiors

Another image Chögyam Trungpa often used to illustrate the real meaning of hierarchy is a garden in which a large number of flowers can be found, some taller than others, which does not mean they are superior to others. The point of hierarchy is to allow each flower to develop. There are no superiors or inferiors, because "the vision of the Great Eastern Sun is based on celebrating life."[41]

The idea of hierarchy, as understood by Chögyam Trungpa, is neither

---

39. Ibid., p. 97.

40. *Orderly Chaos*, p. 3.

41. *Shambhala: The Sacred Path of the Warrior* (Shambhala Library, 2003), p. 46.

intrinsic nor fixed; it is impermanent and shifting. One day you represent the teachings, the next you clean the meditation room. If we think that some positions are superior to others, we have failed to understand what Chögyam Trungpa wanted to convey. Each of us is important just as we are in whatever role or tasks we perform.

Recognizing hierarchy provides the chance to cultivate excellence and authentic presence

Recognizing the existence of natural hierarchy allows us to cultivate *excellence*. This word, which is essential to Greek thought, is defined as what makes human beings stand out from others in such a way that everyone admires them. It is a recognized perfection that creates enthusiasm.

In the language of Shambhala, there is a notion that is similar to Greek excellence (*aretē*): authentic presence (Tibetan *wangthang,* which literally means "field of power"). Authentic presence is the mark of all human beings who acknowledge their nature and therefore display their basic goodness. "When you meet a person who has inner authentic presence, you find he has an overwhelming genuineness, which might be somewhat frightening because it is so honest and real."[42] Authentic presence is the condition that allows excellence to manifest itself. Chögyam Trungpa talked about both outer and inner authentic presence. Outer authentic presence is the sense of charisma or genuineness that we can sometimes experience in great athletes, politicians, or actors. Inner authentic presence is based on egolessness and is a sign of great spiritual maturity: letting go and emptying oneself out.

While I was thinking about these questions, I met a young dancer at the Paris Opera. I mentioned Sylvie Guillem, a ballerina whom I find extraordinary. The young dancer said at once: "She's so far above all the others, in every respect. It doesn't seem human. She's so impressive!" With this reaction, which any of us can have when confronted with manifest excellence that truly affects us, we are saying something essential. Our recognition of a great dancer like Sylvie Guillem is, in a sense, our acknowledgment of

42. Ibid., p. 184.

natural hierarchy. The extraordinary talent and accomplishment of such a person can be recognized as beyond or above what others have accomplished. In terms of popular opinion, this might be scandalous if we hold the belief that everyone should be equal. What is interesting is that the recognition of this kind of excellence is not based particularly on a "value judgment," but it is *apparent* to us—we can see this demonstrated very simply and clearly by the person who has authentic presence of some kind. If we recognize such excellence where it manifests itself, we create an incentive or an aspiration to cultivate our own excellence, and we begin to recognize that everyone has the potential for such excellence in some aspect of their life.

Chögyam Trungpa was concerned with helping his students to develop fully. One of the aims of an enlightened society is to provide opportunities for people to find their place, their genuine spot, in the world, where they can develop fully and feel true to themselves in what they do and how they live. Chögyam Trungpa felt that each of his students had an important contribution to make in order for the vision of the Kingdom of Shambhala to survive.

5. Royalty, Democracy, and Socialism

Paradoxically enough for us twenty-first-century Westerners, Chögyam Trungpa was both a democrat in the finest sense of the term and inspired by the vision of monarchy, understood as the rule of goodness and excellence.

Criticism of democracy

On his arrival in the West, Chögyam Trungpa showed a great interest in democracies. This political approach was quite foreign to Tibet. Initially, he thought it could represent the expression of authentic freedom.

He personally had an extremely democratic way of working with people and considering all as having an innate dignity, to which he seemed to connect effortlessly. He held this view throughout his life. In one of his talks, given in 1980, he even proclaimed: "How many buddhas will there be? How many kings or queens will there be? It is saying the same thing."[43] Each person can become a monarch, someone capable of ruling his or her own world completely, just as each one can become a buddha. A monarch in this sense embodies basic goodness, which according to Chögyam Trungpa should be the basis for political and social order in the world. He connected order in the natural world with order or hierarchy within ourselves and then related that to how one actually rules in society as well. If we want to understand Chögyam Trungpa as a political philosopher, we need to understand that in his view these three aspects are indivisible.

Although Chögyam Trungpa was, as a human being, a democrat, he was nonetheless highly critical of most of the Western democracies he came into contact with. Seeing the extent of political bankruptcy in the West led him to analyze even more deeply the social situation there. His purpose was not to condemn the idea of democracy itself, which he appreciated, but its current appearance, marked by the frenetic rise of excessive individualism. Democracy has become just the sum of various interests and is based only on a crude form of rule by the majority.[44] Duty in public life has disappeared below the horizon, subservient to accomplishment in the private sphere. Chögyam Trungpa called this a loss of the democratic vision. He wrote: "Democracy is built on the attitude that I speak out for myself, the invincible me. I speak for democracy. I would like to get my own right, and I also speak for others' rights as well."[45] But how to live together without a common vision?

In our democracies, this triumph of individualism is linked to the preservation of the ego and adds to the negation of natural hierarchy. And yet, to take another example, an orchestra is not just a group of musicians who play at the same time. They need a conductor to lead them if the

---

43. *Great Eastern Sun*, p. 78.

44. On this subject, it is profitable to read the central part of Hegel's *Philosophy of Right* where he describes bourgeois society as a sort of mad competition, a struggle of each against all, in which people strive for their selfish ends, and which is a close match to our current situation. Is this the purpose of civilization and the meaning of life in society?

45. *Training the Mind and Cultivating Loving-Kindness* (1993), p. 87.

music is going to be played to good effect. The musicians place themselves in the hands of the conductor and so become even freer, since the direction provided by the conductor allows them to do what they really want—to play music. When politicians are constantly worried about getting reelected and thus are willing to seek the approval of the voters at any cost, this considerably weakens their integrity and can weaken the society as a whole. Similarly, if a conductor is powerless to conduct, the instruments cease to play as a unified orchestra. Instead of using a genuine ability to organize and orchestrate society—the ability to actually *govern,* which leads to a society that celebrates everyone's existence—modern democracies are often afraid to exercise any authority, thus denying the positive aspects of hierarchy. Instead, everything is completely flattened out in the praise of mediocrity.

Democracy then becomes a rule that is no longer political but technocratic. As explained by Georges Bernanos (the novelist known to English speakers for his book *The Diary of a Country Priest*) in *La France contre les robots* (1947)—a book as prophetic as it is profound—humanity today "is part of the cattle that plutocratic, Marxist, or racist democracies fatten up for the factory and charnel house."[46] By this he meant the triple expression of one fundamentally harmful form of government. For "Some deny freedom, some still pretend to believe in it or no longer do, but unfortunately all that does not matter much, because they no longer know how to use it."[47]

For Georges Bernanos, democracy is not an essentially just form of government, in which we all freely exercise our responsibilities; it is not even "the worst except for all the others"; it is "a regime . . . in which the multitude dominates the free individual."[48]

Whereas modern democratic leaders speak of equality in a way that is both abstract and unreal, we should instead look at the real democratic basis of society, which is to recognize each person's basic dignity and per-

---

46. Georges Bernanos, *La France contre les robots* (Paris: Robert Laffont, 1947), p. 70.

47. Ibid., p. 47.

48. François Fédier, "Reconstitution," in *Regarder Voir* (Paris: Les Belles Lettres, 1995), p. 316.

sonal gifts. A society that does not recognize its members' gifts, or the possibility of excellence, cannot allow us all truly to thrive. This in essence was Chögyam Trungpa's critique.

Monarchy, or the conception of a sacred power

For all of these reasons, Chögyam Trungpa stressed the possibility of looking to the example of monarchy as a model for leadership, in terms of both how to rule one's life and how to be a leader within society.

It is hard for us to think in such terms, because the kings and queens who exist today do not, in general, personify the ideal of monarchy that attracted Chögyam Trungpa. Many contemporary monarchs are purely figureheads and have no meaningful role to play in governing society. They generally have been reduced to having their love lives splashed across the front pages of tabloid magazines. As Chögyam Trungpa wrote in a poem in 1977:

> Britain experiences cosmic shock with the problem of
>   existence and nonexistence—
> The only saving grace is Her Majesty the Queen in mar-
>   keting her underpants,
> Which might work for a while, but still is questionable:
> Will Charles be referred to as Chuck?[49]

Chögyam Trungpa's idea of the rule of a king or queen was quite different. As he articulated the idea in the Shambhala teachings, the monarch is connected with the sacred character of power, as we have already stated. Chögyam Trungpa explained: "We're talking about monarchy, and monarchy usually is based on the notion of leadership of an individual in which—depending on whether it's in the West or in the East—there is a quality of connection to some higher force. In the East

---

49. "International Affairs," in *First Thought Best Thought*, by Chögyam Trungpa, p. 128. © 1989 by Diana J. Mukpo. Reprinted by arrangement with Shambhala Publications, Inc., Boston, www.shambhala.com. Reprinted with permission of Diana J. Mukpo.

they say heaven, in the West divine right, but altogether the notion of monarchy means that the power of rulership is invested in an individual who would see to the benefit of people."[50] The point here is that the king, or anyone who rules in a situation, does not decide what to do according to a personal whim. He or she is not free to wield power. Chögyam Trungpa always emphasized that the source of genuine power came from the Rigdens, who represent primordial vision and power that arises from the most nonconceptual level of our experience, which is called the cosmic mirror in the Shambhala teachings. In more down-to-earth terms, the ruler's power comes only from authenticity—so much so that this authentic presence can be experienced by everyone. From a spiritual point of view, one who rules on the highest level has to be the incarnation of the truth of the teachings. He or she must embody the teachings.

Following his long retreat in 1977, Chögyam Trungpa began to emphasize the Shambhala teachings and the Shambhala world as his most important focus and project. In many of the photographs of Chögyam Trungpa taken from 1977 on, he begins to look strikingly regal. He no longer resembles the pleasant, friendly young man he was when he arrived in the West. Nor does he look like the elegant man in a suit and tie that he then became. He now radiates an extraordinary kingly dignity. If in the Shambhala vision, everyone is called on to become a king or queen, Chögyam Trungpa became a striking example of this.

In 1982, Dilgo Khyentse of the Nyingma lineage, who had been one of Chögyam Trungpa's teachers in Tibet, conferred a Shambhala empowerment on Chögyam Trungpa and his wife, Diana Mukpo. This ceremony is usually reserved for secular rulers and was indeed also conferred by Khyentse Rinpoche on Jigme Singye Wangchuck when he became the king of Bhutan. It is unusual to perform this ceremony for a spiritual teacher. After the ceremony, Chögyam Trungpa made remarks in which he explained the meaning of the ceremony and how it connected with his desire to establish the Shambhala world. From this time on, he assumed an additional title. As a result of this empowerment, he was called

---

50. Chögyam Trungpa, "Dekyong Council Retreat," May 25, 1985, unpublished.

the Sakyong, literally "protector of the earth." This ceremony recognized the union between spiritual and temporal activity, in a profound and traditional manner. The Sakyong abhisheka allowed Chögyam Trungpa to make a further connection with his desire to manifest the principles of the Kingdom of Shambhala—not just as the embodiment of an ancient fantasy but as a practical way to live now, here on earth.

It was not personal pride that pushed Chögyam Trungpa into assuming this role. He recognized that remaining a simple spiritual teacher would have been far more comfortable: "Sometimes you might think I'm crazy: 'Why doesn't he just teach pure Buddhism and have a good time in America and not bother with all this further hoo-hah?' Maybe you're right. Maybe I should have done that. But it is against my principles. My principles throughout my whole life and my basic demeanor are not to take a rest but to keep working, keep on working continuously [for the good of others]."[51]

He also explained that the relationship that exists between the Sakyong and his subjects is more complete than the one between teacher and disciple. As the Sakyong, Chögyam Trungpa was saying that his entire life was devoted to realizing the teachings, with no private corners exempted. And therefore, he was also implicitly encouraging his students to bring their whole awareness and life to the teachings. All aspects of their lives concerned him, whether spiritual, psychological, economic, cultural, or social: "The whole kingdom is the domestic situation—and fear comes from that."[52] There is no private sphere where the Shambhala vision ceases to be applied.

The parliament and the role of the dekyongs

Although Chögyam Trungpa believed in having strong leaders within Vajradhatu, he wasn't trying to establish some sort of absolutist kingdom for himself. He felt that each member of the community should

---

51. Chögyam Trungpa, *1978 Kalapa Assembly Transcripts* (Boulder: Vajradhatu Publications), p. 185.

52. Ibid., p. 7.

play an important role in how the situation was ruled, and he developed and encouraged various approaches and institutions to accommodate that. In addition to having many departments and committees within Vajradhatu beginning in the early 1970s, and in addition to encouraging people to become professionals, start businesses, and raise families—all of which made people feel that they had important roles in society—he also tried to create a kind of parliamentary system that would provide feedback and input into how the Shambhala world was governed. Parliamentary democracies were not something he would have experienced in Tibet, but he had become quite familiar with them in the West, and they struck him as having a great potential to further communication and to bring decision making much more in touch with the needs of the individual in society.

Chögyam Trungpa wanted to create a political situation, essentially, within the community he founded in which each practitioner is involved in the entire community. For this reason, in the 1980s he set up the deleks. This Tibetan term means "place where peace and happiness can occur." A delek is a group of practitioners from the same neighborhood who get together each month in a friendly atmosphere. In this way, practitioners would have a real sense of sangha, or community.[53] Building commitment to and involvement in such communities can help build people's ability to concretely apply the mahayana vision of taking care of one another and thus avoid the individualism of practitioners concerned only with their personal development.

The delek system was first set up during the Kalapa Assembly of 1981. During this ten-day period, each person was assigned to a delek based on the physical area where they were staying in the hotel where the program was held. Deleks met several times during the program and worked on different problems. The work assignments at the Kalapa Assembly were divided among the deleks in a way that encouraged people to find the

---

53. Note that the existence of a sangha still means that each path is an individual one: "Sangha doesn't necessarily mean dependence. It means that each individual is practicing with the encouragement and involvement of the entire sangha." Vajra Regent, "The Delek System," March 1981, *Dekyong Manual* (Boulder: Vajradhatu Publications, 1982), p. 12.

means to work together. After this experiment, which people found invigorating and challenging, the delek system was initiated in Boulder and then spread to other communities established by Chögyam Trungpa. Members of the Boulder community were divided into thirty-seven deleks, based on where they lived. Each delek contained approximately twenty-five members. On June 9, all the deleks met, and each was asked to choose a dekyong by "spontaneous insight," or consensus. The dekyong was the representative of the delek, who attended the Dekyong Council, which was like the infant form of a parliament. The dekyong was also expected to take an interest in each person in the delek and to help them with any problems they might encounter. Dekyongs were asked to communicate information to the delek and to convey the ideas and concerns of the delek back to the Dekyong Council and from there to the higher levels of leadership within Vajradhatu. Chögyam Trungpa explained his project: "The delek system cuts down the extraordinary hypocrisy of dictatorship, as well as the idea of too much democracy. It brings us a middle path, which is somewhat democratic: your individual contributions could become very positive and excellent through the delek system, and the dictatorial aspect of society could be cut down. Our notion of hierarchy is more like a flower than a lid. It is more like a waterfall than a volcano. Hierarchy can help people organize their lives in such a way that they can contribute individually—every one of them. You as dekyongs have the possibility of uplifting people. You have the possibility of bringing people up and cheering people up genuinely."[54]

In a number of Shambhala communities where there are a sufficient number of practitioners, deleks still exist today. While some might argue that they have not realized their potential as a major political force within the community, they continue to provide a concrete and lively way for people to come together as members of the community.

Following his yearlong retreat in Nova Scotia (from mid-1984 to April 1985), Chögyam Trungpa began to suggest to the dekyongs that they play more of a political role within the mandala of the sangha. He wanted the Dekyong Council to become much more of a parliament, with a real role

---

54. Chögyam Trungpa, "Dekyong Oath Ceremony," June 15, 1982, unpublished.

in the leadership and governance of the community. During the last two years of his life, this political emphasis—how to create a society in which people could genuinely join together and dedicate themselves to encouraging bravery and confidence—became his main preoccupation. He devoted the greatest part of his time to it.

At a celebration of his birthday, after his return from this long retreat, on April 28, 1985, Chögyam Trungpa gave an address reflecting all of these concerns. To close this chapter, it seems appropriate to quote from it:

> Thank you, everybody. This is such a wonderful celebration that you have created. It has become more polished and much better than ever before.
>
> One of the things that I'm concerned about is your own economic situation and your understanding of cultural and social ability—how we could organize this particular society, which is known as enlightened society.
>
> I would appreciate it very much if you could work harder or lesser, depending on your capabilities. Intelligence is the most important thing. It is very sweet of you all that you have made this offering to me, that you are all here to celebrate this situation. But on the whole I would like to see you survive properly and respectfully.
>
> We don't have to put too much emphasis on philosophy as such; I think you do understand that much. But we should work on practicality. How do we survive ourselves and how do we support our families in a manner that would make the greatest contribution to the world in general? Because it makes us more skillful, I would suggest that you study the political situation in the world altogether and how we can fit into it and how we could actually serve the rest of the world.
>
> I would like to thank you, everybody, very much in your love affair with me and your love of the buddhadharma, but you had better watch your step. Otherwise you might get too involved in watching too much of a sort of happy-lovely situation whatever

that may be. So in other words, you all are invited to join and work with me, but in a very pragmatic sense.[55]

In this speech, Chögyam Trungpa remained faithful to his 1972 decision to found Vajradhatu, and to all the proclamations made since 1976 concerning the Shambhala vision. Once again he reaffirmed the importance of not reducing the spiritual path to one of purely personal development. The desire he expresses here to create an enlightened society, which had become central to his work at the beginning of the 1980s, took on an increasingly concrete form in the last years of his life.

---

55. Chögyam Trungpa, "Birthday Address," Elks Lodge, Boulder, April 28, 1985, unpublished.

Chapter Twenty

THE MAIN FIGURES
IN THE MANDALA
OF CHÖGYAM TRUNGPA

I know each of your eccentricities, your sanity and your beauty and your weakness. We have had personal relationships with each other through all this time, and every one of you is a personal friend, a very good friend, and a great student of mine.[1]

—CHÖGYAM TRUNGPA,
speaking to the community
of vajrayana students

1. The Students

Instead of magnetizing and working with a small group of students, Chögyam Trungpa set up an immense organization. He had several thousand students who considered him their principal, or root, teacher. He tried to involve all of his students closely in his work, by giving them responsibilities. He wanted all of them to find a place where they could flourish in the world, and more particularly in the world that he was creating, a world dedicated to wakefulness, which was his constant concern. He thus helped many students to manifest their own qualities, and nurtured each person's own inspiration.

However, more fundamentally than cultivating individuals, Chögyam

1. Chögyam Trungpa, *Collected Vajra Assemblies*, vol. 1 (Halifax: Vajradhatu Publications, 1990), p. 3.

Trungpa cultivated *situations* that would allow everyone to develop and train according to their own interests. During the previous chapters, we have stressed some of the organizations that he set up: the Kalapa Court, Vajradhatu, various regional meditation and practice centers, Vajradhatu Seminary, the Naropa Institute, and so on. All of these were environments that could convey his teaching. (They were also powerful containers for the study and practice of Buddhism and the propagation of the Buddhist teachings in general.) One of his most effective but unusual methods (*upaya*) was his use of his administrative organization as a vehicle to work with people. Because of the way he set up the organization, its aim was not maximum efficiency but instead to build the greatest loyalty among his students—not loyalty to him personally but to the basic space of wakefulness or enlightenment. From this viewpoint, Chögyam Trungpa did not view education purely as an act of transferring information from one person to another, but as the creation of situations that allow everyone to develop fully, as who they are. It is for this reason that we can call Chögyam Trungpa a social visionary: the space he molded was not merely a container for his students' heartfelt devotion, nor was it simply a space where students could experience their own richness and dignity; it was the very space of society itself.

Chögyam Trungpa constantly affirmed and displayed how relating with society is not distinct from authentic spirituality. He taught that spirituality is far from being closed in on itself, but instead must entail a true and constant concern for others.

If we restrict ourselves to a spiritual path cut off from any concrete social commitment, we are limiting ourselves and forgetting about our dedication to our dharmic brothers and sisters. But if we affirm that only the social perspective matters, we will not have the resources to truly help others and may only increase the confusion that reigns in the world.

Assigning responsibilities

From his earliest days in the United States, Chögyam Trungpa's approach was to empower his students and involve them as much as possible in his work. For example, when he moved to Boulder in the fall of 1970, those students who remained at Tail of the Tiger, where he had first lived when he arrived in the States, were worried about how they would make their community vibrant without his being in residence full time. They also regarded him as the main source of ongoing interest and financial support for the community. People came to Tail to attend his seminars. He attracted most of the new students.

So it was quite shocking to the young residents of the center when Chögyam Trungpa suggested: "Why don't you teach yourselves?" Even from this early date, he expected his students to assume some responsibility and to begin to present the practice of meditation and the elementary Buddhist teachings to others. In this way, he encouraged everyone to bring the path to life in their own way. Over time, this led to the creation of a well-established administration and the introduction of simple but precise rituals, which were helpful to the community and provided an inspiration for each individual to work with their responsibility to transmit the teachings.

An examination of the establishment and development of Vajradhatu and Shambhala Training, two of the principal administrative or organizational vehicles created by Chögyam Trungpa, shows that this development did not conform to a predetermined plan. Instead, these organizations changed in numerous ways over time, according to the inspiration and understanding of those involved in the administration. One of Rinpoche's main students, the Dorje Loppön, Lodrö Dorje, recounted how Chögyam Trungpa asked him to organize a Christian-Buddhist conference, together with some other senior students. But apart from providing the barest indication of what he had in mind, Chögyam Trungpa gave no instructions about what should be done and who should be invited. The Loppön and his associates had to devise a way to carry out the mission they had been given. This was quite typical of how Chögyam Trungpa worked with many of his students.

Chögyam Trungpa was constantly providing a vision. We can easily misunderstand this notion, by viewing it in opposition to a pragmatic or realistic view of things. But in this case, the presentation of a vision is not a projection into the future that must be accomplished; instead, Chögyam Trungpa was able to express the most intimate aspirations of his students, what they really wanted here and now. The path of the warrior or of the practitioner is a matter of remaining faithful to that kind of vision and cultivating it in each of our actions.

Allowing everyone to find their place

Chögyam Trungpa was always devising responsibilities, titles, functions, obligations, and duties for his students, even if they had not studied with him for very long. Many relatively new students were asked to present the Buddhist teachings in seminars and study groups, while others were asked to assume responsibilities within the organizations being set up. Although many, if not all, of these students were beginners on the path, Chögyam Trungpa happily placed his confidence in their ability to help him propagate the buddhadharma in America.

For example, beginning around 1976, he appointed representatives from Boulder to head up the various centers that had been established across North America. He generally chose students who had worked closely with him for a period of four or five years. He gave the title of ambassador to the students who represented him in this way. Since *ambassador* is generally used for the representative of a nation in a foreign country, it might seem a surprising term for someone whose role was largely as a representative of a spiritual lineage. Moreover, it was a somewhat grand title for a job that was often quite limited: there were sometimes fewer than fifty members in a center. But, as in everything Chögyam Trungpa undertook, he was not afraid to express a vision that at first sight might appear excessive. When we look closely, we can see that he used this title to impress on these students that they were the representatives of the enlightened world—and the term then takes on a deeper meaning.

The trust that Chögyam Trungpa expressed in his students is similar, in some respects, to what is transmitted to the students who receive a tantric empowerment, or abhisheka. During an abhisheka, the practitioners are recognized as potential (or even actual) buddhas, as practitioners who are already accomplished. They are thus asked to change their usual viewpoint, to transcend doubt and discover the enlightenment already inside them: "The idea is to develop the pride of being a buddha. You are one in fact; there's no doubt about that. It is a very important point at the beginning that you *are* the gods, you *are* the deities, you *are* the buddhas. There's no question about that."[2]

Students are recognized as their fundamental selves, even when they have not yet experienced their real inner qualities. The obstacle to students' development is not only their egocentric pride, but more crucially their lack of confidence in their own nature, which is shown by an absence of dignity, or even a lurking depression.

On the other hand, in a situation where one is treated as fully realized, as remarked by Ron Stubbert—a senior student of Chögyam Trungpa's and one of the members of the Vajradhatu Board of Directors during Chögyam Trungpa's lifetime—the risk is that we will manufacture false confidence. If we believe we are important, we can play at being open and pretend that we are up to the task that we have been given. Ron Stubbert commented that this was sometimes true of people who were given responsibilities or positions of authority by Chögyam Trungpa. There is in fact a huge difference between giving a good talk, because we have learned the right techniques to do so, and manifesting authentic understanding in accordance with who we are. Chögyam Trungpa invited his students to reveal themselves and transcend their limitations, for the benefit of everyone. But it was up to each of them to confront and live up to this responsibility.

Chögyam Trungpa created a world and a path for his students that would allow them to manifest themselves fully and to develop real leadership skills. He did not want to have submissive students who would feel belittled by the brilliance of his enlightenment. On the contrary, he showed the human aspect of enlightenment, that it is always available to us, and that we can all contribute to the propagation of an enlightened society.

Diana Mukpo said that a profound part of her relationship with her husband was that he always tried to help her develop the qualities and gifts she had. This was his aim in the relationships he had with each one of his students. Once he had given them important responsibilities, he also

---

2. *The Lion's Roar*, pp. 148–149.

helped to train them. James Gimian remembers that during the first two years that he was in charge of the Dorje Kasung, his authority came directly from Rinpoche, who attentively supported him. Then Chögyam Trungpa stopped directing him, so that he could develop his own abilities.

Chögyam Trungpa showed his respect and love for his students in the most fundamental ways, thus encouraging them to become confident, not only in the work they had accomplished, but more generally in their own capacities. In Chögyam Trungpa's presence, everyone felt buoyed up by his unique brilliance and gentleness, as though space itself had been transformed. Then the students had to learn to keep up the same enthusiasm without their teacher's presence there to support and encourage them.

Chögyam Trungpa often asked his students to undertake ventures that were completely new to them. He was constantly putting them on the spot, pushing them further. Such situations often exposed people's emotions and neurosis, and could give rise to rivalries or even bitter jealousy. Chögyam Trungpa was not trying to create some ideally comfortable condition, but instead promoted a situation in which everyone felt completely challenged and could thus progress beyond their limits. Working closely with Chögyam Trungpa inside the Vajradhatu mandala was sometimes like being in a pressure cooker. In such a volatile situation one has to be willing to bare one's heart.

Chögyam Trungpa was not chiefly preoccupied with results, as most organizations are today. He was not at all put out when someone made a mistake, if this could help the students deepen their relationship with the teachings. The people who were given important responsibilities were not chosen solely because of their qualifications, specific talents, or even experience, but the activities also were designed to help people discover their latent talents and bring out their authenticity. Within this field of genuineness, Chögyam Trungpa was ready to give people a space where they could commit their own errors on their spiritual path and thus expose their confusion, so that it could be fundamentally transformed.[3]

---

3. This section is based on an extremely telling way Chögyam Trungpa described the Padmasambhava principle. See *Crazy Wisdom*, p. 50.

Among the many students who were closely involved or in charge of some project or activity during their association with Chögyam Trungpa, a few stand out because of the importance of their roles and the time and effort that Chögyam Trungpa put into working with them. We are going to look at the examples of a few of the heart disciples or close students of Chögyam Trungpa during the last ten years of his life: the Vajra Regent Ösel Tendzin; the Kasung Kyi Khyap, David I. Rome; and the Dorje Loppön, Lodrö Dorje. The Vajra Regent was his dharma heir; David Rome was his private secretary, who chaired the Board of Directors of Vajradhatu for many years and who was also head of the Dorje Kasung, a controversial but important organization that provided security for Vajradhatu and Chögyam Trungpa himself; and the Dorje Loppön was considered to be a very senior pracitioner and was the head of the Office of Practice and Study. He was in charge of overseeing many aspects of ritual, ceremony, and education in the community. Chögyam Trungpa's wife, Diana Judith Mukpo, and his firstborn son, Ösel Rangdröl Mukpo, had vital administrative and spiritual roles.[4]

2. Diana Mukpo, Sakyong Wangmo

While Diana Mukpo's primary role was not within the official administration that Chögyam Trungpa established, she made a decisive contribution to his world and his work.

In England, she strongly encouraged her husband to leave behind the difficult situation he was embroiled in. In 1982, at a birthday party given for him, Chögyam Trungpa publicly addressed his thanks to Diana for her role in bringing him to North America:

---

4. Although limiting ourselves to these few figures is unjust, because a huge number of students made important contributions to Chögyam Trungpa's work, it is just not possible to go into all the riches of Chögyam Trungpa's mandala, which would fill another book. Furthermore, I have decided to limit the discussion to Chögyam Trungpa's lifetime and have thus not dealt with the years after his death, for that would have led to an analysis of his legacy, which lies beyond the scope of the book.

I would like to offer enormous thanks and appreciation to Her Highness Lady Diana. You have cheered me up many times. In the past, I have gone through all kinds of depressing occasions and dungeons and an unspeakably unliberated world, pure and simple, a world that was not purified at all. We went through that together, with you leading the way ahead of me. I appreciate that very much. You are an extremely brave lady, I must say.

Such an extremely kind lady and an extremely resourceful lady as well, she managed to get us to this goddamned place called America! [*Laughter.*] Now we are going on, going further to Nova Scotia. At this point, she feels she can do it, and she's leading me. Usually any pioneering job is done by a man. This time, the pioneering job is being done by a woman, and I have no doubt at all that she'll do the very best job. I await her extraordinary pioneeringship. Her goodness and bravery will lead us and help us to promote enlightenment in that particular society, that particular world that we are moving up to.

On the whole, I would like to thank you very much for bearing our children, and thank you very much for being a pioneer. Thank you very much for having endless intelligence and endless fortitude. Thank you, my lady, thank you. Without you, I could not have come to America. Because of you, we did, and we did all this. So look at what we have done! [*Laughter.*] Now we will keep on going. Thank you. Thank you very much, young lady. [*His voice cracking with emotion.*] Thank you. Thank you so much.[5]

One of Diana Mukpo's most prominent qualities is the complete and constant confidence she had in everything Chögyam Trungpa undertook. Even when something seemed outrageous, she shared his vision.

As his wife, her relationship with him was, of course, different from the one he had with his students. She could speak to him directly, without feeling intimidated, in a way that few people could. Chögyam

---

5. Chögyam Trungpa, *True Command: The Teaching of the Dorje Kasung*, vol. 1, *The Town Talks* (Halifax: Trident Publications, 2004).

Trungpa liked having people around him who were not "yes men," who did not swallow everything he said, and who would challenge him and thus open up authentic communication. In a poem dedicated to Diana, Chögyam Trungpa wrote: "You never hesitate to tell the truth when you see the falsity."[6] This seems to have been Diana Mukpo's most secret and vital role, which connected her husband to the reality of the West in a very direct way.

Although Chögyam Trungpa very much wanted Diana Mukpo to have a role within the world he was establishing, he also encouraged her independence. When she demonstrated a passion for riding, he urged her to devote herself to the discipline of dressage. She became one of the only women ever to be accepted at the Spanish Riding School in Vienna. She also took part in many international dressage competitions. Through such excellence in her equestrian studies, Diana Mukpo displayed the dignity, discipline, and elegance of a true warrior. Chögyam Trungpa was very proud of his wife's accomplishments in this area.

On another level, within the Shambhala world, Diana Mukpo was known as the Sakyong Wangmo, the head of the mother lineage, with Chögyam Trungpa himself being the Sakyong, or the head of the father lineage. In presenting the Shambhala teachings, Chögyam Trungpa explained that a community needs strong leadership and skillful means, which represent qualities of the masculine principle. These are not necessarily carried out by men, incidentally. The influence of the feminine principle, however, is essential. It is the binding principle. Without the influence represented by the Sakyong Wangmo, a situation remains disjointed and people remain a mere set of individuals. As water unifies the flour and yeast and so makes bread, the Sakyong Wangmo principle provides harmony, which binds together the various parts of the enlightened world or the kingdom. Chögyam Trungpa believed not only that this principle was important, but that the actual Sakyong Wangmo, Diana Mukpo, could provide this binding factor in his world.[7]

---

6. Chögyam Trungpa, "Hunting the Setting-Sun Moon," July 10, 1981.

7. Chögyam Trungpa and Diana Mukpo had two children. Tendzin Lhawang Tagtruk David Mukpo—nicknamed Taggie, the diminutive of Tagtruk ("Tiger Cub")—was born March 9,

3. Ösel Rangdröl Mukpo, Sawang and Future Sakyong

Ösel Mukpo, the firstborn son of Chögyam Trungpa, was in his early twenties when his father died, so his role within his father's world became much more prominent after Chögyam Trungpa's death. However, Chögyam Trungpa knew that his son would play an important part in the future and worked to educate and prepare him for his future role.[8]

Ösel Rangdröl Mukpo was born in India in 1962. His mother was a young Buddhist nun who had met Chögyam Trungpa in Tibet and who escaped with him to India. Ösel spent the first years of his life with his mother in a village of Tibetan refugees in northwestern India. At the age of seven, he joined his father in Scotland, at the Samye Ling meditation center. In 1972, he joined his father and stepmother, Diana Mukpo, in Boulder, Colorado. There, he began his Buddhist studies with his father and his father's senior students, while also receiving a Western education. He also trained in various contemplative arts, such as Japanese archery, calligraphy, and horsemanship. During Chögyam Trungpa's retreat in 1977, when he worked on the presentation of the Shambhala teachings,

---

1971, and later recognized by His Holiness Karmapa as the rebirth of one of his teachers, Surmang Tendzin Rinpoche. At around two years of age, Taggie began to demonstrate behavioral and physical problems that were eventually diagnosed as the onset of autism. Taggie lives in a somewhat secluded environment in a private home connected with Karmê Chöling. He has never played a role as a teacher.

Gesar Tsewang Arthur Mukpo was born April 26, 1973. In 1976, Gesar was recognized by Dilgo Khyentse as the incarnation of Chögyam Trungpa's root guru, Jamgön Kongtrül of Sechen. The Karmapa confirmed this news the same year. As Gesar explained to me: "I think that my birth and the fact that I have been recognized as a tülku was a kind of confirmation or even sign that my father's work is an integral part of the traditional Buddhist lineage which he was trying to implant in the West." In his will, Chögyam Trungpa stated: "Gesar should assume his seat as a Buddhist leader."

8. Although in this book I have decided to limit the discussion of his students' roles to what took place during the lifetime of Chögyam Trungpa, it is still important to point out that after the death of the Vajra Regent Ösel Tendzin, the Sawang Ösel Rangdröl Mukpo became the head of Vajradhatu and Shambhala in August 1990. In 1995 he was enthroned as the Sakyong, in a ceremony that confirmed his role as the head of the Shambhala organization. Without his courage and compassion, the organization founded by his father might easily not have survived.

the Sawang joined him for several months. During a ceremony in 1979, Trungpa Rinpoche gave Ösel Rangdröl, who was then seventeen, the title of Sawang, which means "earth lord" in Tibetan. In this ceremony, Chögyam Trungpa recognized him as his Shambhala heir, in particular for the propagation of the Shambhala teachings.

The Sawang also participated in a large number of training opportunities and activities organized by the Dorje Kasung, with whom he had a great connection. Beginning in the 1980s, he often attended Seminary, and it was there that he took his refuge and bodhisattva vows, and started practicing his ngöndro, or vajrayana preliminaries. Through his experiences at Seminary he also became expert in the Japanese practice of oryoki. The Sawang also became one of the accomplished students of the Japanese archery or kyudo master Kanjuro Shibata Sensei. When Chögyam Trungpa made a visit to Japan in 1983, at the request of Shibata Sensei it was the Sawang who conducted a ritual kyudo purification ceremony, called the shihobarai, at an important imperial temple in Japan.

During the years when Chögyam Trungpa was setting up his outer mandala with such brilliance, the Sawang displayed genuine dignity beyond his years. Handsome, elegant, and charming, he manifested like a young prince.

Julian Nadel told a lovely story that perfectly illustrates this regal quality: "At age twelve, I was the youngest at the Magyal Pomra Encampment [an intensive outdoor education program. On the final day, the Sawang rode up to me on a pure white stallion and, without a word, with one arm and one motion, scooped me up onto the saddle in front of him. We took off—the world whizzing by. I remember being concerned that my head kept bumping into his chin. I remember wanting to go forward forever. . . . When he returned me to where my jaw-dropped mom still stood, he placed me down, one motion, and rode off, without even a smile goodbye. This was not goodbye; this was hello—the following week I began training to be his Kusung."[9] This story is a good example of the way the Sawang is able to connect with the heart of each person at a very deep level. Sometimes without even a word he touches one profoundly.

---

9. Julian Nadel, "Gallop," *Shambhala Annual Report*, 1999, Halifax, pp. 11ff.

Chögyam Trungpa wrote numerous poems to his son, including this one, composed on January 19, 1979:

> Be fearless and consume the ocean.
> Take a sword and slay neurosis.
> Climb the mountains of dignity and subjugate
>   arrogance.
> Look up and down and be decent.
> When you learn to cry and laugh at the same
>   time, with a gentle heart,
> All my belongings are yours,
> Including your father
> Happy birthday.[10]

In this poem, Chögyam Trungpa expresses his deep affection for his son. In the first part, he gives him advice, asking him to display a master warrior's courage, while recognizing the difficulties involved in accomplishing such an ambition. Then, in the second part, the tone of the poem changes. Chögyam Trungpa expresses his fatherly love. The great question for the Sawang at the time of his adolescence was how to find his place in relation to his father's. When Chögyam Trungpa arrived in the West, he already had a profound attainment and had long ago finished his education. But the Sawang was still a child when he arrived in the community and had to complete his education. Chögyam Trungpa's older students looked at him as a young teenager. Chögyam Trungpa is telling him with infinite tenderness to be authentically who he is as he faces this challenge. In this poem, he is saying that there is no need for the slightest comparison, because everything he has belongs to him. The Sawang's task was not to imitate anybody. Instead, as Chögyam Trungpa himself insisted, he was to be himself.

The day after this poem was written, a party was organized in a Chinese

---

10. From *First Thought Best Thought*, by Chögyam Trungpa, p. 155. © 1989 by Diana J. Mukpo. Reprinted by arrangement with Shambhala Publications, Inc., Boston, www.shambhala.com. Reprinted with permission of Diana J. Mukpo.

restaurant in Denver to celebrate the Sawang's birthday, at which Chögyam Trungpa said: "I have been raising several sons, as you know. There is the dharma heir, and there is the blood heir. I have been very busy raising both of them. It's quite a full-time job. I've been working quite hard, with delight, of course."[11] He was referring here to the Sawang as his blood heir and to Ösel Tendzin, his Vajra Regent, as his dharma heir.

4. The Vajra Regent Ösel Tendzin

Among the many students, the Vajra Regent Ösel Tendzin held a special place as Chögyam Trungpa's spiritual son, his dharma heir. Given that devotion lies at the heart of the path in the Kagyü lineage, an examination of the relationship between Chögyam Trungpa and his regent provides an opportunity for us to understand more about the nature of this bond.

The first encounter

"He was known as Narayana, a colourful personality with lots of smiles, possessing the charm of American Hindu diplomacy. From the first, I felt some definite sense of connection with him,"[12] wrote Chögyam Trungpa about the first conversation that he had, in February 1971, with the man who was to become his regent. At this time, Thomas Rich, then known as Narayana, was studying with the Hindu teacher Swami Satchidananda and living in one of Satchidananda's centers in Los Angeles. Satchidananda asked Narayana and Ken Green, known as Krishna, to visit Chögyam Trungpa in Boulder and invite him to an event called the World Enlightenment Festival. Both of these young men later became close heart disciples of Chögyam Trungpa.

Thomas Rich, too, told of that moment: "I met the Vajracarya on a Sunday afternoon at his home in Four Mile Canyon. I was wearing a red

---

11. Chögyam Trungpa, *True Command: The Teaching of the Dorje Kasung*, vol. 1, *The Town Talks* (Halifax: Trident Publications, 2004).

12. Chögyam Trungpa, "Epilogue," in *Born in Tibet*, 4th ed. (2000), p. 258.

ruffled shirt and red velvet pants, à la L.A., and I was sporting long hair and a beard. I was ushered into the sitting room, where I was confronted by a person much younger than I had expected, surrounded by several students, some of whom I had known from my previous stay in Boulder. With a piercing gaze, which seemed to comprehend my entire history, he greeted me courteously."[13]

Once the interview was over, Narayana kept wondering: "How could anybody be solidly there like a rock, like a monument, and yet be empty at the same time?" Profoundly moved by this first meeting, Narayana wrote him a letter, which begins:

> During our first visit last week I remarked that you were not what I expected. What I am now attempting to do is to communicate to what degree that was true for me. This is the third attempt to write to you, the other two being inadequate expressions of what I had experienced through our contact. I have met many saints and teachers, but only one had the ability to change my state to a noticeable degree just through darshan. Swami Satchidananda was the one, but now you are the other. I am telling you this because I realize that it was a significant encounter and one that may have bearing on how I approach life and spirituality.
>
> After our talk I found myself in a state of quiescence. In itself that is not new for me but this calm was deeper, more weighty. The people around me remarked that I seemed different. All I could reply was that our contact was such that all my petty concerns about life became unreal. I have been talking about you ever since.
>
> First I noticed that your physical body was no more than your thought to express yourself, that thought of body being so pure that I understood it (the physical) to be only your creation. Your motions and movements, being unobstructed by manipulative intentions, looked almost automatic. Yet I knew the consciousness attended to each action. Someone had asked me to ask you why you

---

13. This and the following quotation are from *1976 Seminary Transcripts: Vajrayana* (Boulder: Vajradhatu Publications), p. 72. Reprinted by permission.

smoked or drank but the question was absurd in light of your consciousness of the truth. And like any real contact with another, I became again conscious of my own infinite self. Later on I was eating, just dwelling on you and our meeting. As I ate I became conscious again of Maya—what I was eating became nothing, it was going into nothing. Then the motion became nothing. I became more aware of the depth of your consciousness. Forgive this clumsiness. All I am trying to say is that I am open to you and I have been deeply touched by your divinity, so much so that all I have to do is think of you and my mind clears and thoughts subside. This creates in me a willingness to experience you more fully. I am aware that an opening like this is rare in my life.[14]

The future Gampopa

When they next met, a month later, Chögyam Trungpa offered him a glass of liquor. This young student of Swami Satchidananda, always dressed in white, had taken vows to remain pure according to Hindu practice. He had vowed never to drink alcohol. Nevertheless, he accepted the glass and drank it down.

Such a meeting could be likened to that which occurred between Milarepa and his disciple Gampopa, two of the major figures in the history of the Kagyü school, to which Chögyam Trungpa belonged. One night, Milarepa, the lineage holder and by then an aged meditation teacher, dreamed that a disciple would come to see him who would be his spiritual heir. Gampopa was already an accomplished practitioner of Buddhist meditation, but he was not a follower of the Kagyü school at that time, to which Milarepa belonged. He remained attached to a very formal ascetic discipline.

The crucial moment in the meeting was when Gampopa agreed to drop his formal adherence to this outer discipline and join the sacred world by accepting the drink of alcohol that Milarepa offered him. The

14. Letter published in "Ten Years in North America," a supplement to the *Vajradhatu Sun*, September/October, Boulder, 1980. Reprinted by permission.

fact that he drank it down was the sign to Milarepa that Gampopa would integrate all of the teachings his guru would give him.

After their initial meetings in Boulder, Chögyam Trungpa asked Thomas Rich to move with his wife to Tail of the Tiger. Ken Green and his family also moved there. After a period of time living in the "pressure-cooker" discipline at Tail, an important meeting took place between Chögyam Trungpa and Thomas Rich. A conversation took place, which was described a number of years later by the Regent as follows:

> The Vajracarya turned to me.
>
> "I have something to ask you," he said. "Do you know what it is?"
>
> I was slightly dumbfounded and made some vague stab at it. "Well, you want to send Ken [Green] somewhere and keep me here in Vermont."
>
> "Well, somewhat," he said, and laughed. "This is slightly embarrassing, somewhat like proposing marriage. Can you guess?"
>
> My mind was blank. "No," I said.
>
> "Then I'll tell you. I want you to be my Gampopa, my successor."
>
> I was utterly shocked. "Me? Are you sure?"
>
> "Quite sure. Do you accept?"
>
> "Yes," I said.
>
> "Just like that?" he said.
>
> "Just like that," I said.
>
> "Good, from now on there is no turning back. If you do, you will be destroyed by the dakas, dakinis, and dharmapalas."
>
> The Vajracarya talked about his eventual death. I made some feeble remarks about how awful that would be, and he laughed. "For me that is no problem at all," he said.[15]

Chögyam Trungpa then asked Thomas Rich to pay attention to any dreams he had that night. The next day, Rich described how, in his

---

15. Vajra Regent, "Letter," in Chögyam Trungpa, *1980 Seminary Transcripts: Vajrayana* (Boulder: Vajradhatu Publications), pp. 53–54. Reprinted by permission.

dream, he had wanted to eat an egg, and after everyone had told him it was impossible, he finally found one that he ate entirely. Chögyam Trungpa was delighted with this good omen: "The egg symbolizes the unborn wisdom within, like the garuda's egg. When it hatches, the garuda is fully formed."[16]

Chögyam Trungpa asked Thomas Rich to keep this decision to empower him secret. During the following six months, he made no further mention of the event, which surprised and worried Rich. He even wondered if had dreamed it all. Then, in the summer of 1972, during a meeting at Tail of the Tiger, where Rich was a member of the executive committee, Chögyam Trungpa turned to him and asked what he thought about the matter they were discussing. He replied, "I think we should do whatever you want, and it will be fine." That evening, Chögyam Trungpa called for Thomas Rich and told him, "It wasn't good enough what you said at the meeting today. You should always remember who you are."

Little by little, Thomas Rich began working alongside Chögyam Trungpa, quickly becoming one of his main administrators. But, as usual, Chögyam Trungpa gave him very little concrete advice about what to do: "Working as a Vajradhatu director [as of 1973 when Vajradhatu was formed] was extremely confusing at first. The Vajracarya had given me no definite guidelines. . . . The Varjacarya was away, giving seminars."[17]

Thomas Rich officially becomes the Vajra Regent

By 1976, the community had developed and had accepted the idea of having a board of directors and a more formal organization—its period of adolescence was over. Chögyam Trungpa decided to make an official announcement of his choice of regent. "In April, 1976, The Vajracarya announced my Regency publicly for the first time, at a party for the entire Vajradhatu/Nalanda staff. . . . I was thoroughly surprised by the

---

16. Ibid., p. 55.

17. Ibid., p. 56.

announcement myself since the Vajracarya hadn't told me in advance that he would be making it."[18]

Such an event was an opportunity for Chögyam Trungpa to share more openly the direction that he wanted his work to take. For, as he explained: "to ensure that everything will not stop at my death, it is necessary to have one person as an inheritor, someone whom I can train and observe over a period of many years. For a long time it was in my mind to appoint Narayana to this role, and in the summer of 1976 I did so, empowering him as Dorje Gyaltsap, Vajra Regent."[19]

The appointment of the Regent created a situation where Chögyam Trungpa's students were now placed within the continuity of lineage—a lineage presumably with a future as well as a past. This was very helpful in the situation of that time, in which hundreds of students were asking for training and joining Vajradhatu.

During a talk given to the tantrikas on the very afternoon of Thomas Rich's empowerment as Regent, Chögyam Trungpa explained: "As far as the corporate Vajradhatu is concerned, he worked exactly in accordance with what the real vajradhatu, the ultimate vajradhatu should be. His work is giving, all the time letting go and giving, giving out territory and pushing people and sharing sympathy. . . . To individuals who would like to have any kind of consultation, I would say that I think at this point his vision is grown-up enough to answer your questions as much as the old-hat Vajracarya can."[20]

Chögyam Trungpa always perceived the potential that was waiting to blossom in his students. His work with Thomas Rich is a prime example of that. When he first met Thomas Rich in 1971, he knew that this young man could become his regent. He then observed him attentively, until 1976 when he officially empowered him.

Chögyam Trungpa's choice of an American to become the regent of a Tibetan Buddhist lineage is a potent declaration that the dharma is not

---

18. Ibid., p. 57.

19. Chögyam Trungpa, "Epilogue," in *Born in Tibet*, 4th ed. (2000), p. 263.

20. Chögyam Trungpa, *Collected Vajra Assemblies*, vol. 1 (Halifax: Vajradhatu Publications, 1990), pp. 82–83.

bound by culture and that Westerners can fully understand and realize it. As Chögyam Trungpa himself explained: "Many Oriental advisors have said to me: 'Do not make an Occidental your successor, they are not trustworthy.'"[21] With the agreement and recognition of the sixteenth Karmapa, he broke away from their conservative outlook.

The Regent's activities

In November 1976, just a few months after his official empowerment, the Vajra Regent Ösel Tendzin attended the Vajradhatu Seminary in Wisconsin. The Vidyadhara asked him to explain the meaning of devotion to all the students present. In his teaching, the Regent said: "The point is that in the feeling of devotion you have vast space because there is literally no concern for yourself. When that occurs there is a complete environment of precision. In my relationship with the Vidyadhara, that's how it works. Because of intense longing for him, there's nothing in my mind when I'm *there*. So whatever he says or does is teaching: the words of, the feeling of, the act of wisdom. That's how you should be."[22]

Explaining devotion, especially during periods of teaching devoted to vajrayana in Chögyam Trungpa's seminars, became one of the Regent's specialties.

As the years went by, the Regent's role became increasingly important. During the Vidyadhara's yearlong retreat in 1977, he became the acting director of Vajradhatu, overseeing all activities of the practice centers and Dharmadhatus. He gave refuge and bodhisattva vows, as well as instruction and transmissions for vajrayana practice, and was the main teacher during the summer sessions at the Naropa Institute. There, he presented his commentary on Gampopa's *Jewel Ornament of Liberation*, the book that the Vidyadhara had given him on the day he asked him to be his successor.

During the years after Chögyam Trungpa's 1977 retreat, he and the

---

21. Chögyam Trungpa, *True Command: The Teaching of the Dorje Kasung*, vol. 1, *The Town Talks* (Halifax: Trident Publications, 2004).

22. Chögyam Trungpa, *1980 Seminary Transcripts: Vajrayana*, p. 50.

Regent went on long tours, visiting dharma centers in the United States, Canada, and Europe, where they often taught together. The Regent made many teaching tours on his own and taught seminars to beginning and advanced students within Vajradhatu.[23]

5. The Dorje Loppön, Responsible for the Three Yanas

Eric Holm was appointed the Dorje Loppön in 1978 and began using his refuge name, Lodrö Dorje. In *Born in Tibet*, Chögyam Trungpa explained how a loppön is in charge of the details of the vajrayana rituals, while the khenpo presents "philosophical teaching." But the role given to Lodrö Dorje as the Loppön was much larger. He became a high-level teacher, responsible for supervising the training of meditation instructors and future teachers. (That Chögyam Trungpa never appointed a khenpo was presumably because he did not find anyone suitably educated for this responsibility.) While at each Seminary the Regent presented a talk on devotion and how to connect with the teacher, the Loppön presented one on samaya, or the vows that the practitioner makes when entering the vajrayana. Appointed as head of the Office of Three Yanas Studies, he was in charge of training teachers and meditation instructors at all levels of Buddhist practice and study.

The responsibilities of the Loppön grew with time. For example, in 1985, during the abhisheka of Chakrasamvara, one of the most important initiations Chögyam Trungpa gave, the Loppön was empowered as Dorje Loppön. He henceforth had the authority to give refuge and bodhisattva vows and tantric transmissions. It confirmed the importance of

---

23. After Chögyam Trungpa's death in 1987, the Vajra Regent succeeded him as president of Vajradhatu and Nalanda Foundation. He traveled and taught extensively, bestowed the Vajrayogini abhisheka in Colorado, and presided over the 1988 Seminary. During the same period, his health was declining from AIDS, and fundamental disagreements concerning the leadership of Vajradhatu surfaced within the sangha, which entered a chaotic, turbulent period. On the advice of Dilgo Khyentse Rinpoche, the Vajra Regent went into retreat in Ojai, California, accompanied by his family and a number of students. He died in San Francisco in 1990, and the Sawang Ösel Mukpo succeeded him as leader of Vajradhatu.

what he had achieved. On this occasion, Chögyam Trungpa took the title Vidyadhara (*rigdzin* in Tibetan, the "holder of rigpa," or "awareness") and abandoned that of Vajracharya, which he had used since the Karmapa's first visit.[24]

6. David Rome

David I. Rome became one of Chögyam Trungpa's students in 1971: "I think he started noticing me when I was part of the earliest theater group—he liked my voice and the way I did his sound cycles and poems. I was invited to the first Seminary in 1973 (I think because they knew I could afford to pay for it—I think it cost $300 for three months!). Right after that, in January 1974, I was asked to assist in scheduling interviews for Rinpoche. Quickly it became a full-time job, or more than full-time."

David Rome began attending to Chögyam Trungpa's needs day and night. He was not the first person to do this in America, but he was certainly one of the most dedicated. "This schedule didn't last too long—

---

24. Larry Mermelstein explained the following points: "When His Holiness Karmapa XVI first came to the United States in 1974, he wrote a proclamation in which he referred to Rinpoche as a Dorje Dzinpa, which means 'vajra holder.' Rinpoche was very fond of using Sanskrit for important titles and terms much more than Tibetan. And he knew that the correct Sanskrit for this is Vajradhrik—a rather difficult word to pronounce, not to mention its resemblance to either the Yiddish *drek* [garbage] or English *dick*, neither of which endeared him to this. So he decided to adopt a much lesser (in terms of traditional hierarchy) and easier to handle (for Westerners) title: Vajracharya, 'vajra master,' which is the Sanskrit for the Tibetan *dorje loppön*.

"Vajracharya as a title seemed to suffice until Venerable Tenga Rinpoche came to teach us about Chakrasamvara in late 1985. Tenga Rinpoche was for many years the Dorje Loppön of Rumtek Monastery, and he still often does that title. When Lodrö and I first greeted him upon his arrival in Boulder, Tenga Rinpoche kept calling Lodrö 'Dorje Loppön,' which I'm sure was meant to be respectful and acknowledging of his appointment. It was I who was rather confused about our use of various titles, especially after Lama Ugyen Shenpen confirmed my suspicion that in his experience there was really no difference between *loppön* and *dorje loppön*, the latter just being the fuller form of the title in traditional monastic contexts.

"So when Lodrö and I returned to RMDC (we were all attending the first four-karmas fire offering with Rinpoche) after greeting Tenga Rinpoche, I took the matter up with the Vajracharya. Mitchell Levy and I were serving as Rinpoche's attachés for this period, so I had soon there were drivers and Kasung and Kusung and secretaries and attendants and consorts who all took a piece of what I originally did by myself—but those early times were wonderfully intimate. Chögyam Trungpa was very kind to me, very gentle and protective and affirming—as time went on he also became challenging, occasionally fierce with me. Chögyam Trungpa loved to use me as a guinea pig—he picked my wife for me, which he was very proud of (of course he didn't force her on me, he was much too skillful for that). He created the Shambhala wedding ceremony for us and got us all dressed up in formal kimonos for the event, which took place at sunrise!"

Until his departure to work in his family business in New York in 1982, David Rome was executive director of Chögyam Trungpa's office. As such, he was responsible for supervising all of Chögyam Trungpa's activities.

In addition to his role as executive director and private secretary, David Rome played a decisive role on the Vajradhatu Board of Directors as the chair of the meetings. He was also appointed to a senior leadership role with the Dorje Kasung (see chapter 21). Together, the Vajra Regent, the Dorje Loppön, and David Rome, along with Jeremy Hayward and, in later years, James Gimian and Martin Janowitz, made up a Privy Council established by Chögyam Trungpa as a senior leadership group with whom he consulted about all administrative, educational, and spiritual affairs.

---

relatively easy access to him. I explained how odd it seemed to me that we had Dorje Loppön Tenga Rinpoche, Dorje Loppön Lodrö Dorje, and Vajracharya (Sanskrit for *dorje loppön*) Chögyam Trungpa Rinpoche. Surely there was meant to be a better way to distinguish these three people, especially Chögyam Trungpa, in my not-so-humble opinion.

"This turned into quite a fun and interesting revisiting of H. H. Karmapa's 1974 proclamation and related ideas. Rinpoche still did not want to use either the Sanskrit Vajradhrik or the Tibetan Dorje Dzinpa. Finally, he remembered that Dudjom Rinpoche had in 1979 referred to him as *vidyadhara* in the longevity supplication he wrote and offered to Rinpoche. We were all quite accustomed to chanting this supplication daily, and *vidyadhara* was not too difficult to say."

7. The Board of Directors, the Sangyum, and the Dapöns

The board of directors

At Vajradhatu, the role of the board of directors was quite different from the one it usually has in companies, where it is distinct from the management team. Most of the members of the Vajradhatu Board of Directors worked for the organization full time, and the board was more like a cabinet (Kashag) or council of ministers, as conceived of in the Tibetan system of government.

Each of its members had a specific responsibility. There was a finance minister, a minister of internal affairs, a minister of external affairs, a minister of education, a minister of publications, a minister of legal affairs, and several other departments. In this sense, Chögyam Trungpa's organization was more like the political administration of a state than that of a company, and he drew on English examples as well as Tibetan models. The objective of a company's board is to make a profit, while the purpose of the board established by Chögyam Trungpa was to help set up and govern a community.

Among the board's responsibilities was to aid the development of the various meditation centers that were being opened in most North American and European cities, and to organize Chögyam Trungpa's travels, seminars, and domestic life.

The board of directors was thus a group of very close students with whom Chögyam Trungpa worked. They were his representatives, and he trained them with this in mind. It was with them that he first introduced a formal protocol, well before it became the general community style. For example, he attended meetings in a tie, without comment; soon, all the other men did likewise.

Chögyam Trungpa was the chairman of the board, although the actual business of the board was chaired by David Rome, as mentioned above. Generally, the board met every week, often when Chögyam Trungpa was out of town. All aspects of the life of the organization were discussed at these meetings. Jeremy Hayward, who was a member, recalls expressing his frustration to Chögyam Trungpa: "I'd like to be closer to you, but I'm constantly taken up by the administrative tasks I have to do." Chögyam Trungpa replied that the same was true for him. But the part played by the board seemed to him all the more important because it allowed for the creation of a true organization. By dividing responsibilities among his students, it allowed Chögyam Trungpa to radiate his vision to the greatest number possible.

The role of such a body is even more crucial when everything is new. This board was involved in establishing many new forms and procedures. It had to invent just about everything: the form of the shrine, the way that various programs would be conducted, the way to receive a teacher, to teach, and so on. A common culture for the students was thus created. In addition, the board had to oversee finances and worry about fundraising. They tended to set policy and procedure while leaving implementation up to the individual ministers or directors and their department staff.

Chögyam Trungpa often expressed his appreciation for the courage of those who agreed to devote themselves so fully to making his vision into a practical reality. In 1979, at his birthday party ceremony, he said: "These gentlemen are known as the directors of the Vajradhatu and Nalanda organizations. They are wearing pins, in case you haven't noticed, which denote that they are warriors and what particular kind of warriors they are. Their warriorship has never given up. They are constantly willing to be warriors."

The Sangyum

In the last years of his life, Chögyam Trungpa appointed more and more women to positions of importance and authority within his organization. He consistently chose women as the deans or the heads of the Naropa Institute, and he gave women leadership roles in more and more areas. However, it was only very late in his life, in 1985, that he appointed women to the board of directors and gave them the highest authority within the organization. In 1985, Chögyam Trungpa appointed seven women to the top layer of his organization, not to replace members of the board of directors but to oversee the board. These women were referred to as the Sangyum. The term is usually reserved for the wife of the teacher, but in this case it was used for a group of women with whom Chögyam Trungpa had a particular heart and mind connection, such that he trusted them to oversee and help to shepherd key areas of his work.

Chögyam Trungpa often stressed that this choice was not his, but had been made by the Rigdens, the kings of Shambhala. In that sense, he was saying that the role of feminine energy within Shambhala was on a primordial and fundamental level. To stress the importance that he gave to these appointments, Chögyam Trungpa recognized the Sangyum as members of his family, not just members of his administration. By so doing, he showed that he was thinking of the Sangyum's influence as not being "job" oriented but as being on a much broader level.

The way Chögyam Trungpa worked with the Sangyum was very much the way he worked with all of his closest students for periods of time: he asked them to stay in his presence and share his everyday life. In this form of training, the student did not have to learn anything in particular; instead, education was based on their experience of a way of being—which is perhaps the deepest of all teachings.

The appointment of the Sangyum was announced in a very low-key way in the June/July 1985 edition of the *Vajradhatu Sun*. An announcement entitled "Kalapa Court Appointments" read: "The Kalapa Court announces the appointment of five private secretaries [the group grew to seven later] to the Vajracarya's personal staff. . . . several of the appointees are already on staff at Vajradhatu or Nalanda, and all of them are receiving personal training from the Vajracarya for the responsibilities they are being given."

In the last years of his life, as indicated above, Chögyam Trungpa placed ever more emphasis on the importance of feminine energy and the role that women could play in the transmission of his teachings and his world. The intellectual brilliance that dominated the earlier years was broadened and replaced by an ever more heartfelt sense of the teachings. In some way, it was the preeminence of the energy of devotion over and above the energy of intellect. While both are needed for the transmission of the teachings, he seemed to feel that the heart was more essential than the brain in the later days. Buddhism sees feminine energy as a complete opening, an ability to accommodate everything that occurs, a panoramic awareness that can appreciate the slightest detail, a universal passion-compassion unaltered by the slightest partiality.

According to their descriptions of how their training affected them, by being with Chögyam Trungpa, the Sangyum developed a full allegiance to the abrupt and limitless opening of enlightenment. He himself was the space free of all reference points, of "accommodation without trying, without effort."[25] An unforeseeable quality emerges from this vast space, which the Sangyum experienced and had to learn to trust.

When the Sangyum asked Chögyam Trungpa what they should study in order to carry out their functions, he advised them to learn and study *The Letter of the Black Ashe* and *The Golden Sun of the Great East* (two of the root texts of Shambhala), learn to have good elocution, practice ikebana, not look on his work as a burden, maintain a royal attitude, avoid being frivolous, resist being Americanized, and have the generosity to govern and manifest a sense of dignity. This provides us with a precious indication of what Chögyam Trungpa meant by governing and the training he thought necessary for those who wanted to become authentic statesmen or politicians. For Chögyam Trungpa, governing primarily consisted in maintaining one's dignity and place, rather than being mainly concerned about the effectiveness of a given action.

As a part of their work, Chögyam Trungpa asked the Sangyum to attend the meetings of the board of directors and to try to acquire an overall vision of the situation. They were to represent him there.[26] In the very last years of his life, having gone through a period when he introduced great formality, which included the creation of the Court and other Shambhala institutions, Chögyam Trungpa's teaching took on yet another quality. He now became inscrutable, like space. In some sense he was returning to the formless quality of his very early years in the West.

---

25. *Glimpses of Space: The Feminine Principle and Evam* (Halifax: Vajradhatu Publications, 1999), p. 27.

26. We should here think back over the notion of power and Chögyam Trungpa's singular understanding of it. As Karen Lavin, one of the Sangyum, so rightly explained: "there is no question then of who has more power. *Power* is not the right word. For feminine principle to fully manifest, it has to be above the administration hierarchically." *Kalapa Journal*, Halifax, 1998, p. 20.

Yet this final vajra space had a kind of immovable solidity to it. It could be solid, often claustrophobic, intense, and highly uncomfortable to be in his presence, especially in the last year, because the space around him could not be manipulated or penetrated by ordinary conceptual mind. The Sangyum's mission was to remain with him in this absence of reference points, the space of mind where he naturally lived, especially at this time of his life. On a relative level, the Sangyum helped people to be slightly less ill at ease at a time when remaining in the presence of Rinpoche was an incredibly difficult experience.

The Dapöns

When Chögyam Trungpa established the Dorje Kasung, it was at first very loosely organized as a group of students providing personal service to the teacher, including elements of a bodyguard function as well as driving high-profile visitors, organizing motorcades, and acting as liaison with local officials and police departments when teachers traveled around the country. For example, members of the Dorje Kasung worked very closely on the first visit of His Holiness the Dalai Lama to America in 1979, in these various capacities. Almost from the beginning of the Dorje Kasung, Chögyam Trungpa realized that it would be necessary to have leadership for this organization. So quite early on, he established the post or the position of Dapön. *Dapön* literally means "arrow chief" and was used in Tibet to refer to military leaders, roughly the equivalent of generals. Initially there was one Dapön, who was called the Dorje Dapön, or "indestructible general."

Later, as the organization grew and matured, further levels of leadership were added. The head of the whole Dorje Kasung organization became known as the Kasung Kyi Khyap, which roughly translates as the "overall command protector." Within the Dorje Kasung, divisions eventually were formed, representing specialization. Those who worked in the household of Chögyam Trungpa and provided personal service to him or to other teachers became known as Kusung, body protectors, and a Kusung Dapön was appointed. The first Kusung Dapön was John Perks. When he resigned around 1981, Martin Janowitz became the Kusung

Dapön. A Kasung Dapön was appointed for those who continued to specialize in the more "outer" practice of Kasungship. James Gimian held this position from 1977 to 1995.

In addition to their responsibilities for the Dorje Kasung organization, the Kasung Dapön and the Kusung Dapön, as well as the Kasung Kyi Khyap, were members of the core leadership group that Chögyam Trungpa relied on in later years to help in the running of Vajradhatu as well as in the formation of policies and discussion of new initiatives. This group was called the Privy Council and consisted of the Vajra Regent Ösel Tendzin, the Dorje Loppön, Lodrö Dorje, the Kasung Kyi Khyap, Director Jeremy Hayward, the Kasung Dapön, and the Kusung Dapön. The Kasung and the Kusung Dapöns also had a strong personal connection with Chögyam Trungpa and spent a great deal of time in his direct personal service. In the last few years of his life, at least one of them or his physician, Mitchell Levy, was always on duty with Chögyam Trungpa. He affectionately referred to these three men as "the Three Musketeers." Several years before his death, he promoted the Kasung Dapön and the Kusung Dapön each to the rank of Dapön Kyi Khyap.

In describing the importance of the basic Dorje Kasung energy, Chögyam Trungpa often spoke of it as "military" energy. Clearly, it was an important element for him in how he presented the dharma, and it was also a significant element in other aspects of his life. He seemed to draw strength from the Kasung energy. In a talk to the members of the Dorje Kasung he described this as follows:

> Obviously, we are not going to wage war or organize a war against anybody at all. We're not going to attack or kill anybody. We're not talking about that kind of military. But we are simply talking about being the military which has structure, discipline, fearlessness, and good head and shoulders.
>
> In my past experience, when I've visited certain Dharmadhatus [meditation centers] where the military leaders don't have good head and shoulders, I can't instruct the students properly because the students don't have any reference point for creating the atmosphere that I would like to teach in. I find myself just a wick with the

flame burning without a container. In certain other places where I've visited, where there is a good, strong military situation, I can contain myself in it thoroughly and teach properly. That is not because everybody runs around being a busybody, driving me around and providing lots of valets and cooks and all the rest of it. It's simply that the particular presence of your militariness helps me to teach a lot, to teach further. Then I feel very comfortable. Mind you, the need for this atmosphere is not based purely on my comfort, but rather that the dharma can be taught properly and fully with this kind of structure. Otherwise, the whole teaching situation becomes like a giant wick with its flame burning, but there's no lamp to hold the oil, and I find myself stupid, wasted.[27]

---

27. Chögyam Trungpa, *True Command: The Teachings of the Dorje Kasung*, vol. 1, pp. 64–65.

Chapter Twenty-one

THE DORJE KASUNG

AN EXEMPLARY PATH

He who couldn't care gains victory.
He who couldn't care gains beyond bondage.
He who is beyond doubt and fear is truly profound
 and brilliant.
He who no longer needs reference point is just and
 powerful.
He who is unconcerned about gain and loss is truly
 all-victorious.
Profound brilliant just powerful victorious—
Be to you as the Vajra Kasung.[1]

—CHÖGYAM TRUNGPA

1. The Dorje Kasung, the Kasung Kyi Khyap, and the Dapöns

If the center of the mandala is the pure presence of the deity, of the monarch, of the master who embodies the truth of its principles, the border is made up by the Kasung; their "post," so to speak, is the point where the outside meets the inside. If we liken the teacher to a burning candle, we may say that the light becomes brighter when it is contained by a surrounding lamp. The container principle is the role of the Kasung, who both contain and magnify the light of the center. Without the Kasung,

---

1. Chögyam Trungpa, excerpt from "Glory Be to the Kasung" in *Warrior Songs* (Halifax: Trident Publications, 1991). Copyright © 1991 by Diana J. Mukpo. Used by permission.

without a border, it is more difficult to promulgate the teachings and to create a situation in which people can wake up. For these borders can change people's states of mind, by establishing a sacred space.

The Kasung answer the basic imperative that the propagation of the teachings needs to be safeguarded. Because the dharma proclaims the truth of non-ego or unconditional openness, dharma can be a threat to ego. Thus ego may react violently to the propagation of the dharma. It is thus vital to protect the teacher who proclaims the dharma and the situation in which it is proclaimed. To put it another way, anyone who has a profound connection with the truth is a threat or menace to the status quo, if the status quo is based on conventional mind rather than allegiance to truth. To understand this point, it is sufficient to remember how some of the great Western philosophers have been treated by their societies: Socrates was accused of impiety and condemned to death, Aristotle had to flee to avoid the same fate, Spinoza was excommunicated from the Amsterdam Synagogue at the age of twenty-four, Giordano Bruno was burned at the stake, Nietzsche lived in the greatest solitude and had to leave the university, and Heidegger was accused of being a Nazi and his teachings were outlawed. There are other, similar examples of great thinkers or artists.

The Buddhist teachings aim to expose students and cut through their hypocrisy in order to show them that they can be themselves, free of habitual conditioning and lines of thought. When confronted with such openness, most students experience a deep feeling of relief at being face to face with their own hearts, but some are not ready for such an ordeal and can react violently. One of the stories that is often told to students of Buddhist tantra is that of Rudra: "He and a fellow student, a dharma brother, were studying with the same master. They had a disagreement about how to interpret the master's instructions. They were taking opposite extremes in carrying out their practice, and each of them was sure that he was right. They decided to go to the teacher and ask for his comment. When the teacher told Rudra he was wrong, Rudra became so angry that he drew his sword and killed his teacher on the spot."[2]

---

2. *The Lion's Roar*, pp. 70–71.

Thus Chögyam Trungpa wrote in a "Letter to the Vajra Guards":

A charlatan's job is, to begin with, to protect himself and his ego. While he is always conning people, he must be careful not to make enemies so that he won't be exposed to any threats. He must preserve his façade, or his falsity will be seen through. He is buying people in order to win their support, and he only enters a situation when it seems to be to his advantage.

In our case, I am not concerned with winning people over, so I am not afraid of insulting people's ego trips and cutting through them. My interest is not in selling the dharma. There is no fear in telling the truth, to attempt to secure my own personal position.

Some people are open to this and become friends and practitioners like yourselves. Other people are horribly insulted and threatened. Some of these people run away to preserve their hypocrisy, but some are haunted by the inevitable truth. Perhaps they freak out and try to strike out in defence of their belief in egotism. Another possibility arises from those who are disillusioned by other teachers and spiritual scenes, who develop a general vendetta towards spirituality.

Both of these dangerous situations have already manifested, through threatening phone calls, letters, and visits. For example, last summer a person who had become disillusioned and angered by Guru Maharaj Ji suddenly appeared at Karma Dzong to check out our organization. In his green backpack he carried a number of hand grenades. Fortunately, someone was able to cool him out and persuade him to leave. At the time, I was unaware of this event. I was in my office, down the hall, giving interviews.[3]

The dorje, or Buddhist scepter used in rituals, symbolizes the basic principle of protection offered by the Dorje Kasung. The sharp prongs of the dorje repel aggression and correspond to repelling what needs to be re-

---

3. "Letter to the Vajra Guards," November 6, 1975, in Chögyam Trungpa, *True Command: The Teachings of the Dorje Kasung*, vol. 1, *The Town Talks* (Halifax: Vajradhatu Publications, 2002).

pelled. Between the prongs there is a space, which represents the space through which practitioners can enter into the mandala. This space also represents the ability to accept whatever occurs. Thus, while aggression is repelled, what is free of aggression is invited inside. At the center of the dorje is a sphere that represents the immutable and indestructible nature of vajra, the truth of the teachings, the nature of the mind.

The protection provided by the Dorje Kasung is not purely physical but also includes the integrity of the declaration of the truth of egolessness itself.

The creation of the Dorje Kasung

The creation of the Dorje Kasung goes back to His Holiness the sixteenth Karmapa's first visit to North America in 1974, which was, as we have already stressed, a turning point in the way rituals and ceremonies were presented. A small number of students, who were called Vajra Guards at that time, helped to provide service and security for both the Karmapa and Chögyam Trungpa during this historic visit. After this visit, seeing the benefits of the mind training the activity provided, Chögyam Trungpa decided to keep the Dorje Kasung as an element in his teaching mandala.

A Kasung is one who protects (*sung*) the lineage or sacred command (*ka*). But it was quite unusual for Chögyam Trungpa to apply the term *kasung* to the functions and activities of the Dorje Kasung. In Tibet the term *kasung* has never been used to describe a human being, but rather a dharmapala, a spiritual being whose function is to protect the teachings.

David Rome becomes the head of the Kasung

When Chögyam Trungpa first established the Vajra Guard, he came up with a sort of military hierarchy that eventually included a number of different ranks and officers. The first leader of the Dorje Kasung was Gerry Haase, who was appointed the Dorje Dapön, or the Indestructible General. A few years later, David Rome was appointed the overall leader or commander of the Dorje Kasung. David Rome explained the conditions of his appointment: "I was Chögyam Trungpa's personal secretary.

Being a humble intellectual, I was ready for this kind of responsibility. Everyone wanted to see him. So my job was to act as a filter, which I tried to do as honestly as I could. Sometimes he wanted to see people, other times he thought it better to wait for the right moment. When the Kasung were created, I didn't like the idea and so I didn't take part. During the 1976 Seminary in Wisconsin, I was asked to teach a class. One day I was particularly depressed, so I decided to stay in my room. Because I was frightened they'd come and get me, I decided to drink enough Scotch to be sure that they'd leave me alone. The next day, there was going to be a big celebration. I was still feeling depressed and ashamed of myself and didn't want to go. My wife insisted and I finally went along, hoping I wouldn't be noticed. But Chögyam Trungpa saw me at once. He called to me, then in a very soft voice he asked my permission to 'undermine' me. I had no idea what he had in mind, but I said OK. Nothing ever happened—or so I thought until I realized years later that it was about one week after that conversation that he appointed me Dorje Kasung—head of the guards and 'Protector of the Sacred Command'—and instructed me that it would be my duty to remove any corrupt officials in the future, and then took me down to a cold dark room of the hotel late at night and made me call the Regent and inform him of all this, including that I would have to remove *him* if he ever went bad. So this was his way of undermining a bookish, shy Jewish young man—make him General of the Army!" David Rome thus became the head of the Kasung. He later was given the title Kasung Kyi Khyap, and the Vajra Guard became known as the Dorje Kasung.[4]

2. The Path of the Kasung

We have mentioned the Dorje Kasung several times in earlier chapters, to emphasize the mind training they received in order to develop their at-

---

4. Gerard Haase-Dubosc and John Perks were respectively appointed Dapön and Rupön. *Dapön* literally means "chief of place." It is the Tibetan word for "army general." *Rupön* means "regiment chief." The rank of Dapön is higher, directly followed by Rupön.

tention to the slightest details, and their sense of presence. Their role in the society Chögyam Trungpa created is also of interest.

This role was to become increasingly important. Beginning in 1978, Chögyam Trungpa held regular summer outdoor training programs with the senior members of the Dorje Kasung. These were called Magyal Pomra Encampments. It was during one such program in 1979 that the practice of oryoki was first introduced. It was also at an Encampment that Chögyam Trungpa introduced the use of a lhasang as a ceremony and purification. In this ceremony, juniper smoke is burned and offered to create a sacred space. A lhasang is often held at the beginning of a practice program. Chögyam Trungpa considered the Magyal Pomra Encampments of such significance that he invited all the members of the Vajradhatu Board of Directors, including the Regent and the Dorje Loppön, to participate in several of them.

We must now examine how being a Kasung opens a path into the heart of the teachings in a highly intimate and direct manner.

This path can be presented in three ways: learning to be, working directly with aggression, and providing service to the teacher.

Learning to be

The way of the Dorje Kasung exposes one of the basic characteristics of Buddhism and of the Shambhala vision: training your mind and finding your place in the mandala, or the kingdom, can be very direct and very simple. The main point is learning to be. As Chögyam Trungpa wrote: "There are all kinds of approaches toward being. Being good, being bad, being sensible, being crazy. Beatitude [be-attitude]. All kinds of notions of being. But when we talk about being in relation to awareness, we are talking about unconditional being. You just be. Without any questions about what you are being. It is an unconditional way of being."[5]

A member of the Dorje Kasung often had to stand or sit in a "cool

---

5. *The Path Is the Goal*, p. 35.

boredom, refreshing boredom, boredom like a mountain stream."[6] This would occur when a Dorje Kasung had a post, such as sitting outside of a lecture hall during a teacher's presentation, or sitting at the desk of a Shambhala center providing a presence in the evenings. Often, very little happened. A Dorje Kasung was to regard these situations, however, as practice, rather than just "hanging out." The instruction was that one should be alert rather than daydreaming, physically relaxed, ready for anything, but without expectations.

As described by James Gimian, one of the main leaders of the Dorje Kasung who worked closely with Chögyam Trungpa on this aspect of the teachings: "To my mind a lot of other teachers present Tibetan Buddhism basically as a religion—'If you do these things, you will be a good person.' That's not what Buddhism is about. Buddhism is about: you as a human being possess basic goodness. Everybody does. And it doesn't take mumbo jumbo for you to understand that—it takes hard work. That hard work has to be as familiar to you as your blood, not something laid on top of you. And Chögyam Trungpa tried to find ways to do that."[7] With the establishment of the Kasung, Chögyam Trungpa created what is certainly one of the profoundest forms of meditation in action.

Overcoming aggression

In his work with the Dorje Kasung, Chögyam Trungpa introduced the use of uniforms. This was in part purely practical. If you are going to have security personnel or even ushers, you need to identify them in some way. The use of uniforms has long been one way to enable a group providing service to stand out. For their in-town service duties, the Kasung wore a navy blue blazer, a white shirt, and gray pants or skirt. For some special events and also during the Magyal Pomra Encampments, the

---

6. *The Myth of Freedom*, p. 56.

7. Quoted in David Swick, *Thunder and Ocean: Shambhala and Buddhism in Nova Scotia* (Lawrencetown Beach, Nova Scotia: Pottersfield Press, 1996), p. 114.

Kasung wore a khaki uniform, which had obvious similarities to military wear. Chögyam Trungpa himself had a whole wardrobe of uniforms, which he loved to wear on many occasions, including some occasions when he gave a talk to senior students who had no affiliation with the Dorje Kasung.

Many people were shocked that Chögyam Trungpa wore uniforms and created them for members of the Kasung. There were many reasons for people to be suspicious of a spiritual path that seemed to have militaristic influences.

Chögyam Trungpa undoubtedly knew that he would awaken these kinds of feelings in people. In fact, he was interested in exploring people's relationship to their own aggression and wanted to work on how we experience conflict and then overcome it, with gentleness rather than aggression as a weapon. He also liked uniforms because they reminded him of monastic discipline. A monk's robes wipe away individual expression in dress and allow the wearer to rediscover a more naked simplicity, which is at the heart of all forms of discipline.

One day, he explained this in a marvelously intriguing way: "I feel extremely good that I have dressed up in a military costume this evening so that I can share my nakedness with you. This costume is part of my skin and my nakedness. It is the expression of my mind in some sense."[8]

A military uniform, however, also provides its wearer with a feeling of power. The point of Kasung practice, as taught by Chögyam Trungpa, is that this feeling of confidence and dignity should not degenerate into aggression, as is generally the case, but instead should become an opportunity to express genuineness and to serve others in a more authentic way.

In practical terms, wearing a Kasung uniform in a city center and having to uphold rules of behavior for others, such as not permitting them to casually enter a room while a talk was going on, meant that the Dorje Kasung often become the focus for people's irritation and other forms of conflict. The Kasung were often in a position of having to confront the

---

8. Chögyam Trungpa, remarks during a ceremony organized by the Kasung for his birthday, February 24, 1978, in Chögyam Trungpa, *True Command*.

aggression of those they had to turn away.[9] But the conflict or even violence the Kasung experiences is above all his or her own, one's own reaction to the irritation of others. Working with aggression and conflict in this way, one can learn to develop true gentleness.

In an environment devoted to the practice of mindfulness and awareness, the path of the Dorje Kasung can help one to connect with one's state of mind and recognize its nature.

Serving the teacher

One of the aspects of the path of the Dorje Kasung is to provide service to the teachers of the lineage. This expression of devotion is the very heart of vajrayana Buddhism. The lineage of the Trungpas is particularly known for its perfection of the practice of devotion and its reliance on devotion as the fuel or heart of the path.

The Trungpa lineage was founded by one of the disciples of a great Tibetan teacher named Trung Ma-se. Trung Ma-se had eleven heart disciples, called the "eight realized ones" and the "three idiots." The "idiots" were his closest disciples because they provided personal service. They were known for their devotion rather than their learnedness; thus they were called idiots. Among the three idiots was the first Trungpa, Künga Gyaltsen. As he was Trung Ma-se's attendant, he received the title "Trungpa," an honorific term meaning "he who is close to the teacher." By staying close to the teacher, the first Trungpa actually received a high level of instruction in that realm of learning that lies beyond words and is above all a direct experience. Living in the presence of a teacher is one of the most powerful sources of attainment. The path of the Dorje Kasung is intimately related to this tradition, which is at the heart of the Trungpa lineage. It brings together both extremely strict discipline and a certain freedom, which is part of the devotional path.

---

9. In addition to aggression, the other two poisons, or kleshas, are passion and ignorance. Aggression consists in rejecting what happens to you, while passion tries to attract what ignorance pretends not to see. The three poisons are all ways to avoid connecting with things as they are. The Kasung path particulary works on aggression.

As we have already said, being close to Chögyam Trungpa meant being exposed and open to the absolutely unexpected. So the Kasung were in the first row, close to that experience. One of them explained this beautifully: doing this work "was to be in the presence of such exquisite awareness that could come like a punch in the stomach or a kiss on the cheek."[10]

There are no breaks in this kind of service, either for the Kasung or for Chögyam Trungpa. He was available continuously, and his service to sentient beings was nonstop: "I want to share my world, right from the point when I arise from my bed and take my next in-breath or out-breath, from when you begin knocking at my door and come in to my bedroom. From that point until I lie down and fall asleep in the evening, you share my life. In the role of Kasung or Kusung, you have no restrictions on sharing my life at all. I regard it as a tremendous accomplishment, in some sense, that we can develop enlightened society and that the person who is leading that enlightened society does not have any privacy at all. . . . I have stretched myself out, revealed myself utterly without any reservations. There is no such thing as private life of the Dorje Dradül—none whatsoever."[11]

3. Encampment

Chögyam Trungpa started a specific summer outdoor training program for the Dorje Kasung, called the Magyal Pomra Encampment. This program was held from the beginning in tents, inspired by the Tibetan nomadic tradition, which included the practice of whole monasteries being set up in tents that moved from one area to another throughout much of the year.

In 1978, the first Encampment had thirty-five participants. The largest Encampment during Chögyam Trungpa's lifetime occurred in 1984, with three hundred twenty-five attending.[12]

---

10. Joe Rinehart, *The Iron Wheel*, August 1993, p. 12.

11. Chögyam Trungpa, *True Command*, vol. 1, p. 118.

12. While Chögyam Trungpa was in retreat for a year, this was the only public program he took part in. Thus, many students wanted to attend this Encampment.

The Encampment, a twenty-four-hour-a-day training experience, was an extremely intense opportunity for individuals to deepen their understanding of the path of the Dorje Kasung: "The Encampment provides a very profound education, and we should receive it properly and fully. Such an occasion is similar to entering a monastery and accomplishing your full ordination within ten days."[13]

The program lasted seven to nine days and was based on principles from the three yanas of the Buddhist path. The hinayana training corresponded to what is considered basic training at Encampment. This is designed to increase mindfulness and awareness. The main discipline is the practice of drill, or marching, which is done as an exercise to synchronize mind and body. Training in oryoki and other disciplines is also part of the experience at the Encampment. The second part corresponded to the mahayana, a feeling of relaxing into the discipline by adopting a broader perspective.

The vajrayana aspect of Encampment includes service to the teacher, which is an expression of loyalty and devotion, both basic qualities of vajrayana. In addition, some of the disciplines practiced at Encampment involved connecting directly with one's emotions and working to overcome hesitation and fear. During the third Encampment, in 1980, Chögyam Trungpa organized a skirmish between two teams. This has continued as a basic part of the Encampment format since that time, although there are occasionally more than two teams. A skirmish, as developed by Chögyam Trungpa, is a very direct way for all the participants to experience many aspects of conflict and aggression that otherwise remain conceptual. While many people might agree in principle that conflicts should be resolved without violence, this remains just a theory unless it is tested in real situations. During the first skirmish ever held at Encampment, Chögyam Trungpa appointed the Vajra Regent as the commander of one army and David Rome, the Kasung Kyi Khyap, as the other commander. Before the action began, Chögyam Trungpa asked each of the commanders to agree to a number of rules. The two opposing armies

---

13. Chögyam Trungpa, "Gentleness Comes from Harsh Training," August 1980, unpublished transcript of a talk given at the Magyal Pomra Encampment.

marched up into a series of highland meadows where the skirmish took place. Each participant had a certain number of bags of flour that they could use as weapons. When someone was hit with a flour bag, he or she was "dead" and had to remain out of action. There were other rules; for example, if the opposing team gave water to someone who had been hit, that person could join the opposing army. One rule, the most important rule, was only visible on the carbon copies of the document signed by the heads of the armies. Either commander could have noticed the rule, but neither did because it was hidden from them on the top copy they signed. During the battle, the two commanders were responsible for their armies' strategy, and the soldiers were expected to follow their commands. The Regent's strategy was very aggressive, and he had his army attack the other group. He had many hits with the flour bags and "killed" many of the opposing team. David Rome seemed to be quite lost and somewhat fearful in his approach, and, as a result, he marched his army into the hands of the opposing team, where they were largely slaughtered. A small band from his army did escape the first battle and spent hours trekking around a mountainside, trying to avoid capture or death. In the end, they staged a final, futile assault on the Regent's army and were all slaughtered. Watching one's comrades falling down in the midst of the hazy flour smoke was quite realistic and devastating.

At the end of the day, following the final battle in the skirmish, a huge rainbow filled the entire meadow where the last action took place. Chögyam Trungpa had spent the afternoon on a rock there watching the drama unfold. He took all of the Dorje Kasung back down to the main camp, where in a downpour that soaked everyone, he discussed the result of the day's skirmish. Chögyam Trungpa told the assembled students that in fact they had all lost. They had missed the point of the skirmish. At this point, he revealed the hidden rule, which was the fundamental message he was trying to convey. This rule read: "Lack of proper strategy, causing greater loss of life, is cause for loss of battle." Then he explained to everyone that the dictionary should be rewritten and the word *war* defined as a victory over aggression.

This was a moment of profound shock for everyone present. Many of those assembled started sobbing, recognizing the aggression they had put into the exercise and the problems they had overcoming it. Chögyam Trungpa told everyone that they would have to go back the next day and conduct the entire skirmish again. People were exhausted, but he was not interested in how tired they were. Indeed, both armies marched back up the hill the next morning and conducted a skirmish without a shot being fired.

In later years, strategy progressed and there were many more skirmishes, some with no "killing" and some with minimal "loss of life." However, the first and most fundamental message, that victory over war could not come out of aggression, was perhaps the most profound.

4. An Army Dedicated to Wakefulness and Helping Others

The Dorje Kasung is doubtless one of the most misunderstood and controversial projects that Chögyam Trungpa instigated. The existence of the Kasung sometimes gave rise to concern, especially from people outside the community who did not know what the point of the Kasung organization was. There were attacks in the media on Vajradhatu and Chögyam Trungpa personally, based largely on the misperception of the Dorje Kasung. Seen from the exterior, practitioners dressed in army uniforms and marching in formation seemed a long way away from the Buddhist principles of gentleness and compassion. They recalled people's worst memories of violence and fanaticism.

But in reality, the Kasung embodied a form of bodhisattva activity.

Nevertheless, we must still recognize the provocative nature of using a military uniform and discipline in this way. In the hands of a less wise or less skillful teacher, an organization like the Dorje Kasung could indeed become a miscarriage of the true nature of the Buddhist path. But by now, it must be quite clear to the reader that this approach of "standing ego on its head" was precisely how Chögyam Trungpa taught in many situations. He used the most deeply rooted preconceptions and forms within Western culture to communicate basic Buddhist principles. Chögyam Trungpa was far from naive and was never the prisoner of the sort of fine sentiments that often conceal cowardice.

In the hands of a great tantric master such as Chögyam Trungpa, membership in an army thus transfigured by the recognition of basic goodness could lead a practitioner to a nonreligious monastic experience. Like soldiers, as we have noted, monks also wear uniforms and lead a highly disciplined existence. During Encampment, each practitioner's life was simplified and reduced to the essential.

Even more radically, Chögyam Trungpa saw that wisdom can exist, at least latently, within even the most extreme form, such as the military. Aspects of the military, such as the creation of such an ordered and precise organization with a clear chain of command and respect for power and hierarchy—all these qualities can be very powerful in an activity such as disaster relief or peacekeeping. This indeed seems to have been one of the ideas that Chögyam Trungpa would have liked to pursue in the future. What once seemed to many as one of Chögyam Trungpa's stranger fancies now appears to be coming true, as the role of many armies is now to help others.

Chapter Twenty-two

DEPARTURE
FOR NOVA SCOTIA

No other place will be suitable but here alone, Nova Scotia, where we can actually develop our sense of fearlessness, and gentleness can be practiced perpetually.
— CHÖGYAM TRUNGPA[1]

As early as the summer of 1976, while introducing the Shambhala teachings, Chögyam Trungpa told some of his close students that he had decided to move to Nova Scotia, because he considered that the headquarters of Vajradhatu International should be set up there. When people heard this, many of them expressed disbelief. It seemed a totally unlikely decision.

His students did not know it yet, but in the years to come a large number of them would move to that isolated province on the Atlantic coast of Canada, which is considered to be one of the economically less fortunate and most socially conservative areas of the North American continent.

---

1. Chögyam Trungpa, "Community Talk," Halifax, October 3, 1982, unpublished.

1. Integrating Practice into the Local Economy and Politics

Although Chögyam Trungpa did want to create a world for his students that would fully integrate practice and study with everyday life, he did not want to set up a closed community where all his Buddhist students lived together apart from the rest of the world—in a small village, for example. On the other hand, insisting that all practitioners live normally within the larger society, setting aside time and trying to earn enough money to study and practice during vacations, seemed limited and dualistic to him. This would mean that on the one hand there was the sacred world, which you went to when you had enough time and money, and on the other hand the world of samsara, with which you had to compromise a little. Chögyam Trungpa wanted his students to mix with the local life of where they lived. Buddhism would not be of help to others if it was practiced only in isolated hermitages by the happy few.

In other words, Chögyam Trungpa was faced with a dilemma: should his practitioners be Buddhists discreetly and in private, or should they seek to help the society in which they lived and try to transform it?

Chögyam Trungpa chose the latter alternative. But he then realized that such a project was not workable in Boulder, Colorado, in the middle of the American West. Even though the community in 1979 included more than fifteen hundred members, or one inhabitant out of seventy in a city of approximately one hundred thousand, the Buddhist community could not have any tangible influence on civil society. How was it possible to introduce the Shambhala vision into a town like Boulder, so devoted to pleasure and comfort? And how could they establish the Kingdom of Shambhala in such a huge country as the United States— where, he sensed, the increasing climate of karmic aggression would make it impossible, beyond a point, to make a difference?

Everything that might seem disadvantageous about Nova Scotia—the poor climate, poverty, isolation, few sources of entertainment—was in fact an advantage. In fact, it reminded him of his life in Tibet. Given that

Tibet as a whole is a fairly isolated part of the world, eastern Tibet, where Chögyam Trungpa was raised, was particularly remote, a fact that helped incubate the spiritual tradition to which he was heir. As the Nova Scotia population was fairly small, with just under a million inhabitants in the entire province, it would be possible to achieve something significant. New immigrants would gradually discover that living in a place that, Chögyam Trungpa felt, was characterized by an open, gentle quality suited to a contemplative lifestyle was an opportunity to bring the teachings to life. As Chögyam Trungpa put it: "It's not like Florida. You might have to relate with reality much more so than you have ever had to."[2]

2. Moving to Nova Scotia

Chögyam Trungpa first visited the province of Nova Scotia in June 1977. The weather was often dull, gray, and rainy, as is typical in this region. Part of the reason for the visit was to evaluate whether this was really the place to move to—and to relocate the international headquarters of his organization as well. During the trip Chögyam Trungpa traveled incognito as an elegantly dressed prince of Bhutan, which was somewhat perplexing for the rest of his traveling party. Nevertheless, people played along with this disguise, or manifestation, one might say in his case. At dinner, the women accompanying him often wore long dresses and white gloves, and the men dressed in tuxedos.

The party did not stay more than a night in any one place, because they had decided to tour the entire province. They received a warm welcome everywhere. Jan Watson wrote: "I will never forget this woman in Ingonish Beach who opened up her hotel a weekend earlier than usual because we were going to be there. It was a little place, and she was so hospitable and

---

2. Quoted in David Swick, *Thunder and Ocean: Shambhala and Buddhism in Nova Scotia* (Lawrencetown Beach, Nova Scotia: Pottersfield Press, 1996), p. 27. Remarks of Chögyam Trungpa in this book were taken from an unpublished manuscript; all rights reserved. Used by permission of Diana J. Mukpo.

sweet—she got her mother's silver for us, polished it up, and laid on this beautiful spread. There was a lot of that kind of thing."[3]

Chögyam Trungpa was delighted by the visit. It confirmed his decision. In Nova Scotia he had discovered an atmosphere of gentleness and simplicity, qualities he was trying to nurture in his presentation of the Shambhala teachings. After another short trip to Nova Scotia in April 1979, he made an announcement at a meeting with senior Shambhala students:

> When I first landed in Nova Scotia, I couldn't touch the ground even—it felt too shaky. This time I stepped out on the road, knelt down, and felt the soil—a slightly papal approach maybe: feeling the earth. It was a well-paved road—still, it felt very good. The psychological mentalities of a place are affected by weather, of course. We will take that into account, but we could extend that logic— even if there is severe weather, we still could feel goodness with our palms. So it was a very grounding experience. . . . You can't feel this anywhere else—except that I would feel the same thing if I went back to Tibet and touched the side of a mountain, but I never had such an experience outside of Tibet before. Throughout our journey, I found the island [Nova Scotia] is connected with Tibet. . . . There doesn't seem to be any resistance as far as the psychic level, and the people are very cooperative. In fact, they seem to be starved and need some further energy to be put on them. I felt a general sense of longing for something else to happen. I checked several times, maybe a hundred times when we were there. I looked to see if this sense was my own invention or actually happening. My conclusion was that it is happening on the ground itself.[4]

The situation seemed promising to him. He conceived of the future in Nova Scotia as a marriage of the local culture with the culture of Shambhala. Each had something to give the other. Not all of his students were

---

3. Jan Watson, ibid., p. 10.

4. Ibid., p. 26. From an unpublished manuscript; all rights reserved. Used by permission of Diana J. Mukpo.

eager to embrace this view. For many, moving to a remote corner of the continent felt like going into exile.

Nevertheless, there were some who were ready for this challenge. At Chögyam Trungpa's urging, a group of thirteen students settled in Halifax the next year and opened the first meditation center there; other students began slowly relocating, some of them to smaller towns spread around the province. Six months after the first Buddhist pioneers moved to Nova Scotia, Chögyam Trungpa traveled there to give a seminar, which was attended by more than one hundred students from around North America. The first Canadian Dharmadhatu Conference was held as part of this seminar, which took place in the far northern corner of the province at the Keltic Lodge in Ingonish, on Cape Breton Island.

In 1982, Chögyam Trungpa's wife and several very senior teachers moved to the province. Diana Mukpo stayed for several years and then returned to Boulder to spend more time with her husband. During the time that Diana Mukpo was living in the province, Chögyam Trungpa traveled there a number of times. He spent most of 1984 in retreat in Mill Village, a small town about two hours outside of Halifax. At the end of this year of retreat, Chögyam Trungpa returned to Colorado with the intention of completing business in Boulder and then moving back up to Halifax. Diana Mukpo accompanied him when he made his move to Nova Scotia in the fall of 1986. In 1985, the Vajra Regent Ösel Tendzin and his family moved to Halifax at the request of Chögyam Trungpa to help remodel and expand the Shambhala center there. By this time, several members of the Vajradhatu Board of Directors were already settled in Nova Scotia.

In 1986, Chögyam Trungpa was planning to leave Boulder in the fall and spend a year in Halifax. Throughout the last few months that he was in Boulder, he seemed more than ready to depart. He did not stay till the end of the Vajradhatu Seminary, leaving the presentation of the vajrayana teachings entirely to the Vajra Regent and the Loppön. The Regent had traveled back to Rocky Mountain Dharma Center to spend time at Seminary.

In early September, having spent a few weeks preparing, Chögyam Trungpa decided to leave rather suddenly for Nova Scotia. Some students tried to get him to wait a little bit longer, but he was determined that the time was right. He arrived in Nova Scotia in early September and a few weeks later, he was rushed to the hospital with a heart attack. He never fully recovered from this and died in Halifax seven months later, on April 4, 1987.

During the year before his move, he had traveled widely throughout the United States on his last teaching tour, encouraging everyone to come with him to Nova Scotia. It was his last teaching, which he repeated everywhere: "Come and live in Nova Scotia."

As David Swick remarks in *Thunder and Ocean*, his book devoted to the life of the Buddhist community in Nova Scotia, moving to a new country and a new town is an exhausting experience. When several hundred people make the same effort, for the same reason, it is a major event.[5] The arrival of this new community did not go unnoticed by the inhabitants, but the Buddhists' desire to adapt and to respect the country won over many of their Canadian neighbors. However, the new arrivals still had to face a number of problems. Although people were polite and somewhat welcoming, they also were reluctant to fully accept the community until people had proved themselves to be genuinely committed to life in Nova Scotia. It was also extremely difficult for many of the sangha to find work in a small economy that was not undergoing a great deal of growth at that time.

Chögyam Trungpa's vision and inspiration can be seen in this excerpt from "Farewell to Boulder," a poem he wrote on October 25, 1982, while he was visiting Nova Scotia:

> It is time for us to change to a new planet,
> Fresh planet,
> Extra Planet.
> It is time for us to go elsewhere,
> Where donkeys can talk,
> Horses can play,
> Dogs can run.
> It is time to go where sunshine is not all that frequent,

5. Ibid., p. 15.

It is time to avoid the Flatirons,
It is time to avoid ponderosa,
It is time to come closer to the ocean,
It is time to take pride in the small island,
It is time to be small,
It is not time to be big,
It is time to be modest,
It is time to move to Nova Scotia,
It is time to enjoy the crescent moon, at least a
    croissant!
It is time to be human being.
It is time to be.
Be in Nova Scotia,
Be in little island,
Be in fresh air.
Let us be natural,
Let us not ask any questions,
Let us drop all the questions,
Let us be,
Be, be, be.

Hail to the discovery!
We have discovered something very ordinary
But we have experienced something extraordinary.
Let us be,
Let us discover,
Let us celebrate,
Let us appreciate,
Let us celebrate that we have discovered insignificant
    island,
Let us appreciate the ordinariness of it,
Let us celebrate! [6]

---

6. Chögyam Trungpa, excerpt from "Farewell to Boulder (1982)" in *Royal Songs* (Halifax: Trident Publications, 1995). Copyright © 1995 by Diana J. Mukpo. Used by permission.

This poem gives us very direct access to Chögyam Trungpa's motivations. In the last few years before the move, he had made an enormous effort, creating the Court, setting up Vajradhatu, teaching constantly, meeting thousands of students, and establishing a variety of structures. The result was laying a solid foundation for the future of Buddhism in North America but also creating a certain amount of bureaucratic neurosis. This poem is a call to step beyond this condition and recover a down-to-earth simplicity.

There was a link between the way Chögyam Trungpa experienced Scotland vis-à-vis England at the end of the 1960s and how he experienced Nova Scotia vis-à-vis the United States in the 1980s. In both New Scotland (Nova Scotia) and old Scotland, the landscape and the people provide a kind of primal and deeply felt setting that is in sharp contrast to the dominant cultures of England and the United States. Nova Scotia, although outside of the United States, is still an English-speaking place on the same North American continent. He wanted to ground his North American presence in the solid, somewhat undeveloped world of Nova Scotia, which had not yet been lost to an overly sophisticated and artificial culture.

Chögyam Trungpa may have drawn on elements of just such a culture in the 1970s in order to build a universe dedicated to enlightenment. He employed lawyers to set up corporations, professors to open a university, doctors to launch a new therapeutic approach, and so on. But in the 1980s, he felt rather frustrated by what he had thus far achieved. Cultural neuroses such as personal ambition, or the artificial character of human relations, had not gone away.

Unlike many of his previous poems, this one does not stress the importance of conquering and adopting a wider vision. Instead, it is rather modest: "It is time to be small, / It is not time to be big, / It is time to be modest." The crescent moon invites us to enjoy something young and not yet fully developed. Moving to a new country was a call to make a new departure.

But such a project is not really in opposition to the previous approaches; it completes them. It is like the last piece of the jigsaw puzzle that at last allows us to see Chögyam Trungpa's work clearly. His desire to transform the West by bringing out its dignity, like pounding oil from a sesame seed, here found its full expression. Even if not all of his students moved to Nova Scotia, the fact that such a vision determined the direction of his teaching was an inspiration for everyone. One way or another, being a student of Chögyam Trungpa means having a special relationship with this country.

Chapter Twenty-three

SPIRITUAL MASTER
AND MONARCH

I love all of you very dearly. You might wonder how that is possible since I don't spend time with each one of you individually; nonetheless, I think of each one of you always.

Sometimes I may not even know your name, but I know your face: I know your gaze; I know your expressions; I know when you are making a sad or a happy face. I know all of you, and I am so proud and appreciative of all of you. I personally feel so fortunate that we are able to be together as a community.[1]

—CHÖGYAM TRUNGPA

1. The Teacher Is One with the Nature of Each Being's Mind

At the end of an interview I had with David Sable, one of Chögyam Trungpa's students, he told me that, in his opinion, the written and spoken teachings of Chögyam Trungpa represent only ten or twenty percent of what he manifested. For David Sable, the deepest and most intense way of learning about the dharma was quite simply being with Rinpoche, even for a short instant. Chögyam Trungpa was the living symbol of the dharma.

---

1. Chögyam Trungpa, "Shambhala Day Address, 1982," *Vajradhatu Sun*, April/May 1982, p. 28.

In contrast to the Western view, symbolism in tantric Buddhism is the natural expression of reality. It does not describe anything but the present moment. It allows us even deeper contact with what is. The teachings are transparent, in easy reach; nothing is hidden or secret—everything is fully displayed. Such is the meaning of mahamudra, the culmination of the teachings of the Kagyü school, for which "explanations . . . speak in terms of symbolism, since *mudra* means symbol. But on this level, symbols do not exist as such; the sense of experience ceases to exist. What one perceives is actual reality. That is why it is called *ma*-*ha*mudra, the *great* symbol. It is the symbol born within, wisdom born within."[2]

From this point of view, meeting with Chögyam Trungpa meant experiencing the totality of the teaching. He was a living buddha. It is always possible to publish books, but in the end the teachings that can be expressed in words are not the fundamental expression of truth. There is nothing to say. Buddhism is quite simply a way of seeing things as they are—even if, paradoxically, the Buddha's words were preserved in numerous volumes to describe this simplicity beyond fabrication.

The master is the embodiment of enlightenment. As Dilgo Khyentse explained: "He is the lord of all the mandalas; on the outer level he personifies the Three Jewels, on the inner level, the Three Roots, and on the secret level, the three kayas, or bodies of enlightenment."[3] He embodies limitless love for the infinite wealth of the living present. His presence is constant, yet flexible and alive. To see him is to be in contact with space itself.

When you went into Chögyam Trungpa's office, his bedroom, or the room where he was lecturing, whether it was to give him a glass of water, meet with him, or spend the night with him, or even if you were standing by the doorway through which he was to walk or sitting beside him at dinner, there was a possibility of experiencing that living openness in

2. Chögyam Trungpa, in Herbert V. Guenther and Chögyam Trungpa, *The Dawn of Tantra*, p. 36.

3. Dilgo Khyentse, *Au seuil de l'éveil*, trans. Padmakara Translation Committee (Peyzac-le-Moustier: Éditions Padmakara, 1991), p. 80.

which the slightest tendency of closing our consciousnesses seemed out of place.

Being with someone who is so free from conceptual mind makes us aware of our own prisons, our habitual thoughts, our reflexive behavior. When faced with absolute love, we realize that we do not know how to love. In his presence, the slightest inauthentic action or thought came to the surface and could be abandoned.

Carolyn Gimian told me this about her experience of being in the presence of Chögyam Trungpa: "My first habitual tendency was to feel small and inadequate, but over and over he would cut through that state of mind and instead make me feel wonderful. He made you feel bigger, kinder, and better than you thought you were. When you felt so accepted, loved, and empowered, you could drop a lot of the inadequacies and misconceptions."

The Loppön remembers one of the first conversations he had with Chögyam Trungpa, at the beginning of the 1970s. He had brought along a list of the things he wanted to ask him about, in particular whether he should become a vegetarian and whether it was important to be celibate. It was eleven at night when he was ushered in, and just after the interview had begun, Diana Mukpo came into the bedroom, barely clothed, saying: "Chökyi, are you coming to bed?"

That instant saw the collapse of all the concepts that the Loppön had projected onto Chögyam Trungpa and the meaning of being a Buddhist. He realized that the communication between them had been on a deeper level than in a normal conversation. He noticed that Chögyam Trungpa always had a fascinating ability to sharpen his students' karma. Coincidences like this happened all around him, as though the environment grew more dynamic when he was there. In his presence, the situation taught people as much as the teacher did. Or perhaps it would be more accurate to say: in his presence, you became aware of the way reality is constantly teaching you.

Richard John, another of his students, put this very well: "You could experience Trungpa Rinpoche's compassion by being in the room. Most of what you would perceive, in the room with him, was a vacuum. There would be this tremendous sense of presence, but there was nothing happening. It was sort of the opposite from our usual experience. Usually there's a lot happening, but no presence. And he wouldn't do anything; he would just be there."[4]

In his presence, by all accounts, one was stripped naked. It was an experience of surprising intensity and poignant truth that made people aware of their own aspiration to become their true selves and be free from suffering. Once one is opened to this possibility, it is difficult to pretend that nothing has happened.

Chögyam Trungpa quite movingly described this experience of losing the ground beneath your feet: "Terrifying! You have lost the whole ground. . . . There is the sense that your badges and your uniform have been taken away from you. . . . You are suspended in nowhere. That's the shunyata experience. No ground to walk on, no ground to work with. . . . So the whole process is very scary. You could say that it is a dance, if you like. I'm afraid it is not a particularly musical one."[5]

The teacher makes us drop all our masks. Beyond all you can know or learn lies the ultimate source of wisdom. Chögyam Trungpa entered deeply into the lives of those who met him. Even if you were with him for only a few minutes, he managed to strip you bare, without the slightest regard for social or cultural conventions. This book will have successfully conveyed who Chögyam Trungpa was if it manages to make its readers feel, even for an instant, the living sensation of space in its "ultimate nakedness." In this nakedness "you begin to feel you are just a live brain with no tissue around it, exposed on a winter morning to the cold air. It's *so* penetrating, irritating, and sharp."[6]

To put it another way, to meet a genuine teacher such as Chögyam Trungpa is to be into direct contact with the cosmic mirror: the very vastness from which everything emerges. Generally, all we can experience is the contrast between this absolute space and our confusion. Such a space

---

4. Quoted in David Swick, *Thunder and Ocean: Shambhala and Buddhism in Nova Scotia* (Lawrencetown Beach, Nova Scotia: Pottersfield Press, 1996), p. 34.

5. *Glimpses of Shunyata*, pp. 18–19.

6. *Illusion's Game*, p. 120.

exposes the pathetic way we fight to establish solid ground, something we can hang on to. Such an experience makes many people extremely nervous. But after a time, if we suspend our preconceptions, then the chance of connecting with the world appears. Such a leap is possible—a leap beyond the reference points of our own confusion.

If we keep our head and shoulders straight, as Chögyam Trungpa constantly asked us to do, and we look directly at the space manifested by the teacher, then each of his or her movements and gestures becomes a transmission. Practice and the path simply consist in learning how to face up to the movements of such a rich space.

Even if Chögyam Trungpa constantly changed, altering himself according to the situations he found himself in, metamorphosing over the years, there was always something immutable in him: this quality of continuous transmission. Even in the most mundane situations, he paid attention to everything and everyone.

One day, Chögyam Trungpa visited New York to give some teachings there. He was staying in an apartment in Greenwich Village. The day he left, Irene Woodard, a student who was performing one of her first shifts of service as a Kusung, had the job of simply staying by the elevator to keep it on the right floor. She was supposed to see to it that when Chögyam Trungpa left the apartment, he would not have to wait. She recalls, "I was feeling so pathetic and a bit ridiculous just standing there holding the elevator. Then suddenly everyone came out of the apartment and Chögyam Trungpa walked up to the end of the corridor where I was waiting. He got into the elevator, stopped, looked at me, then kissed me. Then the others followed him in, the elevator went down, and I just stayed there alone, completely stupefied."

He had an astonishing ability to pay attention to everyone, to read the phenomenal world like a wide open book, and to have the presence of mind to do whatever was required.

When you first met him, he was often gentle and kind, or even seductive and enticing, according to the situation. You then felt privileged. Authentic communication of an extraordinary quality was taking place.

But if you started expecting things of him, clinging to the relationship or defining it, Chögyam Trungpa could then become elusive and inaccessible. You might come calling constantly, but every time, a Kusung would tell you that Chögyam Trungpa was busy. Some people projected onto others the responsibility for their not being able to see Rinpoche. For example, they would maintain that the Kusung on duty was responsible.

But as Chögyam Trungpa explained about the relationship with the teacher: "If you stand in his way, you are asking for destruction. If you have doubts about him, he takes advantage of your doubts. If you are too devotional or too dependent on blind faith, he will shock you. He takes the ironical aspect of the world very seriously. He plays practical jokes on a larger scale—devastating ones."[7]

Being with him meant dropping your masks and giving yourself up to this ultimate nakedness that is the meaning of the path.

2. Contact with All Aspects of Students' Lives

Chögyam Trungpa manifested himself like a king. He knew the details of all of his students' lives—in other words, what was going on in the lives of several thousand people. Michael Root, one of the members of the Vajradhatu board, remembers an event when he realized this.[8] Before giving a Vajrayogini abhisheka, the teacher must give a special tantric name to each of those who are about to receive the initiation. Many teachers simply put out a bowl full of small slips of paper with different names written on them, and each student upon completing the abhisheka picks a name from the bowl. Often, Chögyam Trungpa would ask everyone to arrive before the initiation began, and he would see each person for just a few seconds. After they walked through the room, he would write down a name to be calligraphed and given to them. Instead of doing either, this time, Chögyam Trungpa simply looked at the list of names. Then he

7. *Crazy Wisdom*, p. 174.

8. This occurred in October 1985, at Karma Dzong, Boulder, during the last Vajrayogini abhisheka that Chögyam Trungpa gave in the United States.

started talking about each person, mentioning the moment when he had met them and how they had all turned out since. Michael Root was amazed by the extent of his memory and knowledge.

Chögyam Trungpa explained the reason for this during a Kalapa Assembly: "I have earned my relationship with each of you, with everybody in this room without exception. We had our relationships. We have talked together, worked together, cultivated our relationship together— each of you."[9]

Such is the role of the master warrior. He "expresses intense interest in the activities of his students—from the level of what they have for dinner up to the level of their state of mind, whether they are happy or sad, joyful or depressed."[10] If the teacher does not have this intimate relationship with his students, then his teaching, however powerful or precise it is, will probably lead only to an accumulation of knowledge. It can benefit the students, but it cannot overcome the apparent solidity of the ego.

How can one avoid falling into spiritual materialism, without that intimate relationship with the dharma that only an accomplished teacher can offer?

Chögyam Trungpa was involved in minute details of his students' lives at times. On occasion, he liked telephoning a student to wish him or her a cheerful (not a happy) birthday. He often sent his students presents for the big occasions in their lives: a wedding, an important birthday, or the birth of a child. He took care of them. He loved them.

It is an extremely moving and profound experience when a being of such attainment recognizes you as a real friend and not just as a poor soul lost in the suffering of samsara. It's also disarming, because it transcends one's *ideas* about how a spiritual teacher will manifest. The intense humanity that Chögyam Trungpa demonstrated was in itself a very powerful gift

---

9. Chögyam Trungpa, *1978 Kalapa Assembly Transcripts* (Boulder: Vajradhatu Publications), p. 182.

10. *Shambhala: The Sacred Path of the Warrior* (Shambhala Library, 2003), p. 210.

3. An Unconditional and Personal Love

One of his first students, who later became a student of Dilgo Khyentse Rinpoche and then studied with several other teachers, spoke to me one day about Chögyam Trungpa and told me: "No other teacher's ever loved me like he did."

Chögyam Trungpa had an astonishing capacity to love all his students. He had a personal relationship with all of them, and many of them became his friends, or even his lovers. A journalist with the *Boulder Daily Camera* interviewed Chögyam Trungpa and asked him about what he called his "alleged sexual promiscuity." Wasn't it shocking for a spiritual master to behave in such a way? Chögyam Trungpa replied that as far his personal relationships were concerned, he was having a love affair with all his students.[11] He appreciated them so much. He was really interested in their lives. At the end of each Seminary, as in this example from 1979, he told them: "I love you very much. You have been extraordinary students, every one of you, which is almost unbelievable. It is fantastic, and I appreciate it a lot."[12] When he made remarks such as this, many people in the audience were moved to tears.

They wept because they knew it was true. Everyone felt loved in a deeper way than they had ever experienced before.

Such love asks for nothing; it is an unconditional acceptance of what everyone is.

Karen Lavin, one of the Sangyum, remembers a day when she was in a difficult situation and Chögyam Trungpa asked her how she was. She replied, "I'll just have to be brave." He looked at her with infinite gentleness and said, "No, you'll just have to be yourself."

This concrete love, so close to the reality of the dharma, is the main reason so many people decided to become his student and practice the ways of buddhadharma and of the warrior in the Shambhala teachings.

---

11. Quoted in Carolyn Rose Gimian, "Editor's Afterword," in Chögyam Trungpa, *Great Eastern Sun*, p. 222.

12. Chögyam Trungpa, *1979 Seminary Transcripts: Vajrayana* (Boulder: Vajradhatu Publications), p. 68.

For the first time in their lives, they felt loved for what they were and discovered a real possibility of truly being themselves. Beyond any religious conviction, they would learn to be human.

As his son wrote: "When Chögyam Trungpa taught, you always had the impression that he was speaking directly to you. . . . Even if he was talking to hundreds of people, everyone there would leave thinking that Rinpoche had talked about their situation."[13] Such a love is unattached to any norm, rule, or convention. When faced with a love that demands nothing, except that you be what you are, everyone is naturally and almost miraculously pushed into giving the best of themselves.

In our world, Chögyam Trungpa's love and goodness were a miraculous experience. As La Rochefoucauld wrote: "Nothing is rarer than true goodness; those who believe they have it generally have only complacency and weakness."[14] In Chögyam Trungpa, you could see flesh-and-blood goodness. It had nothing to do with our usual images of it.

Chögyam Trungpa's love for his students encompassed the compassion we find in the mahayana. His love was all the more vast and powerful because, in tantric terms, it lay beyond both samsara and nirvana. Chögyam Trungpa did not have the slightest embarrassment about anybody's psychological misery or confusion. He was extraordinarily penetrating and ready for anything.

4. A Man in Constant Transformation

When he arrived in the United States, Chögyam Trungpa was thirty-one but looked eighteen. Two years later, he looked thirty-five. He transformed according to the situation. His voice changed, becoming less measured and refined, and more direct and down-to-earth, like the Americans he lived with. Chögyam Trungpa could lose or put on twenty pounds with little effort.

---

13. The Sawang Ösel Rangdröl Mukpo, forward to *Le coeur du sujet* (French edition of *The Heart of the Buddha*) (Paris: Éditions du Seuil, 1993), p. 8.

14. La Rochefoucauld, *Maximes*, p. 481.

In his early years, he displayed an unrivaled brilliance, finding new ways to transform confusion and speak in an effective way. His seminars of the time were gems struck with a real freedom. He was charming, tender, and accessible.

In the mid-1970s, the introduction of the Shambhala vision and the creation of the Court changed him. He manifested as a king, a completely regal presence.

Beginning around that time, spending casual time with Chögyam Trungpa became more difficult and infrequent. He continued to teach extensively, and people had access to him in various official or service roles, such as being members of the Dorje Kasung. But he no longer "hung out" with people, except on rare occasions.

In 1980, the year that the sixteenth Karmapa was dying from stomach cancer, Chögyam Trungpa's health also began to decline, and he was injured in a fall down the back stairs at the Kalapa Court. He insisted on continuing with official duties such as teaching at the Kalapa Assembly and the Vajradhatu Seminary, but other meetings and celebrations were cut back or canceled. When the annual report was presented at the Shambhala New Year in 1980, Vajra Regent Ösel Tendzin explained: "As we know, this year has produced such shock. . . . The Vajracarya, who introduced us to the noble path of the dharma, has been in very poor health."

Talking about Chögyam Trungpa's health is extremely difficult, in that he showed few of the normal reactions to illness. For instance, his approach to illness was never based primarily on trying to cure himself or prolong his life. As his private physician, Dr. Mitchell Levy, explained: "The most important aspect of Rinpoche's approach to his own health was that he identified fundamental healthiness or well-being as separate from physical well-being. He often talked of 'basic healthiness' and manifested this in a very clear manner. Although his body appeared to be quite ill at times, he was able to communicate a fundamental sense of healthiness, even in the midst of minor and major illness. For him, it seemed that the healing process was involved with making contact with this purity or healthiness first, and then following the advice of physicians or taking medication. This had a huge impact on the manner in which a physician would deal with him. He was not really asking to be 'cured' of anything.

Instead, it was a process of working together with physicians to manifest 'basic healthiness.'"

In 1984, Chögyam Trungpa spent a year in retreat with a few senior students. During this time, he manifested states of mind that were unusual, and, from a normal standpoint, he was somewhat inaccessible for periods of time. Some people believed that he was going to leave his body. Many students began to fear he would die. They consulted with a number of senior Tibetan teachers. From their viewpoint, Chögyam Trungpa, like many great yogis of the past, was out of touch with people around him because he was communicating with another realm—the realm of the dakinis, female deities who represent enlightened energies. Chögyam Trungpa's students were encouraged to do various practices, including the chanting of extensive liturgies, to encourage him to remain on the human plane.

At the end of the year of retreat, Chögyam Trungpa did in fact return to an ordinary state of relating with his students and his world. He came out of retreat and resumed his demanding schedule of teaching. Nevertheless, throughout the last years of his life, his diction and gestures remained quite slow. His way of speaking, which had been so thick with metaphor and brilliant with logic and meaning, took a more austere or pithy form. Each word became an expression of silence surrounded by an ocean of space. Though he was a master of oral invention, playing with language in a refined way, he generally stopped giving long teachings. These changes were difficult for many of Chögyam Trungpa's students to understand. Apparently, superficially he was losing his physical capacities. Dying did not frighten him at all. He had in fact always said that he would not be with his students for very long, and that without their practice and efforts he would have died long ago.

On an outer level, Chögyam Trungpa was suffering from the results of many years of excessive alcohol consumption, as well as the results of refusing to pay attention to how much he slept or make any kind of personal comfort into his reference point. His wife talked about how painful it was to see him sacrifice himself in this way. She did not see it as related to an "addiction" problem but rather that Chögyam Trungpa gave himself completely to accomplishing his task of communicating the dharma to people in the West.

On the other hand, it is not possible to truly explain the life of such a person and how he transformed logically, medically, or pathologically. Chögyam Trungpa was not bound by such limits. He shattered them and broke away from convenient characterizations. Especially for a Western audience, trying to explain the behavior of a spiritual teacher in terms like his existing on another plane is not only difficult but also could easily fall into the very spiritual materialism that Chögyam Trungpa devoted his life to overcoming. Instead, it is more genuine and more helpful to describe the change in his teaching style in his later years simply and attentively. If we examine what was happening, it becomes clear that a spare purity of language was replacing his earlier passion for in-depth transmission of the details of the dharma. He spoke each word as though it were a complete thought during this period, so that one lost track of the continuity of a sentence or paragraph. Words seemed suspended in space. But the experience of his students, who managed to abandon themselves in the space thus created, was of a magnificent environment in which words became as pure as one of Buddha's sutras.

At this time, his connection with the Dorje Kasung became a more and more prominent part of his teaching, and in that connection, as well as his general embodiment of the Shambhala teachings, he chose to wear uniforms much more often and in more public situations. The striking power of his manifestation was intimidating. He entered directly into contact with situations, without the slightest word or concept. He changed all the time and never answered to his students' expectations. Nobody really understood him, because being with him meant losing the ground on which we are used to walking. It was necessary just to be there, with him, which was extremely difficult. At the end of his life, Chögyam Trungpa sometimes remained for hours without apparently doing anything, simply manifesting a presence that was as full as it was disorienting.

He lived in a way that surpassed all conventions. He would not sleep for several days, pushing his students to go beyond their usual limits. Then he would sleep for days nonstop.

To communicate with him properly, it was necessary to abandon all inhibitions and allow one's ego to be dissolved instantaneously: "The ninth yana, maha ati or ati yoga, is the final stage of the path. It is both the beginning and the end of the journey. It is not final in the sense that we have finished making a statement and we have nothing more to say, but final in the sense that we feel we have said enough. At this level, if there are any further words, they are the creations of space."[15]

There was no normal sense of logic or continuity. Being with Chögyam Trungpa surpassed all means of understanding, because everything about him revealed this space. He was not teaching the doctrine of dzogchen. But to be at his side meant being in the space of dzogchen. At once.

Total abandonment

The master reveals the master in us. Without a master, without a teacher, everything we learn is an impediment on the path to enlightenment and stops us from going beyond our usual understanding. Naropa, one of the founding masters of the Kagyü lineage, loved studying. He was very learned, having extensively studied the Buddhist literature, but he did not understand its true meaning. He had to go further. Chaos destroys this blockage. Chaos is nonsense, that which cannot be understood, a gap in our logic that we cannot make ours.

Tilopa asked his disciple Naropa to jump off the roof of a building, which resulted in severe injuries. Such a request makes no sense; it does not allow us to understand anything.

Naropa was one of the greatest Buddhist scholars of his time. But his teacher still had to shatter his ego into pieces before he could really understand. Similarly, but with perhaps less overtly shocking methods, Chögyam Trungpa showed his students how to be in the world without being trapped or trying to leave it behind: "In the tantric tradition, either the experience of life is regarded as an endless ocean, limitless sky, or else it is regarded as just one dot, one situation. Therefore, the idea of not-two, or advaita principle, is one of the most important principles in tantric Buddhism. It's not two. Not-two here does not only mean one; if you don't have two, you also don't have one, either. It's just 'no' rather than even 'not.' So nothing is left behind which might provide a source of a

---

15. *Journey without Goal* (2000), p. 133.

reference point or meditative indulgency or for that matter a source of disappointment at all. It's one value, which means no value."[16]

Chögyam Trungpa was the master of dissolving. The only way to be his student was to live with uncertainty, to make panic and the absence of ground your home. Authentic devotion starts with this gesture of abandonment in the present, and a commitment to work with it.

5. His Death and Continuing Presence

Chögyam Trungpa was increasingly unwell, but very few of his students saw this as a sign of his impending death. His physical appearance had changed so many times that many of his students thought this was just the latest "phase." His students did not really think that he could die, at least not for a long time.[17] He himself spoke many times about extending his life. For example, at the end of the 1985 Seminary, only two years before his death, he said: "Thank you very much, everybody. You have extended my longevity, for at least, I could say quite safely, ten more years."[18]

The cause of his death has been explained in various, not always consistent, ways. According to his personal physician, Dr. Mitchell Levy: "Rinpoche had a history of diabetes and high blood pressure, both of which are chronic diseases that can affect the body in a number of ways. On September 28, 1986, Rinpoche had a cardiorespiratory arrest from complications due to his diabetes and hypertension. Although he was successfully resuscitated from the initial cardiac arrest and lived for another six months after discharge from hospital, Rinpoche never fully regained his health. He

---

16. Chögyam Trungpa, "Zen and Tantra," Karmê Chöling, January 1974, second talk, unpublished.

17. It must be stressed that his wife quickly grasped the gravity of the situation. As she herself says, this no doubt reflects the difference in relationship between a spouse and a student. The latter is there primarily to try to understand the master's teachings.

18. Chögyam Trungpa, 1985 Seminary Transcripts: Vajrayana (Halifax: Vajradhatu Publications), p. 51.

died in April 1987 as a result of an overwhelming bacterial infection." According to this physician, "Alcohol was not the main cause of his death." But in others' opinion, Chögyam Trungpa's health had diminished over the years and worsened because of his heavy drinking.

According to his wife, Diana Mukpo: "I think his death was directly connected to the fact that he gave so much, that he gave everything—that whatever he needed to do to propagate the teachings he did, even if that meant pushing his body to the point where he became sick."[19]

Saturday, April 4, 1987, was an unusually warm spring day in Halifax, with not a cloud in the sky. Chögyam Trungpa was in a critical care facility in the Halifax Infirmary. Late in the day, his breathing slowed, and it became clear that he was extremely close to death. There were quite a number of people gathered in the room, some very close students and family, some less so.[20]

Among those around the bedside were his wife, Diana Mukpo; his eldest son, the Sawang Ösel Mukpo; the Vajra Regent Ösel Tendzin and his wife, Lila Rich; his doctor Mitchell Levy; the Kasung and the Kusung Dapöns; several Sangyum; and other close students. Those who were present spontaneously sang the Shambhala Anthem in hushed voices. There was not a dry eye in the room. Around seven PM Chögyam Trungpa entered into parinirvana—a traditional term used to describe an accomplished teacher's death or the passing of a buddha, when he or she enters into a state of deep meditation called samadhi. During this period, in which the rest of the body grows cold, the heart and the area around it remain warm and the skin supple.

That evening, the Vajra Regent sent out a letter to all the members of the sangha, excerpted below:

The supreme Vidyadhara, Karma Ngawang Chökyi Gyatso Kunga Sangpo, the Eleventh Trungpa Tülku, passed peacefully into parinirvana at 8:05 P.M. today in Halifax, Nova Scotia. The glorious

---

19. Diana J. Mukpo, "Maintaining the Vision," talk given in Boulder, January 4, 1988, *Vajradhatu Sun*, April/May 1988, p. 21.

20. See *Vajradhatu Sun*, June/July 1987.

dharmaraja, sovereign of Vajradhatu, caused light rays of the Buddha's wisdom and compassion to spread throughout the world. Like Lord Padmakara, he planted firmly the victory banner of the incomparable vajrayana in the West. As the Dorje Dradul, the ultimate warrior, he revealed the splendour of the Great Eastern Sun, the glory of Shambhala. Holding the sceptre of the Rigden kings, he conquered the evils of the setting sun, ripened aspiring warriors, and created enlightened society right here on this earth.

We, his students, are eternally grateful.

> The blazing fire of Chandali consumes the kleshas
> As the lord of mahasukha reigns primordially in
> splendour.
> The razor knife of Ashe cuts the aorta of setting-sun
> cowards
> As the warrior of warriors displays the brilliant dance
> of sanity.

> We prostrate to the only father guru.
> Please guide us and protect us.
> Throughout all our lives, may we never be separated
> from your body, speech, and mind.
> We vow to perpetuate your world.

KI KI SO SO ASHE LHA GYEL LO
TAK SENG KHYUNG DRUK DI YAR KYE

In accordance with the Vidyadhara's wishes, upon his passing into parinirvana, his body was bathed in saffron water. The seed syllables of the armor devas [deities] were placed on the appropriate parts of his body, and it was clothed in a formal brocade chuba. The body will remain at the Kalapa Court as long as the samadhi lasts, and then it will be taken to Karmê Chöling for cremation

During the samadhi, the sangha should chant the Guru Yoga for the Four Sessions, and then they should practice either shamatha-vipashyana or mahamudra, depending on the individual's level of practice. If time permits, the sadhakas should perform the Vajra-yogini Sadhana.

Further communications will be issued concerning the details of the cremation ceremony itself.

Although this is a time of great sadness for us, we should remember the Vidyadhara's instructions and keep him constantly in our minds, not wavering in our discipline and devotion. My thoughts are with you.

Yours in the Dharma,
The Vajra Regent Ösel Tendzin

In the hour that followed his entry into samadhi, as stated in the letter above, Chögyam Trungpa was carried to the Kalapa Court and there was bathed with saffron water. Then seed syllables, which represent different qualities of the enlightened energy of the buddhas, were drawn on the appropriate parts of his body. He was dressed in a ceremonial brocade chuba (Tibetan robe), and his body was placed in the main living room at the Kalapa Court in meditation posture on a specially prepared throne. He had explicitly requested that the entire sangha should witness his samadhi, the time following death when the body remains in meditation. In Tibet, only the closest disciples are allowed to be present at the samadhi of their master, which is considered to be an extraordinary moment. But Chögyam Trungpa valued all his students as close disciples and asked that they be present. Because of the limitless confidence and generosity that he had shown, many people did feel like close disciples.

Hundreds of them came to Halifax. In small groups, they came to practice in the room where he remained. They came to witness his samadhi

It is one thing to know in theory that a master remains in samadhi for several days after his death, but it is quite another to experience it, to see with your own eyes a human being in such a state of presence, as though beyond ordinary death. Shortly after this event, Susan Edwards wrote: "As more and more of us saw him, it became apparent that each of us was experiencing a personal and unique response to our guru's samadhi. For some, he was dead. For others, he was wrathful. Someone said the energy was so thick in the room you could cut it into chunks and sell it. He described how the top of his head had flown away after sitting ten minutes in the Vidyadhara's presence. . . . To me, the Vidyadhara seemed peaceful, a warrior in samadhi, a guru for whom death as I had known it didn't exist. I still could not describe what I was experiencing. Longing had set in. I went back again and again. Group after group, we marched in and out of the throne room. Our minds still, our minds busy. He had invited us to see this. To share in this. To practice with him."[21]

The samadhi, which traditionally lasts three days, continued until midweek morning. His body was then transported to Karmê Chöling in Vermont, in a private plane with his family and about one hundred of his close students. His body was placed in a special box covered in brocade in the main shrine room so that people could continue to meditate in his presence. Shrines were set up in front of each cardinal direction, directly in front of this box. Essentially, Chögyam Trungpa's body became the center of an elaborate shrine in the middle of the shrine room. Many of his personal belongings were also positioned in the four corners surrounding the body.

During the weeks that followed, many of the great teachers of the Tibetan lineages arrived to help with the preparations for the funeral and to lead practices with the members of the sangha. Several hundred of Chögyam Trungpa's students lived at Karmê Chöling during this period, preparing for the final ceremonies. People were living in tents and bunking three or four to a room—probably as full as the center had, or has, ever been. Local residents rented out their houses to students as well. About seventy-five members of the Dorje Kasung set up an encampment in the fields near where Chögyam Trungpa's body would be cremated. Twenty-four hours a day there were people practicing in the shrine room, and at all times an honor guard was on duty with his body, composed of members of the Dorje Kasung.

Six weeks later, on May 26, on a misty morning, his body, on a special

---

21. Susan Edwards, "The Samadhi of the Guru," unpublished.

palanquin, was carried by the Kasung Kyi Khyap, the Kasung and Kusung Dapöns, and Dr. Mitchell Levy as pallbearers in a procession that wound its way about a mile through the woods from the main shrine room at Karmê Chöling up to the meadow where the cremation would take place. Behind the palanquin containing the body, a large honor guard of the Dorje Kasung marched in a very slow and dignified manner. After them came the other members of the procession, led by the Vajra Regent, Lady Diana, the Sawang Ösel Rangdröl Mukpo, other members of the family, the board of directors, the Sangyum, monastics, and other sangha members. The body of Chögyam Trungpa was placed by his "attendants" in a purkhang (literally "dwelling place of the body"), a monument over twenty-two feet high that had been built during this period at Karmê Chöling in these fields on top of the mountainside. Then everyone present came forward and offered a kata, a ritual white scarf, as a gesture of respect and to say goodbye to Chögyam Trungpa. Thousands of scarves were offered.

A fire puja ceremony was led by Dilgo Khyentse Rinpoche, in which all present took part. On the four cardinal points around the purkhang, Tai Situ Rinpoche, the third Jamgön Kongtrül Rinpoche, and Gyaltsap Rinpoche, three of the four Kagyü princes—heirs to His Holiness the sixteenth Karmapa—also officiated at the fire puja. The fourth Shamar Rinpoche had visited earlier but was not able to attend the cremation itself. In addition to these great masters of the Kagyü and Nyingma lineages, many other Buddhist teachers were present, including Zen and Theravadin teachers who had been close to Chögyam Trungpa. Over three thousand people attended the ceremony.

The fire was lit around midday, at the appropriate place in the liturgy. The fire had to be lit by a monk who had never known the Vidyadhara. When some time later the fire began to die down, a number of rainbows were seen. A rainbow completely encircled the sun while three hawks flew around the field. Such a phenomenon has often been described in Tibetan texts as a sign of the spiritual attainment of an exceptional master. Then, a spectacularly long train of clouds started to shine, making the sky bright turquoise and pink. But there was no natural explanation for this, because the sun was still high in the sky and not about to set, and there was no pollution in the atmosphere.[22]

It is hard to imagine how great a shock Chögyam Trungpa's death was for his disciples. Many of them cried every day for months. His presence radiated so much warmth that his limitless gentleness bathed even those who were sitting in the back row of the room where he was teaching. How to go on without it?

Many of his students were young adults when they met him, and now had to face once more the society they had left behind. After his death, many went back to their jobs or studies. An alternative: although they had led ordinary secular lives as Chögyam Trungpa's students, in a sense many of his students were so involved with Chögyam Trungpa's world during his lifetime that they had paid little attention to their own. Now, with his death, they had to move on in their lives, completing projects they had set aside for more than a decade, in some cases. People went back to school, looked for good jobs, raised their families—all the time trying to keep their connection to this man who had so transformed their lives.

But for everyone, the main point was to understand how they could keep up a living contact with him now that he was no longer present in the same way.

As the years went by, what should they remember? The openness and warmth that his presence radiated, or the pain of being so exposed? It was impossible to take one's own personal experience and relationship with the teachings and transform them into an external event. How to preserve the astounding innocence of his presence? How, at the same time, could they keep up the institutions he had founded, which were a means for those who had not known him to encounter his work?

Where was Chögyam Trungpa?

For all of us, whether we knew him personally or not, he could be only

---

22. As Tulku Pema Wangyal and Rabjam Rinpoche, who attended the ceremony, explained, many good omens appeared throughout the day: "First, the fog in the morning, which was neither too high nor too low, and which hung like a protective parasol over the area; then the rainbows, then the cloud shaped like katas; and finally the three hawks, dakinis who had taken the form of birds, welcoming the Vidyadhara." *Vajradhatu Sun*, June 1987.

here, in the living present. He is not in the past. He is a memory that opens into the present. To recall Chögyam Trungpa is to see him here and now.

As with space, which is always within reach, it is possible to contact Chögyam Trungpa again and again, not in an objective way but as an actual presence.

At each instant, there is an opportunity to recover an unencumbered moment, the mind's natural freedom. Such is a great teacher. "Always, without question, there is that room, there is that space. It is very powerful and very important and also very intimate at the same time."[23]

In his will, he confirmed his appointment of the Regent and reaffirmed that his son Ösel Rangdröl Mukpo, then known as the Sawang and now called Sakyong Mipham Rinpoche, should succeed him as the head of the Kingdom of Shambhala; he had been educated for this purpose. He asked all of his students to carry on his lineage, to safeguard and care for his teachings and the world he had created.

In this same document, he says:

> Born a monk
> *Died a king*—
> Such thunderstorm does not stop.
> We will be haunting you, along with the dralas.
> Jolly good luck![24]

---

23. Chögyam Trungpa, *1978 Seminary Transcripts: Vajrayana* (Boulder: Vajradhatu Publications), p. 68.

24. From an unpublished manuscript; all rights reserved. Used by permission of Diana J. Mukpo.

AFTERWORD

My French editor asked me to write a conclusion dealing with the heritage of Chögyam Trungpa. But such a conclusion is impossible. The presence of Chögyam Trungpa and the power of his work have never ceased to question me afresh every day.

Thrangu Rinpoche was perhaps right when he said, "These days the buddhadharma is spreading widely throughout the world, and along with that, modern technology is spreading widely throughout the world. In former times, once the guru had died, there would have been no way to see him. But now we have videotapes and cassette tapes and televisions and movie projectors and so forth, and you can actually see him. And you can listen to the tapes that were made of his presentation of the dharma and listen directly to Trungpa Rinpoche teaching the dharma, so that, at this point, whether the guru is here or not doesn't make much difference."[1] Whether we take Thrangu Rinpoche literally or not, it is still striking that the number of Chögyam Trungpa's students has continued to rise since his death, in contrast to what often happens with other teachers. Because of this growing interest, entire areas of his teachings have been rediscovered and explored in depth. The importance of his work has been given its true dimension and seems ever greater.

While Chögyam Trungpa kept changing what he had set up according

---

1. Thrangu Rinpoche, teaching given at Seminary, RMDC, July 27, 1990, p. 15, unpublished transcript.

to different contexts, his intention was always to establish a body of work that would survive him. So the changes he made to his actions do not mean that his work should not be taken seriously, but rather that attention should be paid to the entirety of what he established, so that those, like me, who never knew him will have the opportunity to be exposed to such a startling manifestation of the truth.

Chögyam Trungpa constantly thought about the unity of what he wanted to accomplish: the setting up of a environment that would be not only a place where an authentic transmission of the dharma could help as many people as possible, but also an example of how an enlightened society can transform the world.

So what is Chögyam Trungpa's heritage today?

Will all of his teachings be preserved and kept alive, or will they vanish along with the students who knew him?

Will his influence, which has no equivalent in the West for a Buddhist teacher, continue to grow ever larger?

Will spiritual materialism, which seems to be becoming ever more virulent, erode Chögyam Trungpa's uncompromising vision?

Will we grasp the importance of his work and allow it to really transform our lives and our world?

To answer these questions, all I can say is that Chögyam Trungpa is present in us. He has not passed elsewhere. His heritage is in our hands. It is up to all of us to keep it alive.

As he himself said of Guru Rinpoche: "We are infested with Padmasambhava in ourselves. We are haunted by him. Our whole being is completely made out of Padmasambhava. So when we try to relate with him 'out there,' as a person who lives on a copper-colored mountain on some remote island off the coast of India, that does not make sense."[2]

The same applies to Chögyam Trungpa.

May he never stop haunting us.

---

2. *Crazy Wisdom*, p. 100.

APPENDIX

Organizations Established by
Chögyam Trungpa

A BOOK SUCH AS THIS can deal only with a limited part of Chögyam Trungpa's achievement. This appendix lists some of the organizations set up by Chögyam Trungpa that were not dealt with in the main section of the text but that cannot be left unmentioned.

AMARA

Amara is an association of health professionals founded in 1978. This Sanskrit word means "absence of obstacles." Amara was set up to provide a forum of health studies with a multidisciplinary approach. Its aim is a better understanding of the connection between one's state of mind and physical well-being. In 1981, Amara's activities were organized by the foundation's bureau of health and social well-being, which had just been set up under the direction of Dr. Mitchell Levy, Trungpa Rinpoche's personal physician. Chögyam Trungpa met with the members of the association regularly to discuss all the aspects of its activities. Amara has created a series of training programs in five levels, taking as its model the program of Shambhala Training.

KALAPA VALLEY

Kalapa Valley is a sacred Shambhala site discovered by Chögyam Trungpa Rinpoche in 1979 during his second trip to Nova Scotia. It is situated in the mountains of Cape Breton in northern Nova Scotia, at the mouth of the river Ingonish. The land was bought in 1993 by his students, who have since kept up the property with a view to its future development as a sacred park and place of Shambhala pilgrimage.

NGEDON SCHOOL AND VAJRAYANA SEMINARY

In 1982, Ngedon School was founded for students who have attended the Seminary and wish to deepen their understanding of the dharma and study the foundation texts of the Buddhist tradition. *Ngedön* means "ultimate meaning." The organization of the teaching given here provides an exemplary opportunity for all Western students wishing to deepen their knowledge of the Tibetan way.

This project was supposed to lead to a Vajrayana Seminary, which Chögyam Trungpa was never able to give. He explained to the Dorje Loppön that his idea was to teach there "the great tantric commentaries of Rangjung Dorje, the third Karmapa, and others, and also to introduce fruition tantra and the ati tradition, with an emphasis on outlook and actual practice."

RATNA SOCIETY

After his retreat in 1977, Chögyam Trungpa noticed that his students were participating less in Mudra and Maitri, and instead were starting up businesses, marrying, and having children. So he founded the Ratna Society, an organization aimed at developing a mahayana- and Shambhala-based approach to the economic realm. It is open to everyone who has a business, or even just a job. In this way, Chögyam Trungpa wanted to encourage his students to take part in economic and social life while showing how Buddhist and Shambhala teachings can be applied there. Its members meet regularly to work together on setting up, running, and expanding businesses on both a pragmatic and a visionary level.

Unlike many other spiritual communities, the Shambhala community does not consider that a job should just be a way of earning money and saving up for retirement. It should be something intrinsically noble, providing an opportunity to develop "authentic presence" and to discover more about the absence of ego.

THE UPAYA COUNCIL

The Upaya Council is a forum to help members of the community resolve conflicts. Members of the Council help the conflicting parties to reach a friendly agreement. They do not deliver a judgment, but instead provide a space in which members of the sangha who otherwise would be incapable of talking to each other can cultivate gentleness and kindness in the hope of putting an end to their disputes.

BOOKS BY
CHÖGYAM TRUNGPA

For earlier works, the first date of publication is given in parentheses following the title. Quotations in the text are generally from the current printings. Note that the Shambhala Classics editions are paginated differently from the earlier editions.

The Art of Calligraphy: Joining Heaven and Earth. Boston: Shambhala Publications, 1994.

Born in Tibet (George Allen & Unwin, 1966; Shambhala Publications, 1977). Fourth edition, Boston: Shambhala Publications, 2000.

The Collected Works of Chögyam Trungpa. Edited by Carolyn Rose Gimian. Vols. 1–4. Boston: Shambhala Publications, 2003.

The Collected Works of Chögyam Trungpa. Edited by Carolyn Rose Gimian. Vols. 5–8. Boston: Shambhala Publications, 2004.

Crazy Wisdom (1991). Boston: Shambhala Publications, 2001.

Cutting Through Spiritual Materialism (1973). Boston: Shambhala Publications (Shambhala Classics), 2002.

The Dawn of Tantra (1975), by Herbert V. Guenther and Chögyam Trungpa. Boston: Shambhala Publications (Shambhala Dragon Editions), 2001.

Dharma Art. Boston: Shambhala Publications, 1996.

The Essential Chögyam Trungpa. Edited by Carolyn Rose Gimian. Boston: Shambhala Publications, 1999.

First Thought Best Thought: 108 Poems. Boston: Shambhala Publications, 1983.

Glimpses of Abhidharma (1975). Boston: Shambhala Publications (Shambhala Dragon Editions), 2001.

Glimpses of Mahayana. Halifax: Vajradhatu Publications, 2001.

Glimpses of Shunyata. Halifax: Vajradhatu Publications, 1993.

Glimpses of Space: The Feminine Principle and Evam. Halifax: Vajradhatu Publications, 1999.

Great Eastern Sun: The Wisdom of Shambhala. Boston: Shambhala Publications, 1999.

The Heart of the Buddha. Boston: Shambhala Publications, 1991.

Illusion's Game: The Life and Teaching of Naropa. Boston: Shambhala Publications, 1994.

Journey without Goal: The Tantric Wisdom of the Buddha (1981). Boston: Shambhala Publications, 2000.

The Life of Marpa the Translator: Seeing Accomplishes All (1982), by Tsang Nyön Heruka. Translated by the Nālandā Translation Committee under the direction of Chögyam Trungpa. Boston: Shambhala Publications, 1995.

The Lion's Roar: An Introduction to Tantra. Boston: Shambhala Publications, 1992.

Meditation in Action (1969). Boston: Shambhala Publications, 1996.

Mudra (1972). Boston: Shambhala Publications, 2001.

The Myth of Freedom and the Way of Meditation (1976). Boston: Shambhala Publications (Shambhala Classics), 2002.

Orderly Chaos: The Mandala Principle. Boston: Shambhala Publications, 1991.

The Path Is the Goal: A Basic Handbook of Buddhist Meditation. Boston: Shambhala Publications, 1995.

The Rain of Wisdom: The Essence of the Ocean of True Meaning (1980). Translated by the Nālandā Translation Committee under the direction of Chögyam Trungpa. Boston: Shambhala Publications, 1999.

Secret Beyond Thought: The Five Chakras and the Four Karmas. Halifax: Vajradhatu Publications, 1991.

Shambhala: The Sacred Path of the Warrior (1984). Boston: Shambhala Publications (Shambhala Dragon Editions), 1997; Shambhala Library, 2003.

The Tibetan Book of the Dead: The Great Liberation through Hearing in the Bardo (1975), translated with commentary by Francesca Fremantle and Chögyam Trungpa. Boston: Shambhala Publications (Shambhala Classics), 2000; Shambhala Library, 2003.

Timely Rain: Selected Poetry of Chögyam Trungpa. Boston: Shambhala Publications, 1998.

Training the Mind and Cultivating Loving-Kindness. Boston: Shambhala Publications, 1993. Shambhala Classics, 2003.

Transcending Madness. The Experience of the Six Bardos. Boston: Shambhala Publications, 1992.

RESOURCES

For information regarding meditation instruction or inquiries about a practice center near you, please contact one of the following:

Shambhala International
1084 Tower Road
Halifax, NS
B3H 2Y5 Canada
Telephone: (902) 425-4275, ext. 10
Fax: (902) 423-2750
Web site: www.shambhala.org (This site contains information about the more than 100 meditation centers affiliated with Shambhala, the international network of Buddhist practice centers established by Chögyam Trungpa.)

Shambhala Europe
Annostrasse 27
50678 Cologne, Germany
Telephone: 49-0-700-108-000-00
E-mail: europe@shambhala.org
Web site: www.shambhala-europe.org

Dorje Denma Ling
2280 Balmoral Road
Tatamagouche, NS
B0K 1V0 Canada
Telephone: (902) 657-9085
Fax: (902) 657-0462
E-mail: info@dorjedenmaling.com
Web site: www.dorjedenmaling.com

Karmê Chöling
369 Patneaude Lane
Barnet, VT 05821
Telephone: (802) 633-2384
Fax: (802) 633-3012
E-mail: karmecholing@shambhala.org

Shambhala Mountain Center
4921 Country Road 68C
Red Feather Lakes, CO 80545
Telephone: (970) 881-2184
Fax: (970) 881-2909
E-mail: shambhalamountain@shambhala.org

Sky Lake Lodge
P.O. Box 408
Rosendale, NY 12472
Telephone: (845) 658-8556
E-mail: skylake@shambhala.org
Web site: http://ny.shambhala.org/skylake

Dechen Chöling
Mas Marvent
87700 St Yrieix sous Aixe
France
Telephone: 33 (0)5-55-03-55-52
Fax: 33 (0)5-55-03-91-74
E-mail: dechencholing@dechencholing.org

Audio- and videotape recordings of talks and seminars by Chögyam Trungpa are available from:

Kalapa Recordings
1678 Barrington Street, 2nd Floor
Halifax, NS
B3J 2A2 Canada
Telephone: (902) 421-1550
Fax: (902) 423-2750
E-mail: shop@shambhala.org
Web site: www.shambhalashop.com

For publications from Shambhala International, please contact:

Vajradhatu Publications
1678 Barrington Street, 2nd Floor
Halifax, NS
B3J 2A2 Canada
Telephone: (902) 421-1550
E-mail: shop@shambhala.org
Web site: www.shambhalashop.com

For information about the archive of the Chögyam Trungpa's work—which includes more than 5,000 audio recordings, 1,000 video recordings, original Tibetan manuscripts, correspondence, and more than 30,000 photographs—please contact:

The Shambhala Archives
1084 Tower Road
Halifax, NS
B3H 3S3 Canada
Telephone: (902) 421-1550
Web site: www.shambhalashop.com/archives

The *Shambhala Sun* is a bimonthly Buddhist magazine founded by Chögyam Trungpa. For a subscription or sample copy, contact:

Shambhala Sun
P. O. Box 3377
Champlain, NY 12919-9871
Telephone: (877) 786-1950
Web site: www.shambhalasun.com

Buddhadharma: The Practitioner's Quarterly is an in-depth, practice-oriented journal offering teachings from all Buddhist traditions. For a subscription or sample copy, contact:

Buddhadharma
P. O. Box 3377
Champlain, NY 12919-9871
Telephone: (877) 786-1950
Web site: www.thebuddhadharma.com

Naropa University is the only accredited, Buddhist-inspired university in North America. For more information, contact:

Naropa University
2130 Arapahoe Avenue
Boulder, CO 80302
Telephone: (303) 444-0202
Web site: www.naropa.edu

serve or regard for the usual conventions or precautions, was of great importance for this work and for my understanding of Chögyam Trungpa's achievement. The freedom he showed whenever we met brought this project to life. David Rome proves that it is possible to unite profound humility and stunning brilliance. I would not have been able to complete this task without the real friendship that has blossomed between us.

That Chögyam Trungpa's books are as important as they are, and convey the inspiration of their author, is due not only to Chögyam Trungpa himself but also to his editors, who have put what was said orally into correct written English. For each volume, this huge task requires months or even years of work

In addition to Carolyn Gimian and David Rome, I had the good fortune to meet Chögyam Trungpa's other editors, Sherab Chödzin Kohn, Sarah Coleman, and Judith L. Lief. I often relied on the forewords they wrote to the books they edited as a vital source for understanding the context in which Chögyam Trungpa gave his teachings. Each of them has developed a great familiarity with his teaching and his personal style.

At the beginning of Plato's *Critias*, Timaeus explains: "At present, I pray to the god to whom our words have just given birth, although he has always existed, that he give us the grace to preserve those words of ours that are true, and, if we have unintentionally sung off tune, to inflict on us a just punishment. And the just punition in this case is to put what has strayed back into the right tone." It was bearing these words in mind that I have, in turn, tried to give this book the right tone. When I have succeeded, it is thanks to those students who spent so many hours listening to and learning from Chögyam Trungpa's tone. Every time I spoke to them, I was once again confronted with this precise tonality.

Chögyam Trungpa set up a board of directors of students who worked in close collaboration with him. I met Jeremy Hayward, head of education (to whom I owe so much in my understanding of the teachings of Shambhala, because he has been in charge of its international development for many years; the confidence and goodness he showed me were unfailing); Ronald Stubbert, head of finance; as well as Charles Lief and Michael Root.

The head of Buddhist teachings was the Loppön, Lodrö Dorje. The clarity and precision of his understanding were of inestimable help to me. To be in his presence is to be in direct contact with the heart of Chögyam Trungpa's teachings.

Over the years, the role of the Dorje Kasung and Dorje Kusung grew increasingly important, and the two Dapön Kyi Khyaps, James Gimian and Martin Janowitz, played a vital part by Chögyam Trungpa's side in the 1980s. They not only gave me a better understanding of the purpose of the Kasung teachings in

ACKNOWLEDGMENTS

I STARTED THIS BOOK after meeting Lady Diana Mukpo, who encouraged me to undertake this project and who has not spared her effort or generosity in seeing it through to a conclusion. My meeting with her has been a continual source of inspiration.

The Sakyong Mipham Rinpoche approved of my desire to devote myself to this project. Since I first met him in October 1989, the few times that I have had the chance to be exposed to his presence have been profoundly moving moments for me. He touched my heart so deeply.

This book owes much to his activity. Son of Trungpa Rinpoche, he was uniquely close to his father, and, with the death of the Regent in 1990, he had the heavy responsibility of his father's community and of pursuing the task of establishing a Western Buddhism. Having been recognized as the incarnation of Mipham Rinpoche also gave him a heavy responsibility in connection to the Tibetan community, strongly in crisis. The dignity with which he has taken on this double task and his concern for transmitting the dharma make him a true example of dedication.

Carolyn Rose Gimian has presided over this adventure, constantly helping me to overcome various obstacles and resistance, and devoting her time to reading my manuscript with great attention. All of her suggestions, remarks, and criticism went straight to the point and allowed me to improve my work. As director of the Shambhala Archives, she has played a vital role in preserving Chögyam Trungpa's teachings. Without her vision, devotion, and courage, a large part of his heritage would be lost today, and a book such as this one would be impossible.

I was fortunate enough to meet and work with David I. Rome, who was Chögyam Trungpa's personal secretary and Kasung Kyi Khyap, the head of the Dorje Kasung. For many years, he was closer than anyone to Chögyam Trungpa. The way he shared his experience with me, quite freely, without the slightest re-

Chögyam Trungpa's universe, but also enlightened my understanding of his work of that period because they were such close witnesses of it.

In 1986, Chögyam Trungpa appointed the Sangyum. I had the great good fortune to meet Agnes Au, who was also Resident Director of Shambhala Training in New York, and Wendy Friedman and Karen Lavin. I should also like to thank Ciel Turzanski, because even if I was not able to meet her to discuss my work on this particular book, my memories of our previous meetings were a great help to me in my understanding of the role of the Sangyum. Chögyam Trungpa asked them to bear witness to his life. During all of my conversations with them, they have always managed to convey with great dignity something that transcends language while also making language possible: his naked presence.

For the material related to the Vajra Regent Ösel Tendzin, I must first thank his widow, Lila Rich, who gave me permission to publish extracts of the letters and talks found in this volume. She answered all my questions with great generosity.

I also owe much to the efforts of Cynthia Anderson and Joseph Parent, who selflessly shared their devotion and respect for the Regent.

Translators have played a key role in Chögyam Trungpa's world. The director of the Nālandā Translation Committee, Larry Mermelstein, has been of unfailing assistance. Without showing the slightest fatigue, he answered my innumerable questions, with a constant desire to share and communicate his passion for the world Chögyam Trungpa created.

I must also thank Walter Fordham, master of Kalapa Court, who told me so much about Court life.

For the chapter on Maitri, my thanks go to Antonio Wood, who introduced me to this practice with exemplary clarity and depth. I am also indebted to the work of Irini Rockwell, Allyn Lyon, and Marvin Casper. Finally, I should like to thank Melissa Moore, Helen Berliner, and Barbara Märtens, who all shared their intuition and passion for this practice during the seminars we have led together.

I would also like to thank Jose Argüelles, Steve Brooks, Michael Chender, Tharpa Chötrön, Lama Denys Teundroup, Herbert Elsky, Ken Friedman, Allen Ginsberg, Jerry Granelli, Gerard Haase-Dubosc, Mipham Halpern, Alice Haspray, Karen Hayward, Fenja Heupers, Ashley Howes, William Karelis, Sara Kapp, Andy Karr, Robin Kornman, Dr. Mitchell Levy, Ellen Lieberson, Jack Niland, Robert Rader, Phil Richman, John Rockwell, Martha Rome, Julia Sagebien, Steven Saitzyk, Margaretta Sander, Jill Scott, Steve Seely, Marcia Shibata, Eric Spiegel, Craig Smith, Gina Stick, Donn B. Tatum, Mark Turnoy, Ludwig Turzanski, Francisco Varela, Peter Volz, Shari Vogler, Elaine Yuen, Irene Woodard, Lee

Worley, and the words of Joshua Zim for their help, in the form of interviews they granted me, the articles I have cited, or letters they sent me in answer to my questions.

I have surely forgotten many others who have helped me during these years of work. May they put this down not to my ingratitude, but instead to my feeble memory.

Nor have I mentioned all those who have, at various times, transmitted the teachings of Chögyam Trungpa to me and helped me to understand them—my deep gratitude to them as well.

My thanks also go to Richard Gravel, Stéphane Bédard, Vincent Bardet, and Esther Rochon for their work translating Chögyam Trungpa's books and scriptural writings into French. Without them, this book would have been impossible. I am also grateful to them for the possibility of experiencing the dharma in French.

The origin of this project was a request made by Vincent Bardet. His intuitions about the situation of Buddhism in the West, his desire to preserve it from the falsely religious hypocrisy that threatens it, and his constant loyalty have been greatly encouraging.

But the project seemed beyond my powers. Whenever I considered giving up this adventure, for which I did not feel qualified, having never met Chögyam Trungpa and living in France where he never taught, I returned to my work buoyed up by Chris Tamdjidi's constant encouragement. Driven by his deep devotion for Chögyam Trungpa and the clarity of the vision he has regarding the work that needs to be done for the buddhadharma in the West, he was a constant presence at each phase of the project. His unfailing friendship, generosity, and goodness made it possible for me to undertake this work.

I should like to thank Fabien Ouaki, who with unflagging determination and generosity supported this project from beginning to end.

I owe so much to the tenderness of Bruno Tyszler, who accepted seeing me shut myself up in my study for days on end, then spend weeks at a time in Nova Scotia and the United States to research this book. He gave me daily encouragement throughout this project.

This book has benefited from the advice and remarks of Francesca Carrouch, Yves Dallavalle, Catherine Eveillard, Lionel Fourment, Laurence Poublan, Thibault Santenac, as well as the help of Veronike Bauer and Luca Fiorentino.

I must also thank Sylvie Gojard, who helped me with real gentleness during the birth pains of this book.

One of the challenges in this project was to convey the importance of the

Acknowledgments   523

meeting between the West and the Buddhist East. A dialogue is only possible if we take Buddhism at its summit and the West at its summit too. The problem is that, while we have a totally authentic contact with Buddhism thanks to the work of a teacher like Chögyam Trungpa, we are often bogged down in the West, incapable of perceiving where its greatness might now lie, and we thus run the risk of distorting Buddhism by using shifting Western concepts.

When as a young man I first started to practice and follow the path of Buddhism as it was presented by Chögyam Trungpa, I had already been struck by the decline of the university, where I had learned nothing about how to live in contact with the essential things in life. But as all authentic and ardent desires find a response, I had the good fortune to meet François Fédier, after I too had become a teacher of philosophy. I soon realized that in him I had come across a man who had a profound feeling for the dignity of the West, in a way that I had never experienced before. The seven years that I attended his classes played a considerable role in my education. Such a book would have been impossible without the depth of his understanding of our historical situation, which he shared with a generosity that still moves me and which is, in our era, heroic.

Throughout this book I have tried to make a relationship between the Buddhist perspective and that of the West, in the hope that the practice of Buddhism will not remain a discipline for isolated individuals, and that Chögyam Trungpa's teaching will resonate in all of us, thus transforming our entire culture, as he wished it would, and allowing all human beings to develop their dignity.

This list of acknowledgments is far too brief. There are many whom I have forgotten, and above all it fails to convey all the qualities of those who generously helped me in my work. May it at least bear witness to the fact that this book has sought to bring together what would have remained scattered without their help.

The English Translation

This translation was made possible thanks to Fabien Ouaki. His confidence in the project, and his understanding of Chögyam Trungpa's importance for the future of understanding dharma in the West, has never faltered.

This edition is not a simple translation of the French version; this attempt to imagine the life and work of Chögyam Trungpa includes a number of additions and corrections.

I first want to thank Kendra Crossen Burroughs, my editor at Shambhala Publications. With exemplary precision and immense clarity, she brought this project to completion. She embodies the excellence of the editor's craft. Over the course of the months spent working out the details of the American edition, I often thought of my extraordinary good fortune in being able to work with such a professional.

Larry Mermelstein and Lee Worley checked certain chapters and helped improve them. They have thus contributed to deepening our understanding of some parts of the life and teaching of Chögyam Trungpa.

Ian Monk did the translation, and he has my enthusiastic thanks for the quality of his work.

John Sell, with the intelligence and taste that an honest man embodies, has patiently worked to ensure that this book maintain its intellectual standards.

David Rome, whose friendship and honesty are among the great comforts of my existence, continued to help me right up to the publication of this translation, with endless generosity.

The sharp eye and mind of Tracy Davis, the proofreader, are deeply appreciated by both the publisher and myself.

L. S. Summer produced an excellent, comprehensive index.

I would most of all like to thank Carolyn Gimian. Without her this book could not have been written. Without her, this translation could not have been brought to successful completion. Her instructions, suggestions, and corrections have always been of exemplary relevance; they have not only elucidated the process of writing this work, but have also illuminated my understanding of the life and vision of Chögyam Trungpa and have strongly improved this version of the work. Her generosity, her discipline, the soundness of her analysis, her involvement, and her devotion to the work of Chögyam Trungpa are, for me, an example both staggering and inspiring in equal measure.

All contributions, memoirs, or stories concerning Chögyam Trungpa; cassettes, photographs, or transcriptions; and financial assistance for the work of archiving and conserving Chögyam Trungpa's work should be sent to: Shambhala Archive, 1084 Tower Road, Halifax, Nova Scotia, B3H 2Y5, Canada.

The author can be contacted at fmidal@club-internet.fr.

INDEX

This index is designed to double as a simple glossary of foreign terms, with short definitions or translations in parentheses following the entry word and page references for fuller definitions in the text.

Page numbers indicating photographs are in italic type.